PART-TIME
Princesses

D0973347

AN ONI PRESS PUBLICATION

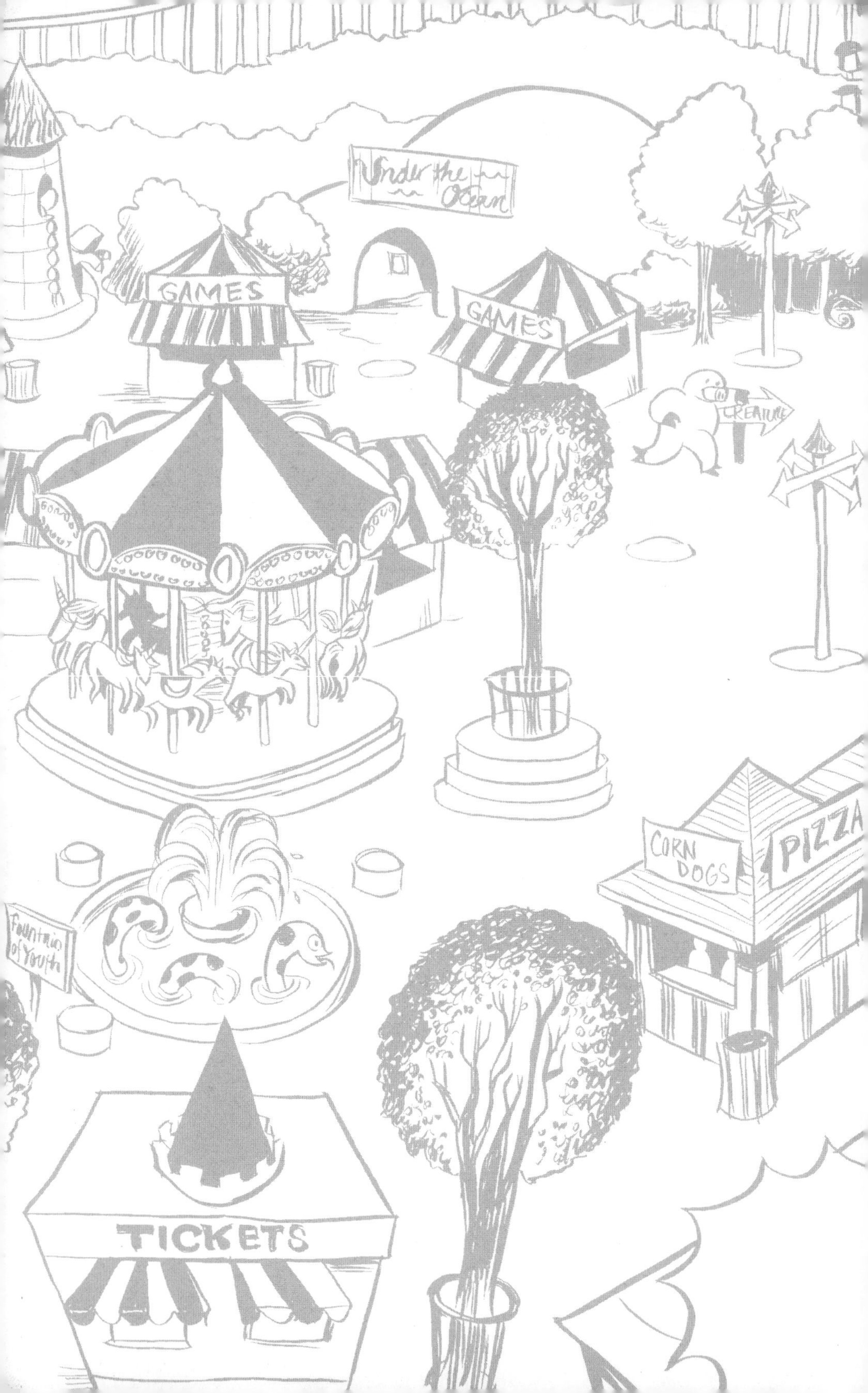
Under the Ocean
GAMES
GAMES
CREATURE
CORN DOGS
PIZZA
Fountain of Youth
TICKETS

PART-TIME Princesses

written and illustrated by
Monica Gallagher

lettered by **Christy Sawyer**

edited by **Jill Beaton** with **Robin Herrera**

designed by **Hilary Thompson**

published by **Oni Press, Inc.**
publisher **Joe Nozemack**
editor in chief **James Lucas Jones**
v.p. of business development **Tim Wiesch**
director of sales **Cheyenne Allott**
director of publicity **John Schork**
editor **Charlie Chu**
associate editor **Robin Herrera**
production manager **Troy Look**
graphic designer **Hilary Thompson**
production assistant **Jared Jones**
administrative assistant **Ari Yarwood**
inventory coordinator **Brad Rooks**
office assistant **Jung Lee**

1305 SE Martin Luther King Jr. Blvd.
Suite A
Portland, OR 97214
U.S.A.

facebook.com/onipress
twitter.com/onipress
onipress.tumblr.com
onipress.com

eatyourlipstick.com

First Edition: March 2015
ISBN: 978-1-62010-217-6
eISBN: 978-1-62010-218-3

1 2 3 4 5 6 7 8 9 10

Library of Congress Control Number: 2014948293

Printed in China

For Jenny

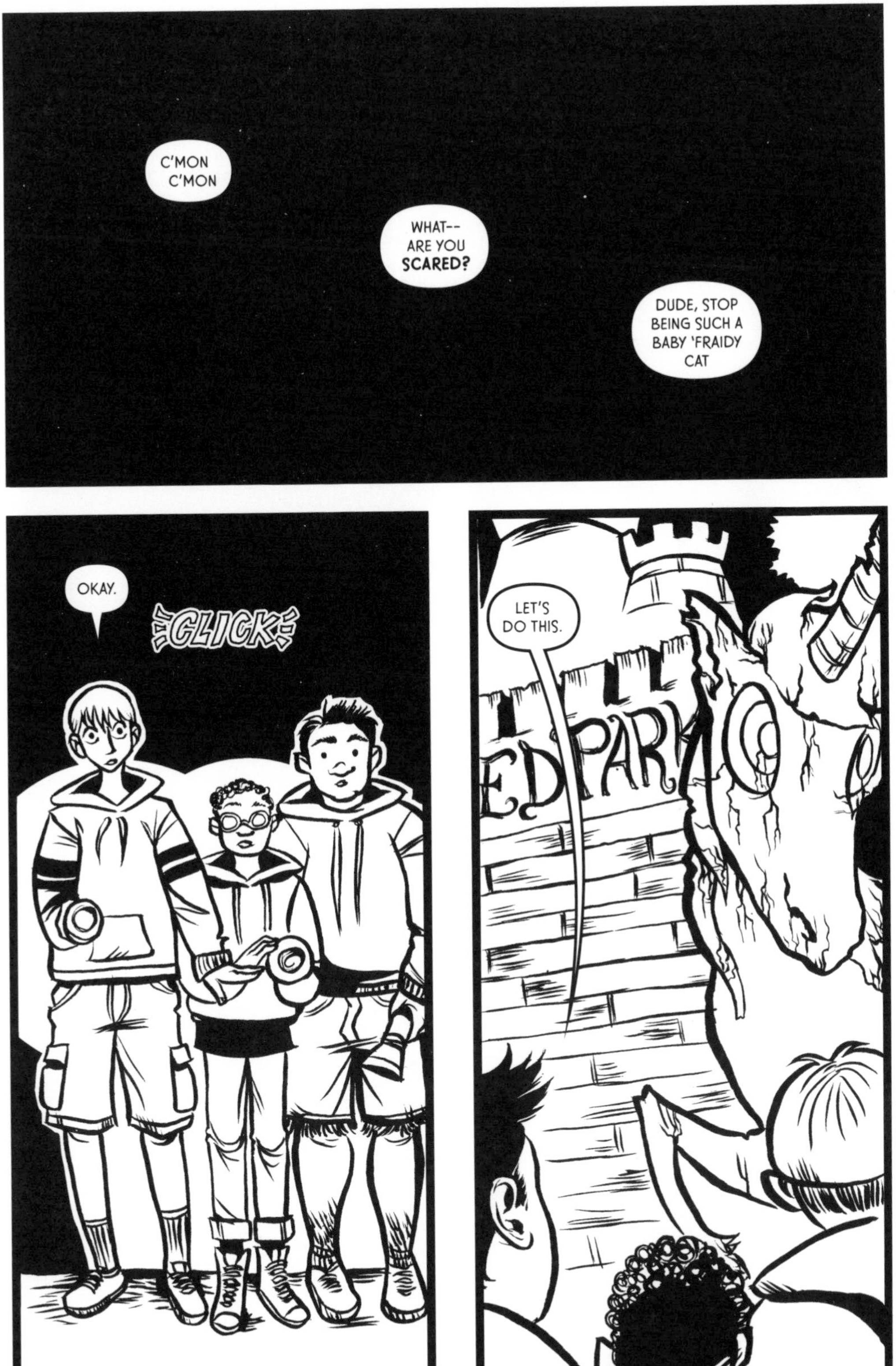
C'MON
C'MON
WHAT--
ARE YOU
SCARED?
DUDE, STOP
BEING SUCH A
BABY 'FRAIDY
CAT
OKAY.
CLICK
LET'S
DO THIS.
ED PARK

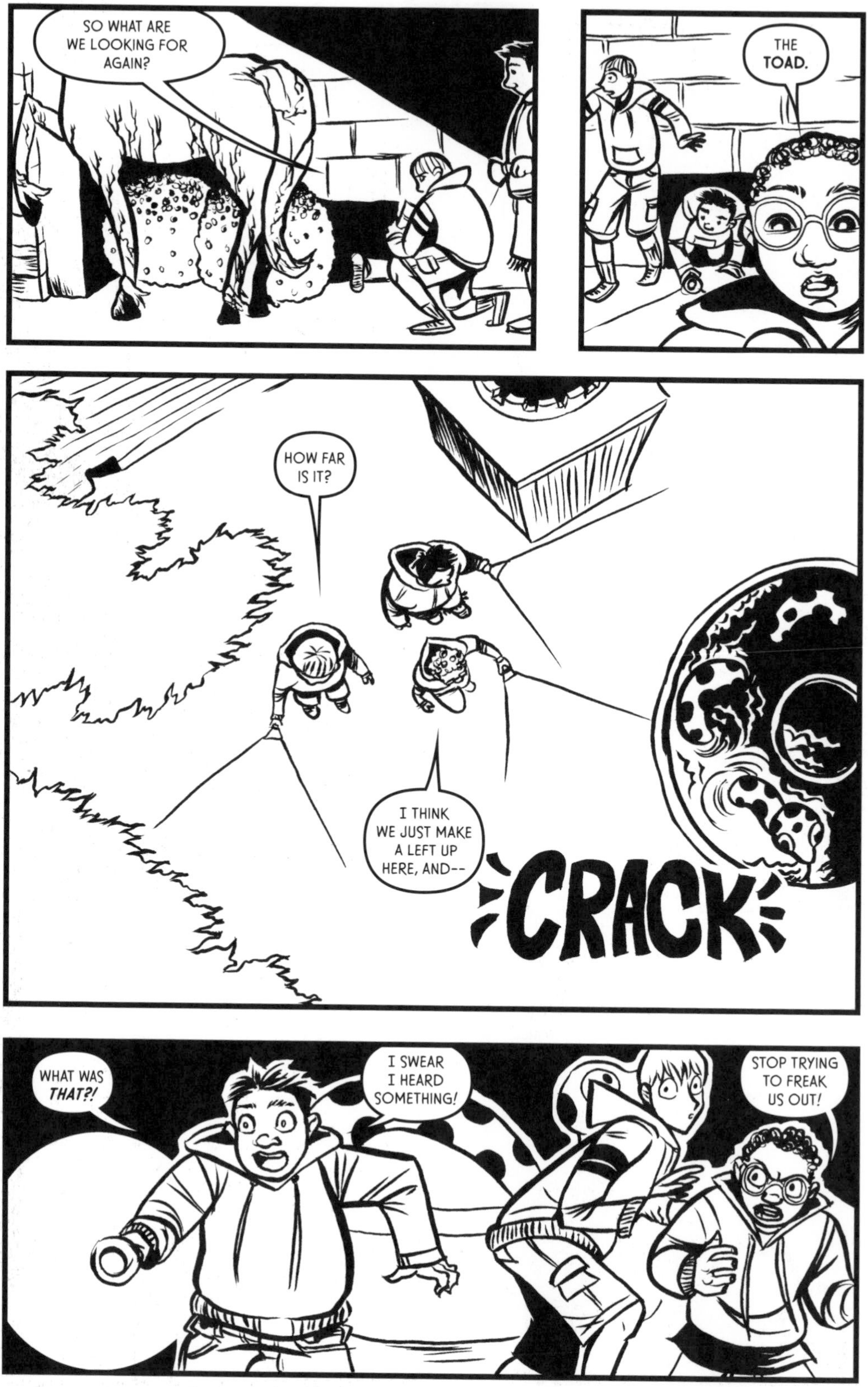
SO WHAT ARE WE LOOKING FOR AGAIN?
THE **TOAD.**
HOW FAR IS IT?
I THINK WE JUST MAKE A LEFT UP HERE, AND--
CRACK
WHAT WAS ***THAT?!***
I SWEAR I HEARD SOMETHING!
STOP TRYING TO FREAK US OUT!

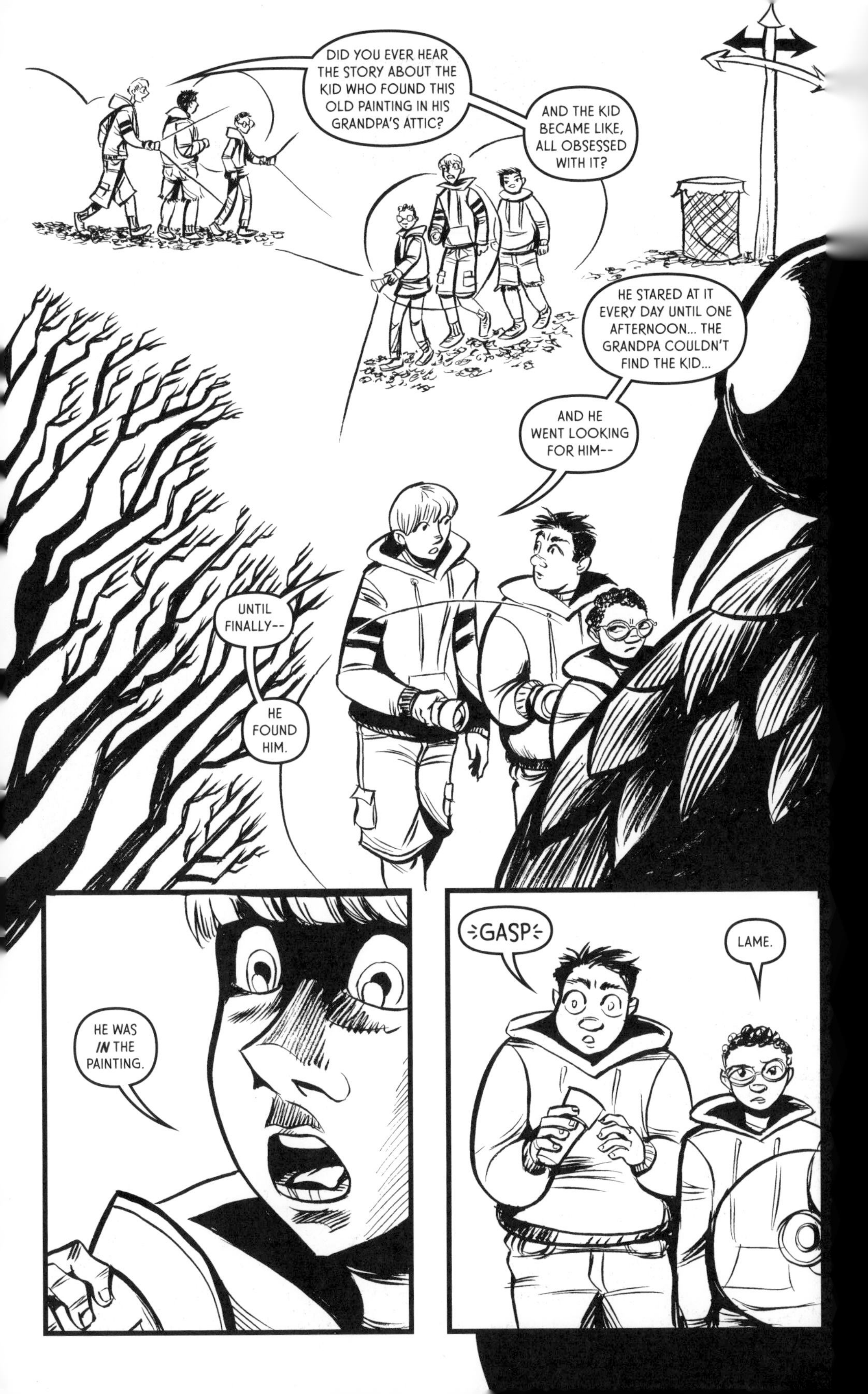
DID YOU EVER HEAR THE STORY ABOUT THE KID WHO FOUND THIS OLD PAINTING IN HIS GRANDPA'S ATTIC?
AND THE KID BECAME LIKE, ALL OBSESSED WITH IT?
HE STARED AT IT EVERY DAY UNTIL ONE AFTERNOON... THE GRANDPA COULDN'T FIND THE KID...
AND HE WENT LOOKING FOR HIM--
UNTIL FINALLY--
HE FOUND HIM.
HE WAS *IN* THE PAINTING.
GASP
LAME.

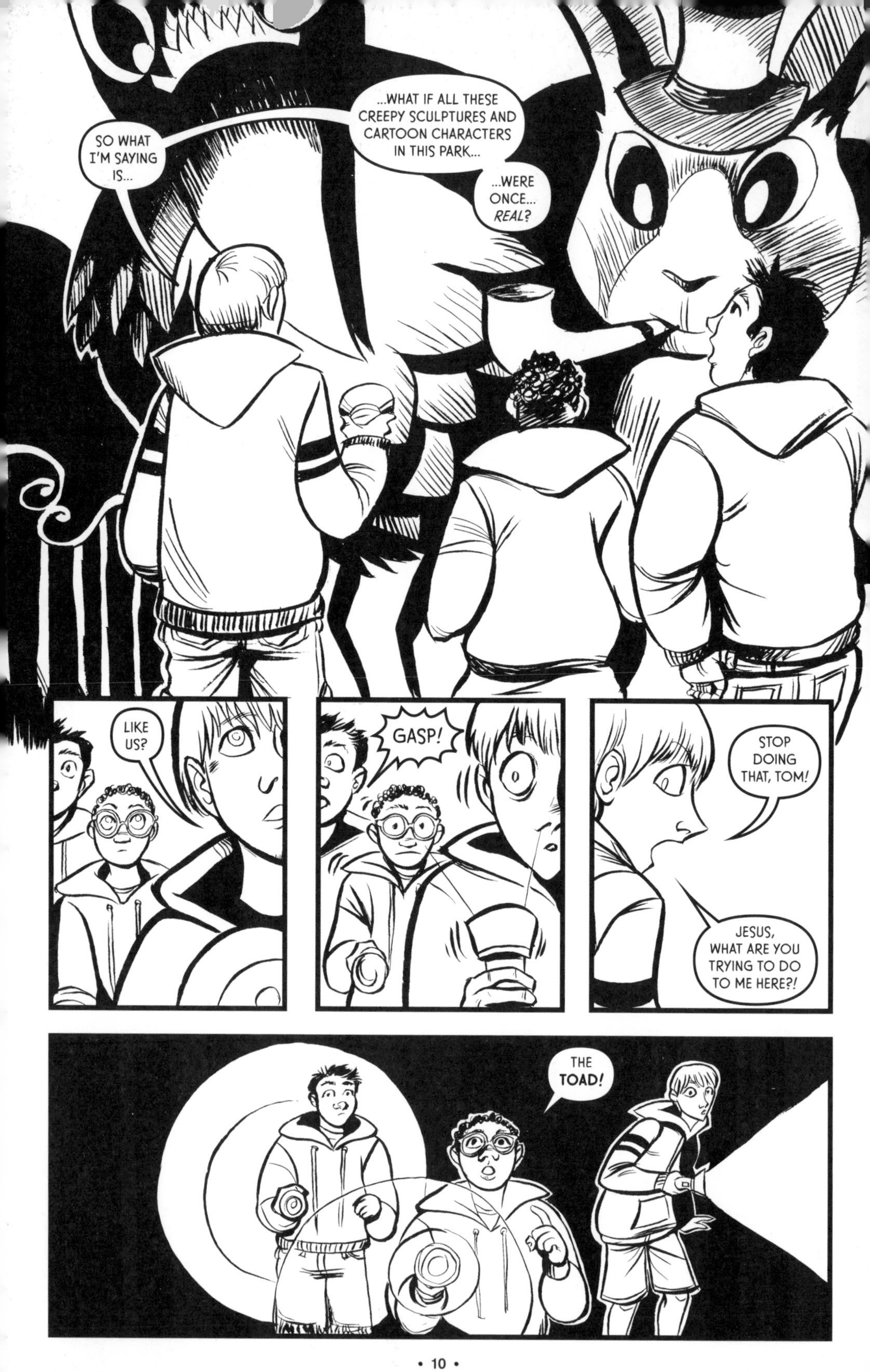
SO WHAT I'M SAYING IS...
...WHAT IF ALL THESE CREEPY SCULPTURES AND CARTOON CHARACTERS IN THIS PARK...
...WERE ONCE... *REAL*?
LIKE US?
GASP!
STOP DOING THAT, TOM!
JESUS, WHAT ARE YOU TRYING TO DO TO ME HERE?!
THE **TOAD**!

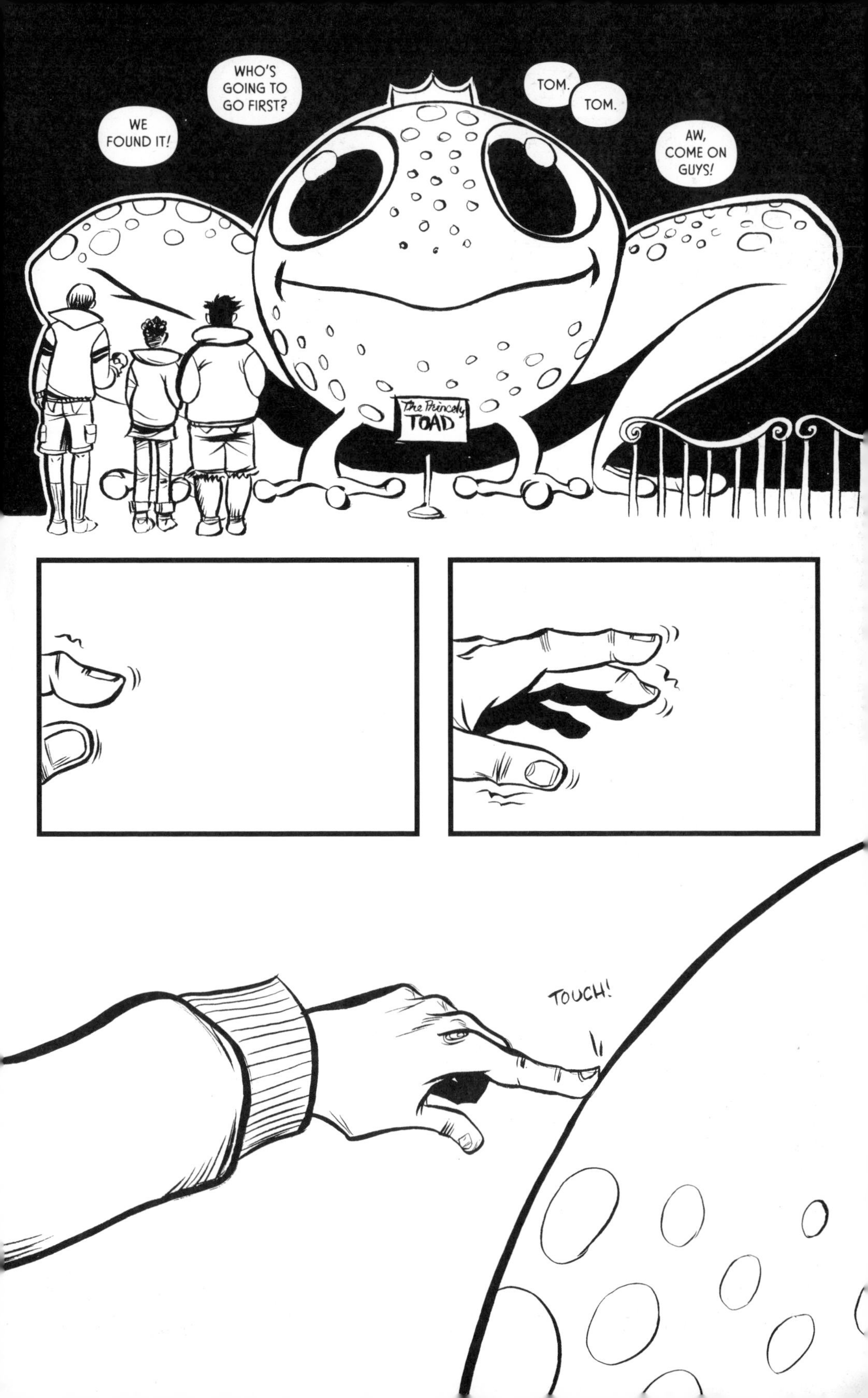
WE FOUND IT!
WHO'S GOING TO GO FIRST?
TOM.
TOM.
AW, COME ON GUYS!
The Princely TOAD
TOUCH!

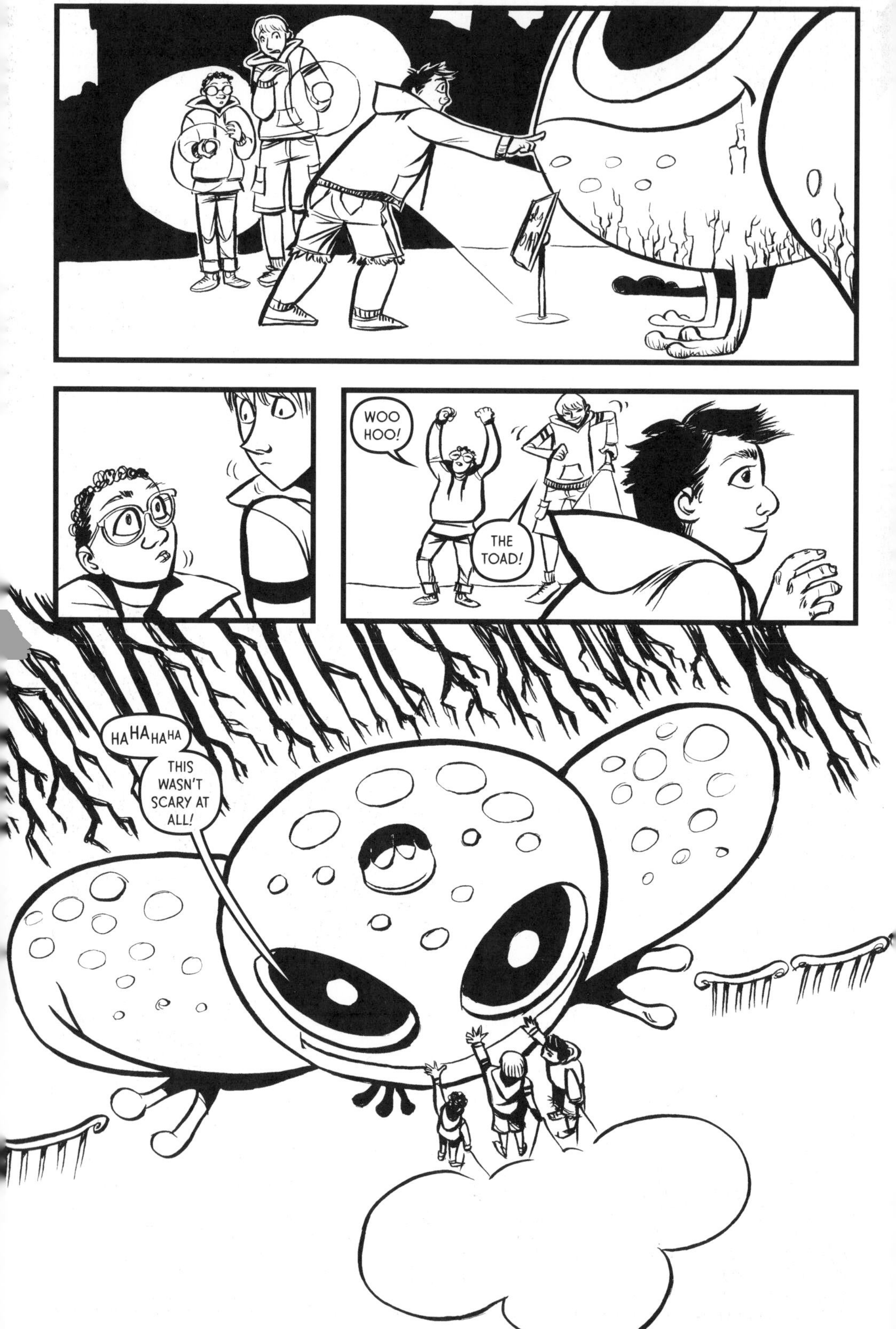
WOO HOO!
THE TOAD!
HAHAHAHA
THIS WASN'T SCARY AT ALL!

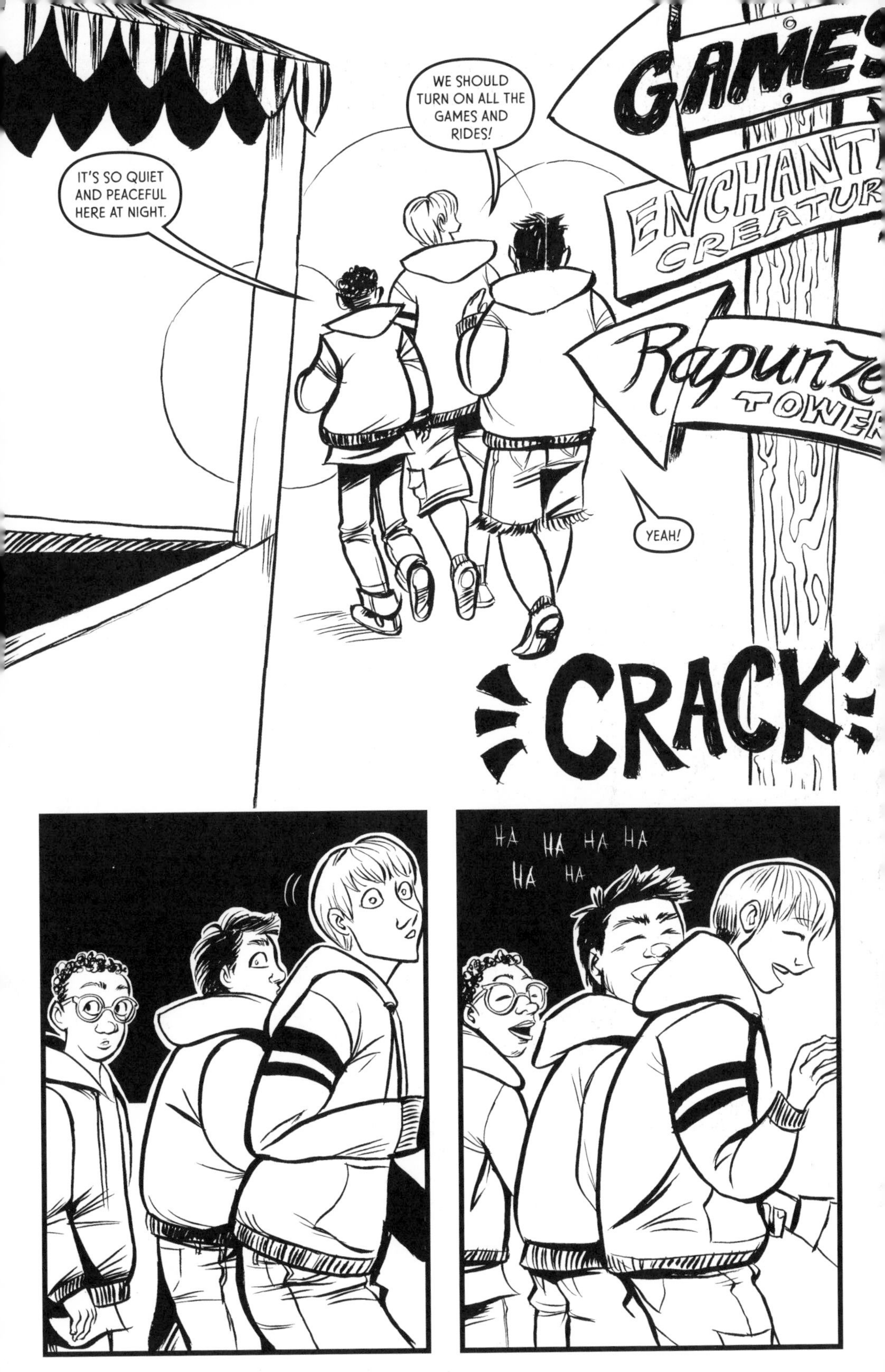
IT'S SO QUIET AND PEACEFUL HERE AT NIGHT.
WE SHOULD TURN ON ALL THE GAMES AND RIDES!
GAMES
ENCHANT
CREATUR
Rapunze
TOWER
YEAH!
CRACK!
HA HA HA HA
HA HA

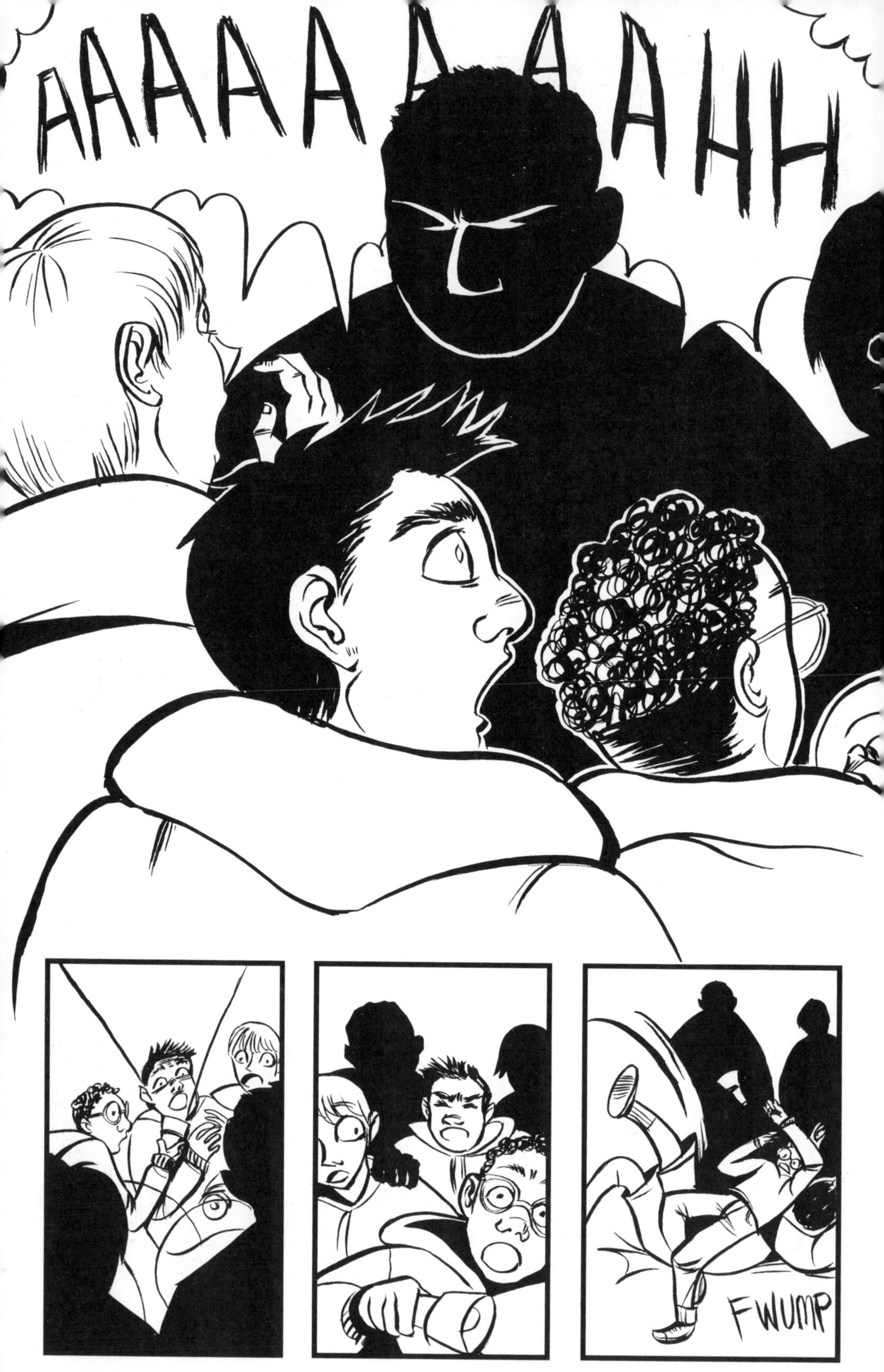
AAAAAAAAHH
FWUMP

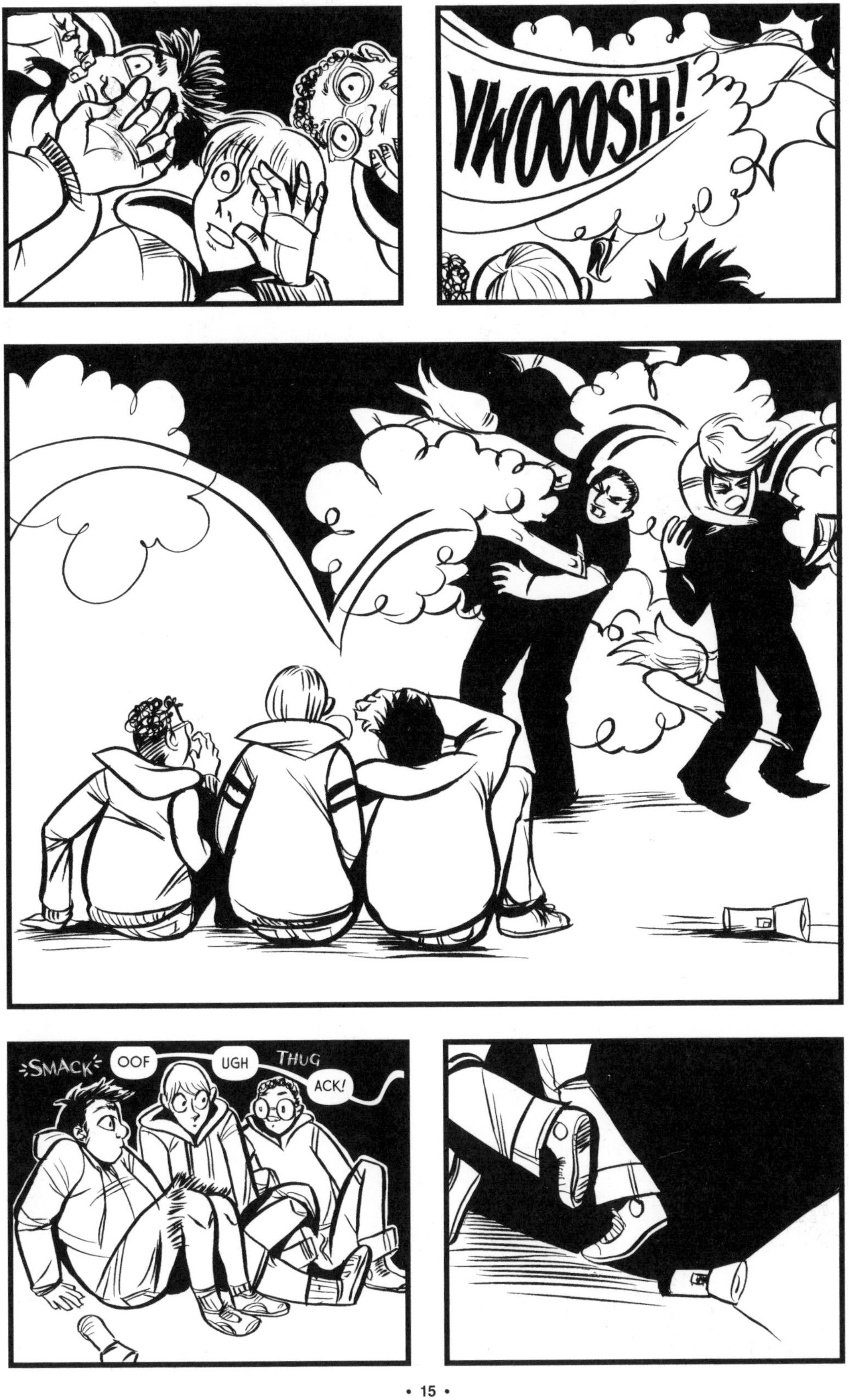
VWOOOSH!
SMACK
OOF
UGH
THUG
ACK!

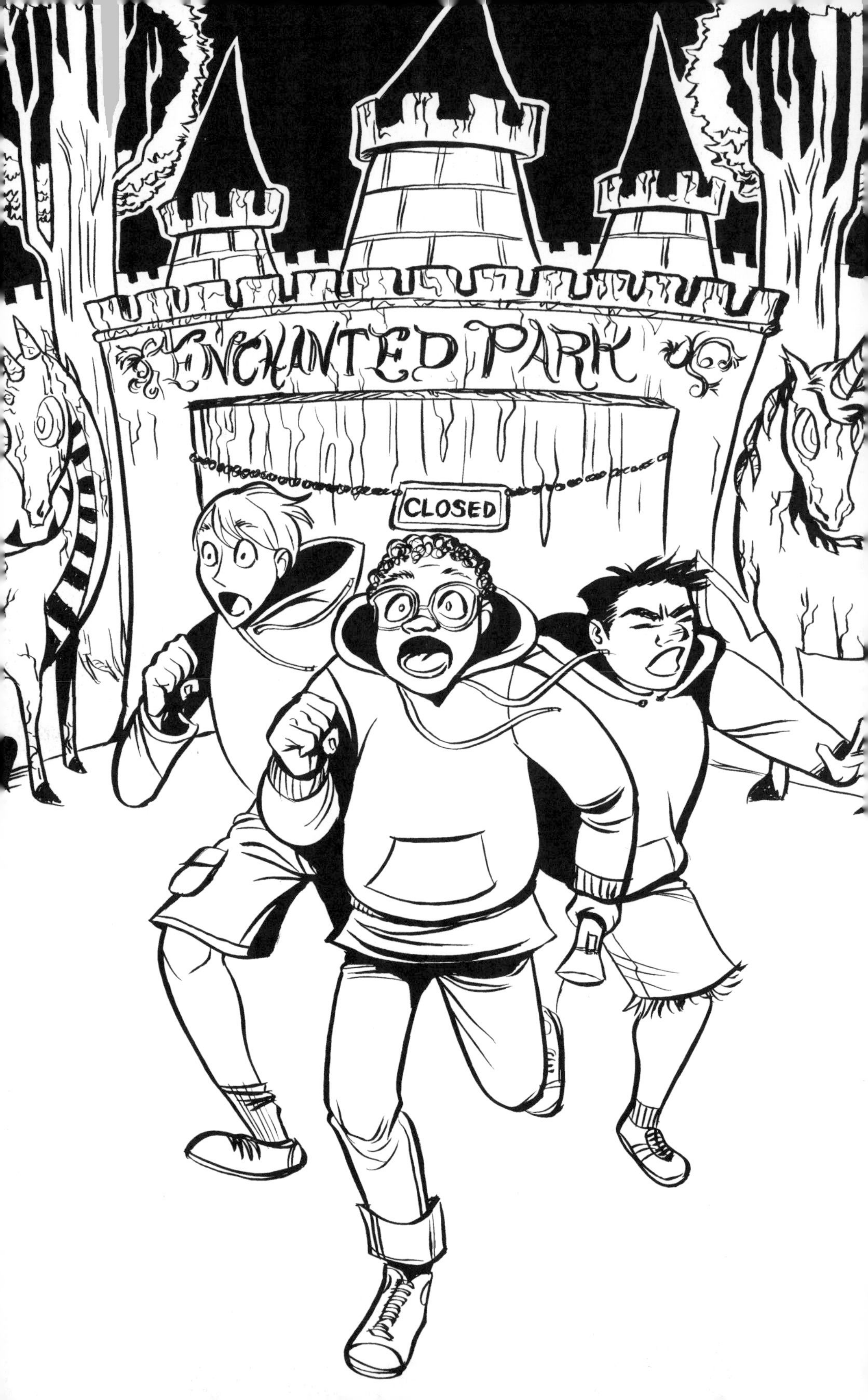
ENCHANTED PARK
CLOSED

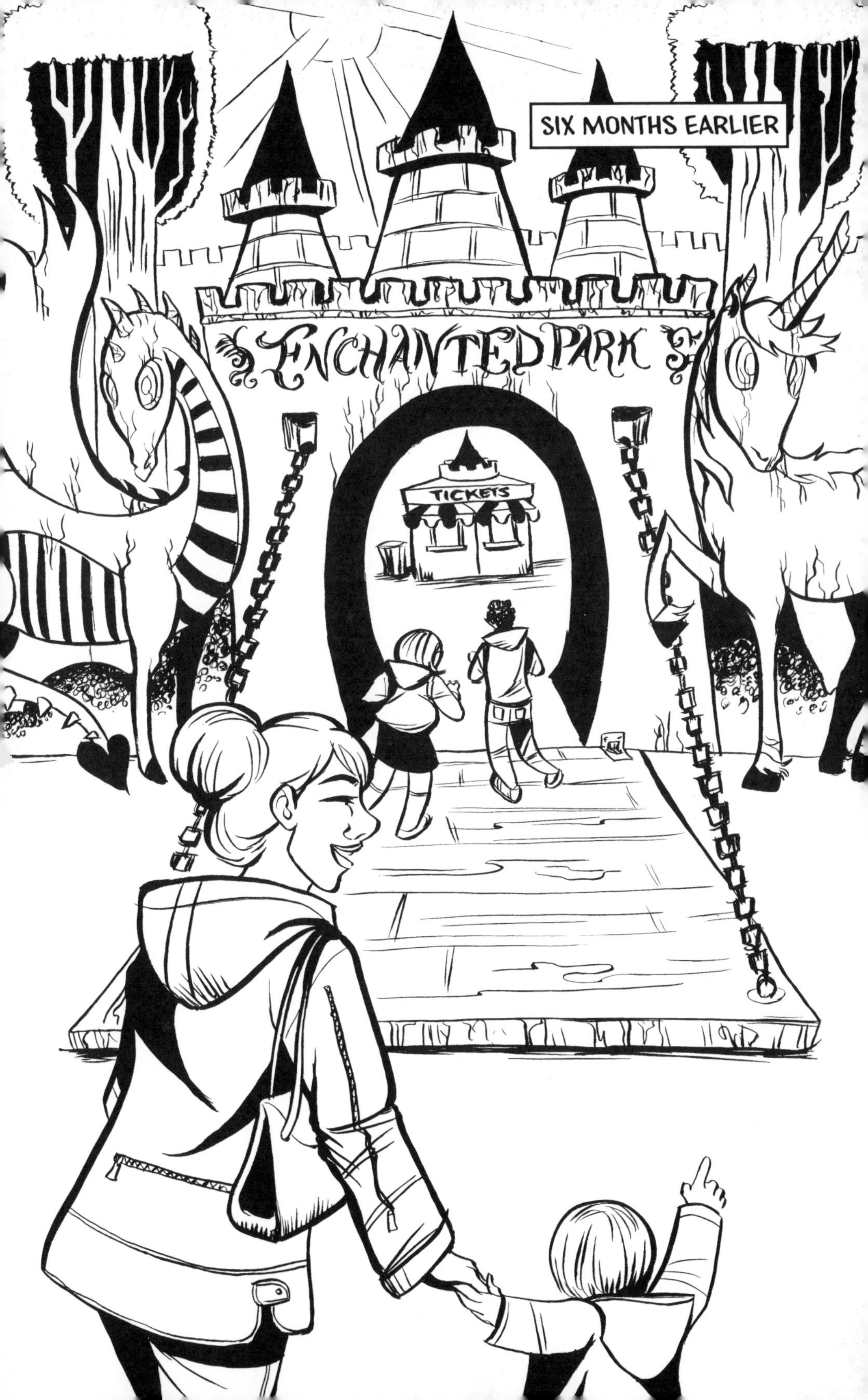
SIX MONTHS EARLIER
ENCHANTED PARK
TICKETS

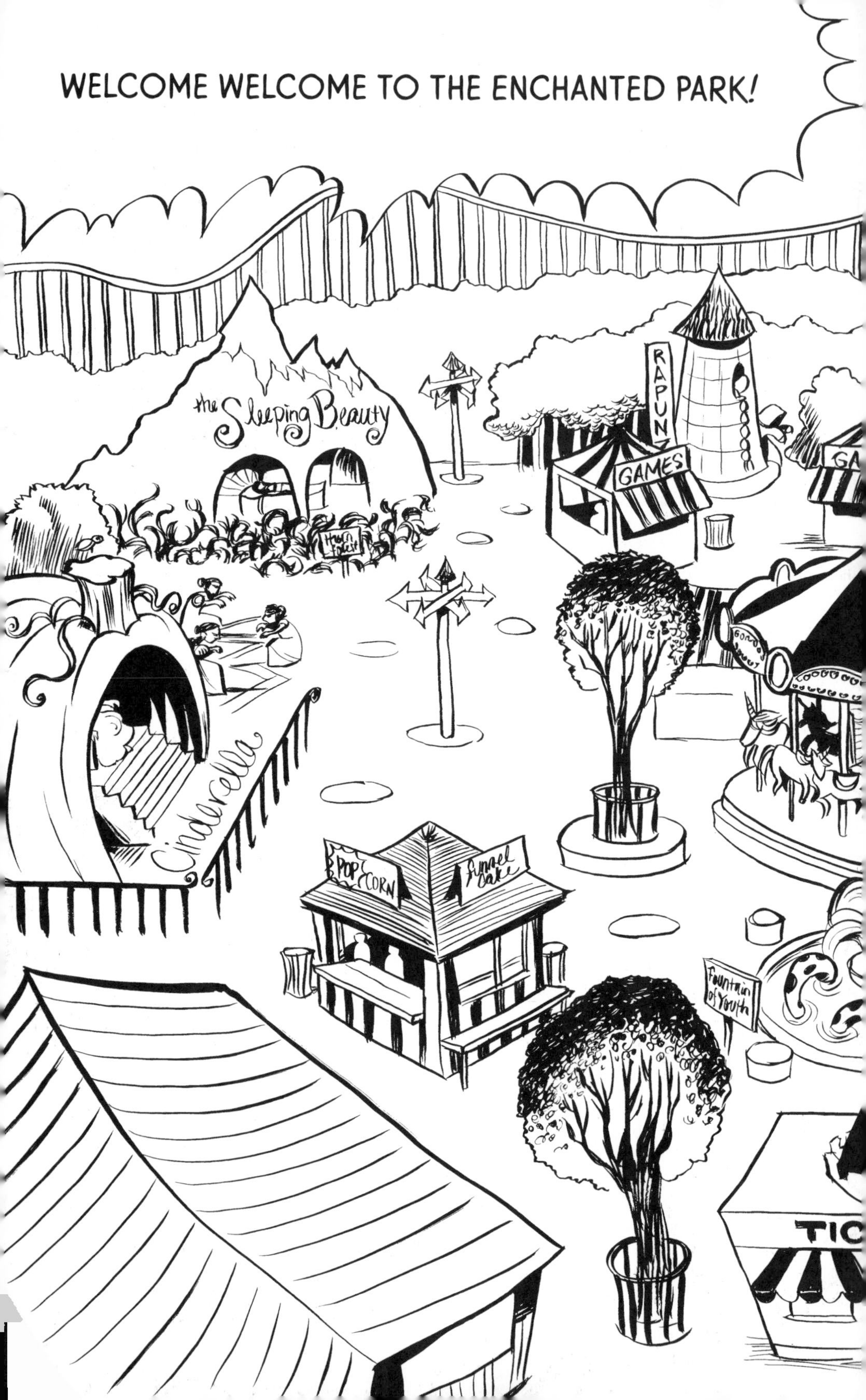

WELCOME WELCOME TO THE ENCHANTED PARK!
the Sleeping Beauty
RAPUNZ
GAMES
GA
Cinderella
POP CORN
funnel cake
Fountain of Youth
TIC

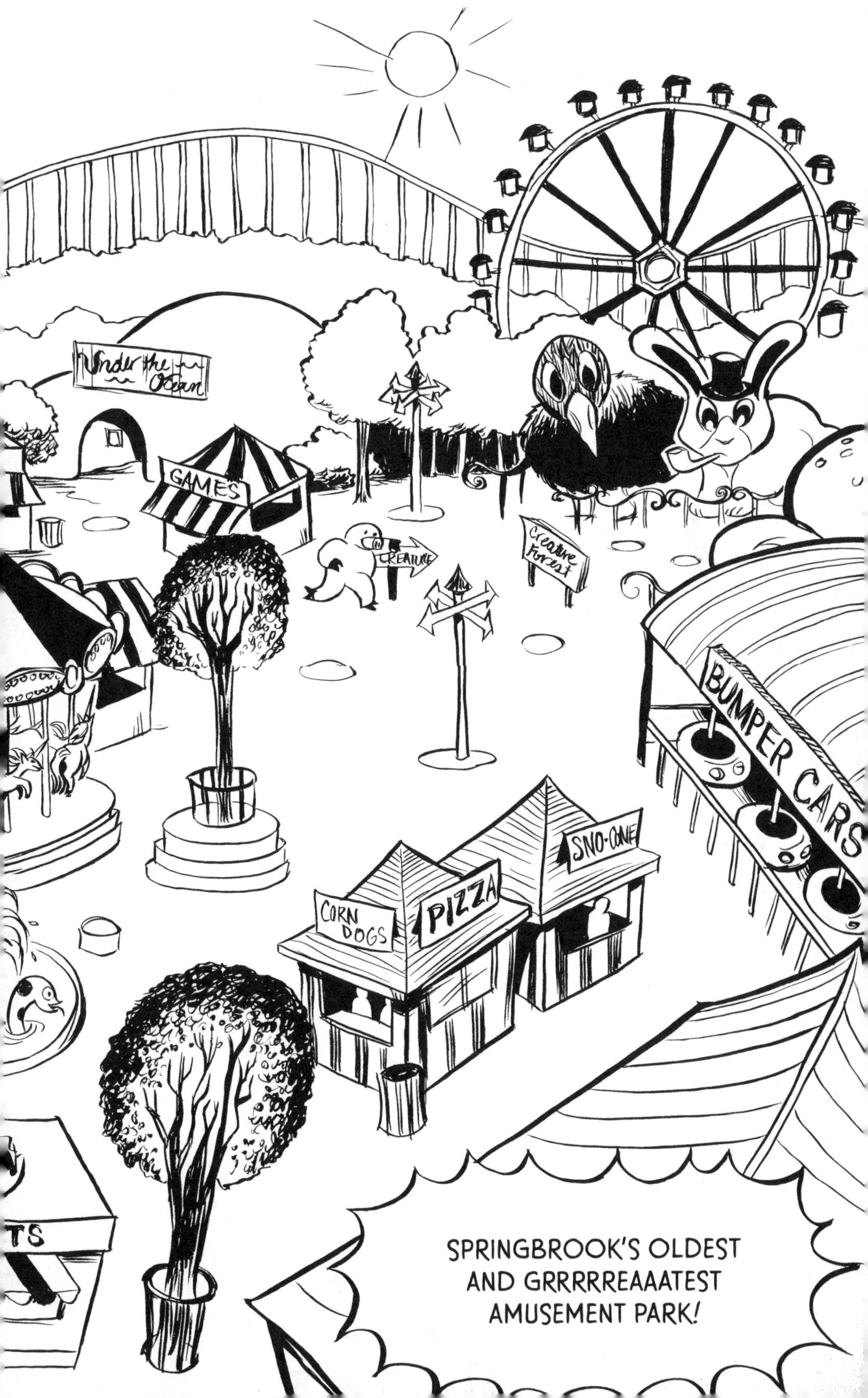
Under the Ocean
GAMES
CREATURE
Creature Forest
BUMPER CARS
CORN DOGS
PIZZA
SNO-CONE
SPRINGBROOK'S OLDEST AND GRRRRREAAATEST AMUSEMENT PARK!

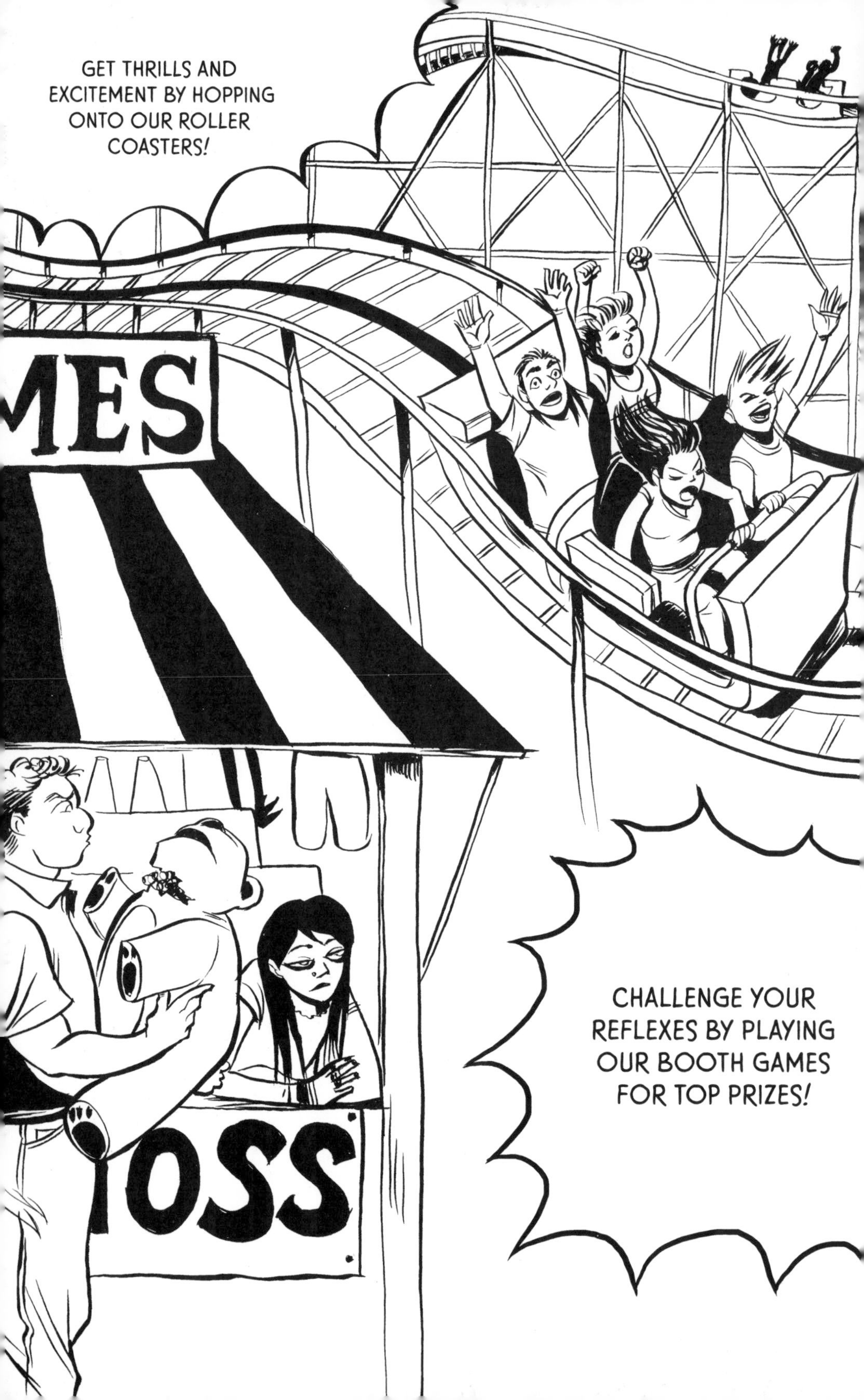
GET THRILLS AND EXCITEMENT BY HOPPING ONTO OUR ROLLER COASTERS!
MES
OSS
CHALLENGE YOUR REFLEXES BY PLAYING OUR BOOTH GAMES FOR TOP PRIZES!

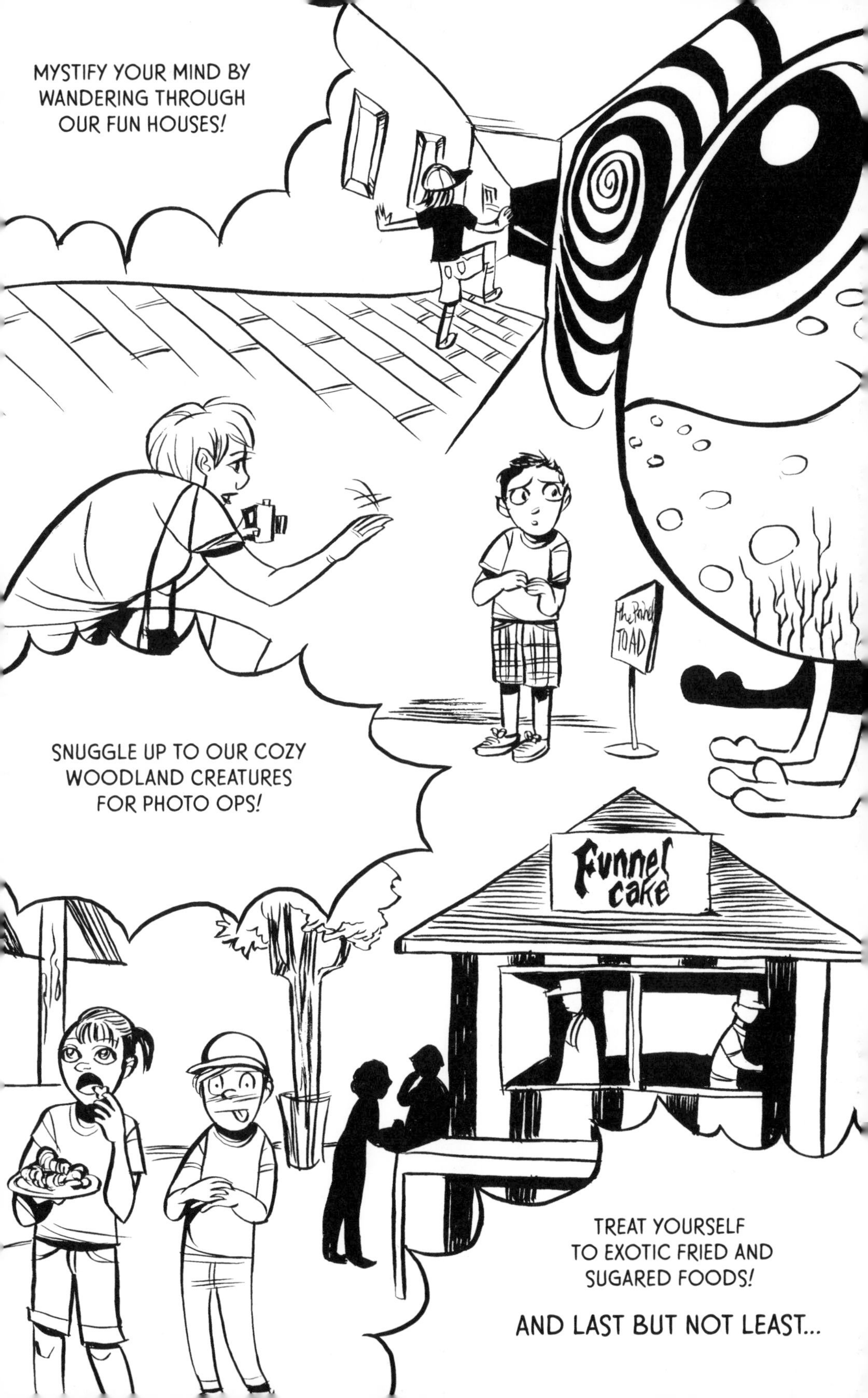
MYSTIFY YOUR MIND BY WANDERING THROUGH OUR FUN HOUSES!
TOAD
SNUGGLE UP TO OUR COZY WOODLAND CREATURES FOR PHOTO OPS!
Funnel cake
TREAT YOURSELF TO EXOTIC FRIED AND SUGARED FOODS!
AND LAST BUT NOT LEAST...

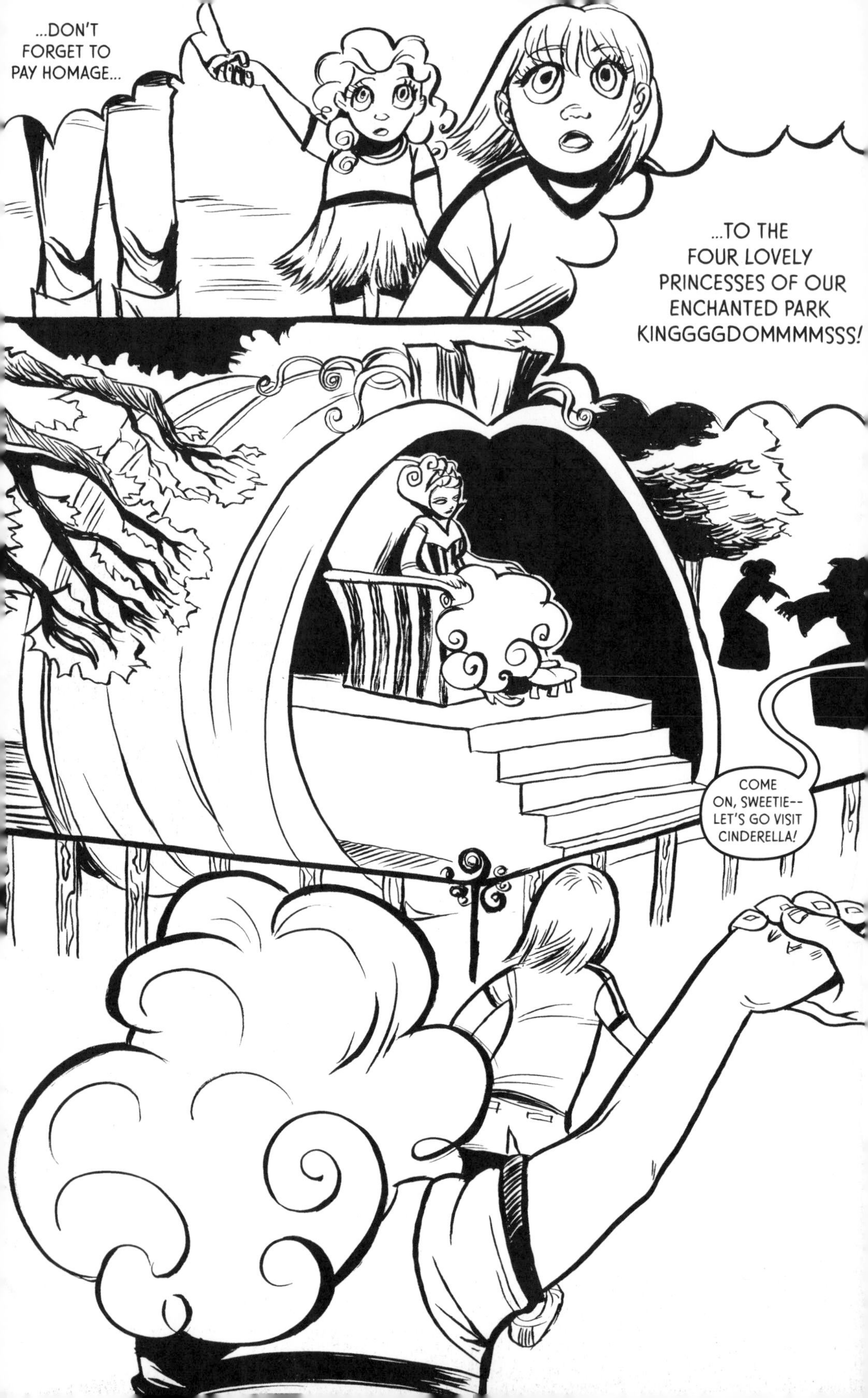
...DON'T FORGET TO PAY HOMAGE...
...TO THE FOUR LOVELY PRINCESSES OF OUR ENCHANTED PARK KINGGGGDOMMMMSSS!
COME ON, SWEETIE-- LET'S GO VISIT CINDERELLA!

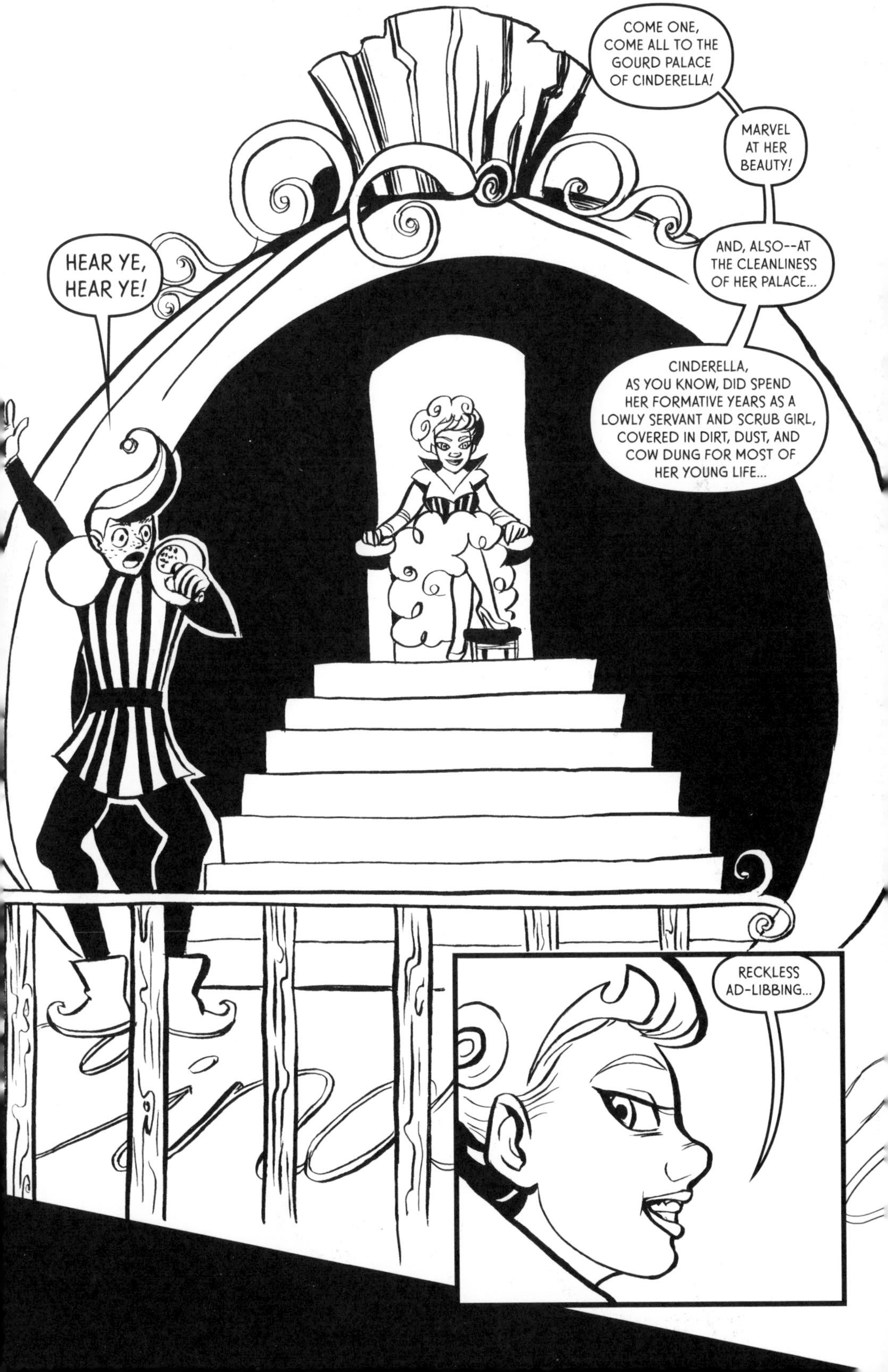
HEAR YE, HEAR YE!
COME ONE, COME ALL TO THE GOURD PALACE OF CINDERELLA!
MARVEL AT HER BEAUTY!
AND, ALSO--AT THE CLEANLINESS OF HER PALACE...
CINDERELLA, AS YOU KNOW, DID SPEND HER FORMATIVE YEARS AS A LOWLY SERVANT AND SCRUB GIRL, COVERED IN DIRT, DUST, AND COW DUNG FOR MOST OF HER YOUNG LIFE...
RECKLESS AD-LIBBING...

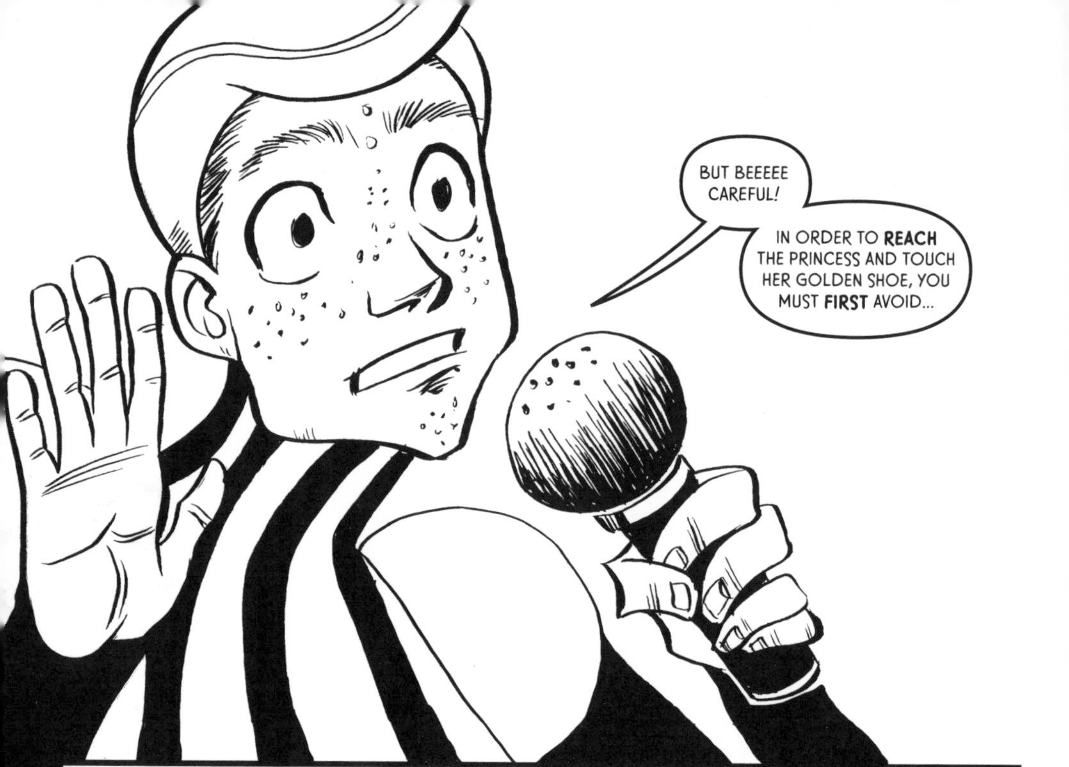
BUT BEEEEE CAREFUL!
IN ORDER TO **REACH** THE PRINCESS AND TOUCH HER GOLDEN SHOE, YOU MUST **FIRST** AVOID...

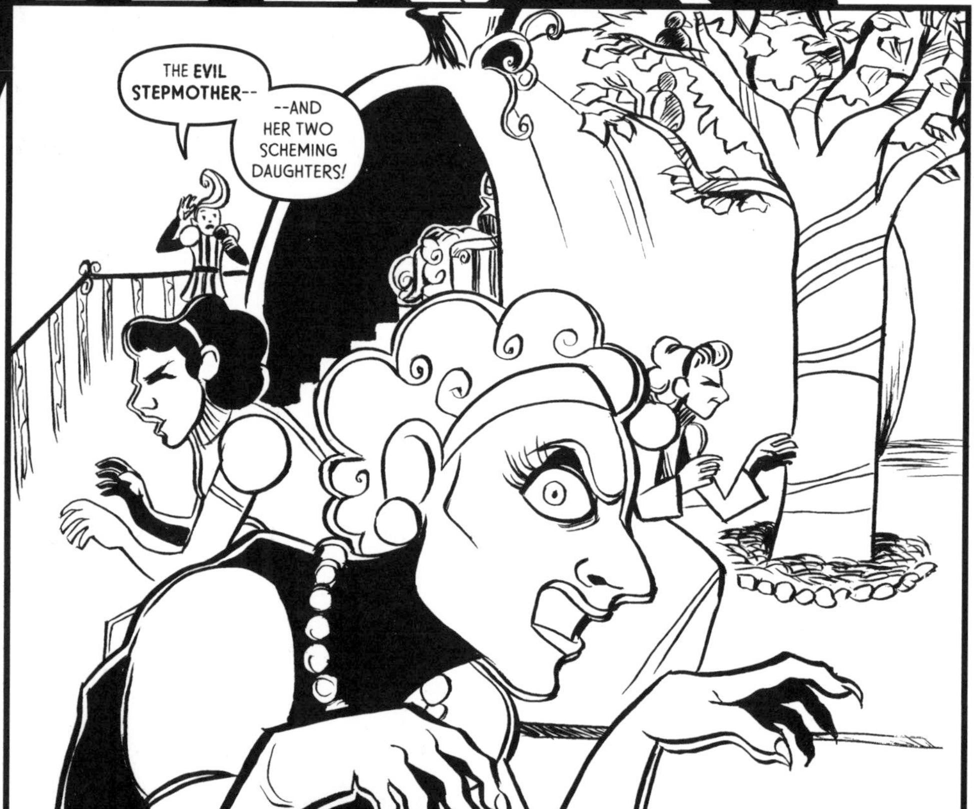
THE **EVIL STEPMOTHER**--
--AND HER TWO SCHEMING DAUGHTERS!

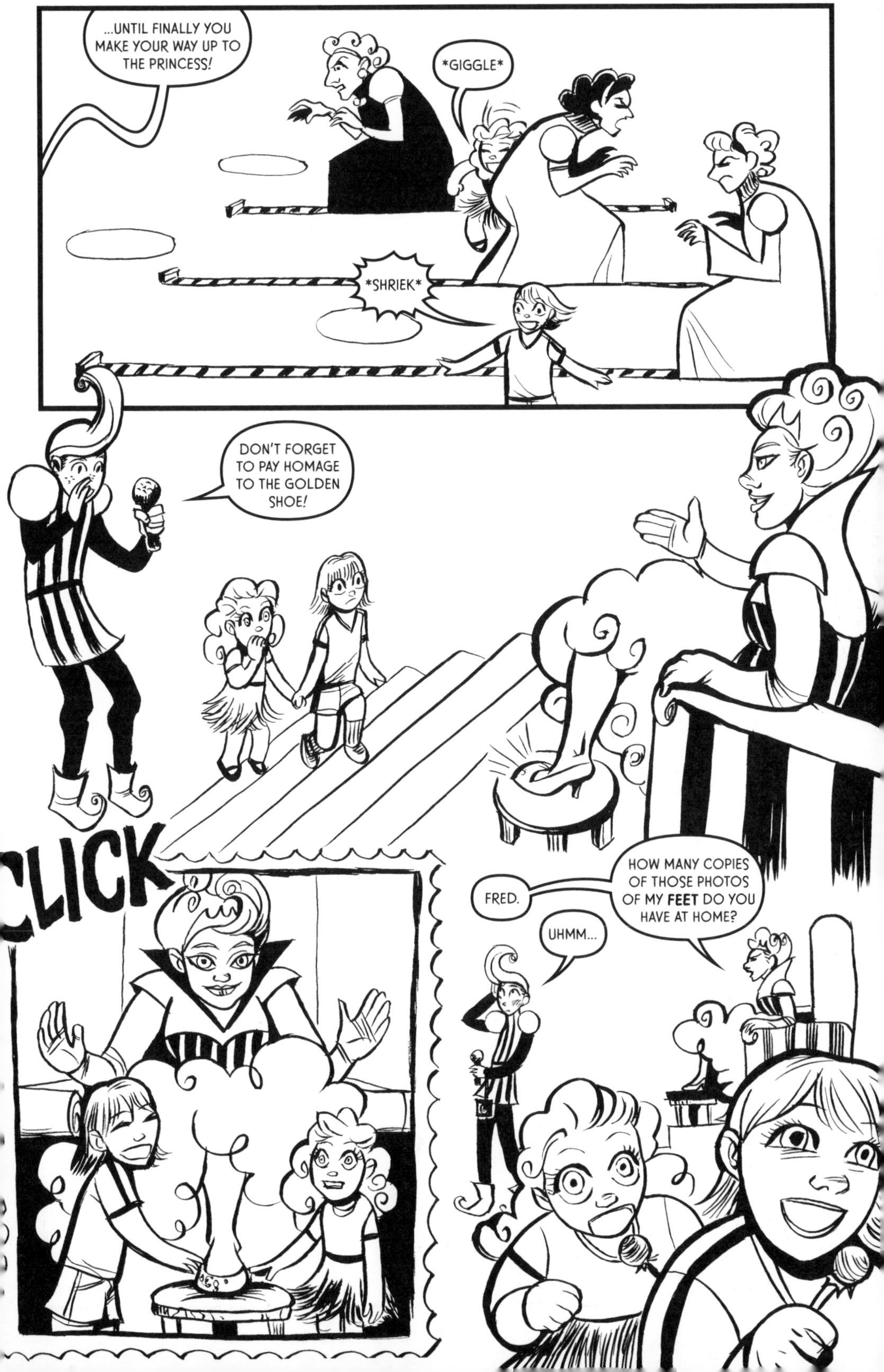
...UNTIL FINALLY YOU MAKE YOUR WAY UP TO THE PRINCESS!
GIGGLE
SHRIEK
DON'T FORGET TO PAY HOMAGE TO THE GOLDEN SHOE!
CLICK
FRED.
HOW MANY COPIES OF THOSE PHOTOS OF MY **FEET** DO YOU HAVE AT HOME?
UHMM...

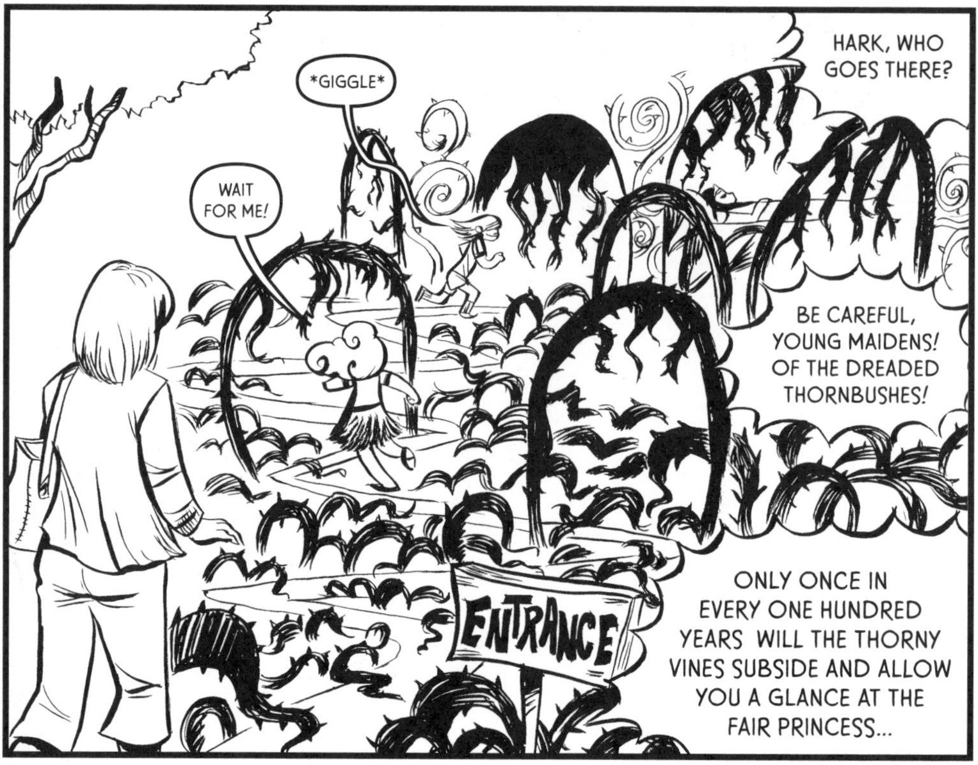
HARK, WHO GOES THERE?
GIGGLE
WAIT FOR ME!
BE CAREFUL, YOUNG MAIDENS! OF THE DREADED THORNBUSHES!
ENTRANCE
ONLY ONCE IN EVERY ONE HUNDRED YEARS WILL THE THORNY VINES SUBSIDE AND ALLOW YOU A GLANCE AT THE FAIR PRINCESS...

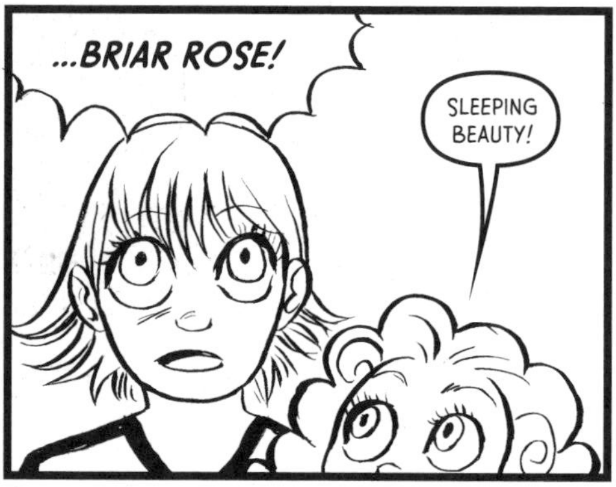
...BRIAR ROSE!
SLEEPING BEAUTY!

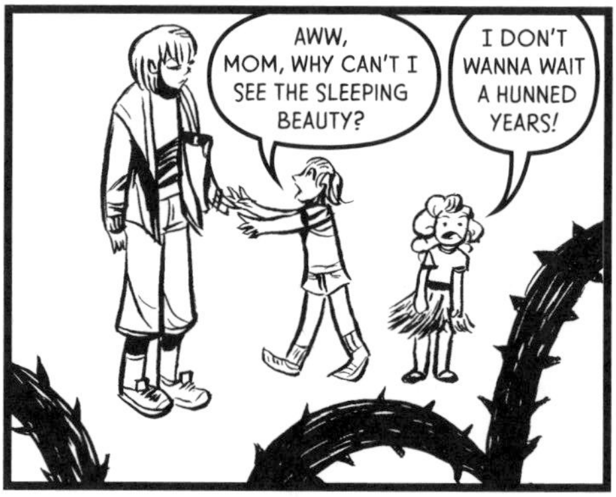
AWW, MOM, WHY CAN'T I SEE THE SLEEPING BEAUTY?
I DON'T WANNA WAIT A HUNNED YEARS!

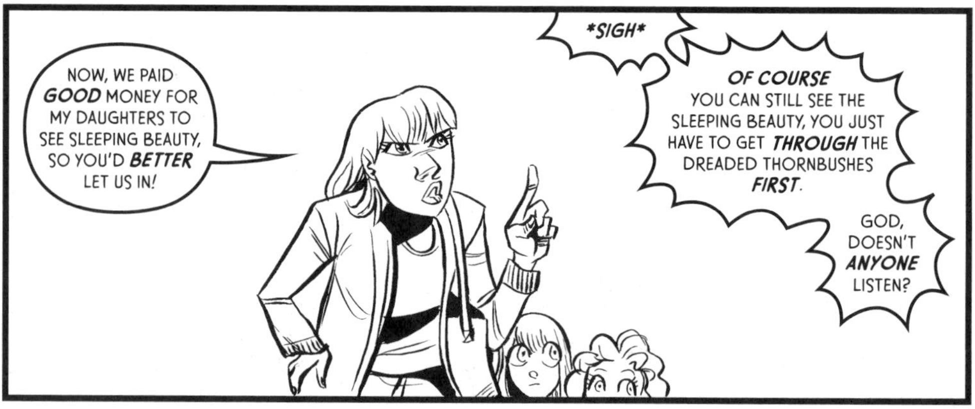
SIGH
NOW, WE PAID GOOD MONEY FOR MY DAUGHTERS TO SEE SLEEPING BEAUTY, SO YOU'D BETTER LET US IN!
OF COURSE YOU CAN STILL SEE THE SLEEPING BEAUTY, YOU JUST HAVE TO GET THROUGH THE DREADED THORNBUSHES FIRST.
GOD, DOESN'T ANYONE LISTEN?

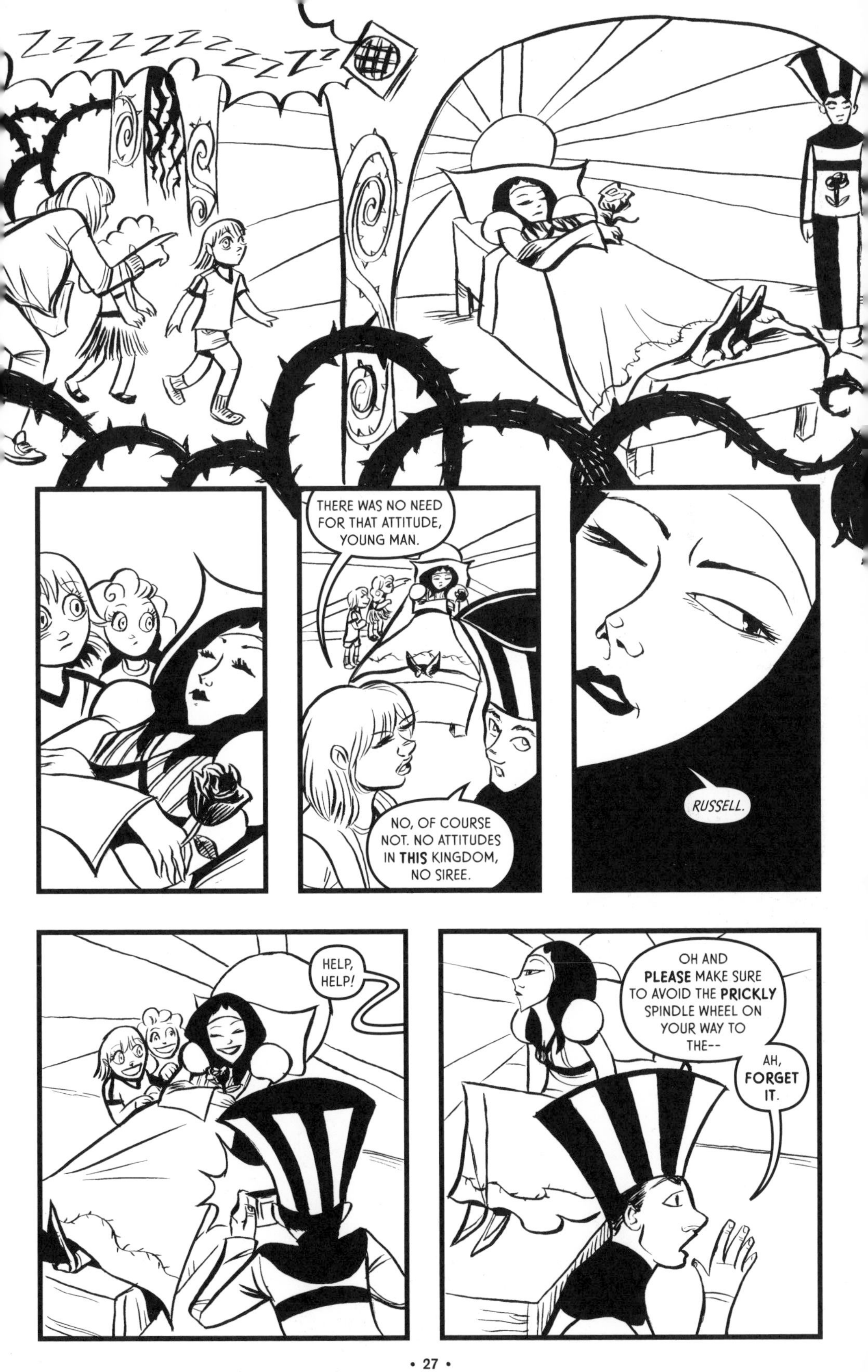
ZZZZZZZZZZZZZZ
THERE WAS NO NEED FOR THAT ATTITUDE, YOUNG MAN.
NO, OF COURSE NOT. NO ATTITUDES IN **THIS** KINGDOM, NO SIREE.
RUSSELL.
HELP, HELP!
OH AND **PLEASE** MAKE SURE TO AVOID THE **PRICKLY** SPINDLE WHEEL ON YOUR WAY TO THE--
AH, **FORGET** IT.

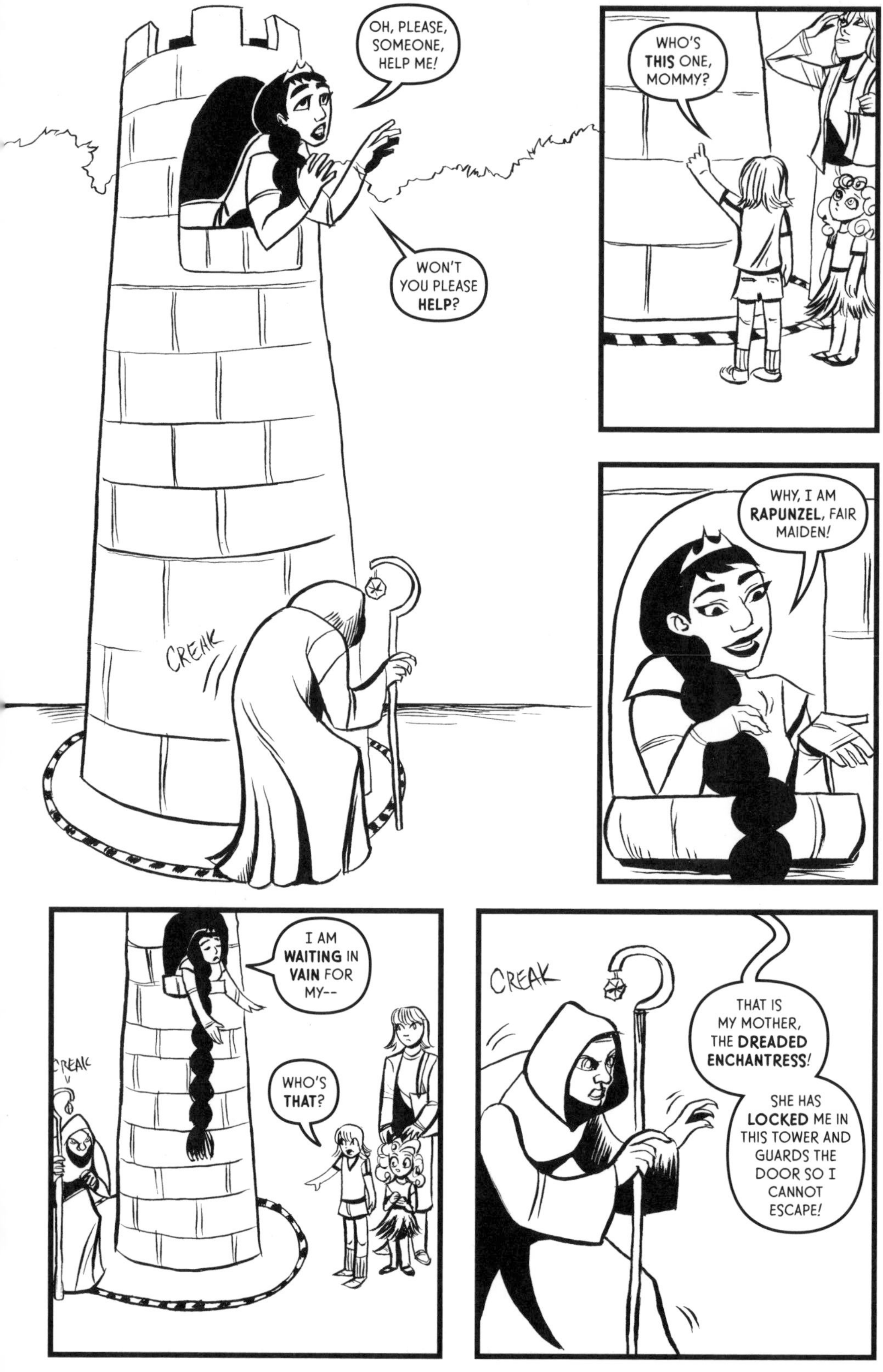
OH, PLEASE, SOMEONE, HELP ME!
WON'T YOU PLEASE HELP?
WHO'S THIS ONE, MOMMY?
CREAK
WHY, I AM RAPUNZEL, FAIR MAIDEN!
I AM WAITING IN VAIN FOR MY--
CREAK
WHO'S THAT?
CREAK
THAT IS MY MOTHER, THE DREADED ENCHANTRESS!
SHE HAS LOCKED ME IN THIS TOWER AND GUARDS THE DOOR SO I CANNOT ESCAPE!

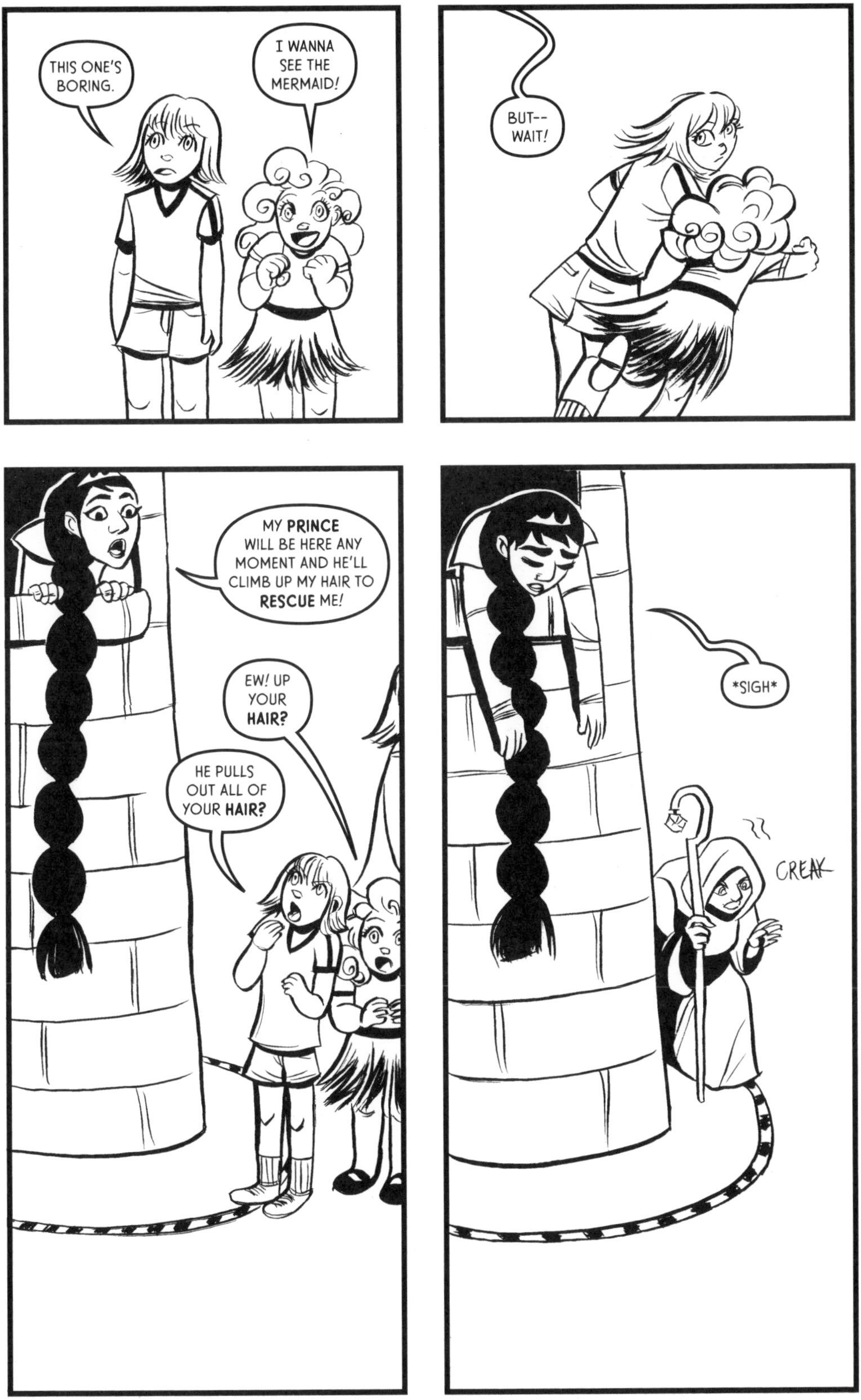
THIS ONE'S BORING.
I WANNA SEE THE MERMAID!
BUT-- WAIT!
MY **PRINCE** WILL BE HERE ANY MOMENT AND HE'LL CLIMB UP MY HAIR TO **RESCUE** ME!
EW! UP YOUR **HAIR?**
HE PULLS OUT ALL OF YOUR **HAIR?**
SIGH
CREAK

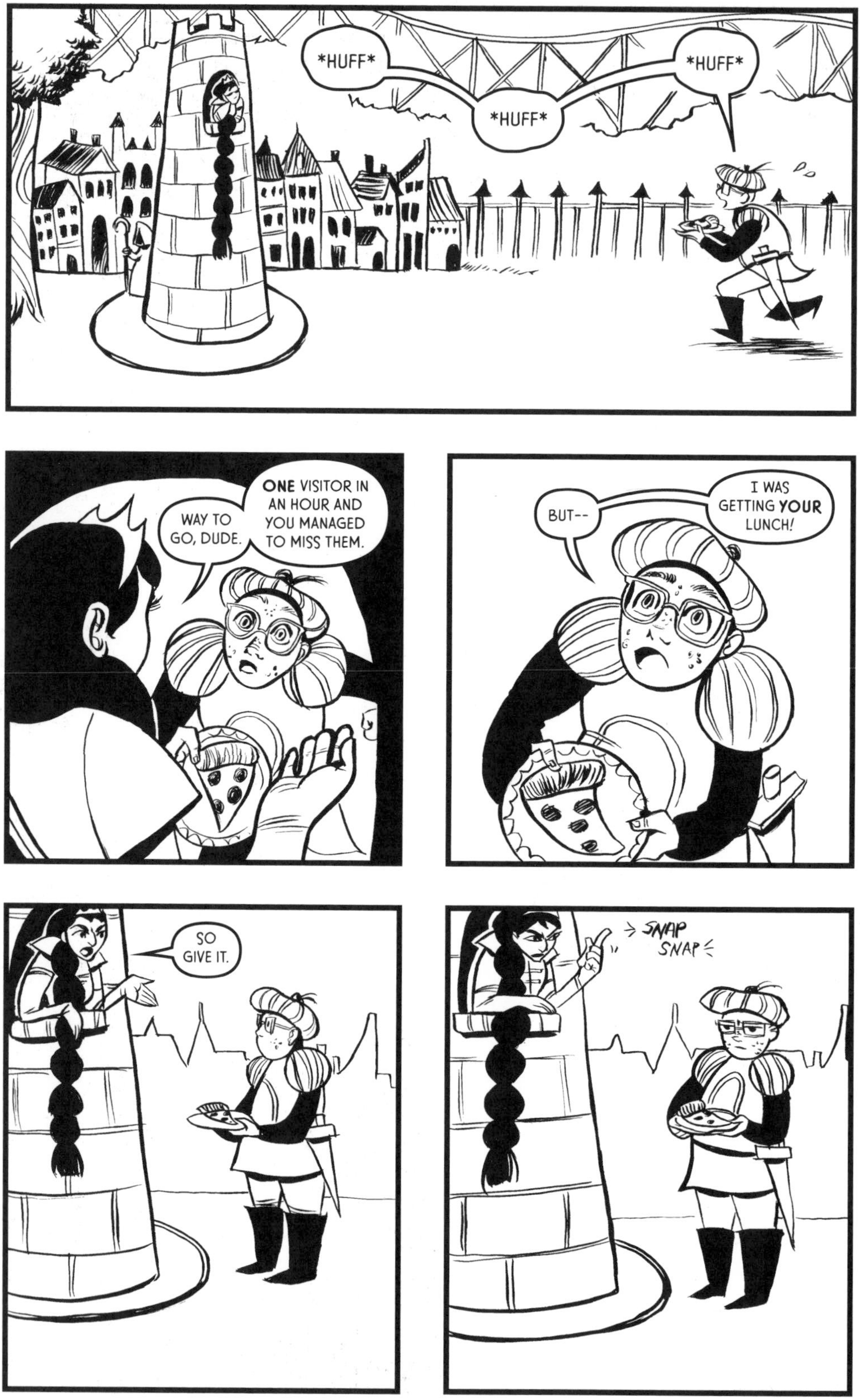
HUFF
HUFF
HUFF
WAY TO GO, DUDE.
ONE VISITOR IN AN HOUR AND YOU MANAGED TO MISS THEM.
BUT--
I WAS GETTING YOUR LUNCH!
SO GIVE IT.
SNAP
SNAP

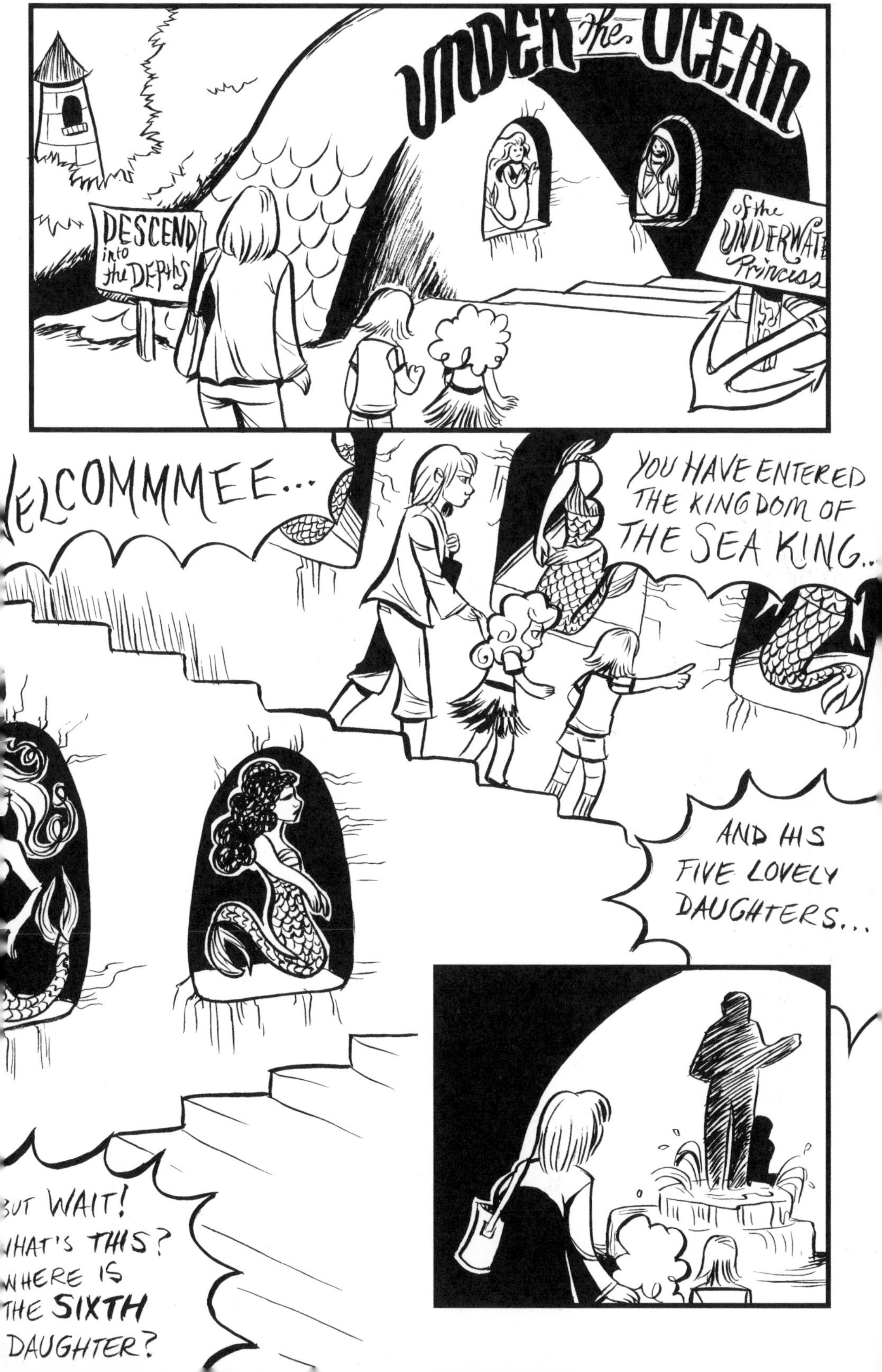

UNDER the OCEAN
DESCEND into the DEPTHS
of the UNDERWAT Princess
ELCOMMMEE...
YOU HAVE ENTERED THE KINGDOM OF THE SEA KING...
AND HIS FIVE LOVELY DAUGHTERS...
UT WAIT! HAT'S THIS? HERE IS THE SIXTH DAUGHTER?

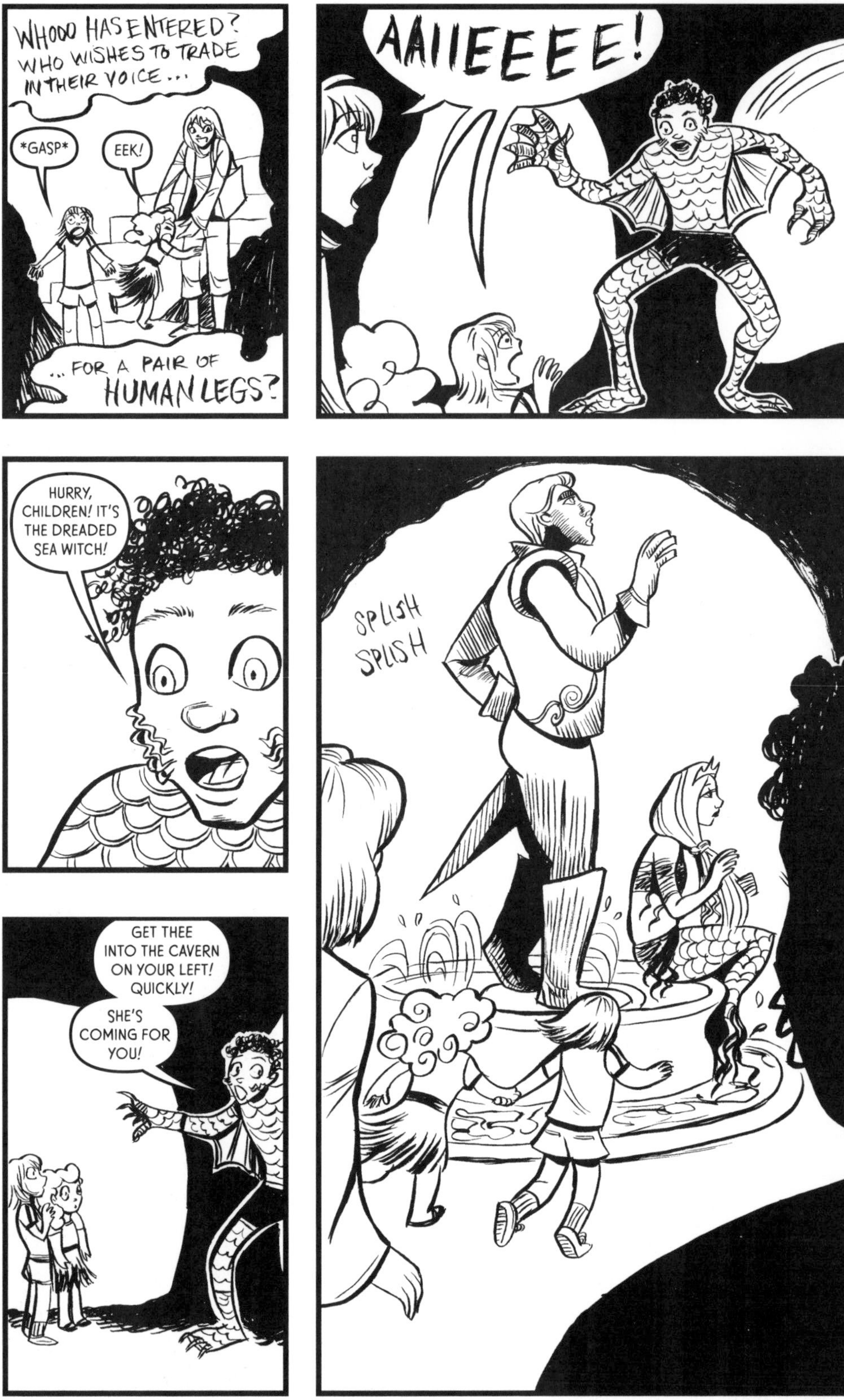
WHOOO HAS ENTERED? WHO WISHES TO TRADE IN THEIR VOICE...
GASP
EEK!
...FOR A PAIR OF HUMAN LEGS?
AAIIEEEEE!
HURRY, CHILDREN! IT'S THE DREADED SEA WITCH!
GET THEE INTO THE CAVERN ON YOUR LEFT! QUICKLY!
SHE'S COMING FOR YOU!
SPLISH SPLISH

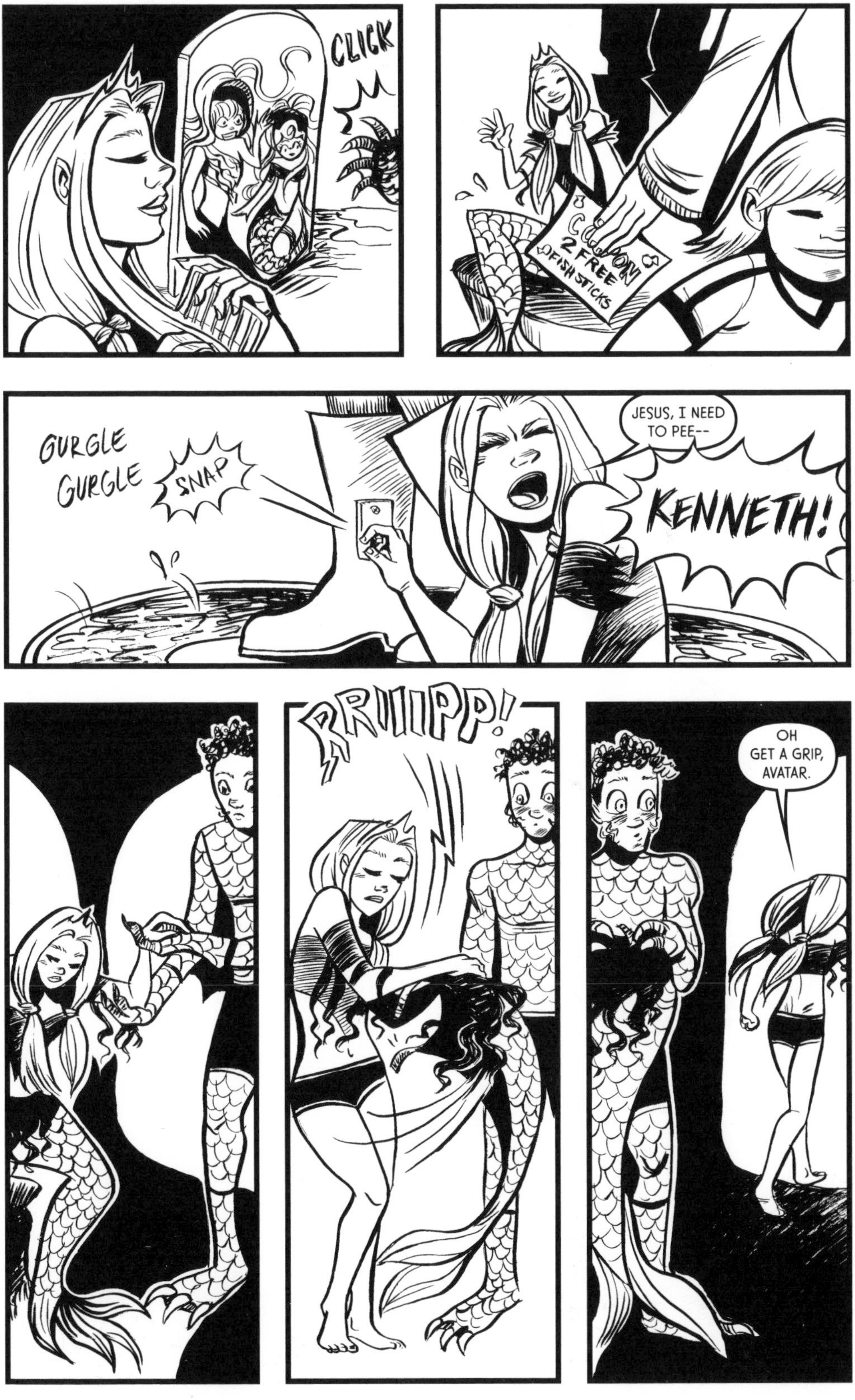
CLICK
2 FREE
FISH STICKS
GURGLE
GURGLE
SNAP
JESUS, I NEED TO PEE--
KENNETH!
RRIIIPP!
OH GET A GRIP, AVATAR.

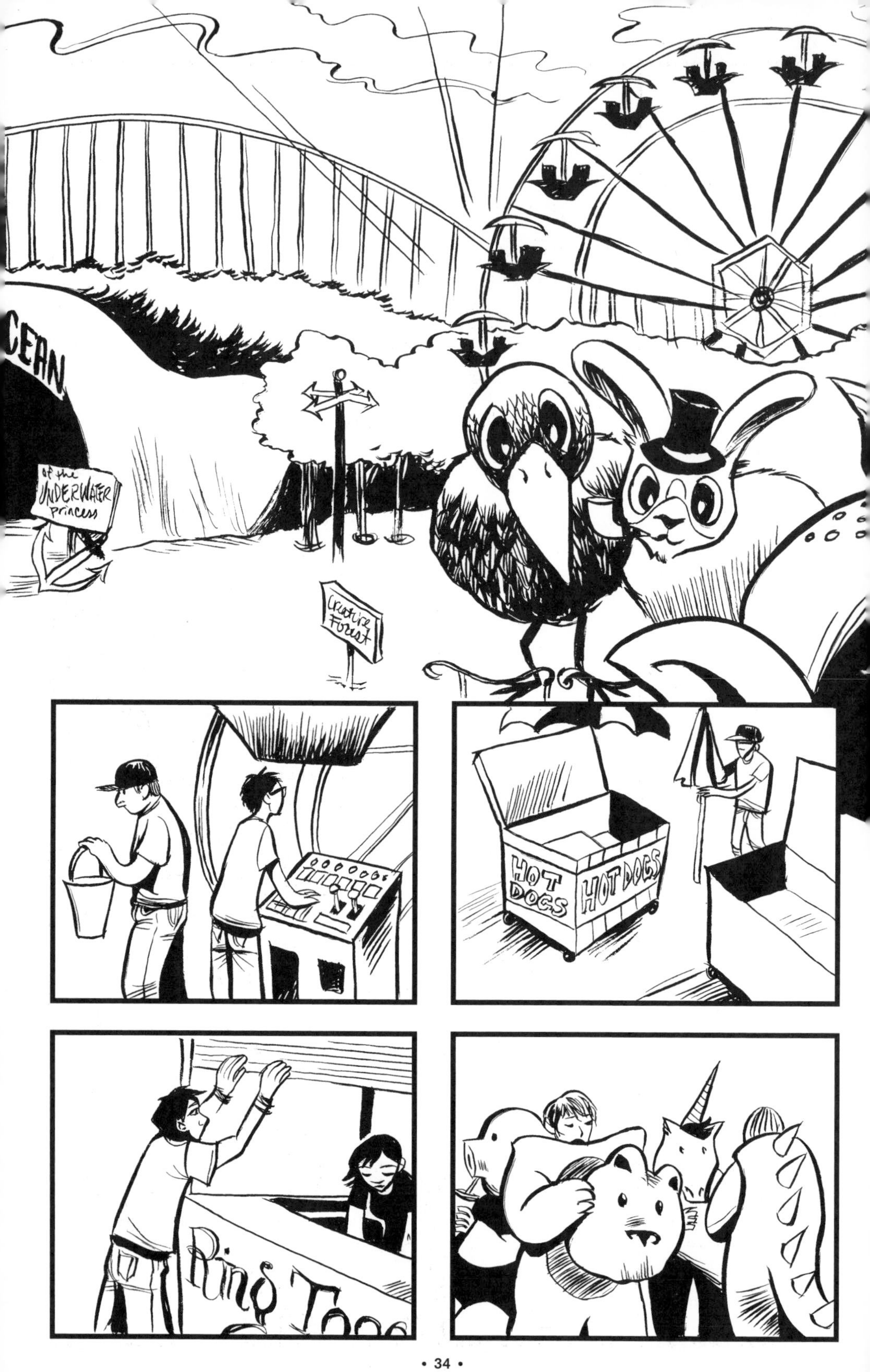
CEAN
of the UNDERWATER princess
Creature Forest
HOT DOGS
HOT DOGS
Ring Toss

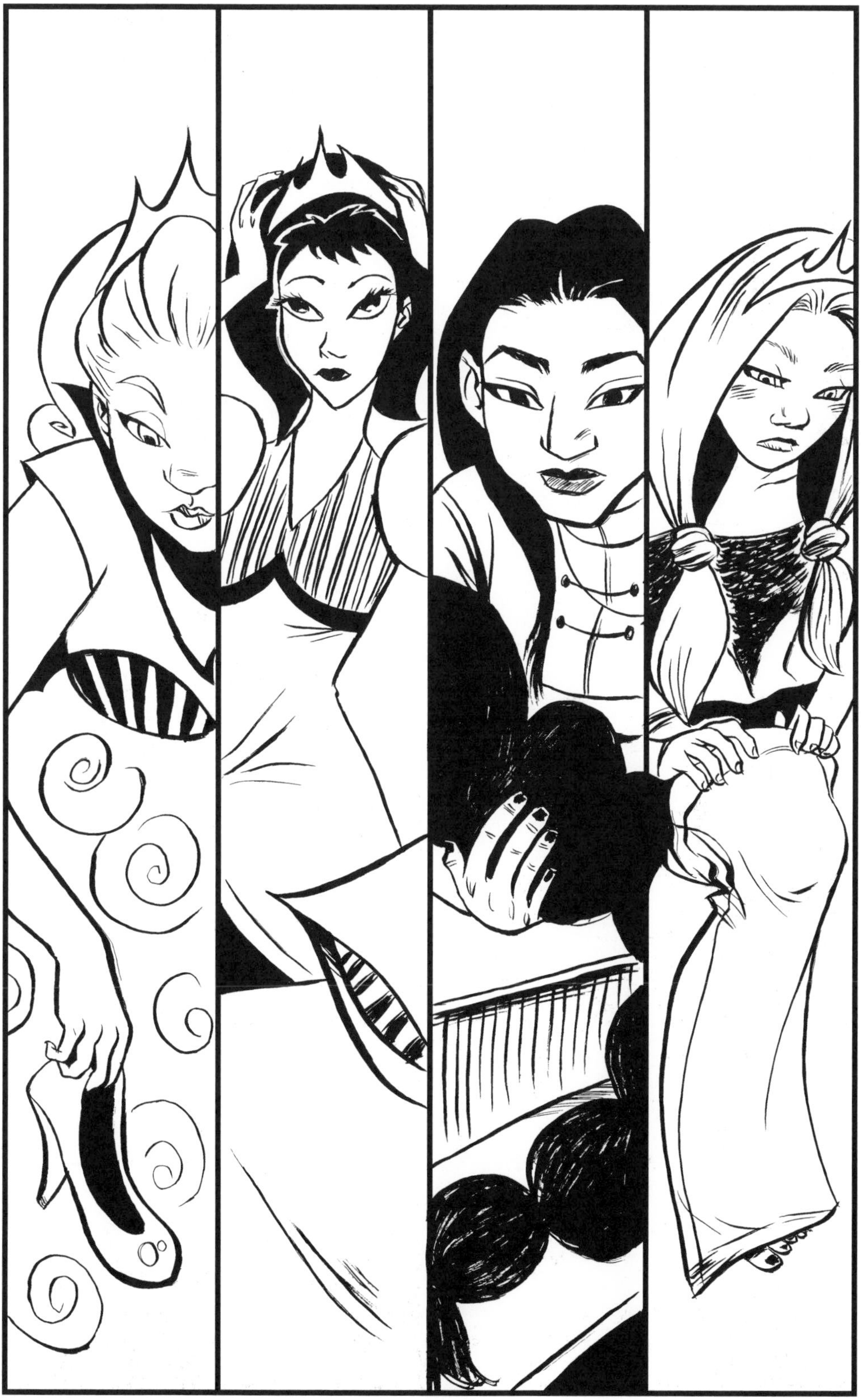

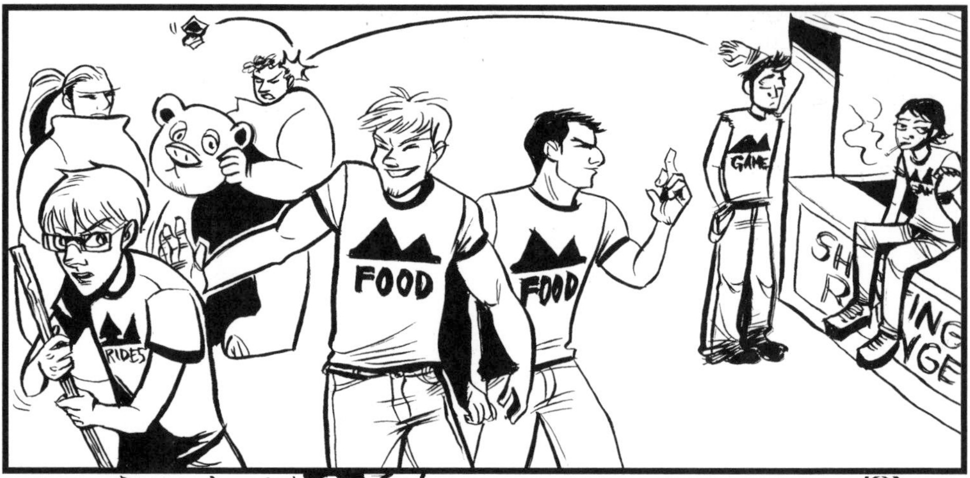
RIDES
FOOD
FOOD
GAME

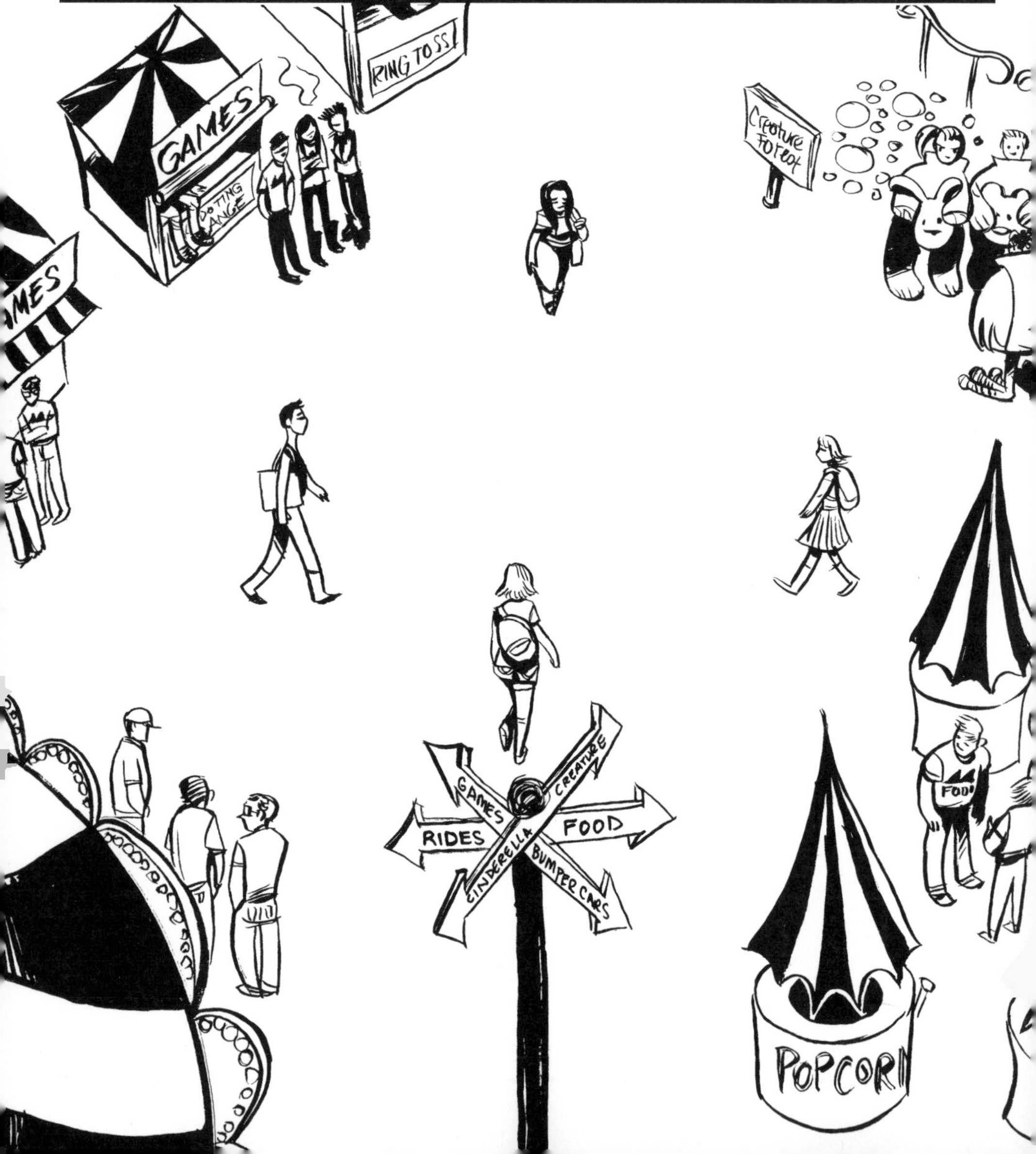
RING TOSS!
GAMES
Creature Forest
RIDES
GAMES
CREATURE
FOOD
CINDERELLA
BUMPER CARS

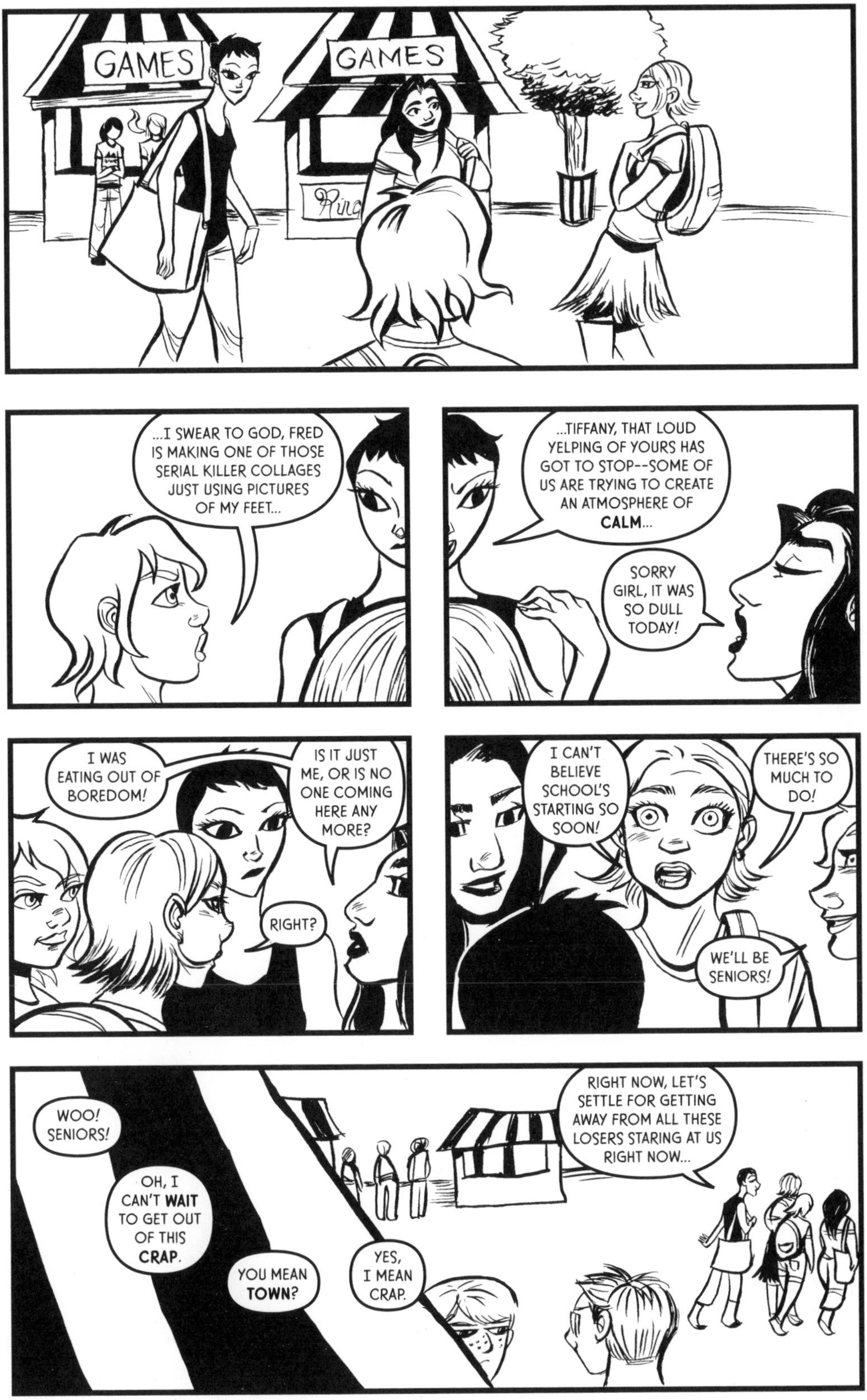
GAMES
GAMES
...I SWEAR TO GOD, FRED IS MAKING ONE OF THOSE SERIAL KILLER COLLAGES JUST USING PICTURES OF MY FEET...
...TIFFANY, THAT LOUD YELPING OF YOURS HAS GOT TO STOP--SOME OF US ARE TRYING TO CREATE AN ATMOSPHERE OF **CALM**...
SORRY GIRL, IT WAS SO DULL TODAY!
I WAS EATING OUT OF BOREDOM!
IS IT JUST ME, OR IS NO ONE COMING HERE ANY MORE?
RIGHT?
I CAN'T BELIEVE SCHOOL'S STARTING SO SOON!
THERE'S SO MUCH TO DO!
WE'LL BE SENIORS!
WOO! SENIORS!
OH, I CAN'T **WAIT** TO GET OUT OF THIS **CRAP**.
YOU MEAN **TOWN**?
YES, I MEAN CRAP.
RIGHT NOW, LET'S SETTLE FOR GETTING AWAY FROM ALL THESE LOSERS STARING AT US RIGHT NOW...

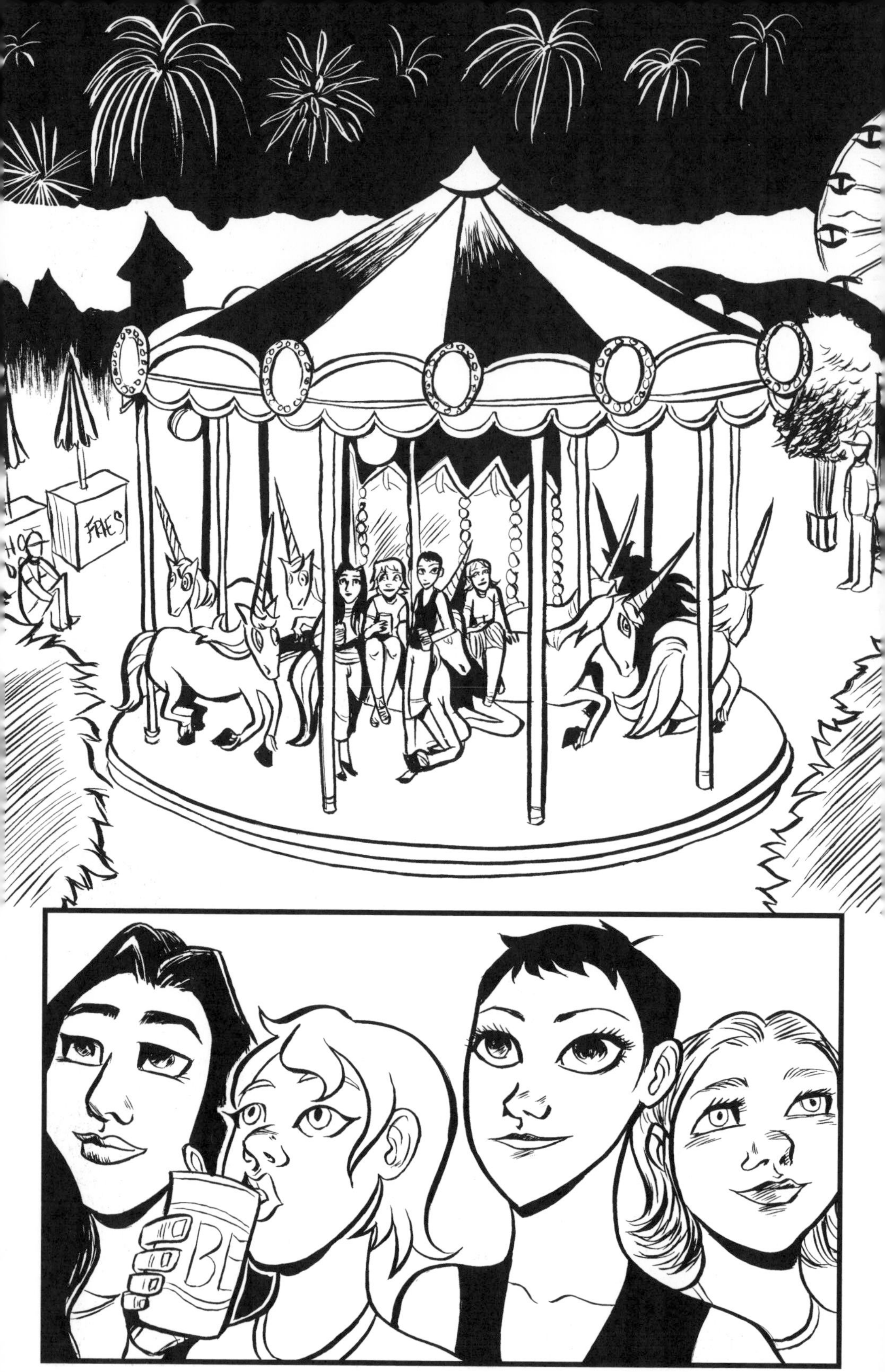
FRIES

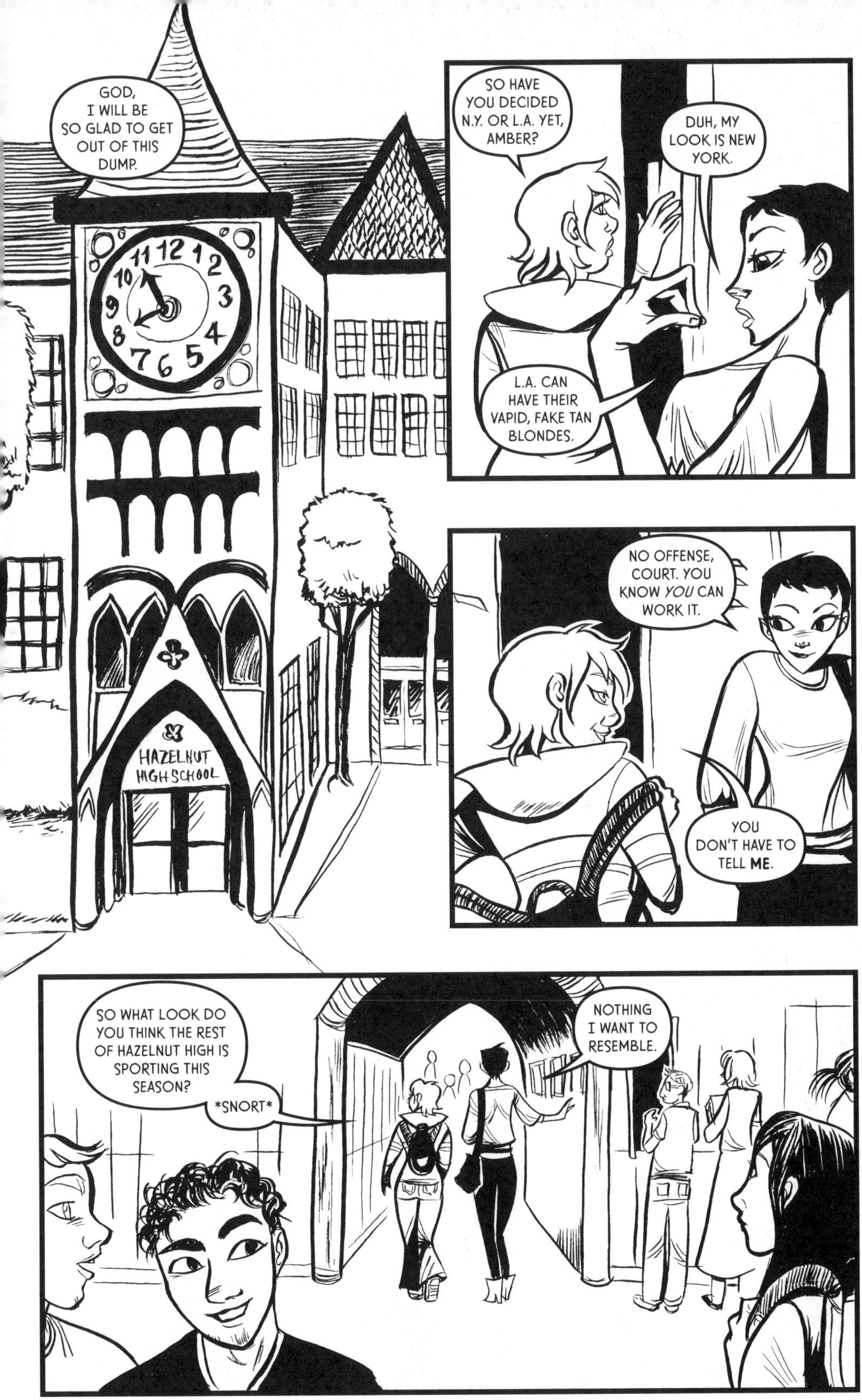
GOD, I WILL BE SO GLAD TO GET OUT OF THIS DUMP.
HAZELNUT HIGH SCHOOL
SO HAVE YOU DECIDED N.Y. OR L.A. YET, AMBER?
DUH, MY LOOK IS NEW YORK.
L.A. CAN HAVE THEIR VAPID, FAKE TAN BLONDES.
NO OFFENSE, COURT. YOU KNOW *YOU* CAN WORK IT.
YOU DON'T HAVE TO TELL **ME**.
SO WHAT LOOK DO YOU THINK THE REST OF HAZELNUT HIGH IS SPORTING THIS SEASON?
SNORT
NOTHING I WANT TO RESEMBLE.

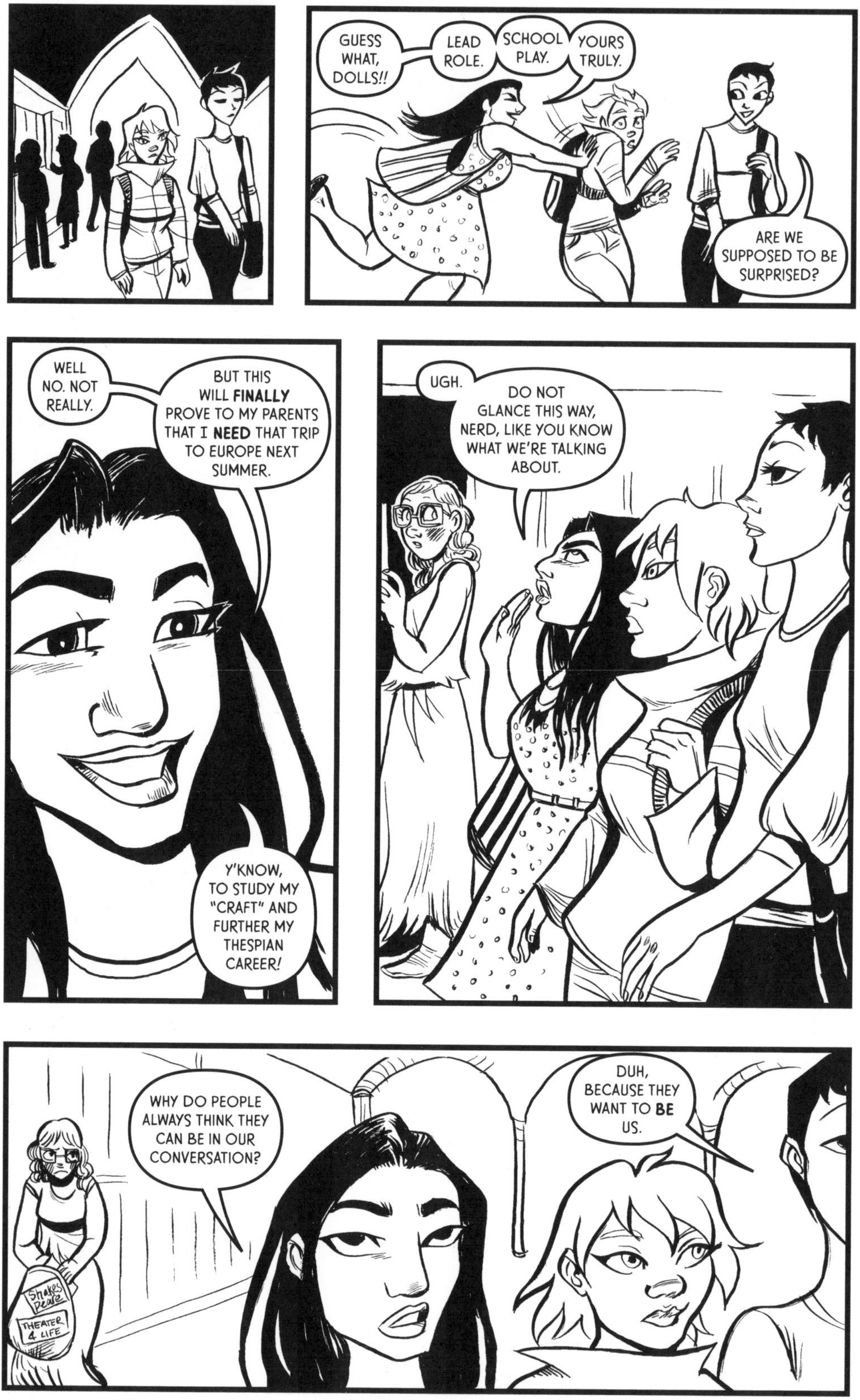
GUESS WHAT, DOLLS!!
LEAD ROLE.
SCHOOL PLAY.
YOURS TRULY.
ARE WE SUPPOSED TO BE SURPRISED?
WELL NO. NOT REALLY.
BUT THIS WILL **FINALLY** PROVE TO MY PARENTS THAT I **NEED** THAT TRIP TO EUROPE NEXT SUMMER.
Y'KNOW, TO STUDY MY "CRAFT" AND FURTHER MY THESPIAN CAREER!
UGH.
DO NOT GLANCE THIS WAY, NERD, LIKE YOU KNOW WHAT WE'RE TALKING ABOUT.
WHY DO PEOPLE ALWAYS THINK THEY CAN BE IN OUR CONVERSATION?
DUH, BECAUSE THEY WANT TO **BE** US.
Shakespeare
THEATER 4 LIFE

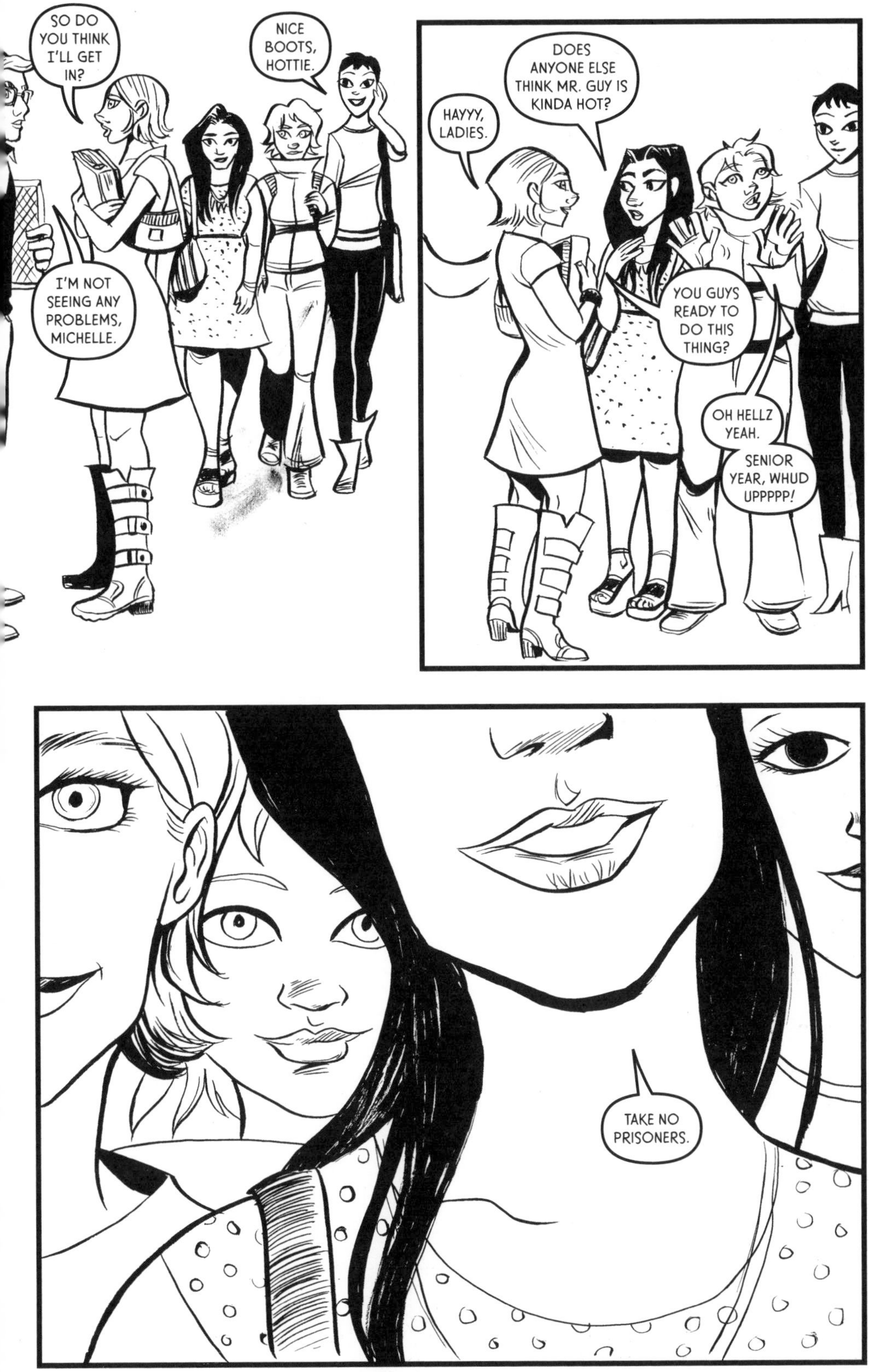
SO DO YOU THINK I'LL GET IN?
NICE BOOTS, HOTTIE.
I'M NOT SEEING ANY PROBLEMS, MICHELLE.
HAYYY, LADIES.
DOES ANYONE ELSE THINK MR. GUY IS KINDA HOT?
YOU GUYS READY TO DO THIS THING?
OH HELLZ YEAH.
SENIOR YEAR, WHUD UPPPPP!
TAKE NO PRISONERS.

SO, WHAT DO YOU THINK ABOUT SWITZERLAND FIRST, **THEN** GERMANY, FRANCE, SPAIN ...AND ENDING IN ITALY?

WHY SWITZERLAND FIRST?

I THOUGHT YOU WANTED TO END UP THERE.

I DIIIIIID...

BUT NOW I'M THINKING OF MY TRIP AS A **RE-BIRTH.**

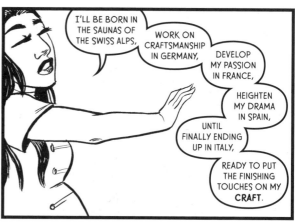

I'LL BE BORN IN THE SAUNAS OF THE SWISS ALPS,

WORK ON CRAFTSMANSHIP IN GERMANY,

DEVELOP MY PASSION IN FRANCE,

HEIGHTEN MY DRAMA IN SPAIN,

UNTIL FINALLY ENDING UP IN ITALY,

READY TO PUT THE FINISHING TOUCHES ON MY **CRAFT.**

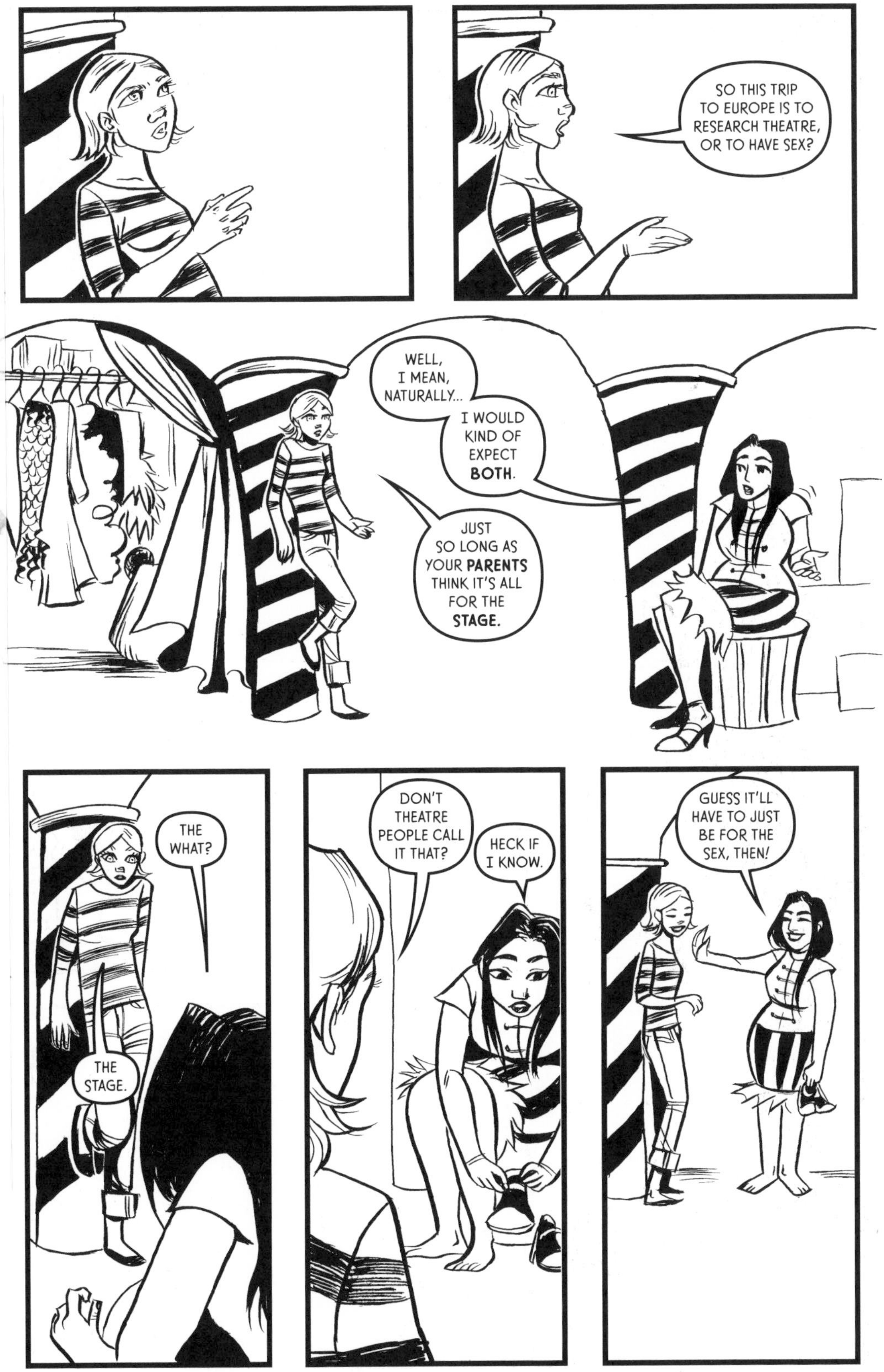
SO THIS TRIP TO EUROPE IS TO RESEARCH THEATRE, OR TO HAVE SEX?
WELL, I MEAN, NATURALLY...
I WOULD KIND OF EXPECT **BOTH**.
JUST SO LONG AS YOUR **PARENTS** THINK IT'S ALL FOR THE **STAGE.**
THE WHAT?
THE STAGE.
DON'T THEATRE PEOPLE CALL IT THAT?
HECK IF I KNOW.
GUESS IT'LL HAVE TO JUST BE FOR THE SEX, THEN!

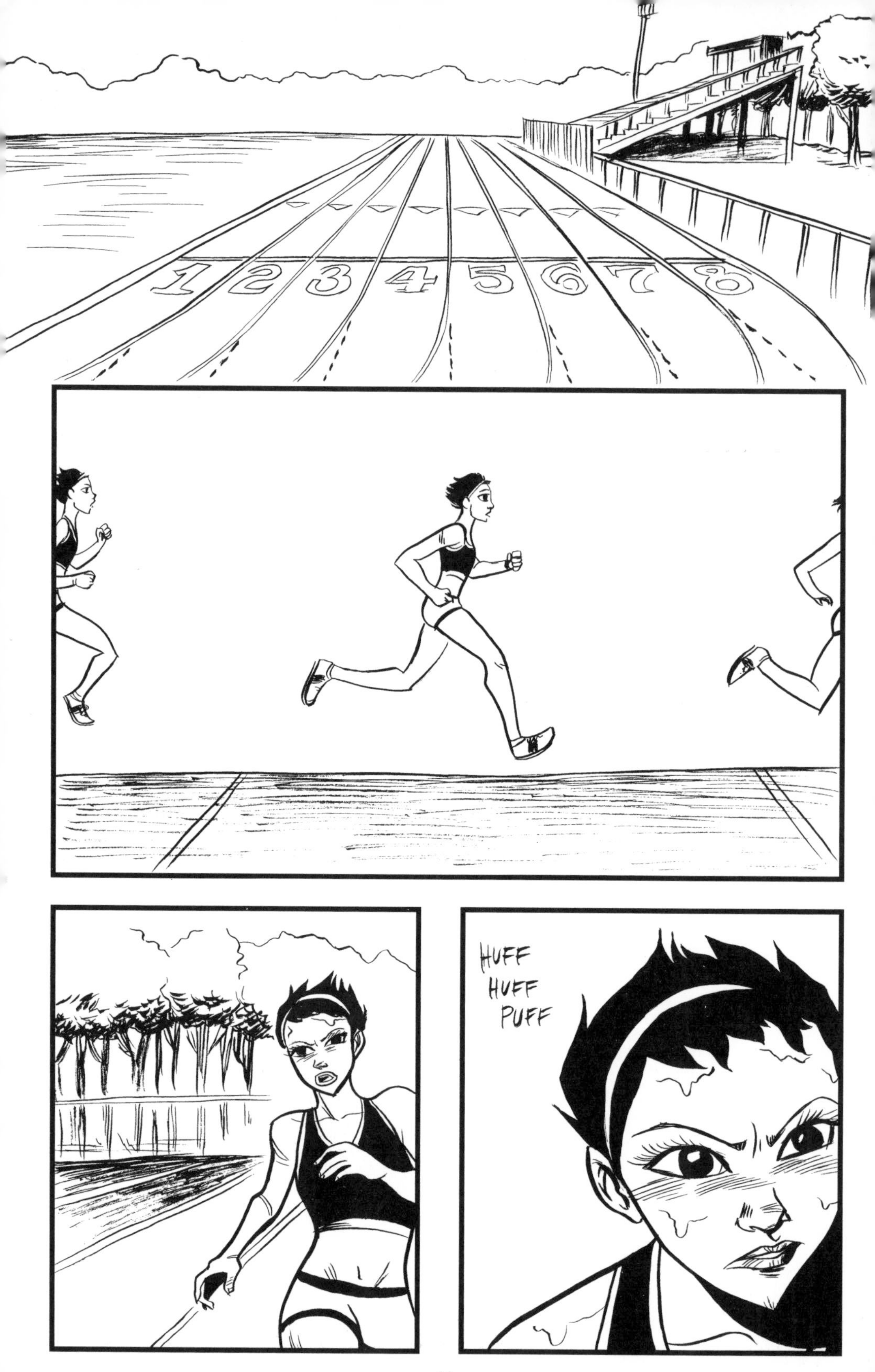
1 2 3 4 5 6 7 8
HUFF
HUFF
PUFF

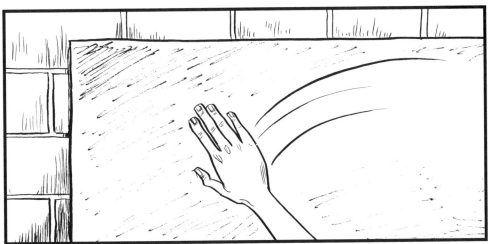

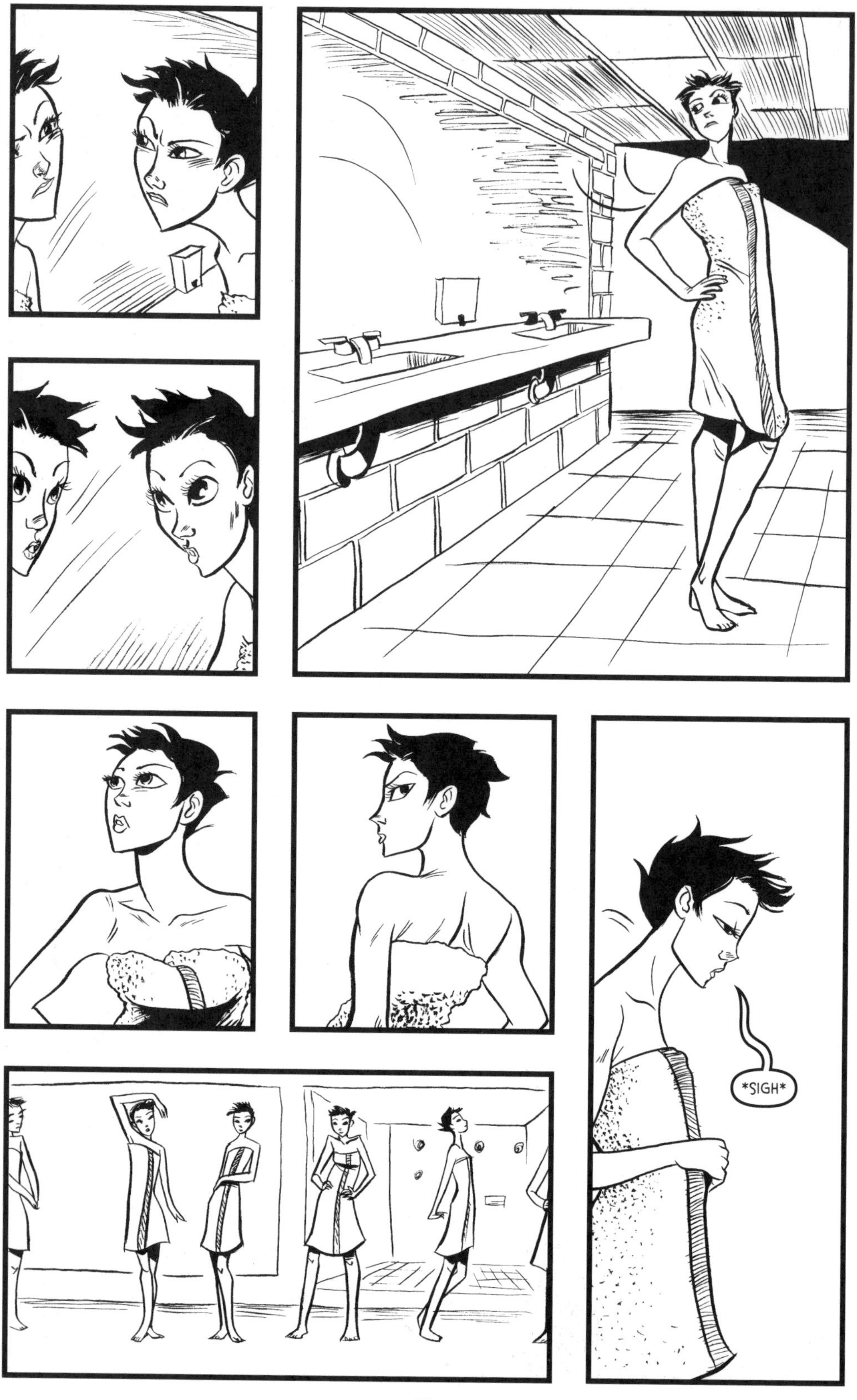
SIGH

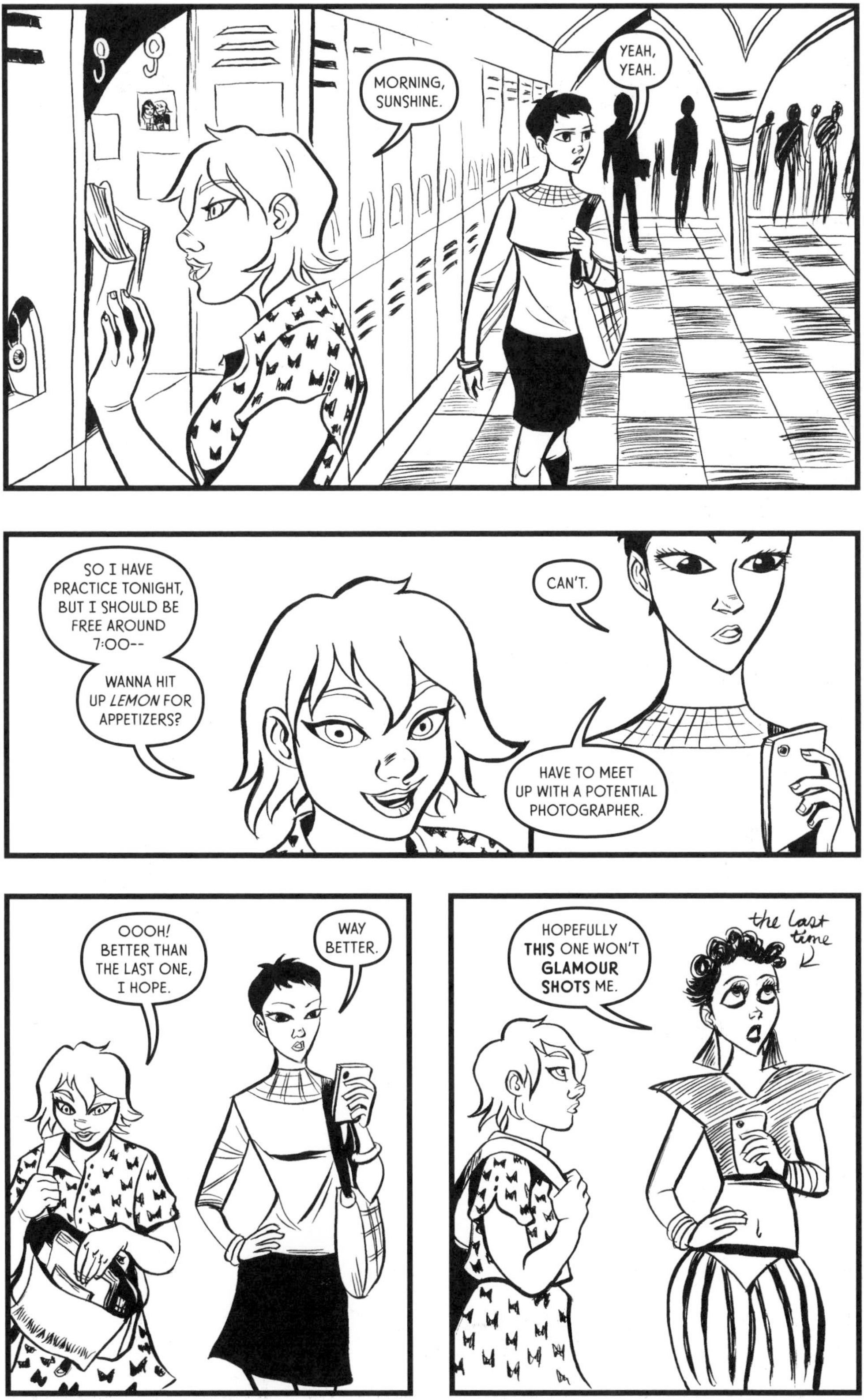
MORNING, SUNSHINE.
YEAH, YEAH.
SO I HAVE PRACTICE TONIGHT, BUT I SHOULD BE FREE AROUND 7:00--
WANNA HIT UP *LEMON* FOR APPETIZERS?
CAN'T.
HAVE TO MEET UP WITH A POTENTIAL PHOTOGRAPHER.
OOOH! BETTER THAN THE LAST ONE, I HOPE.
WAY BETTER.
HOPEFULLY **THIS** ONE WON'T **GLAMOUR SHOTS** ME.
the last time

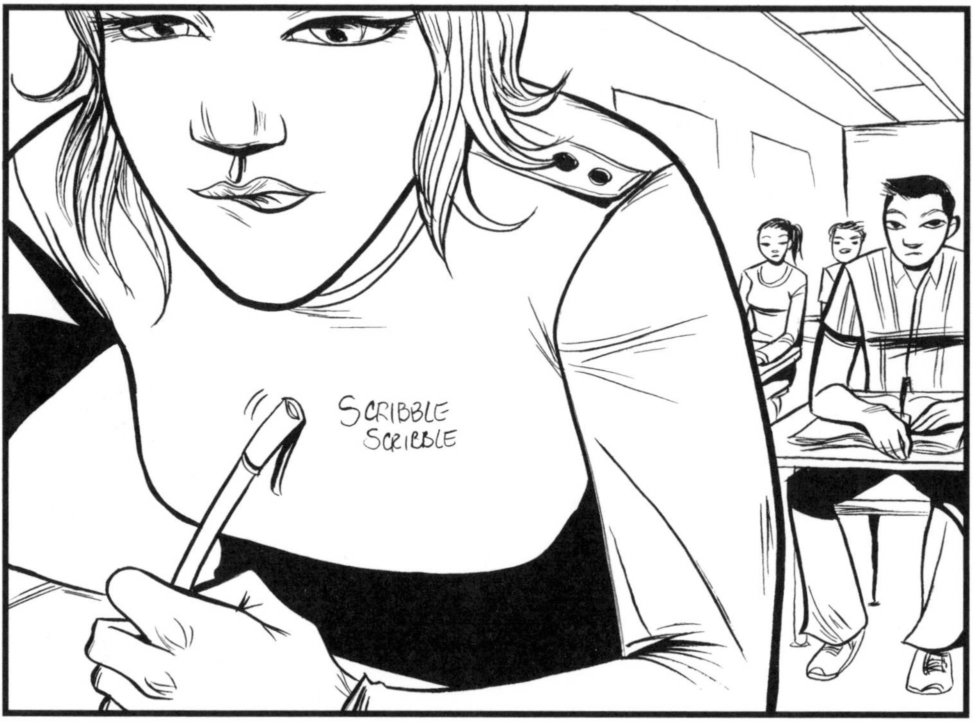
SCRIBBLE
SCRIBBLE

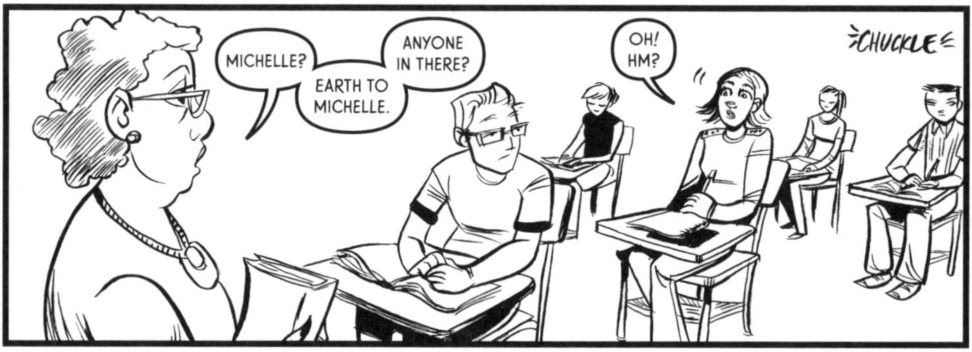
MICHELLE?
EARTH TO MICHELLE.
ANYONE IN THERE?
OH! HM?
CHUCKLE

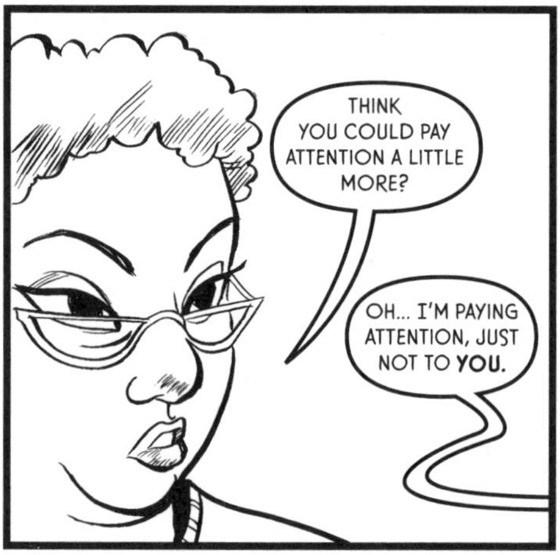
THINK YOU COULD PAY ATTENTION A LITTLE MORE?
OH... I'M PAYING ATTENTION, JUST NOT TO **YOU.**

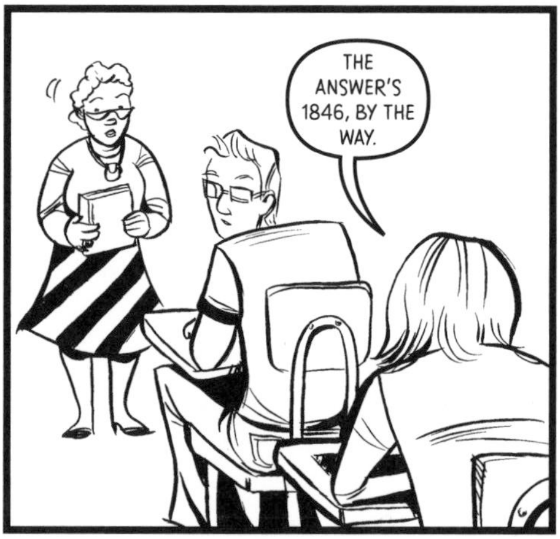
THE ANSWER'S 1846, BY THE WAY.

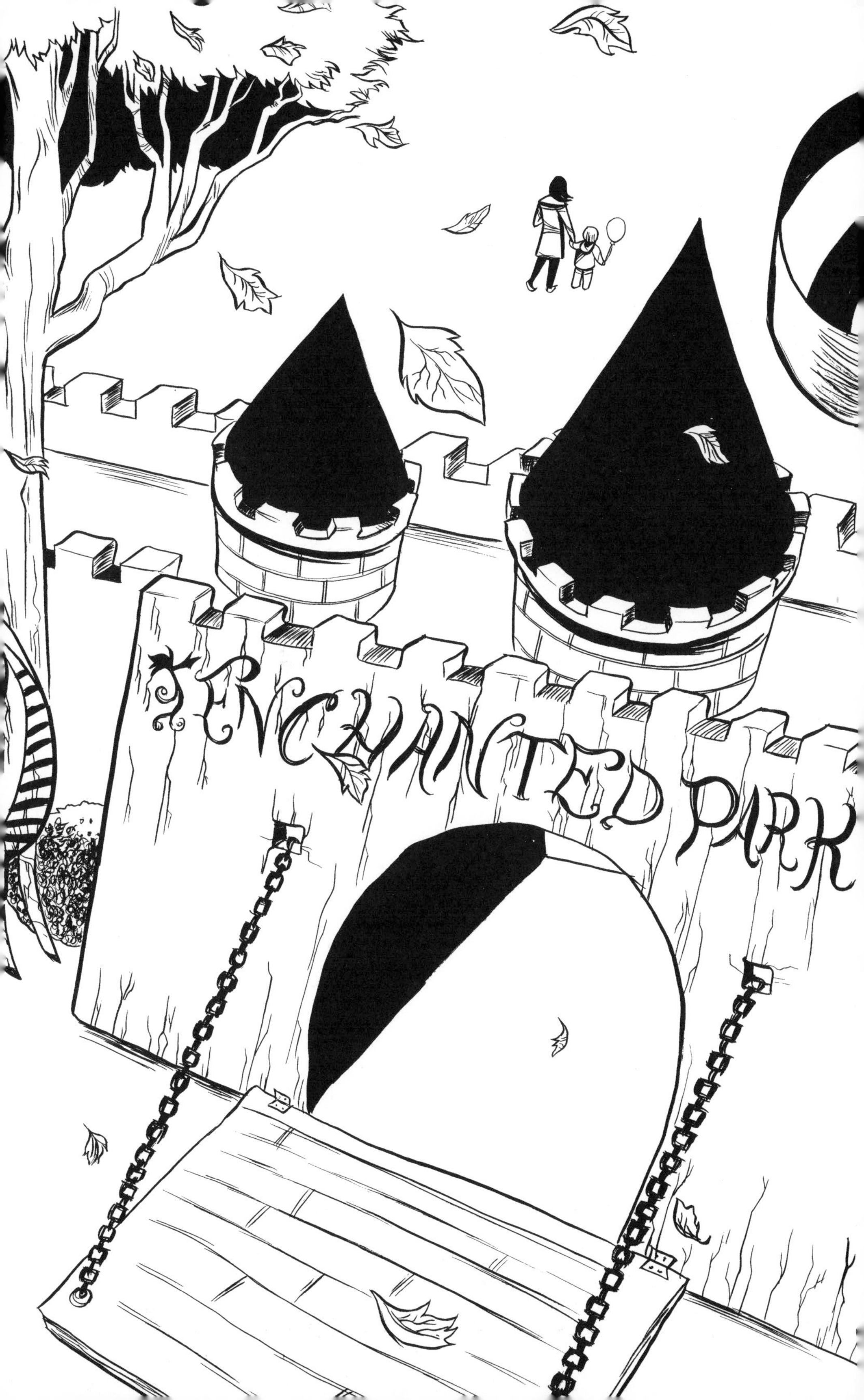
ENCHANTED PARK

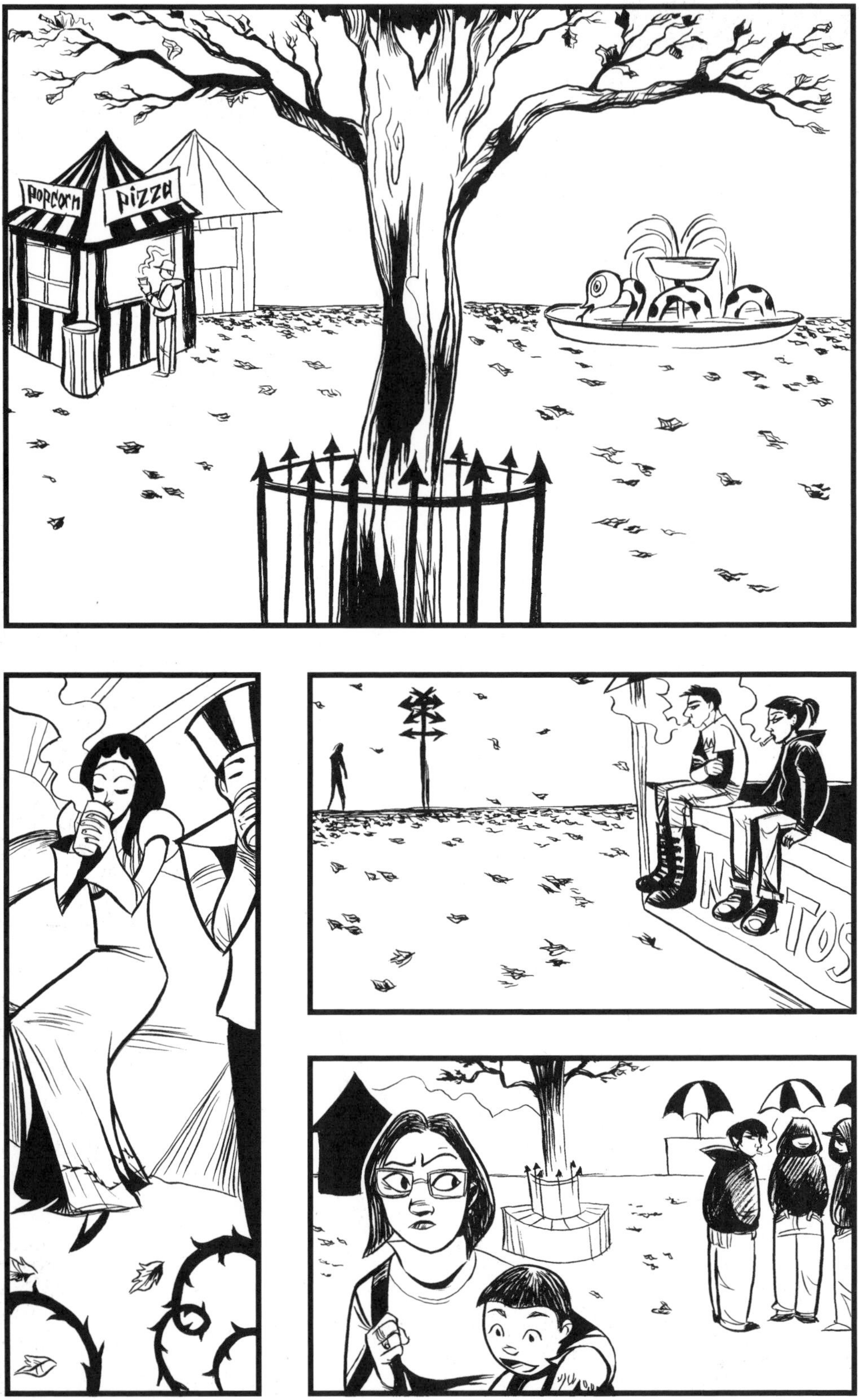
popcorn
pizza

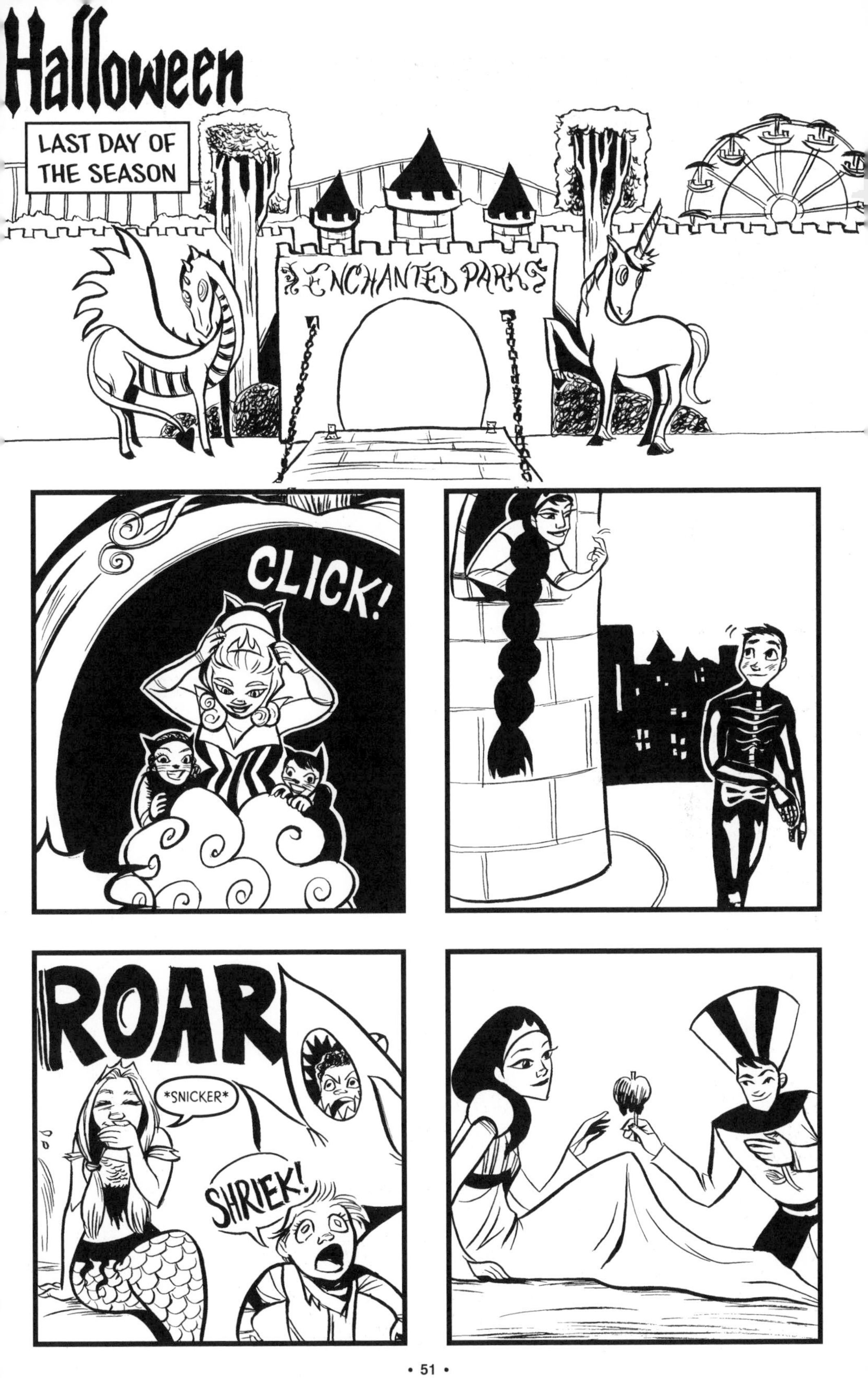
Halloween
LAST DAY OF THE SEASON
ENCHANTED PARKS
CLICK!
ROAR
SNICKER
SHRIEK!

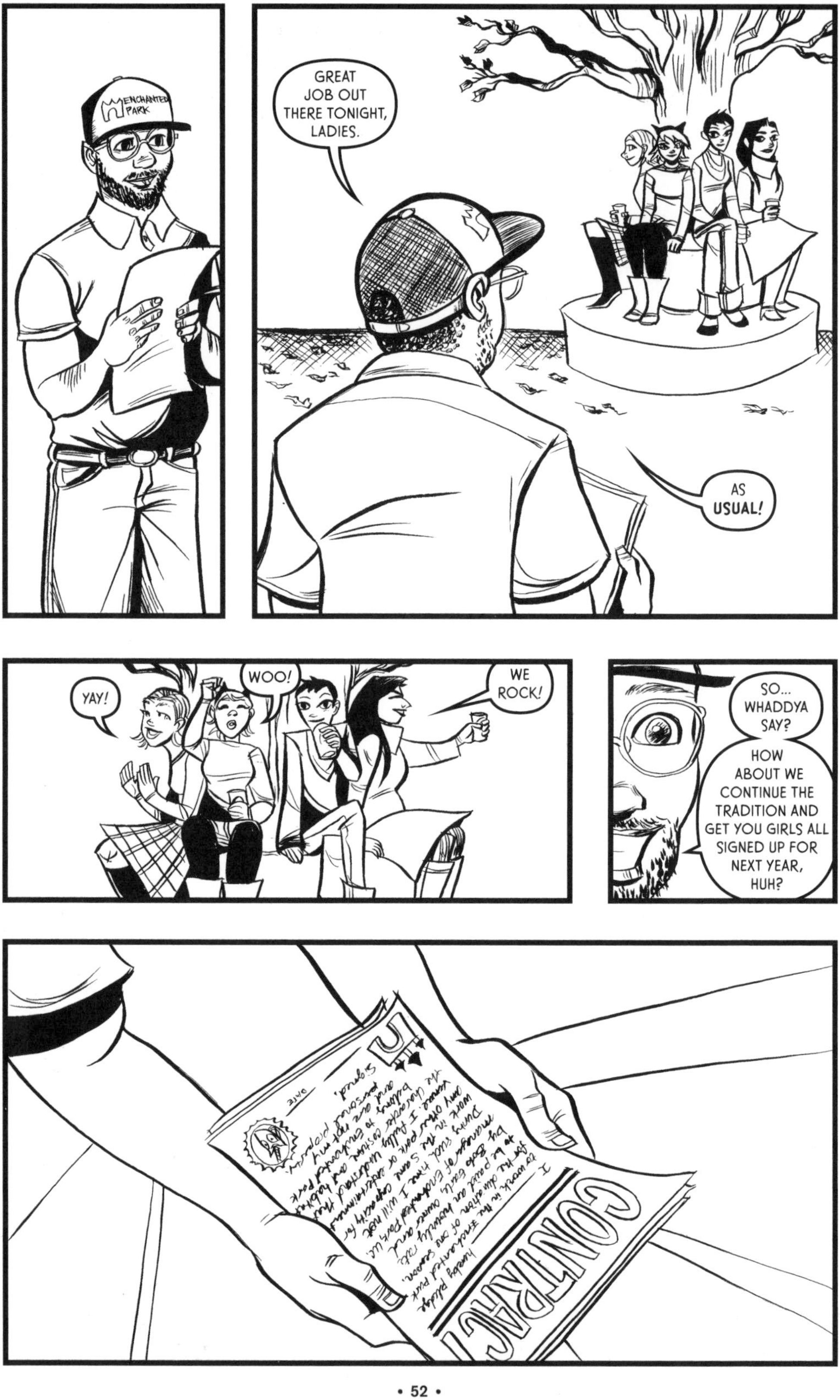
ENCHANTED PARK
GREAT JOB OUT THERE TONIGHT, LADIES.
AS **USUAL!**
YAY!
WOO!
WE ROCK!
SO... WHADDYA SAY?
HOW ABOUT WE CONTINUE THE TRADITION AND GET YOU GIRLS ALL SIGNED UP FOR NEXT YEAR, HUH?
CONTRACT

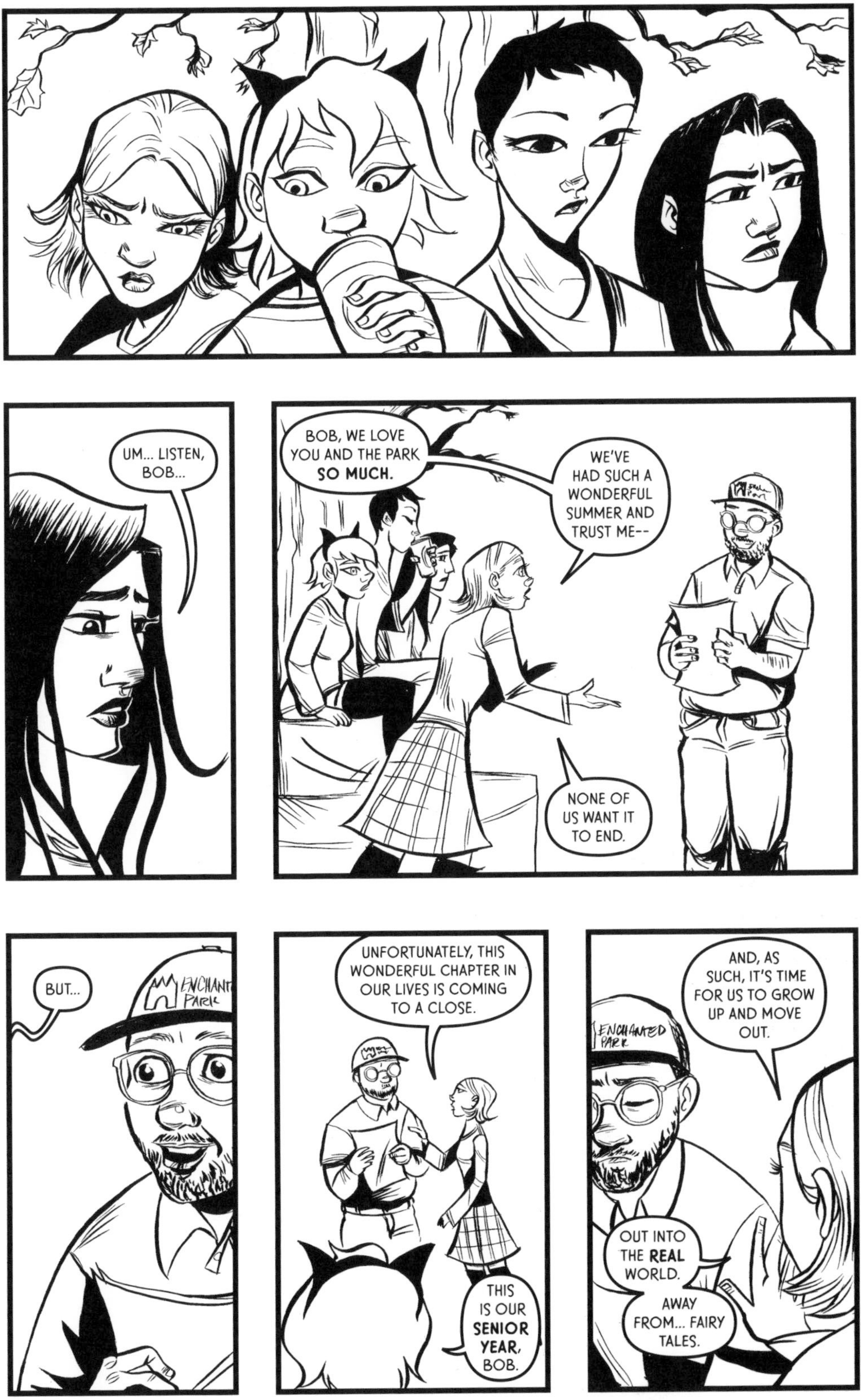
UM... LISTEN, BOB...
BOB, WE LOVE YOU AND THE PARK **SO MUCH.**
WE'VE HAD SUCH A WONDERFUL SUMMER AND TRUST ME--
NONE OF US WANT IT TO END.
BUT...
UNFORTUNATELY, THIS WONDERFUL CHAPTER IN OUR LIVES IS COMING TO A CLOSE.
THIS IS OUR **SENIOR YEAR,** BOB.
ENCHANTED PARK
AND, AS SUCH, IT'S TIME FOR US TO GROW UP AND MOVE OUT.
OUT INTO THE **REAL** WORLD.
AWAY FROM... FAIRY TALES.

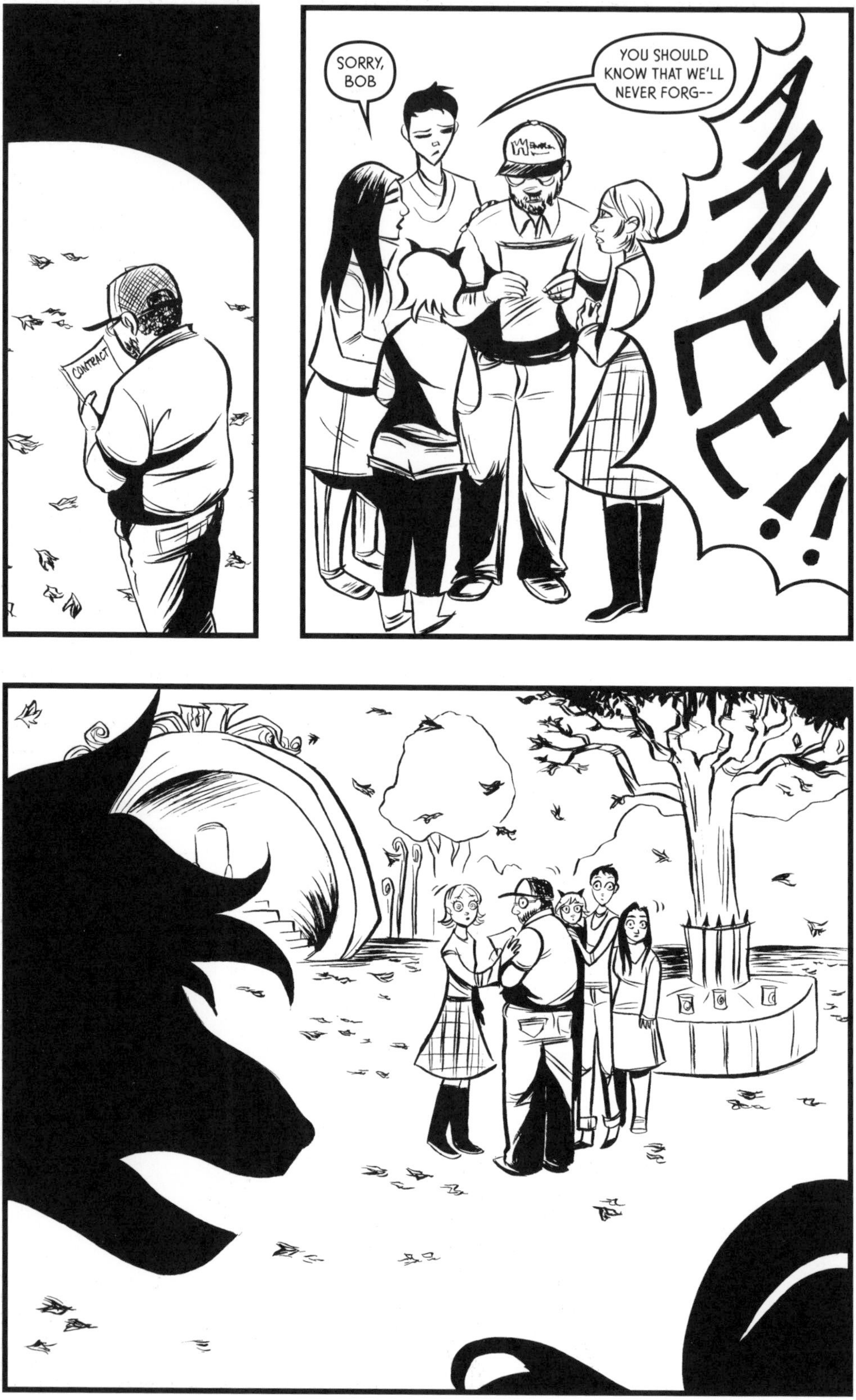
CONTRACT
SORRY, BOB
YOU SHOULD KNOW THAT WE'LL NEVER FORG--
AAIIEEE!!

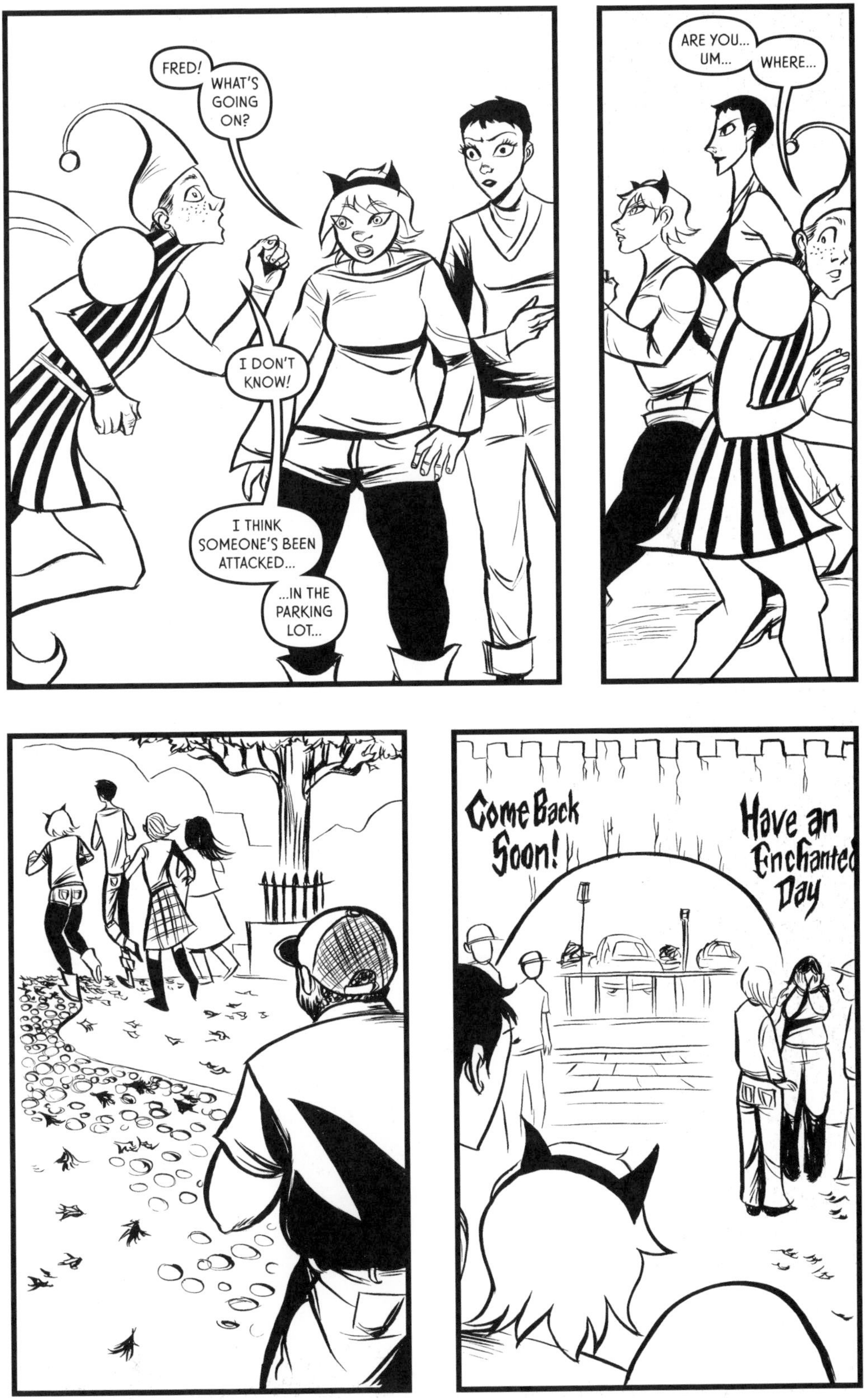
FRED!
WHAT'S GOING ON?
I DON'T KNOW!
I THINK SOMEONE'S BEEN ATTACKED...
...IN THE PARKING LOT...
ARE YOU... UM...
WHERE...
Come Back Soon!
Have an Enchanted Day

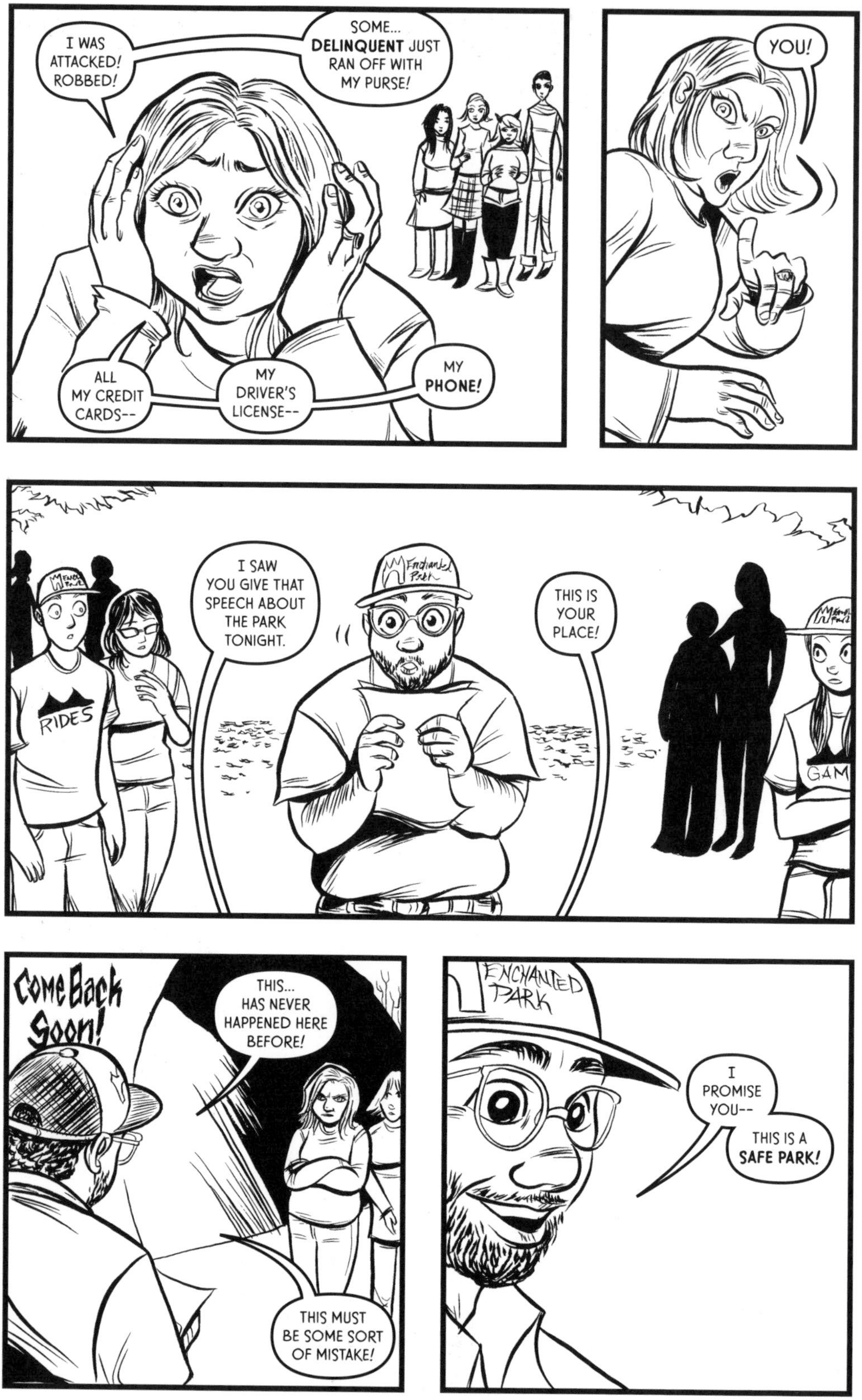
I WAS ATTACKED! ROBBED!
SOME... **DELINQUENT** JUST RAN OFF WITH MY PURSE!
ALL MY CREDIT CARDS--
MY DRIVER'S LICENSE--
MY **PHONE!**
YOU!
I SAW YOU GIVE THAT SPEECH ABOUT THE PARK TONIGHT.
THIS IS YOUR PLACE!
RIDES
GAM
Come Back Soon!
THIS... HAS NEVER HAPPENED HERE BEFORE!
THIS MUST BE SOME SORT OF MISTAKE!
ENCHANTED PARK
I PROMISE YOU--
THIS IS A **SAFE PARK!**

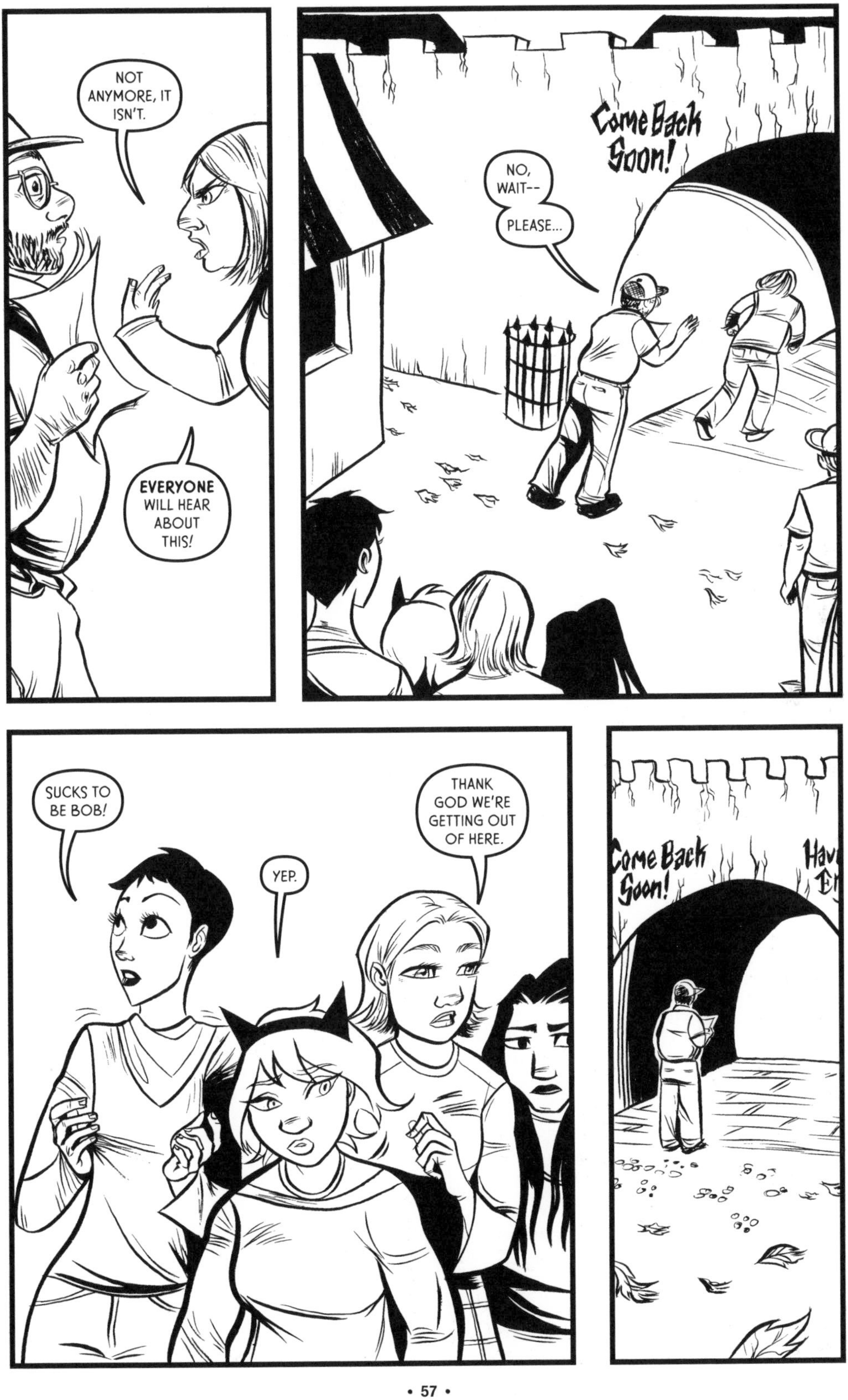
NOT ANYMORE, IT ISN'T.
EVERYONE WILL HEAR ABOUT THIS!
Come Back Soon!
NO, WAIT--
PLEASE...
SUCKS TO BE BOB!
YEP.
THANK GOD WE'RE GETTING OUT OF HERE.
Come Back Soon!

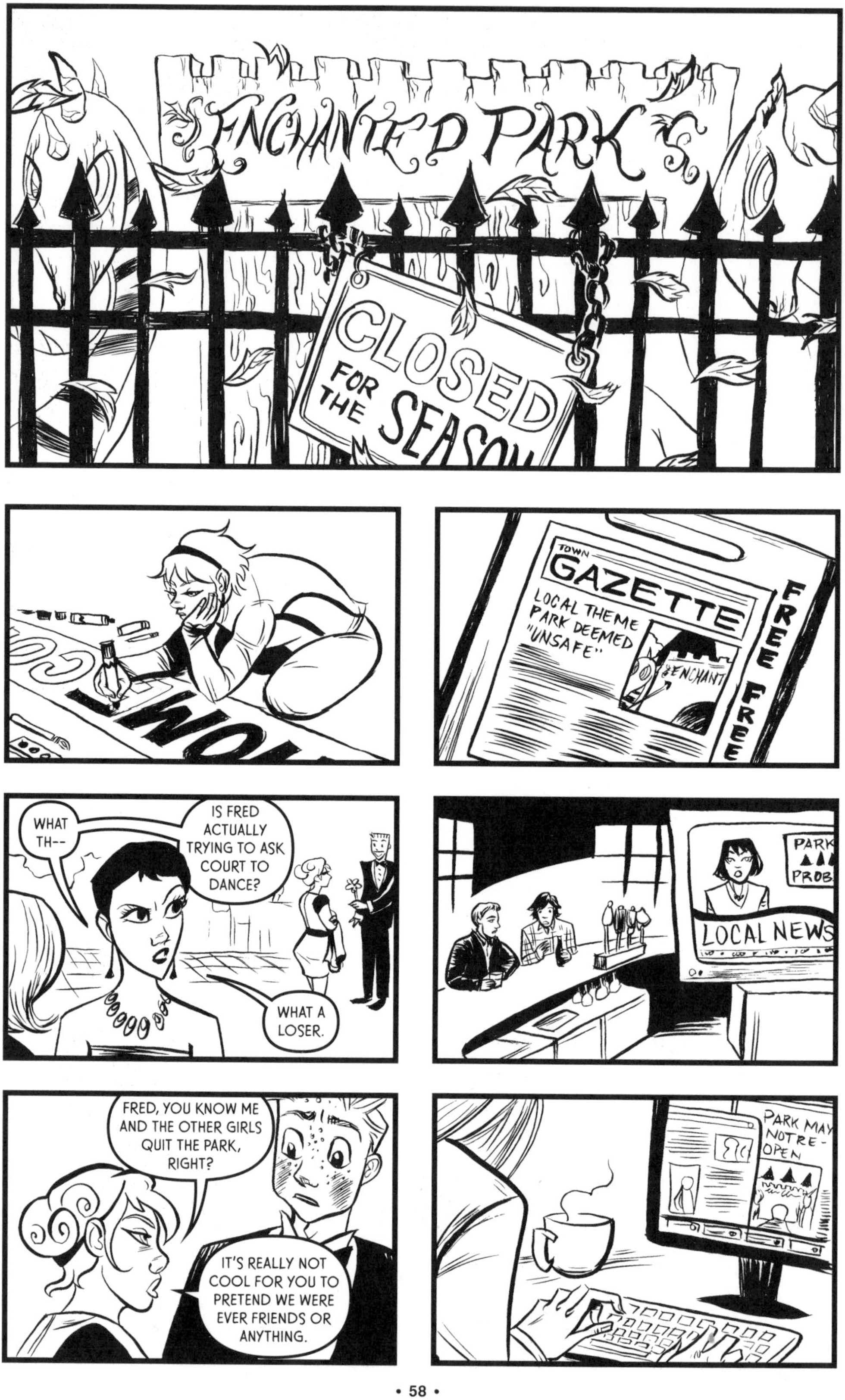
ENCHANTED PARK
CLOSED FOR THE SEASON
TOWN GAZETTE
LOCAL THEME PARK DEEMED "UNSAFE"
FREE FREE
WHAT TH--
IS FRED ACTUALLY TRYING TO ASK COURT TO DANCE?
WHAT A LOSER.
LOCAL NEWS
FRED, YOU KNOW ME AND THE OTHER GIRLS QUIT THE PARK, RIGHT?
IT'S REALLY NOT COOL FOR YOU TO PRETEND WE WERE EVER FRIENDS OR ANYTHING.
PARK MAY NOT RE-OPEN

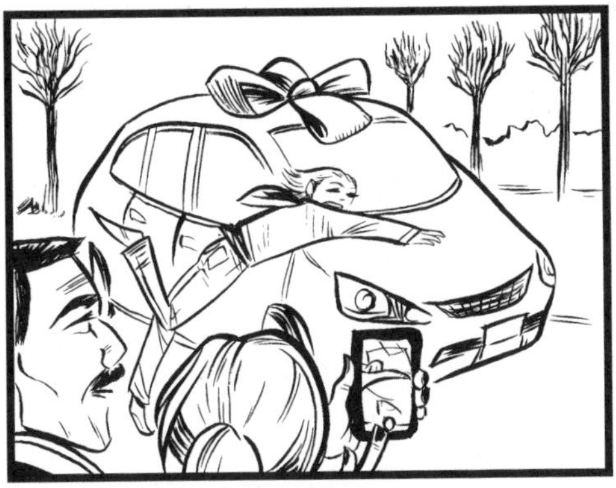

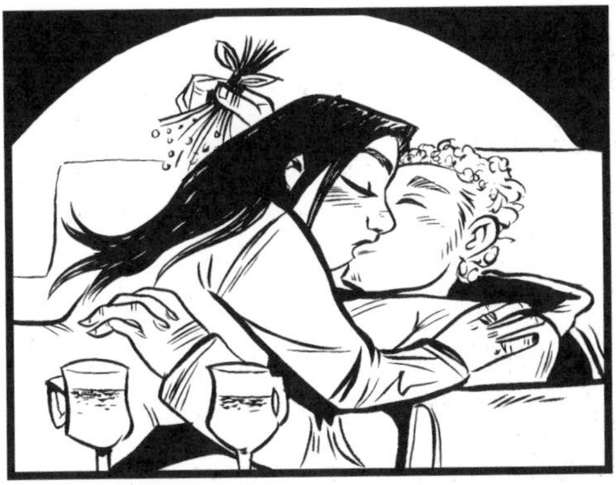

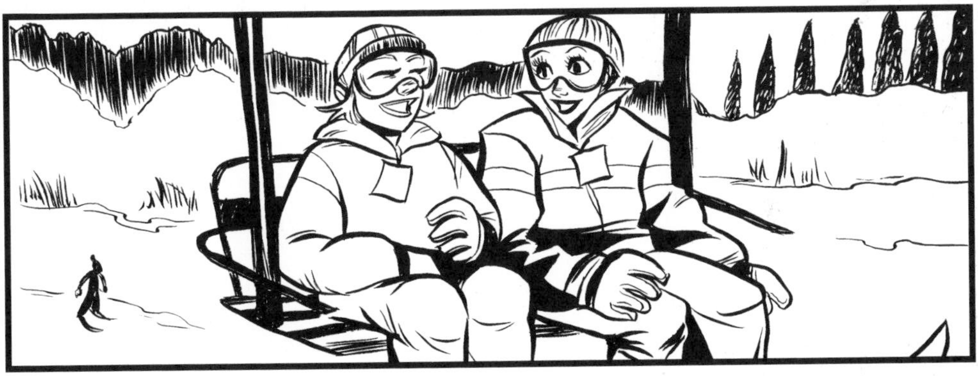

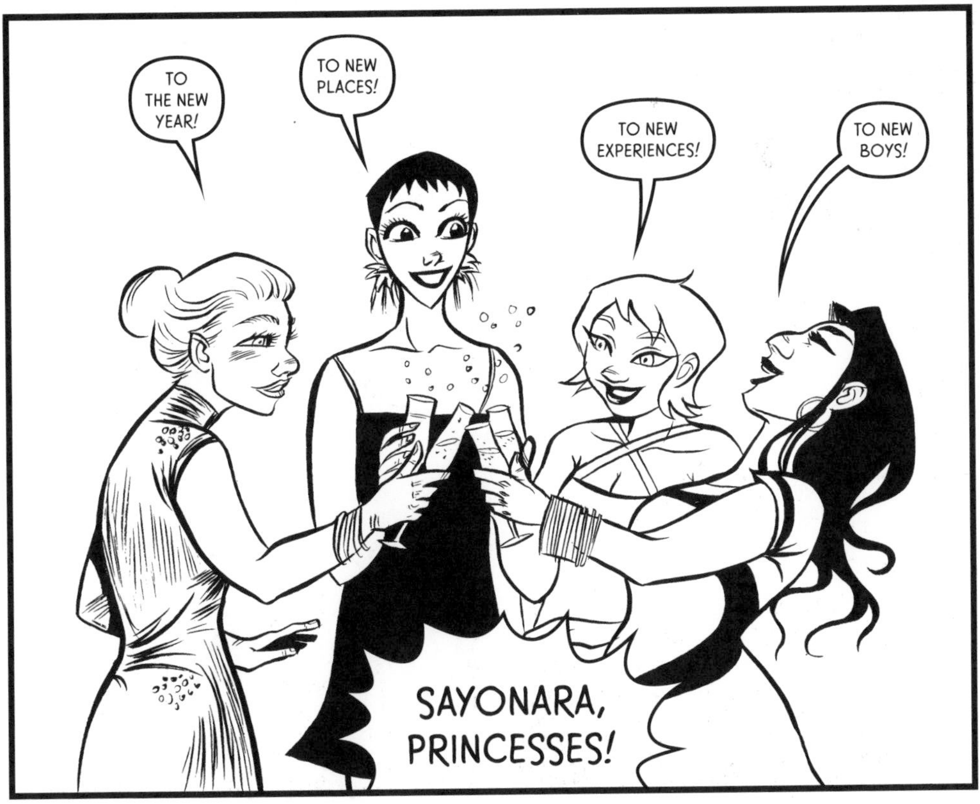
TO THE NEW YEAR!
TO NEW PLACES!
TO NEW EXPERIENCES!
TO NEW BOYS!
SAYONARA, PRINCESSES!

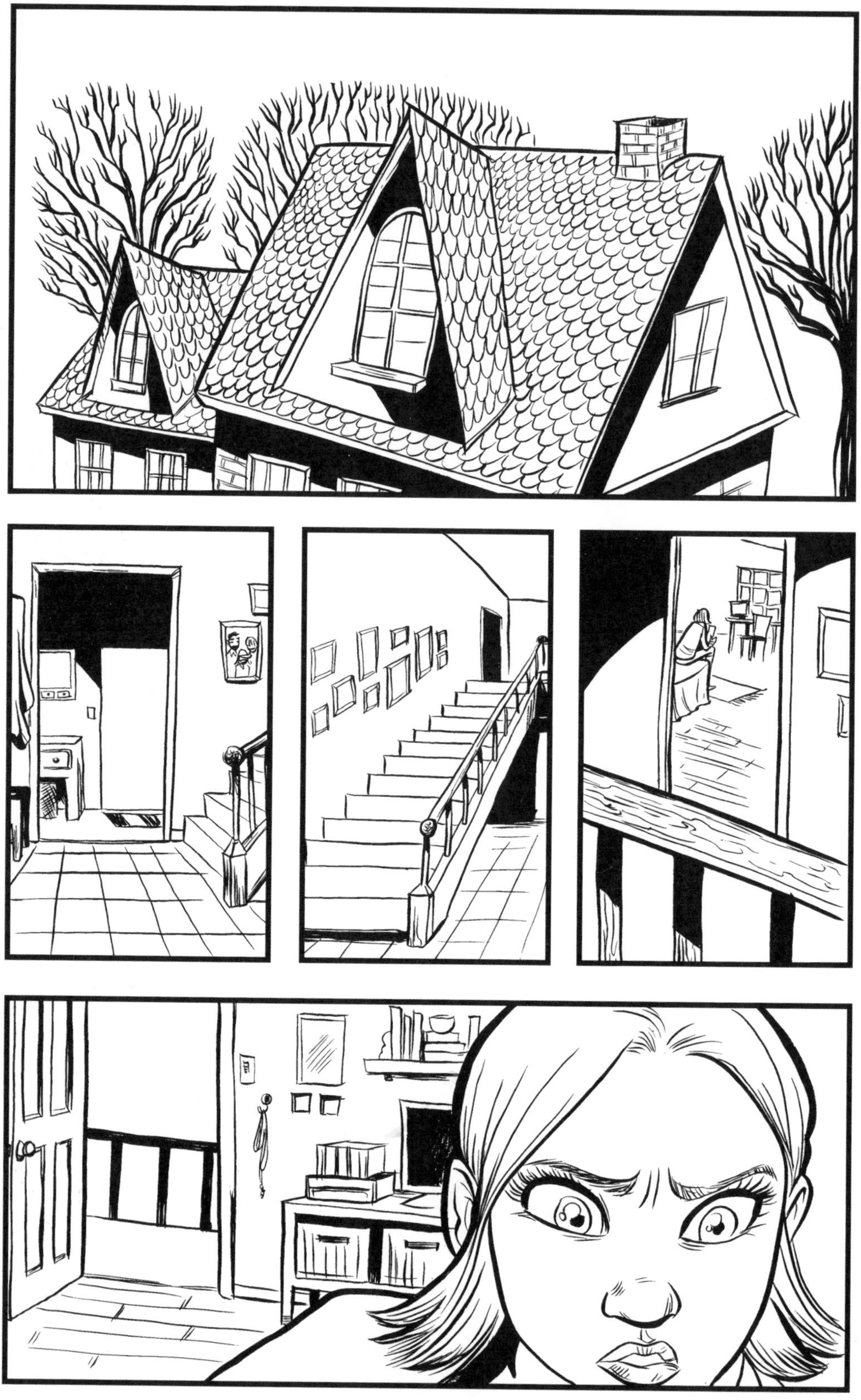

UNIVERS
OF TRITON

January 20, 2013
Michelle Riu
5220 Rustic Ct.
Fairfield, CT

Dear Michelle,
The Admissions Comm
application for the Univ
Consideration, I regr
unable to offer you g
ool was the stron
Tght of this
recogni

KNOCK KNOCK!

READY TO COME DOWN AND HELP SET THE TABLE, SUGAR PIE?

MICHELLE?

HONEY?

ARE YOU ALRIGHT?

...ALL OF THEM...

WHAT WAS THAT, SWEETIE?

SPEAK UP, I'M AN OLD MAN.

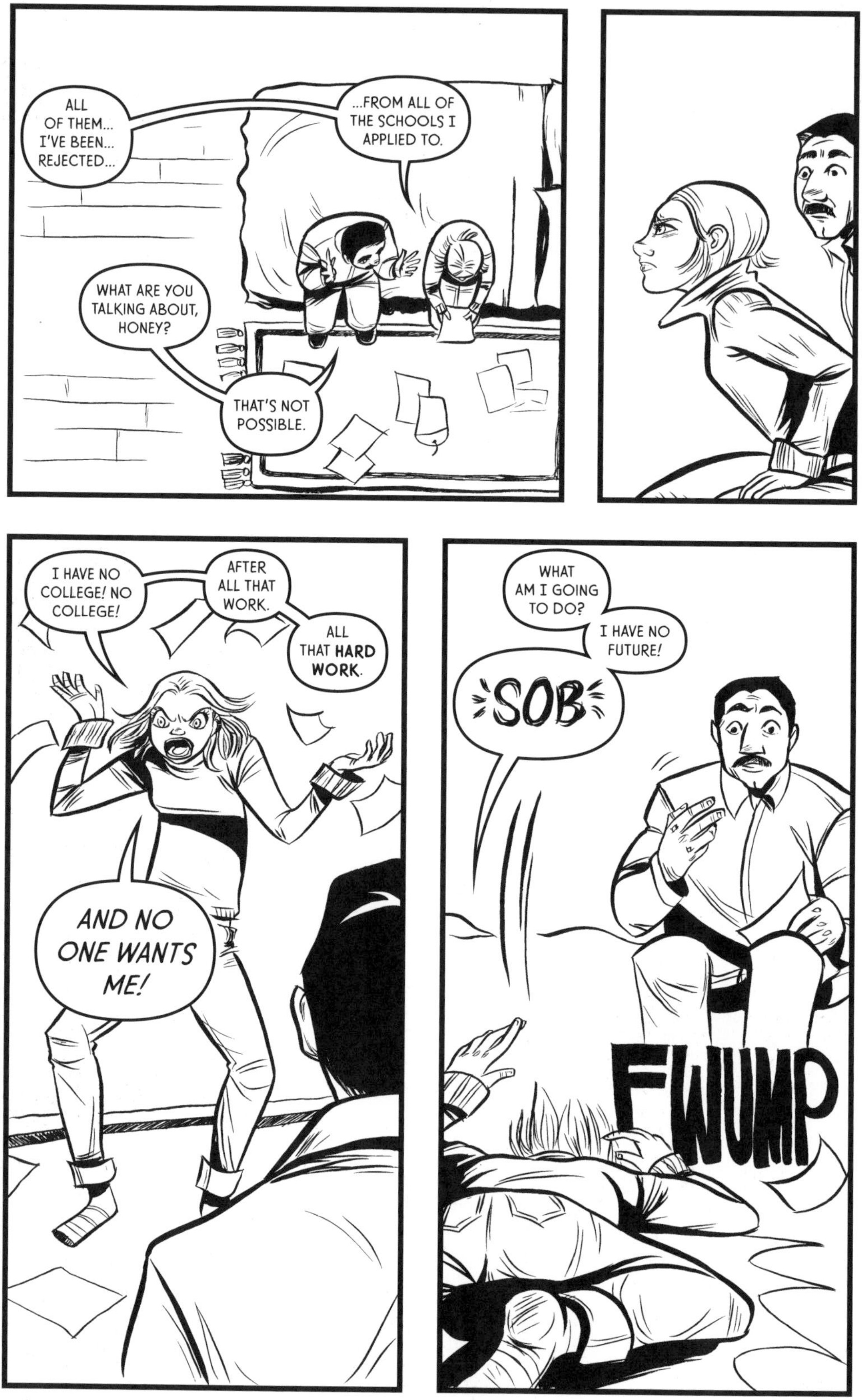
ALL OF THEM... I'VE BEEN... REJECTED...
...FROM ALL OF THE SCHOOLS I APPLIED TO.
WHAT ARE YOU TALKING ABOUT, HONEY?
THAT'S NOT POSSIBLE.
I HAVE NO COLLEGE! NO COLLEGE!
AFTER ALL THAT WORK.
ALL THAT **HARD WORK**.
AND NO ONE WANTS ME!
WHAT AM I GOING TO DO?
I HAVE NO FUTURE!
SOB
FWUMP

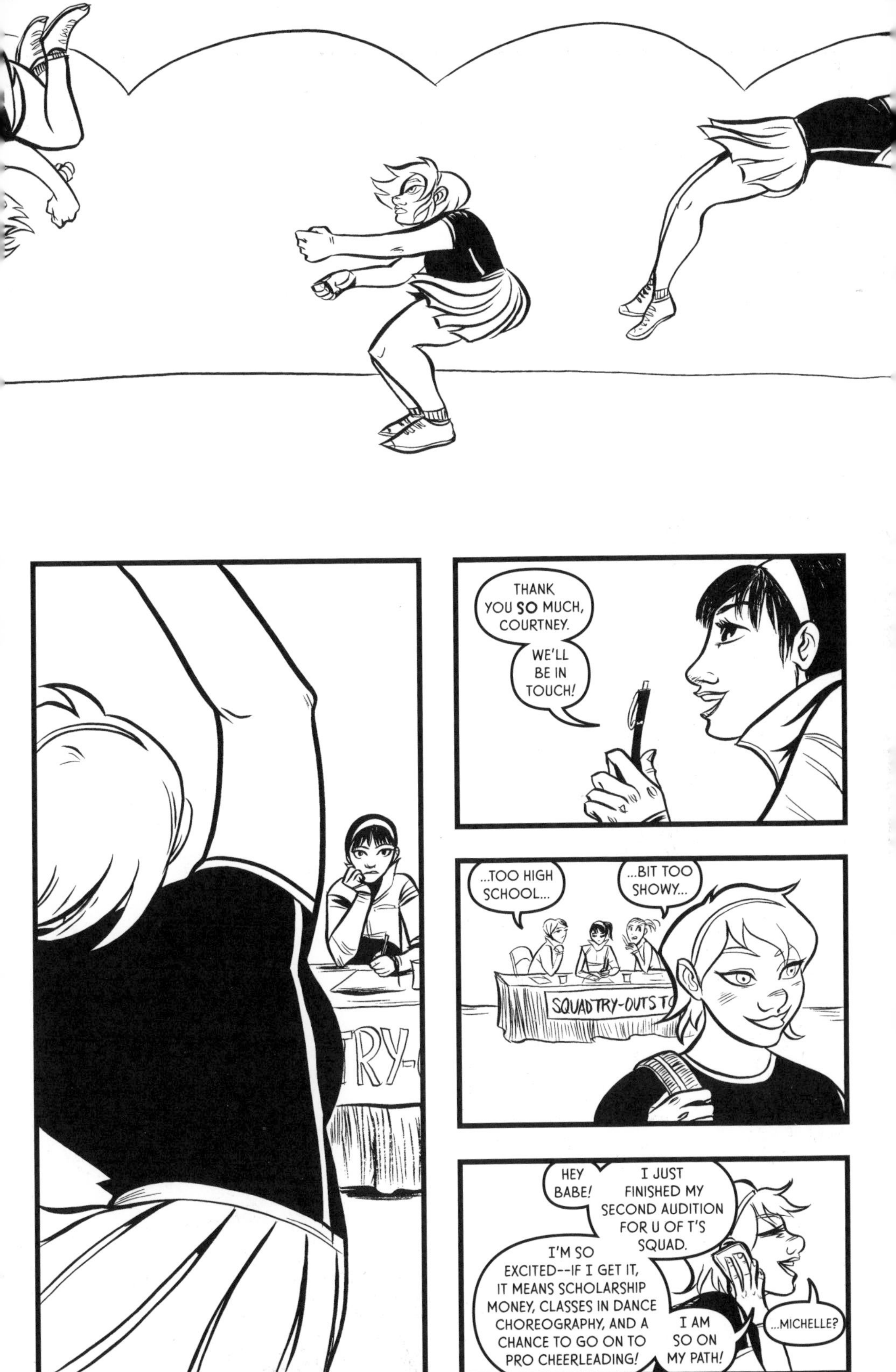
TRY-
THANK YOU **SO** MUCH, COURTNEY.
WE'LL BE IN TOUCH!
...TOO HIGH SCHOOL...
...BIT TOO SHOWY...
SQUAD TRY-OUTS T
HEY BABE!
I JUST FINISHED MY SECOND AUDITION FOR U OF T'S SQUAD.
I'M SO EXCITED--IF I GET IT, IT MEANS SCHOLARSHIP MONEY, CLASSES IN DANCE CHOREOGRAPHY, AND A CHANCE TO GO ON TO PRO CHEERLEADING!
I AM SO ON MY PATH!
...MICHELLE?

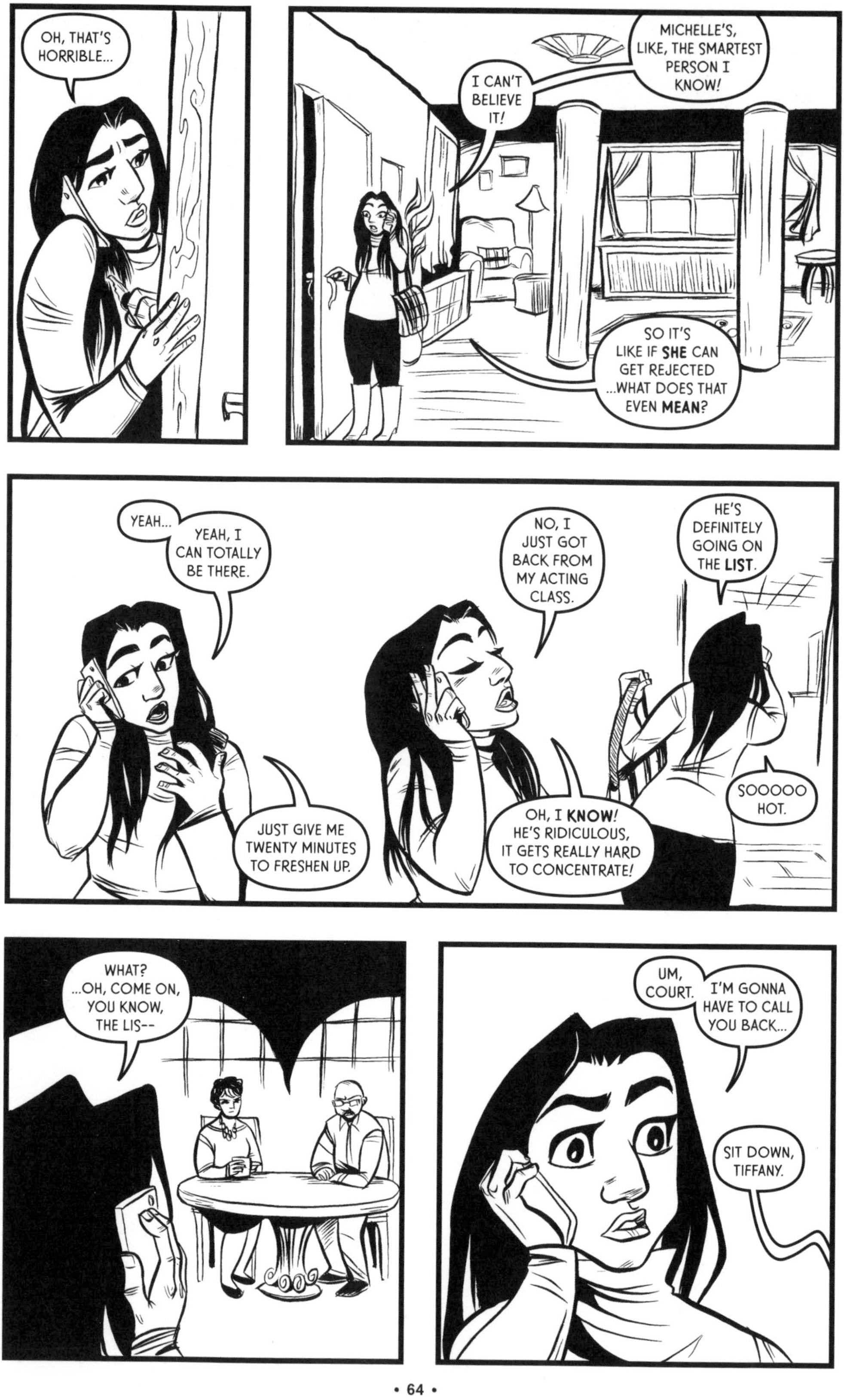
OH, THAT'S HORRIBLE...
I CAN'T BELIEVE IT!
MICHELLE'S, LIKE, THE SMARTEST PERSON I KNOW!
SO IT'S LIKE IF **SHE** CAN GET REJECTED ...WHAT DOES THAT EVEN **MEAN**?
YEAH...
YEAH, I CAN TOTALLY BE THERE.
JUST GIVE ME TWENTY MINUTES TO FRESHEN UP.
NO, I JUST GOT BACK FROM MY ACTING CLASS.
OH, I **KNOW**! HE'S RIDICULOUS, IT GETS REALLY HARD TO CONCENTRATE!
HE'S DEFINITELY GOING ON THE **LIST**.
SOOOOO HOT.
WHAT? ...OH, COME ON, YOU KNOW, THE LIS--
UM, COURT.
I'M GONNA HAVE TO CALL YOU BACK...
SIT DOWN, TIFFANY.

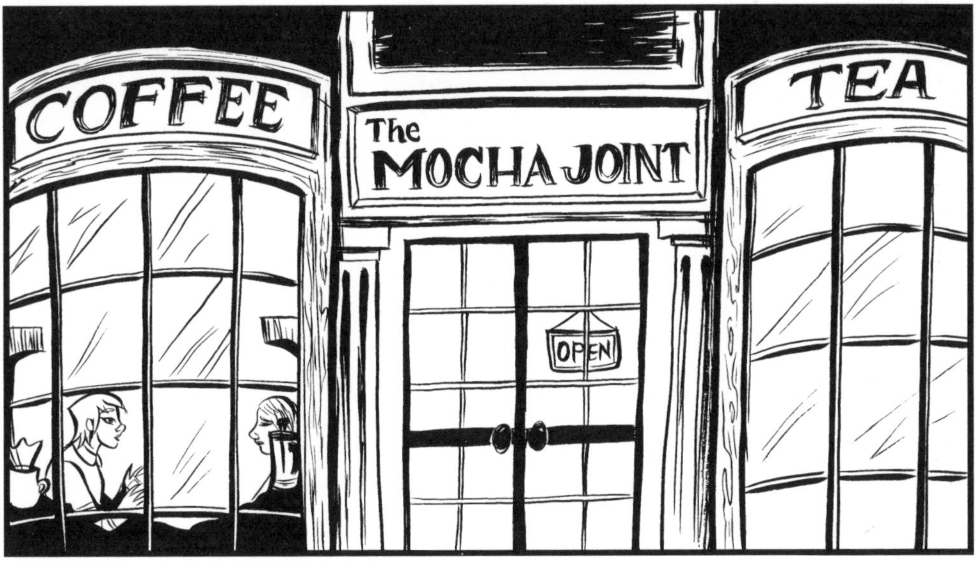
COFFEE
The MOCHA JOINT
TEA
OPEN

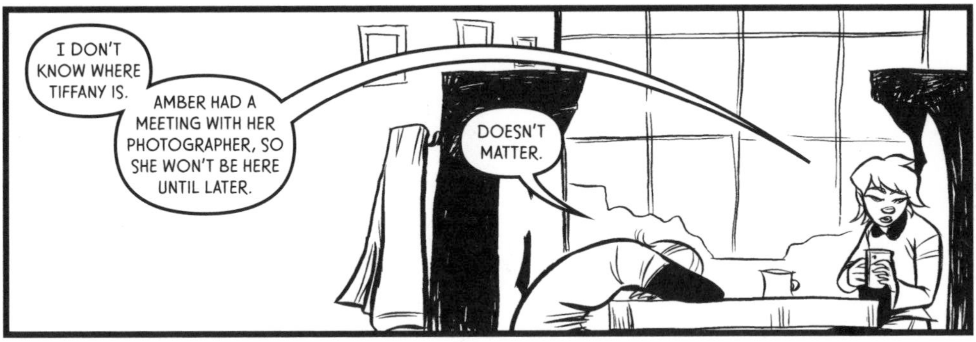
I DON'T KNOW WHERE TIFFANY IS.
AMBER HAD A MEETING WITH HER PHOTOGRAPHER, SO SHE WON'T BE HERE UNTIL LATER.
DOESN'T MATTER.

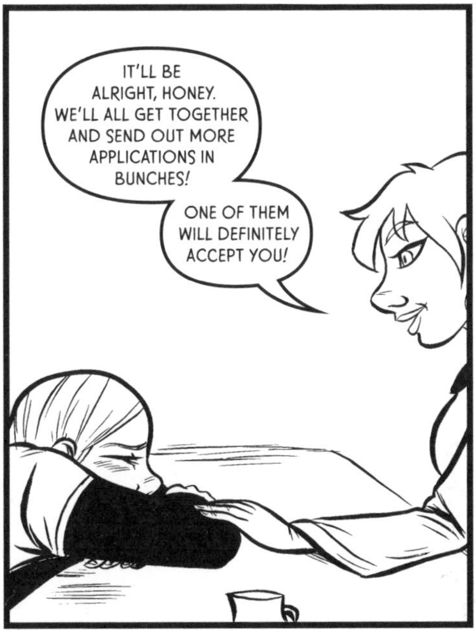
IT'LL BE ALRIGHT, HONEY. WE'LL ALL GET TOGETHER AND SEND OUT MORE APPLICATIONS IN BUNCHES!
ONE OF THEM WILL DEFINITELY ACCEPT YOU!

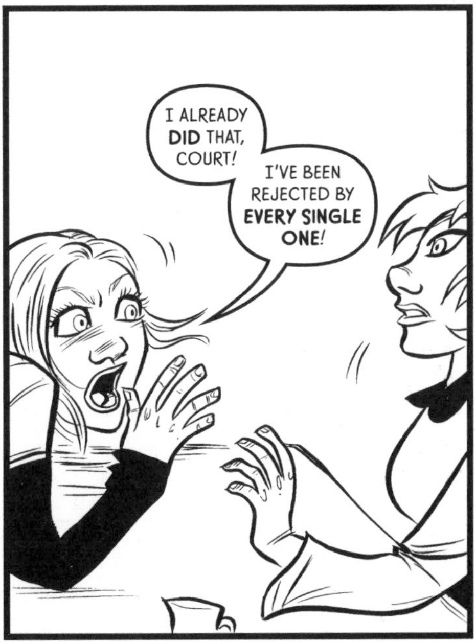
I ALREADY **DID** THAT, COURT!
I'VE BEEN REJECTED BY **EVERY SINGLE ONE**!

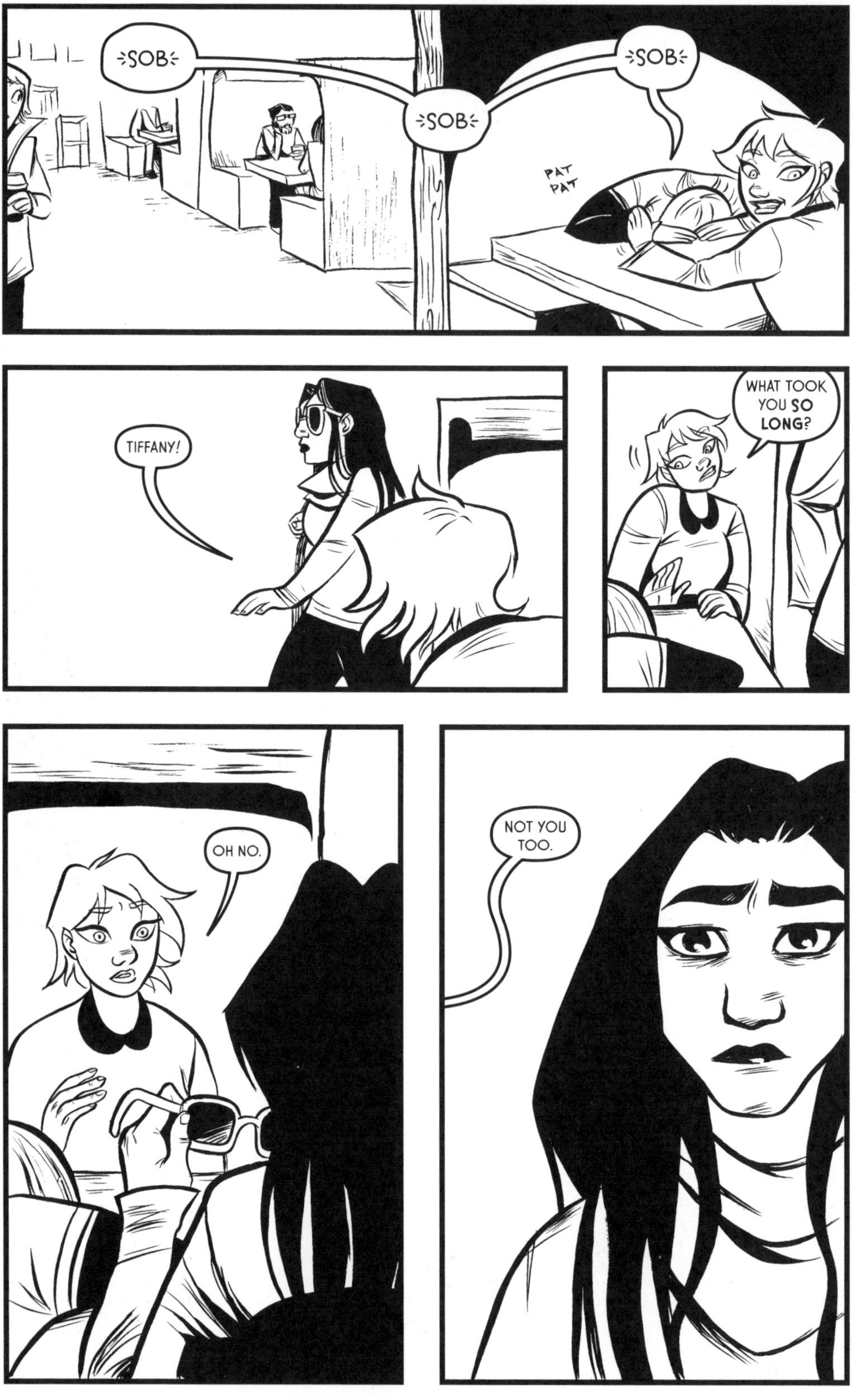
SOB
SOB
SOB
PAT PAT
TIFFANY!
WHAT TOOK YOU **SO LONG?**
OH NO.
NOT YOU TOO.

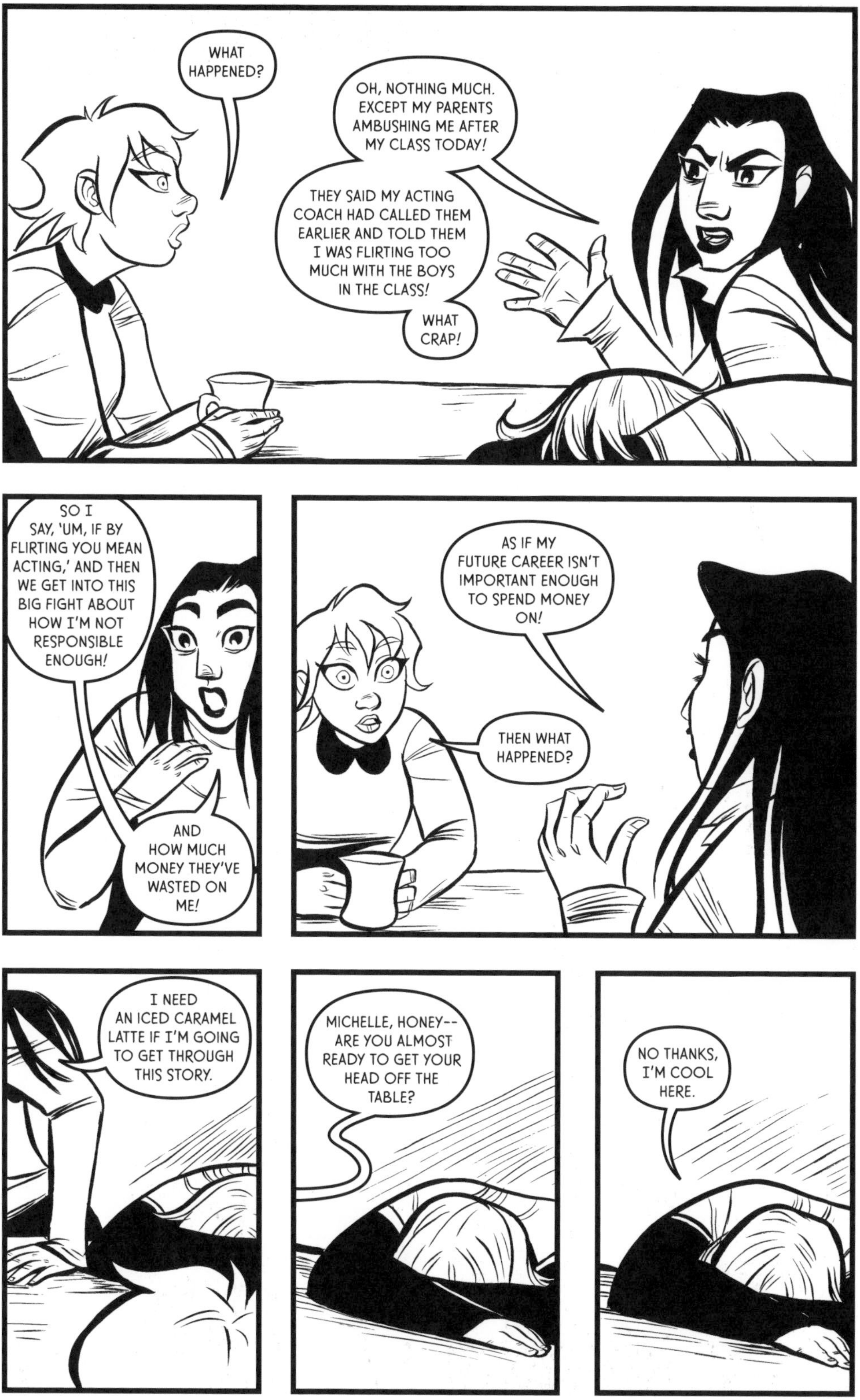
WHAT HAPPENED?
OH, NOTHING MUCH. EXCEPT MY PARENTS AMBUSHING ME AFTER MY CLASS TODAY!
THEY SAID MY ACTING COACH HAD CALLED THEM EARLIER AND TOLD THEM I WAS FLIRTING TOO MUCH WITH THE BOYS IN THE CLASS!
WHAT CRAP!
SO I SAY, 'UM, IF BY FLIRTING YOU MEAN ACTING,' AND THEN WE GET INTO THIS BIG FIGHT ABOUT HOW I'M NOT RESPONSIBLE ENOUGH!
AND HOW MUCH MONEY THEY'VE WASTED ON ME!
AS IF MY FUTURE CAREER ISN'T IMPORTANT ENOUGH TO SPEND MONEY ON!
THEN WHAT HAPPENED?
I NEED AN ICED CARAMEL LATTE IF I'M GOING TO GET THROUGH THIS STORY.
MICHELLE, HONEY-- ARE YOU ALMOST READY TO GET YOUR HEAD OFF THE TABLE?
NO THANKS, I'M COOL HERE.

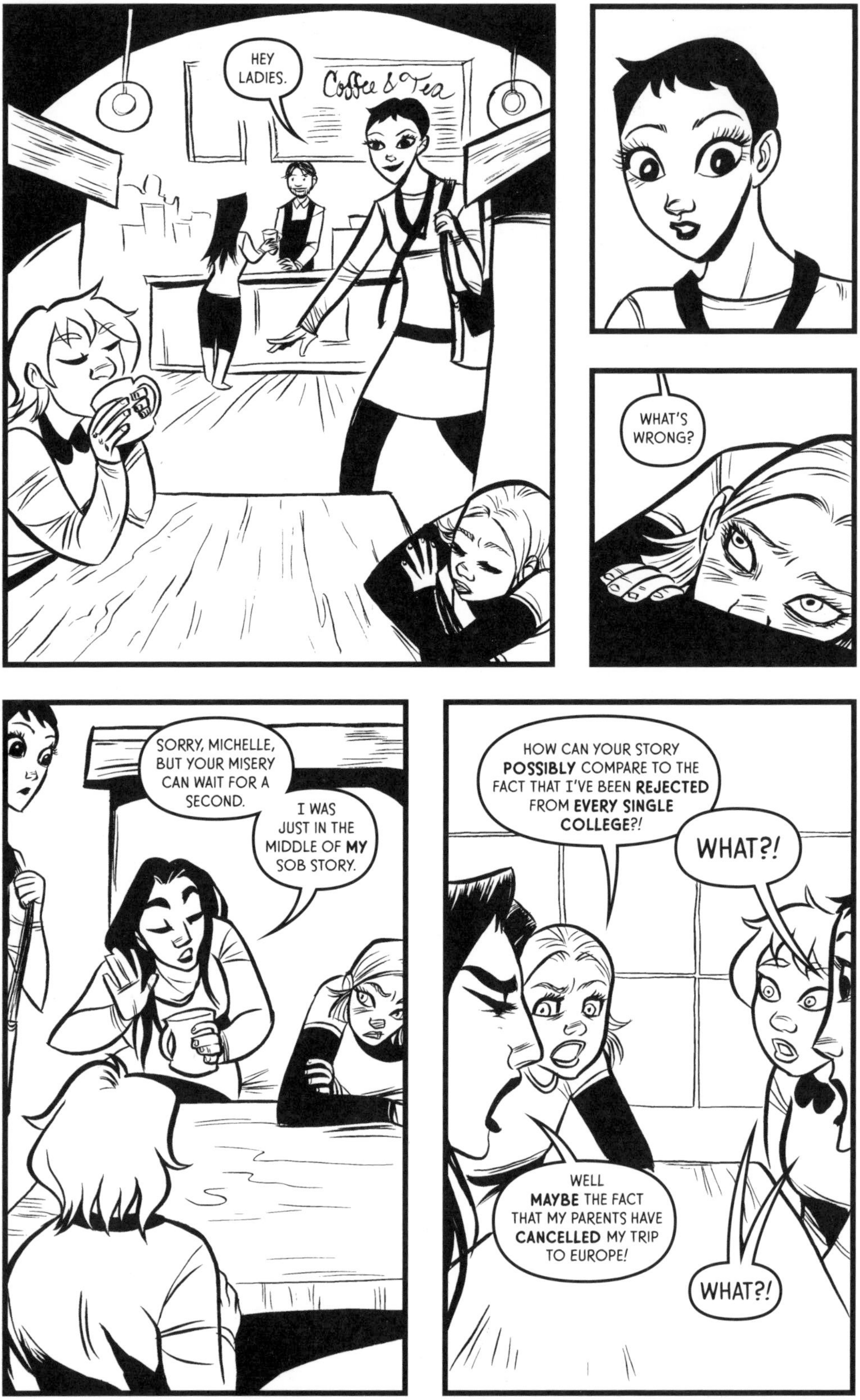

HEY LADIES.
Coffee & Tea
WHAT'S WRONG?
SORRY, MICHELLE, BUT YOUR MISERY CAN WAIT FOR A SECOND.
I WAS JUST IN THE MIDDLE OF **MY** SOB STORY.
HOW CAN YOUR STORY **POSSIBLY** COMPARE TO THE FACT THAT I'VE BEEN **REJECTED** FROM **EVERY SINGLE COLLEGE**?!
WHAT?!
WELL **MAYBE** THE FACT THAT MY PARENTS HAVE **CANCELLED** MY TRIP TO EUROPE!
WHAT?!

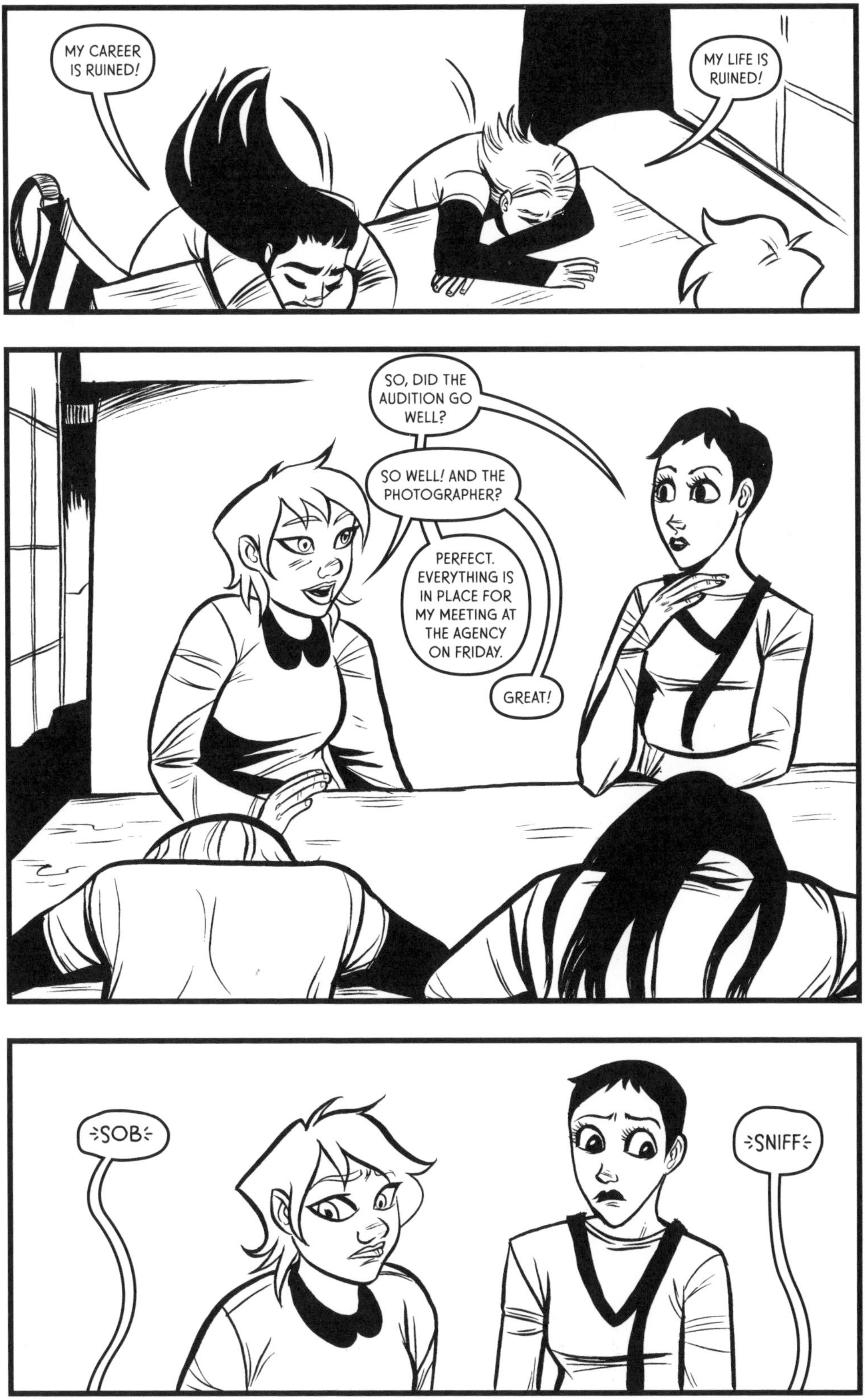
MY CAREER IS RUINED!
MY LIFE IS RUINED!
SO, DID THE AUDITION GO WELL?
SO WELL! AND THE PHOTOGRAPHER?
PERFECT. EVERYTHING IS IN PLACE FOR MY MEETING AT THE AGENCY ON FRIDAY.
GREAT!
SOB
SNIFF

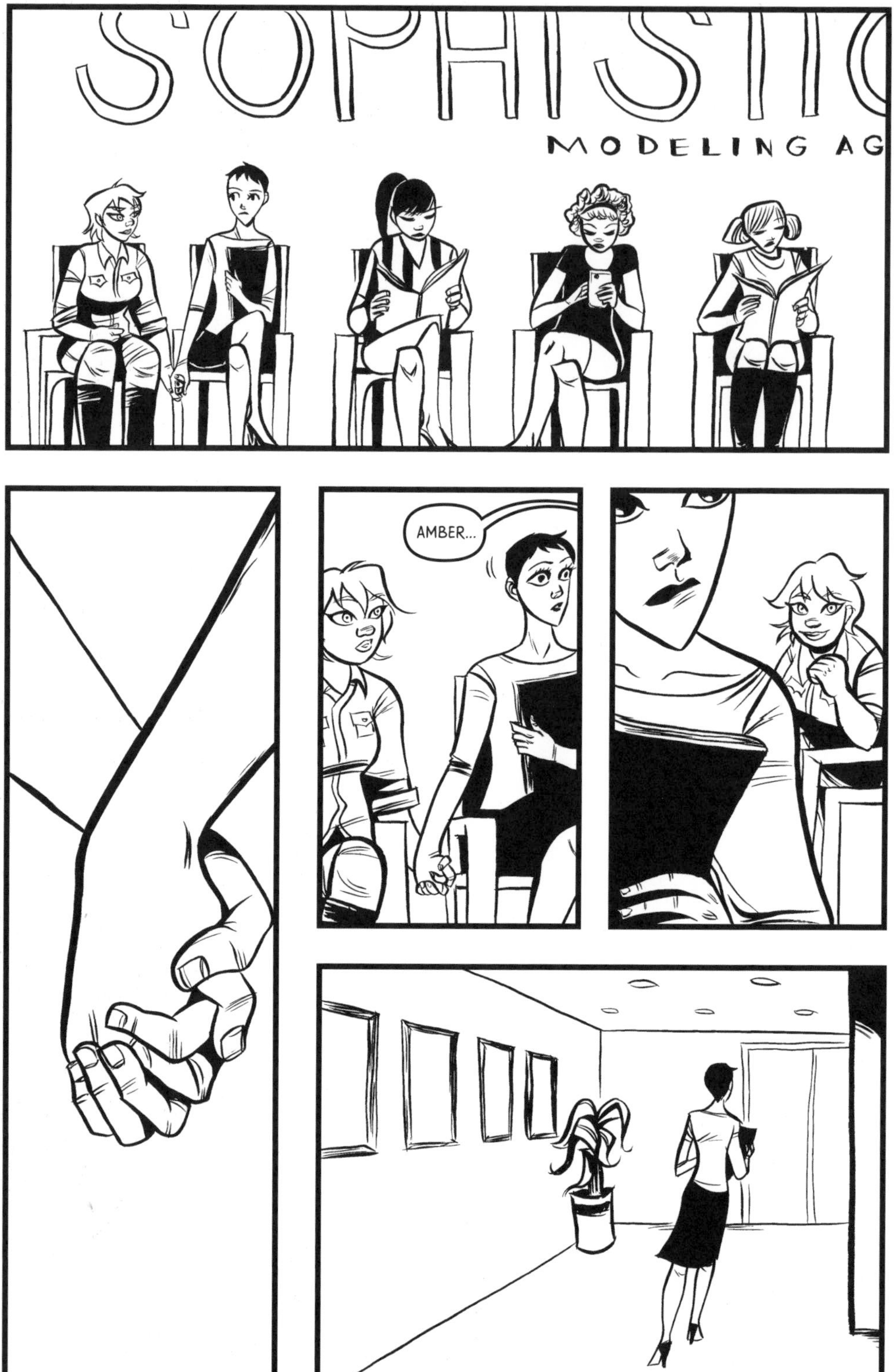
SOPHISTIC
MODELING AG
AMBER...

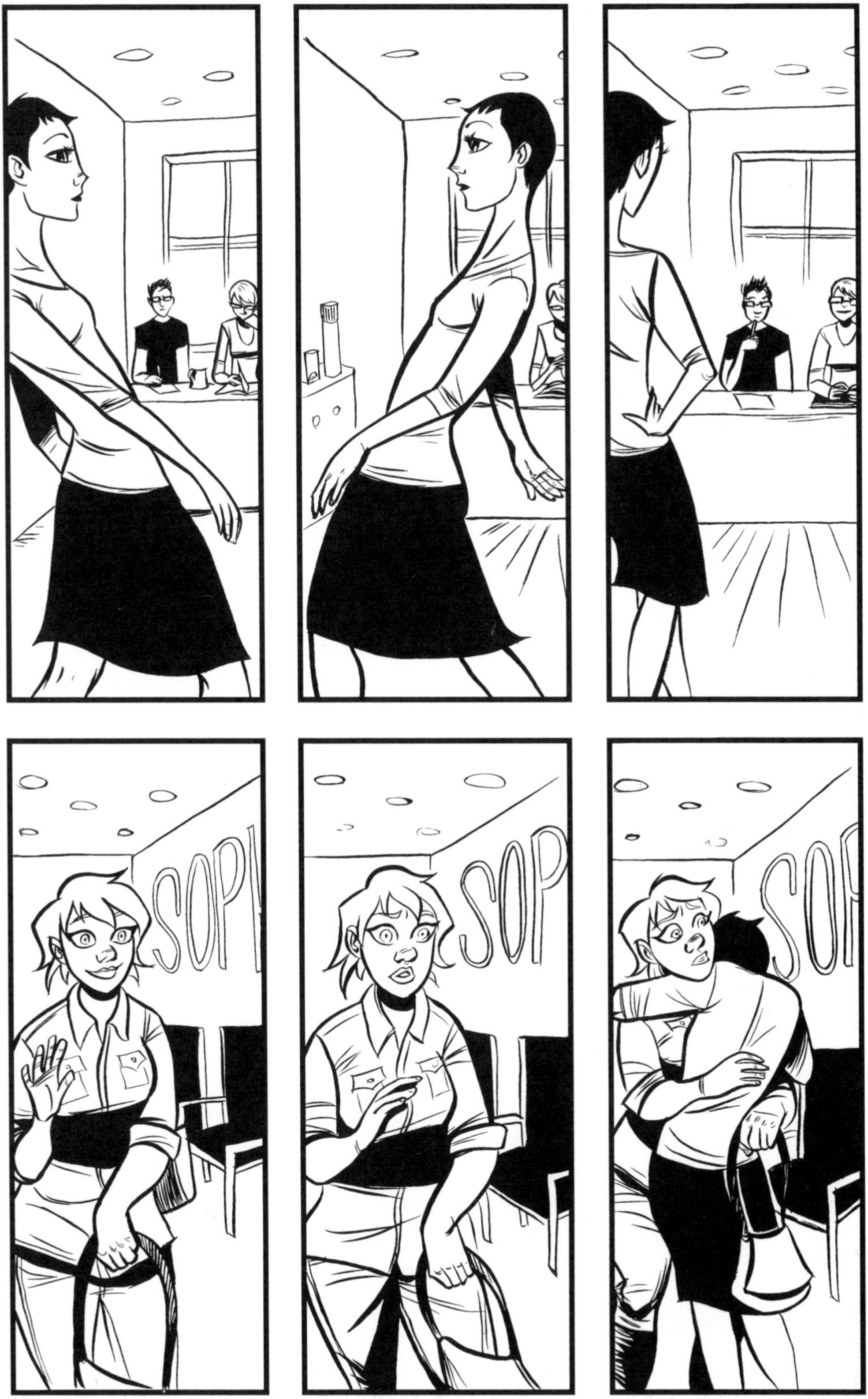
SOP
SOP
SO

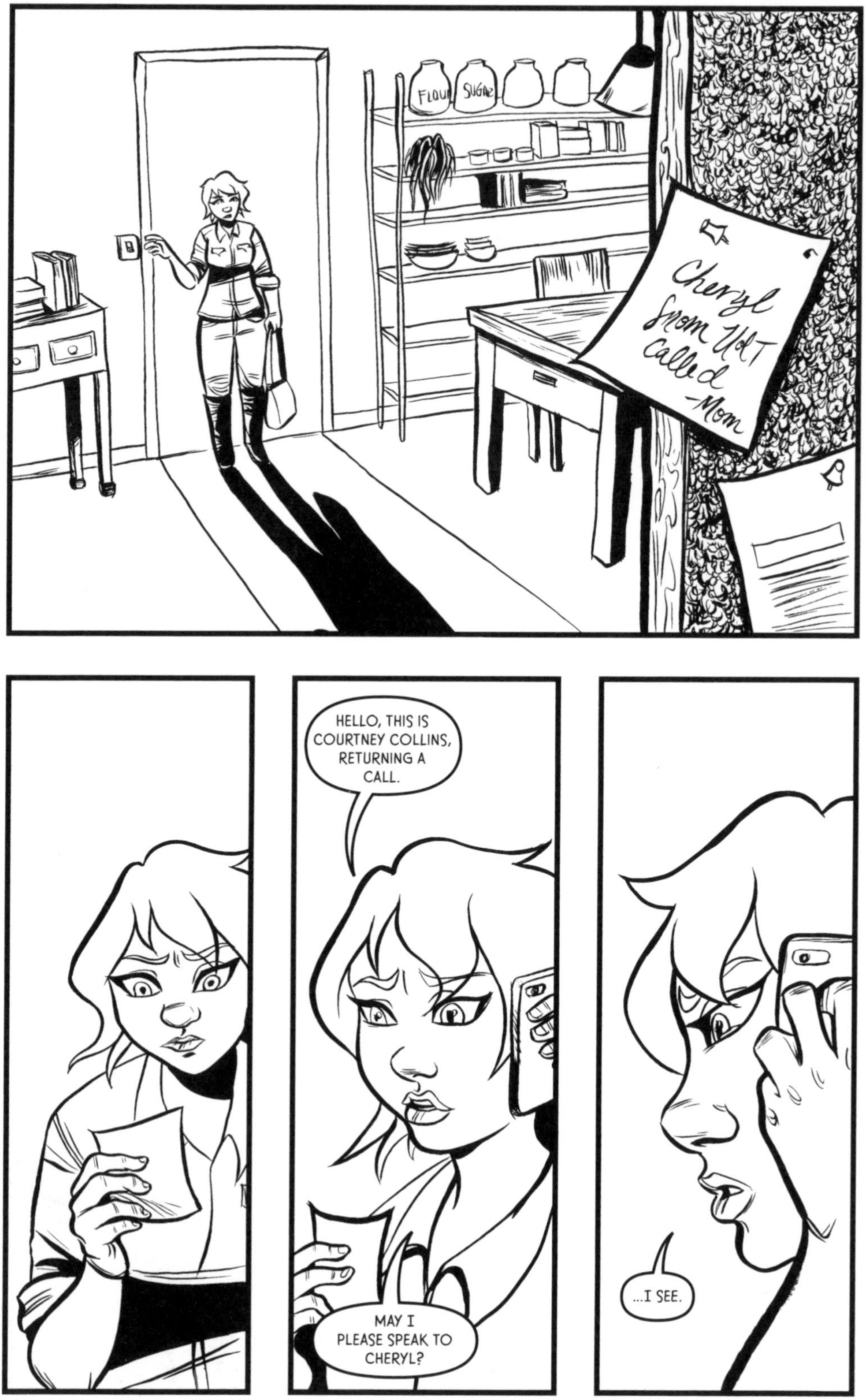
FLOUR
SUGAR
Cheryl from UdT called -Mom
HELLO, THIS IS COURTNEY COLLINS, RETURNING A CALL.
MAY I PLEASE SPEAK TO CHERYL?
...I SEE.

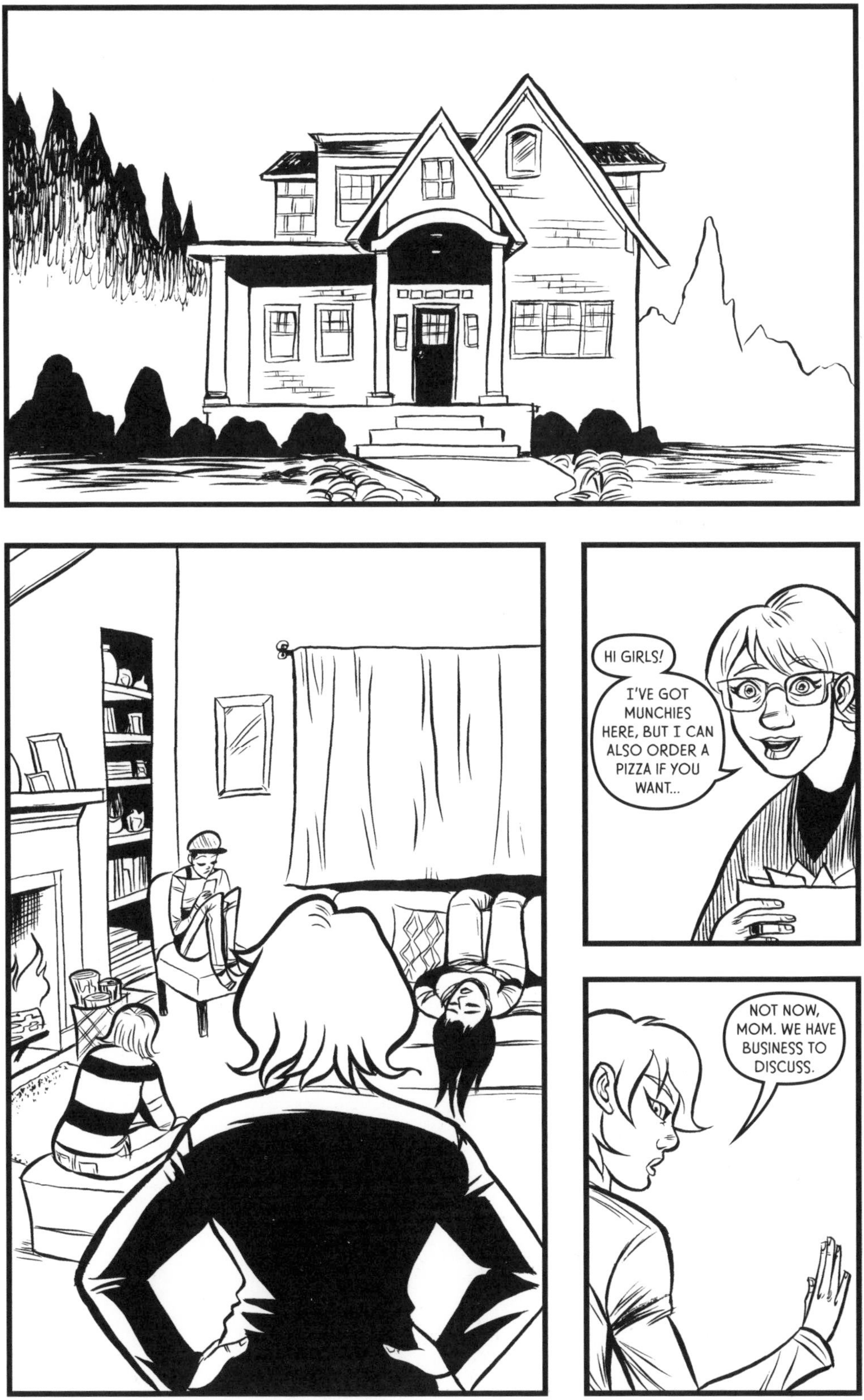
HI GIRLS!
I'VE GOT MUNCHIES HERE, BUT I CAN ALSO ORDER A PIZZA IF YOU WANT...
NOT NOW, MOM. WE HAVE BUSINESS TO DISCUSS.

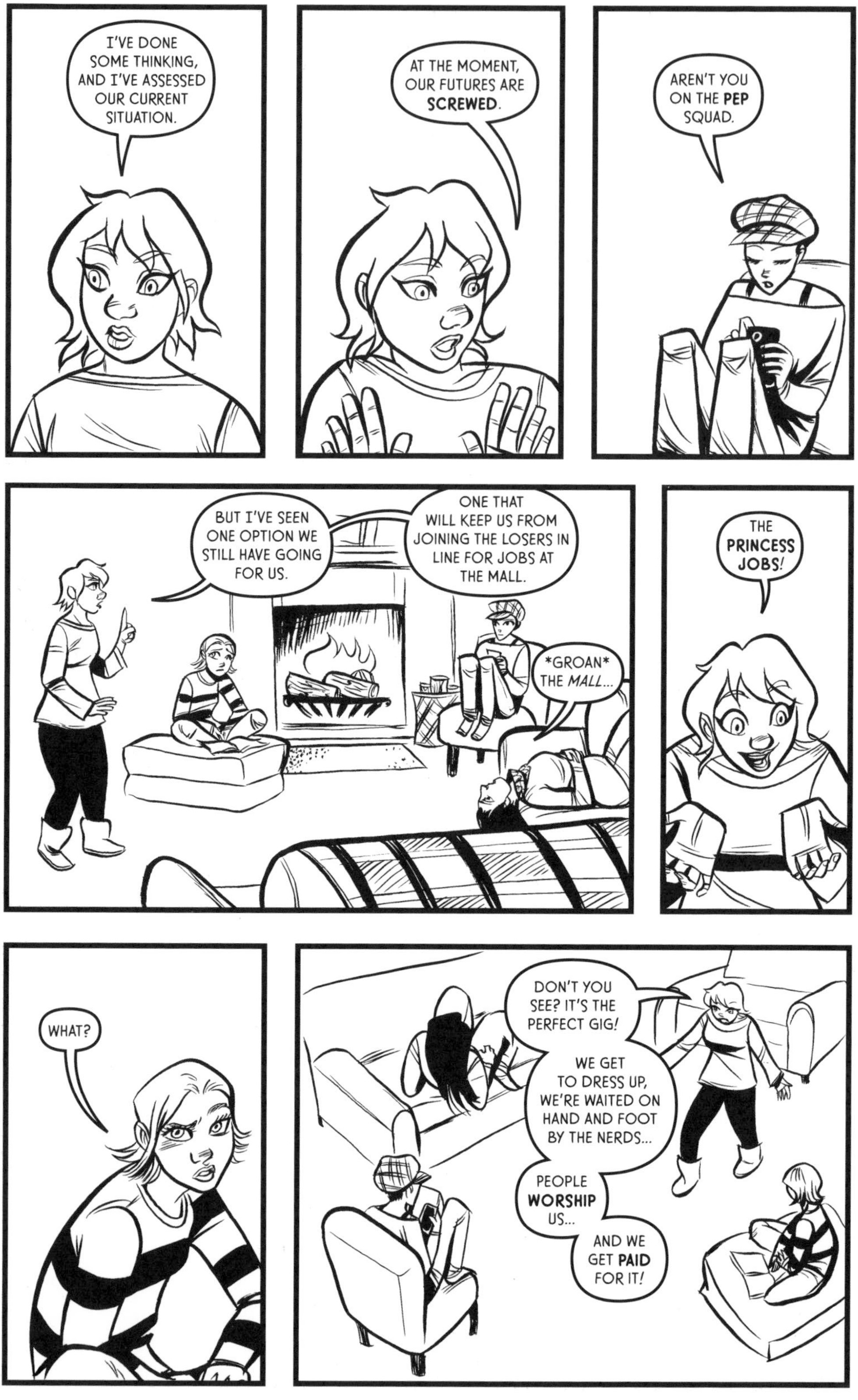
I'VE DONE SOME THINKING, AND I'VE ASSESSED OUR CURRENT SITUATION.
AT THE MOMENT, OUR FUTURES ARE SCREWED.
AREN'T YOU ON THE PEP SQUAD.
BUT I'VE SEEN ONE OPTION WE STILL HAVE GOING FOR US.
ONE THAT WILL KEEP US FROM JOINING THE LOSERS IN LINE FOR JOBS AT THE MALL.
GROAN THE MALL...
THE PRINCESS JOBS!
WHAT?
DON'T YOU SEE? IT'S THE PERFECT GIG!
WE GET TO DRESS UP, WE'RE WAITED ON HAND AND FOOT BY THE NERDS...
PEOPLE WORSHIP US...
AND WE GET PAID FOR IT!

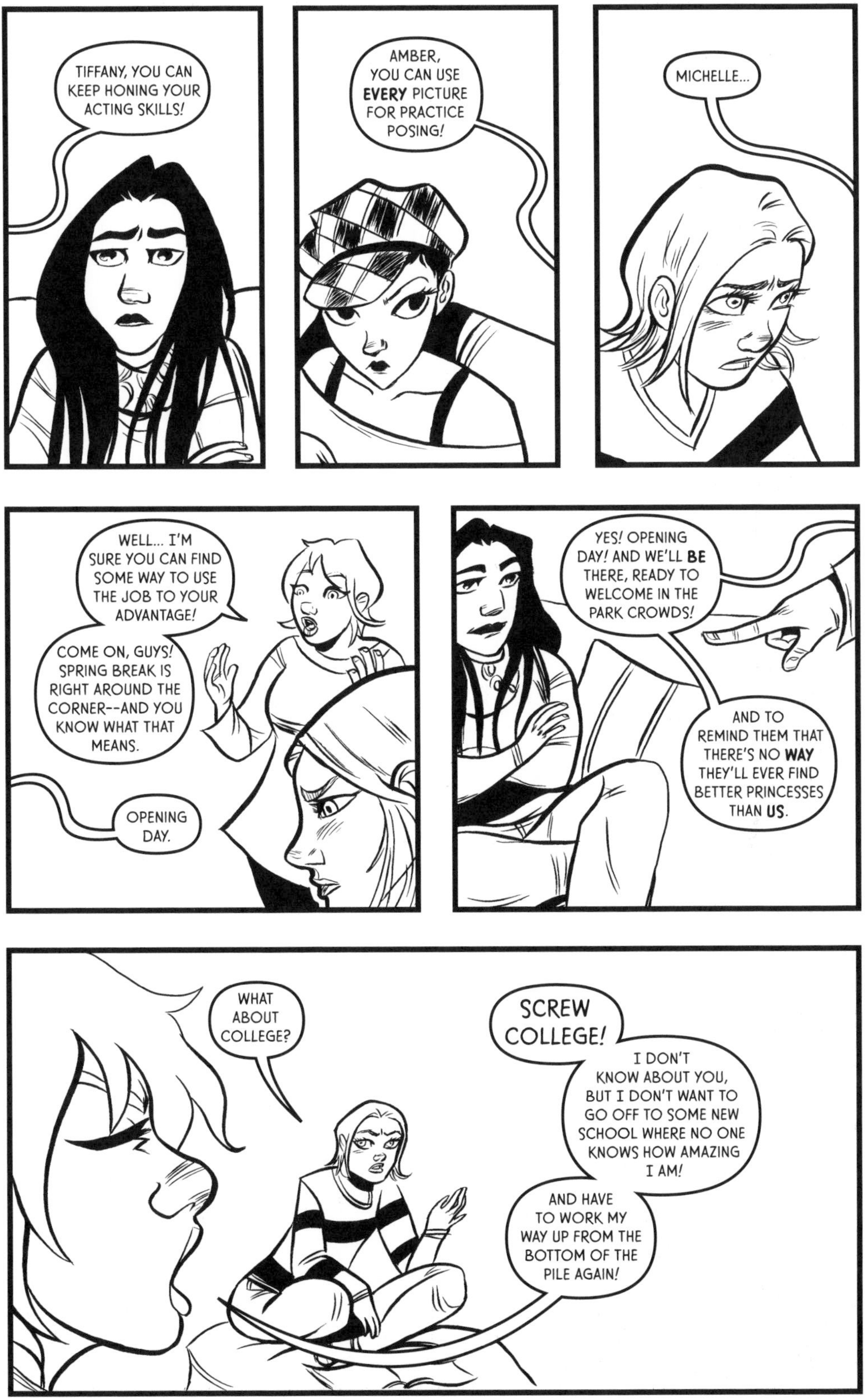
TIFFANY, YOU CAN KEEP HONING YOUR ACTING SKILLS!
AMBER, YOU CAN USE EVERY PICTURE FOR PRACTICE POSING!
MICHELLE...
WELL... I'M SURE YOU CAN FIND SOME WAY TO USE THE JOB TO YOUR ADVANTAGE!
COME ON, GUYS! SPRING BREAK IS RIGHT AROUND THE CORNER--AND YOU KNOW WHAT THAT MEANS.
OPENING DAY.
YES! OPENING DAY! AND WE'LL BE THERE, READY TO WELCOME IN THE PARK CROWDS!
AND TO REMIND THEM THAT THERE'S NO WAY THEY'LL EVER FIND BETTER PRINCESSES THAN US.
WHAT ABOUT COLLEGE?
SCREW COLLEGE!
I DON'T KNOW ABOUT YOU, BUT I DON'T WANT TO GO OFF TO SOME NEW SCHOOL WHERE NO ONE KNOWS HOW AMAZING I AM!
AND HAVE TO WORK MY WAY UP FROM THE BOTTOM OF THE PILE AGAIN!

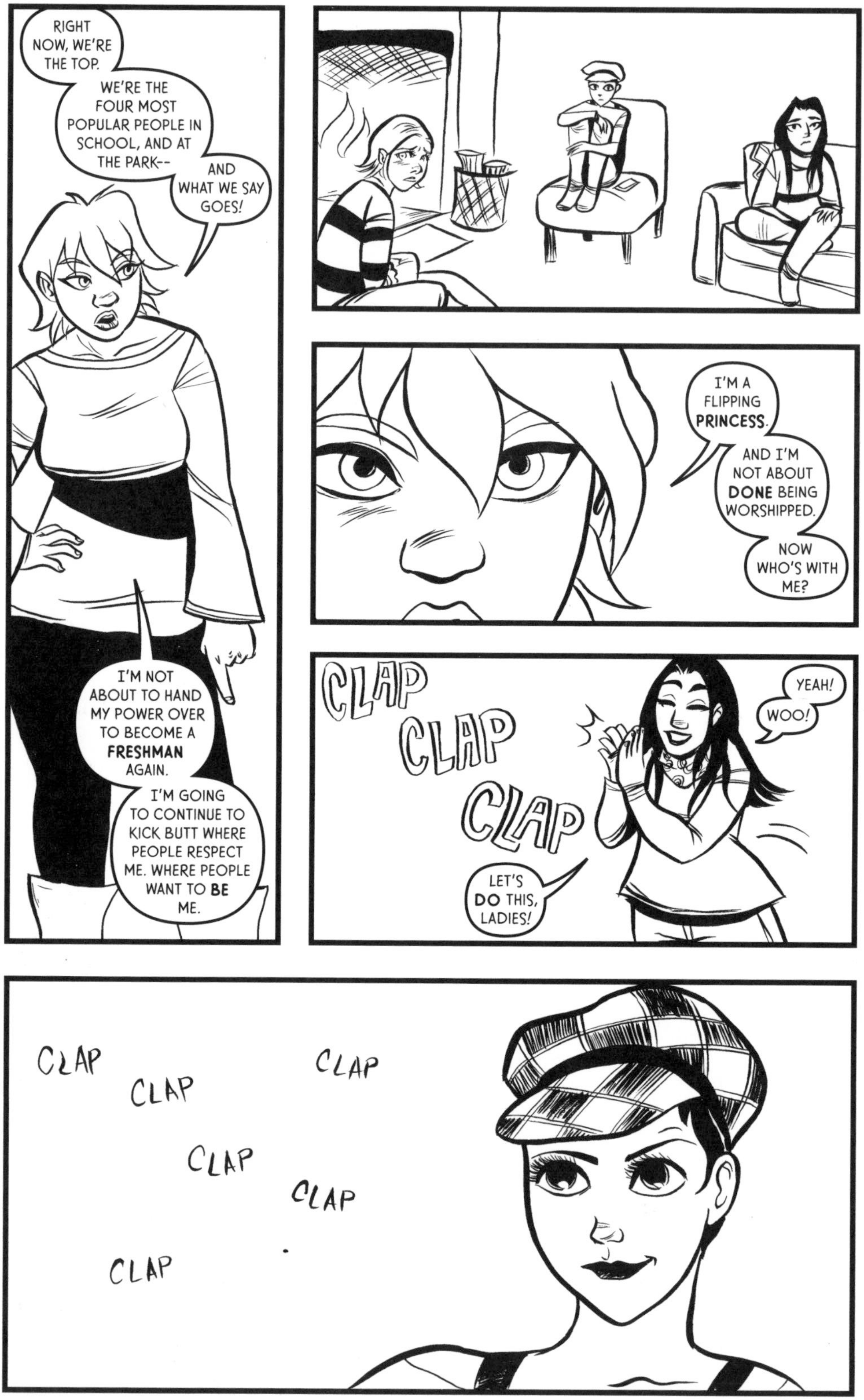
RIGHT NOW, WE'RE THE TOP.
WE'RE THE FOUR MOST POPULAR PEOPLE IN SCHOOL, AND AT THE PARK--
AND WHAT WE SAY GOES!
I'M NOT ABOUT TO HAND MY POWER OVER TO BECOME A **FRESHMAN** AGAIN.
I'M GOING TO CONTINUE TO KICK BUTT WHERE PEOPLE RESPECT ME. WHERE PEOPLE WANT TO **BE** ME.
I'M A FLIPPING **PRINCESS**.
AND I'M NOT ABOUT **DONE** BEING WORSHIPPED.
NOW WHO'S WITH ME?
CLAP
CLAP
CLAP
YEAH!
WOO!
LET'S **DO** THIS, LADIES!
CLAP
CLAP
CLAP
CLAP
CLAP
CLAP

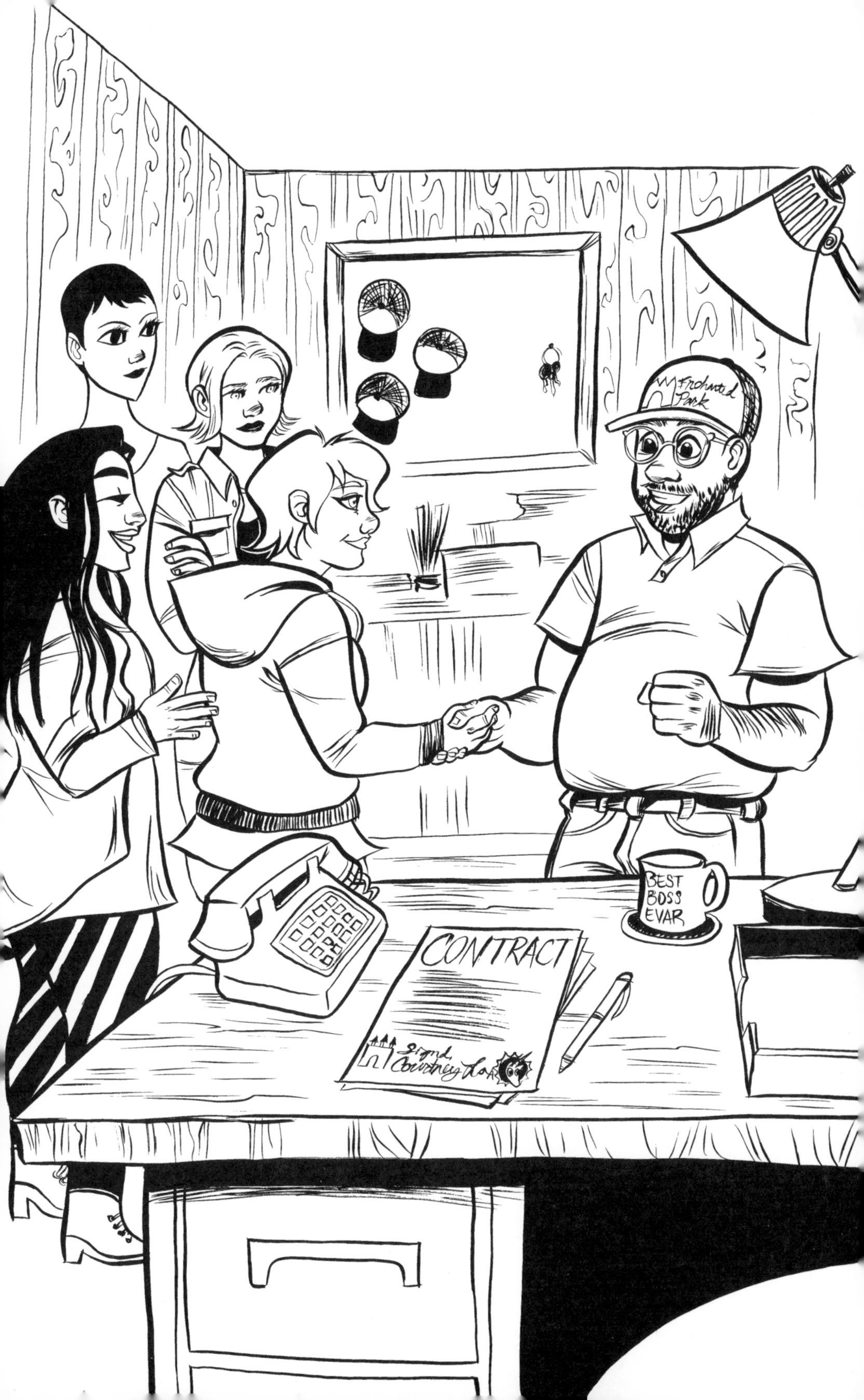
BEST BOSS EVAR
CONTRACT

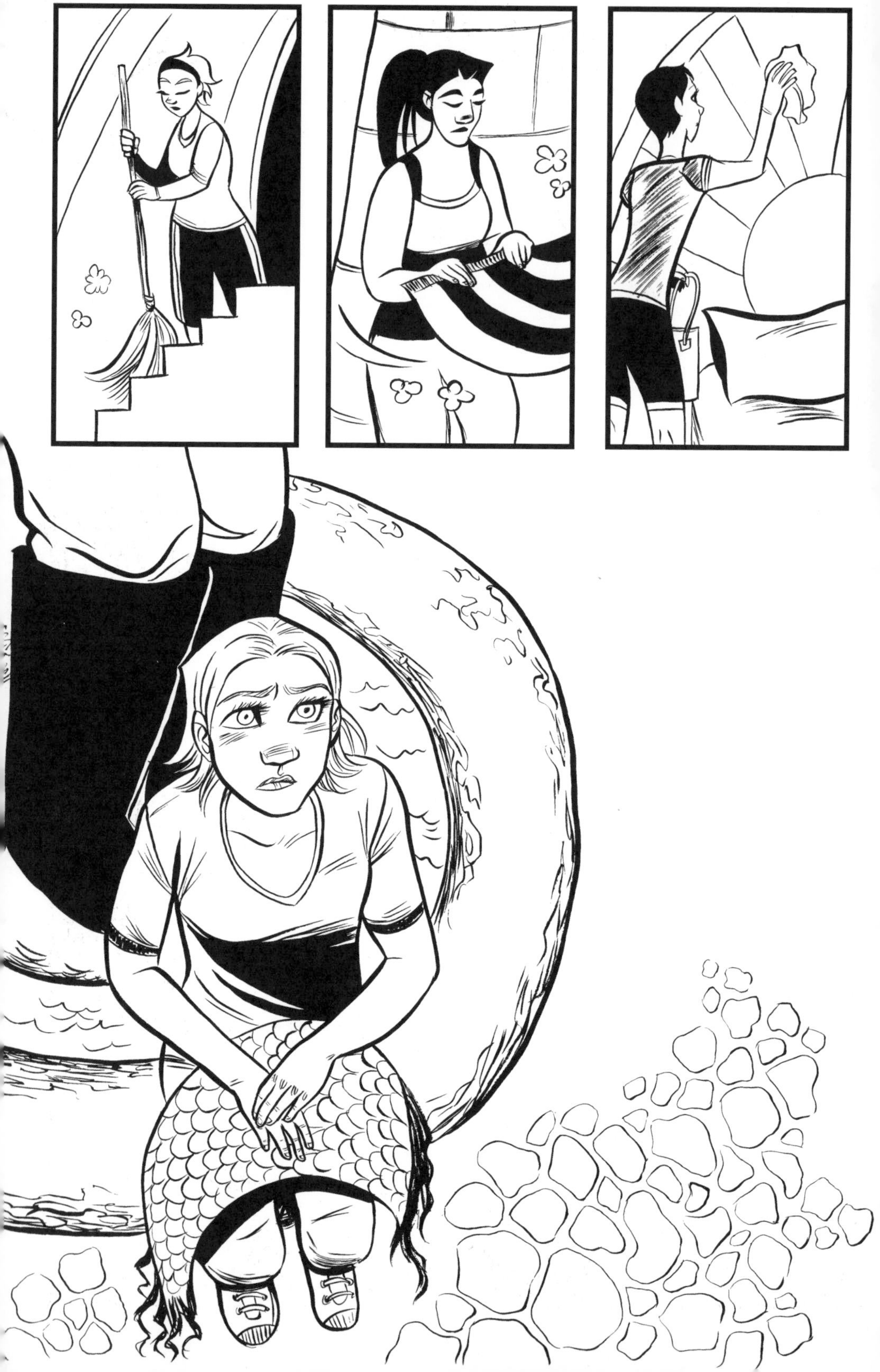

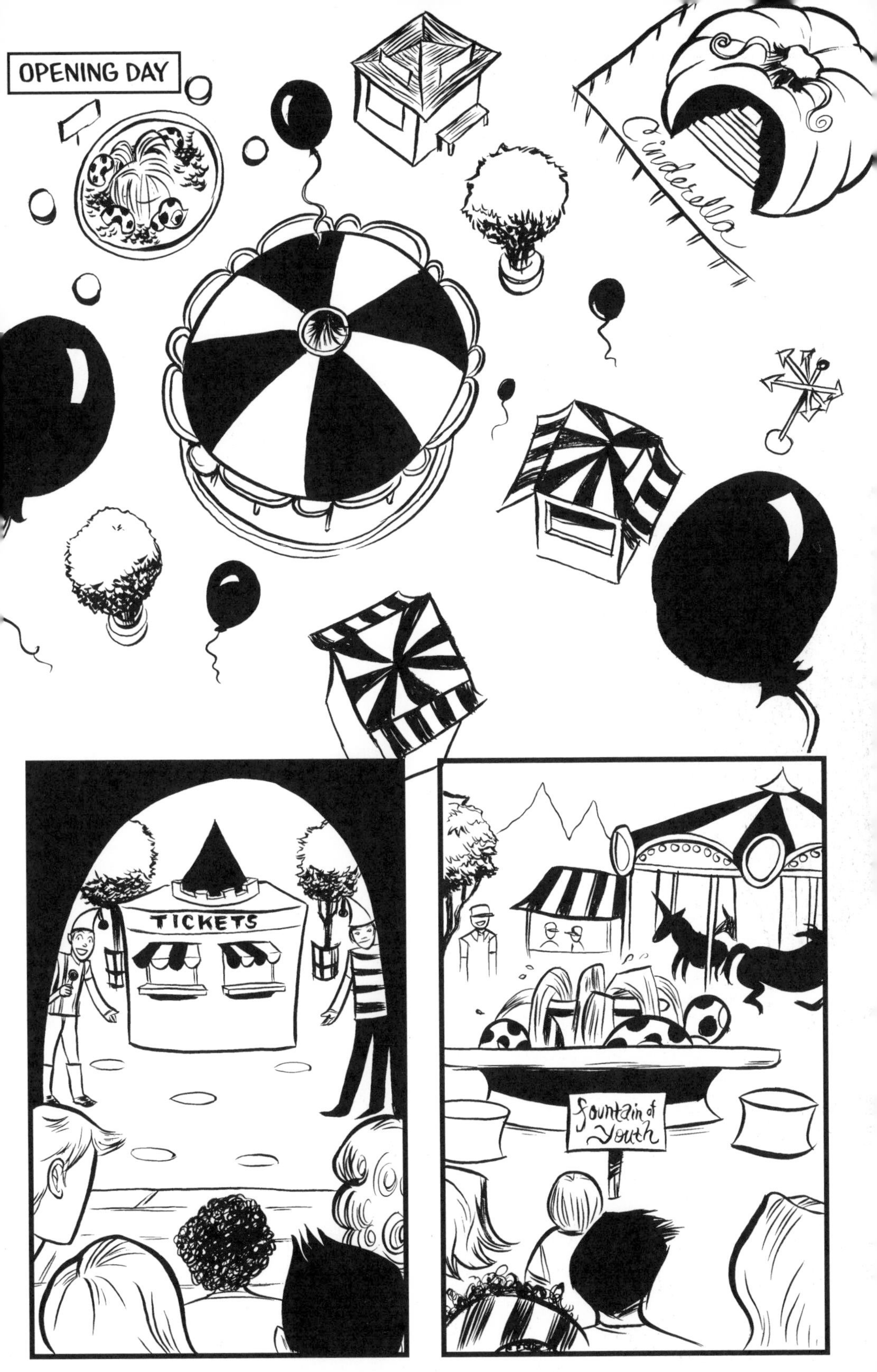
OPENING DAY
Cinderella
TICKETS
fountain of Youth

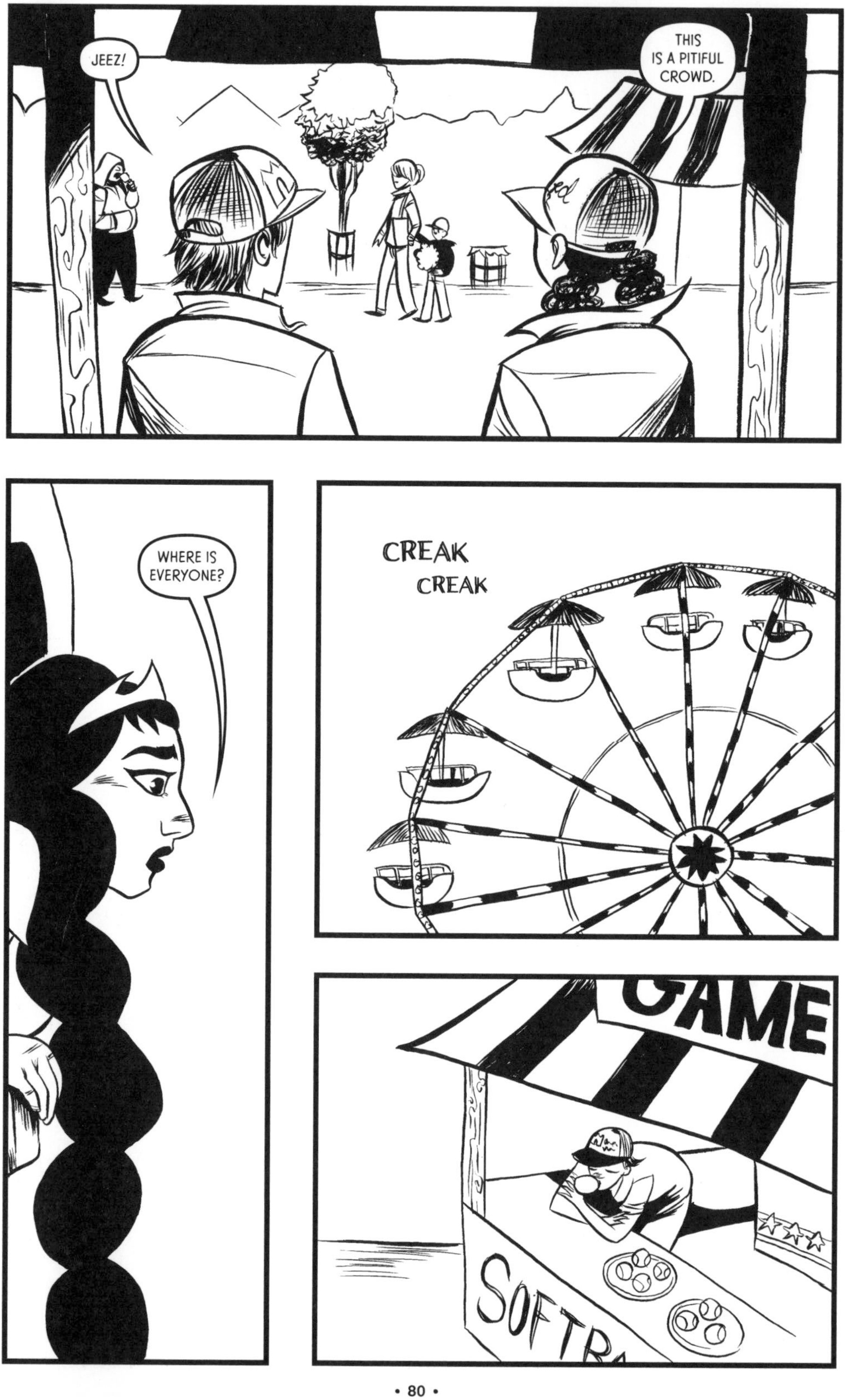
JEEZ!
THIS IS A PITIFUL CROWD.
WHERE IS EVERYONE?
CREAK
CREAK
GAME

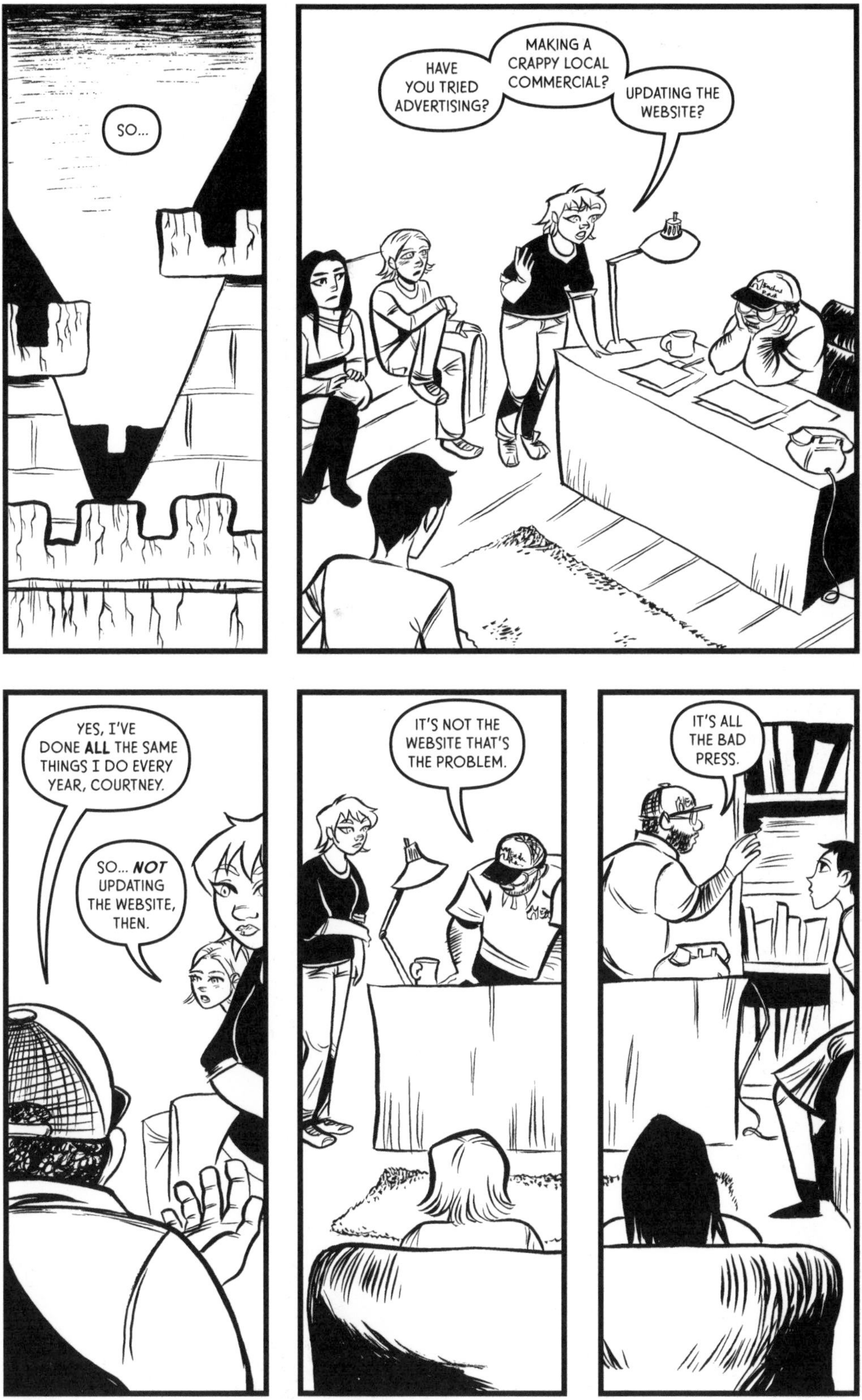
SO...
HAVE YOU TRIED ADVERTISING?
MAKING A CRAPPY LOCAL COMMERCIAL?
UPDATING THE WEBSITE?
YES, I'VE DONE ALL THE SAME THINGS I DO EVERY YEAR, COURTNEY.
SO... NOT UPDATING THE WEBSITE, THEN.
IT'S NOT THE WEBSITE THAT'S THE PROBLEM.
IT'S ALL THE BAD PRESS.

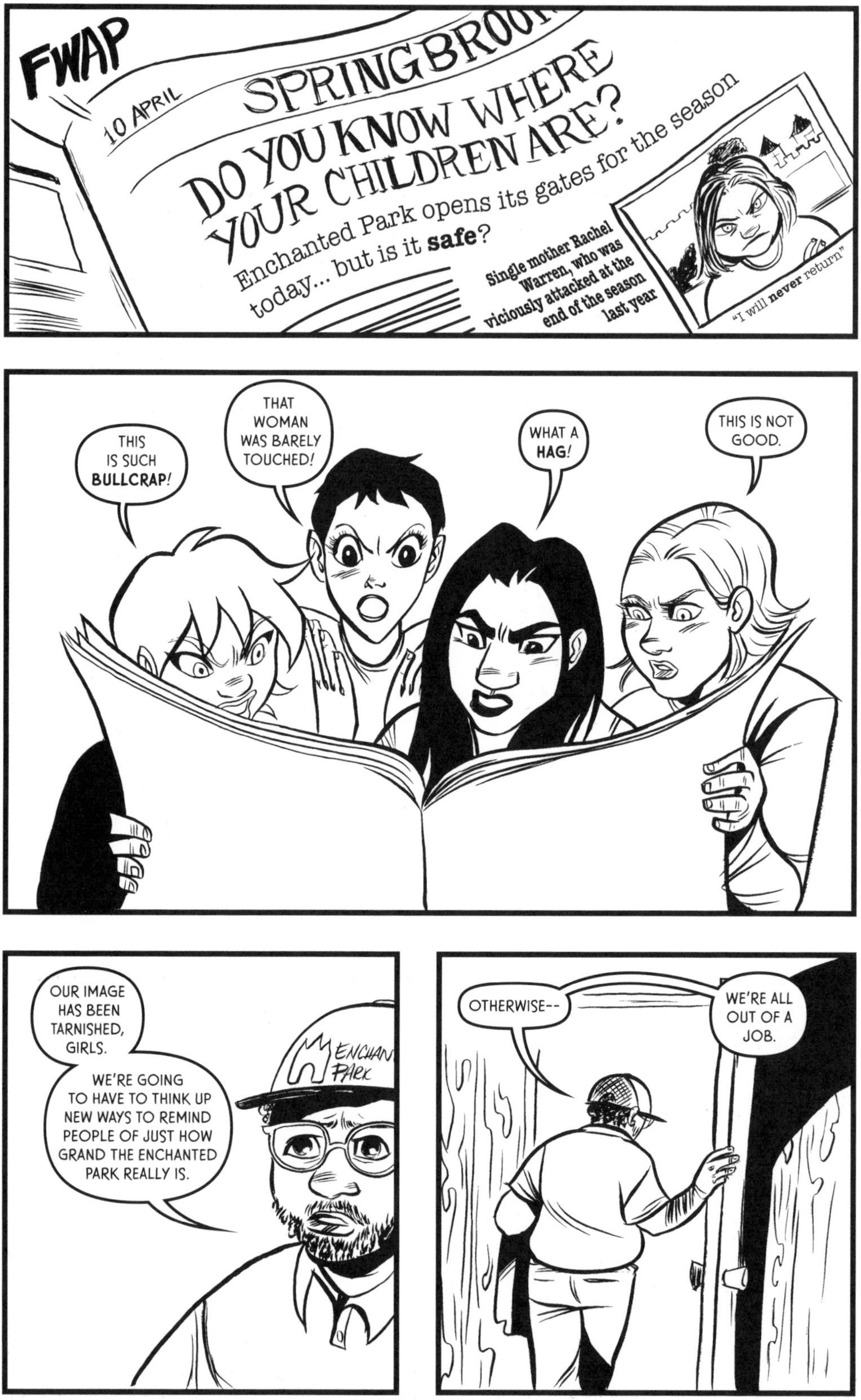
FWAP
10 APRIL
SPRINGBROO
DO YOU KNOW WHERE YOUR CHILDREN ARE?
Enchanted Park opens its gates for the season today... but is it **safe**?
Single mother Rachel Warren, who was viciously attacked at the end of the season last year
"I will **never** return"
THIS IS SUCH **BULLCRAP**!
THAT WOMAN WAS BARELY TOUCHED!
WHAT A **HAG**!
THIS IS NOT GOOD.
OUR IMAGE HAS BEEN TARNISHED, GIRLS.
WE'RE GOING TO HAVE TO THINK UP NEW WAYS TO REMIND PEOPLE OF JUST HOW GRAND THE ENCHANTED PARK REALLY IS.
ENCHANT PARK
OTHERWISE--
WE'RE ALL OUT OF A JOB.

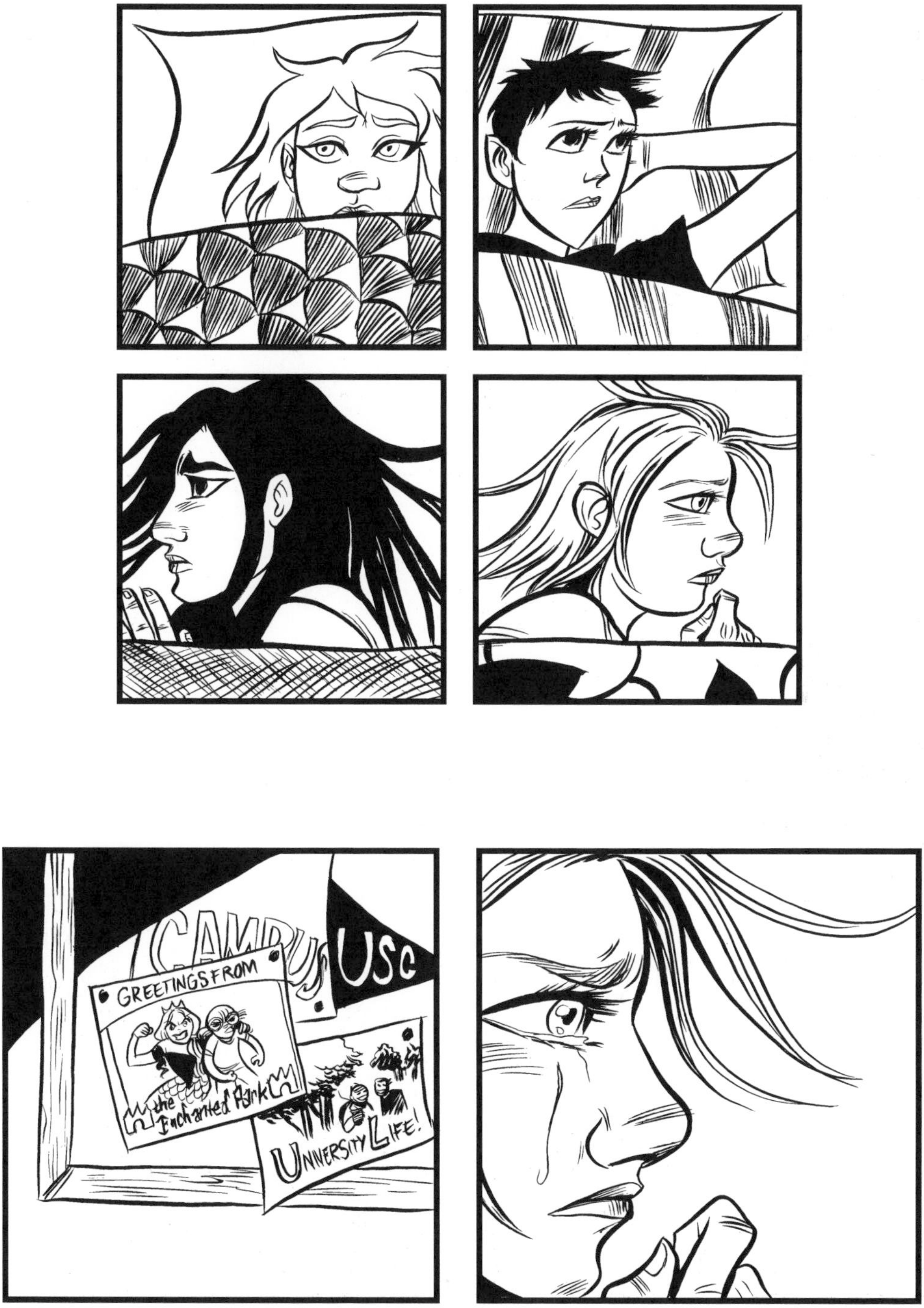
USC
GREETINGS FROM
the Enchanted Park
UNIVERSITY LIFE!

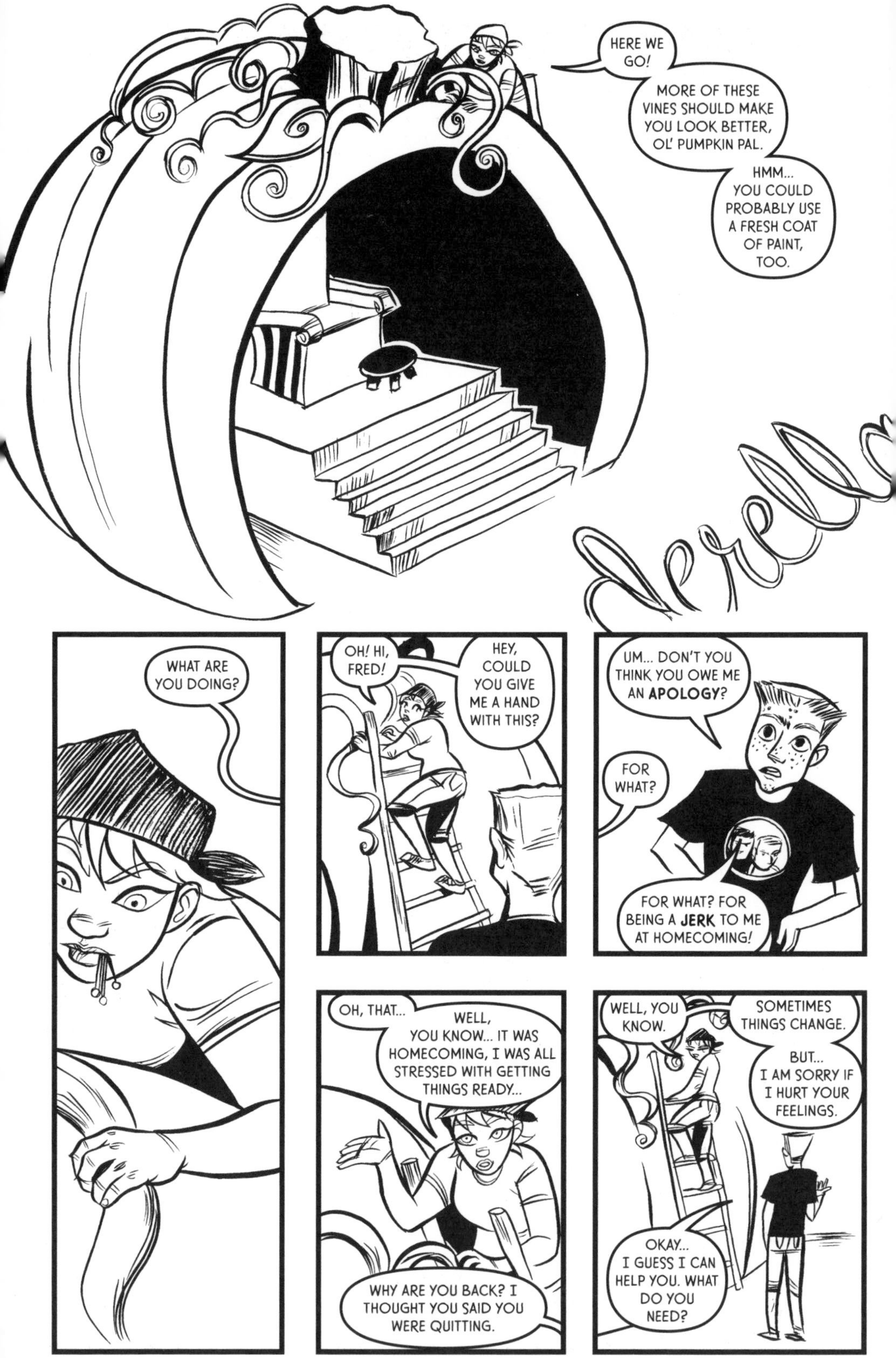
HERE WE GO!
MORE OF THESE VINES SHOULD MAKE YOU LOOK BETTER, OL' PUMPKIN PAL.
HMM... YOU COULD PROBABLY USE A FRESH COAT OF PAINT, TOO.
WHAT ARE YOU DOING?
OH! HI, FRED!
HEY, COULD YOU GIVE ME A HAND WITH THIS?
UM... DON'T YOU THINK YOU OWE ME AN **APOLOGY**?
FOR WHAT?
FOR WHAT? FOR BEING A **JERK** TO ME AT HOMECOMING!
OH, THAT...
WELL, YOU KNOW... IT WAS HOMECOMING, I WAS ALL STRESSED WITH GETTING THINGS READY...
WHY ARE YOU BACK? I THOUGHT YOU SAID YOU WERE QUITTING.
WELL, YOU KNOW.
SOMETIMES THINGS CHANGE.
BUT... I AM SORRY IF I HURT YOUR FEELINGS.
OKAY... I GUESS I CAN HELP YOU. WHAT DO YOU NEED?

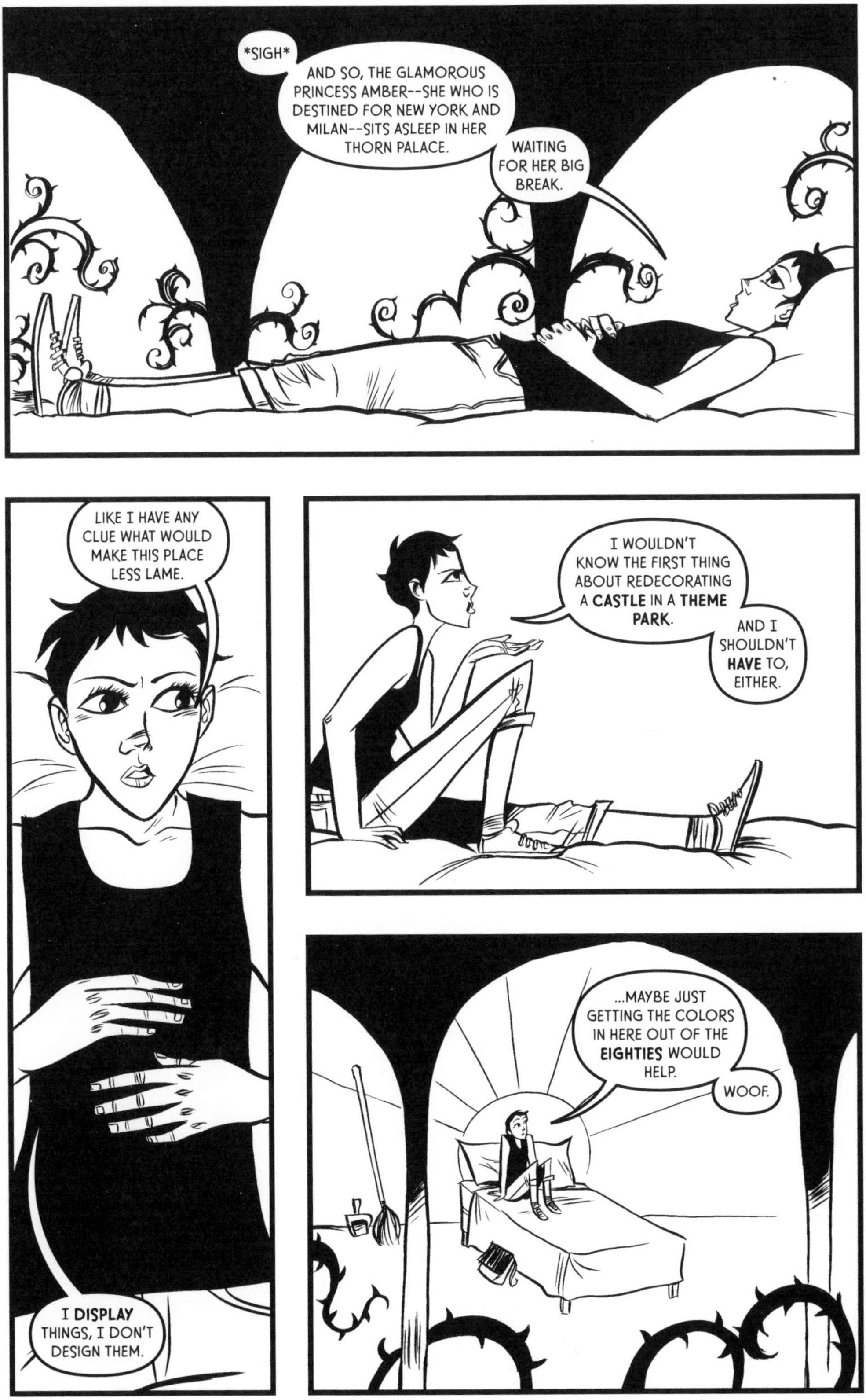
SIGH
AND SO, THE GLAMOROUS PRINCESS AMBER--SHE WHO IS DESTINED FOR NEW YORK AND MILAN--SITS ASLEEP IN HER THORN PALACE.
WAITING FOR HER BIG BREAK.
LIKE I HAVE ANY CLUE WHAT WOULD MAKE THIS PLACE LESS LAME.
I DISPLAY THINGS, I DON'T DESIGN THEM.
I WOULDN'T KNOW THE FIRST THING ABOUT REDECORATING A CASTLE IN A THEME PARK.
AND I SHOULDN'T HAVE TO, EITHER.
...MAYBE JUST GETTING THE COLORS IN HERE OUT OF THE EIGHTIES WOULD HELP.
WOOF.

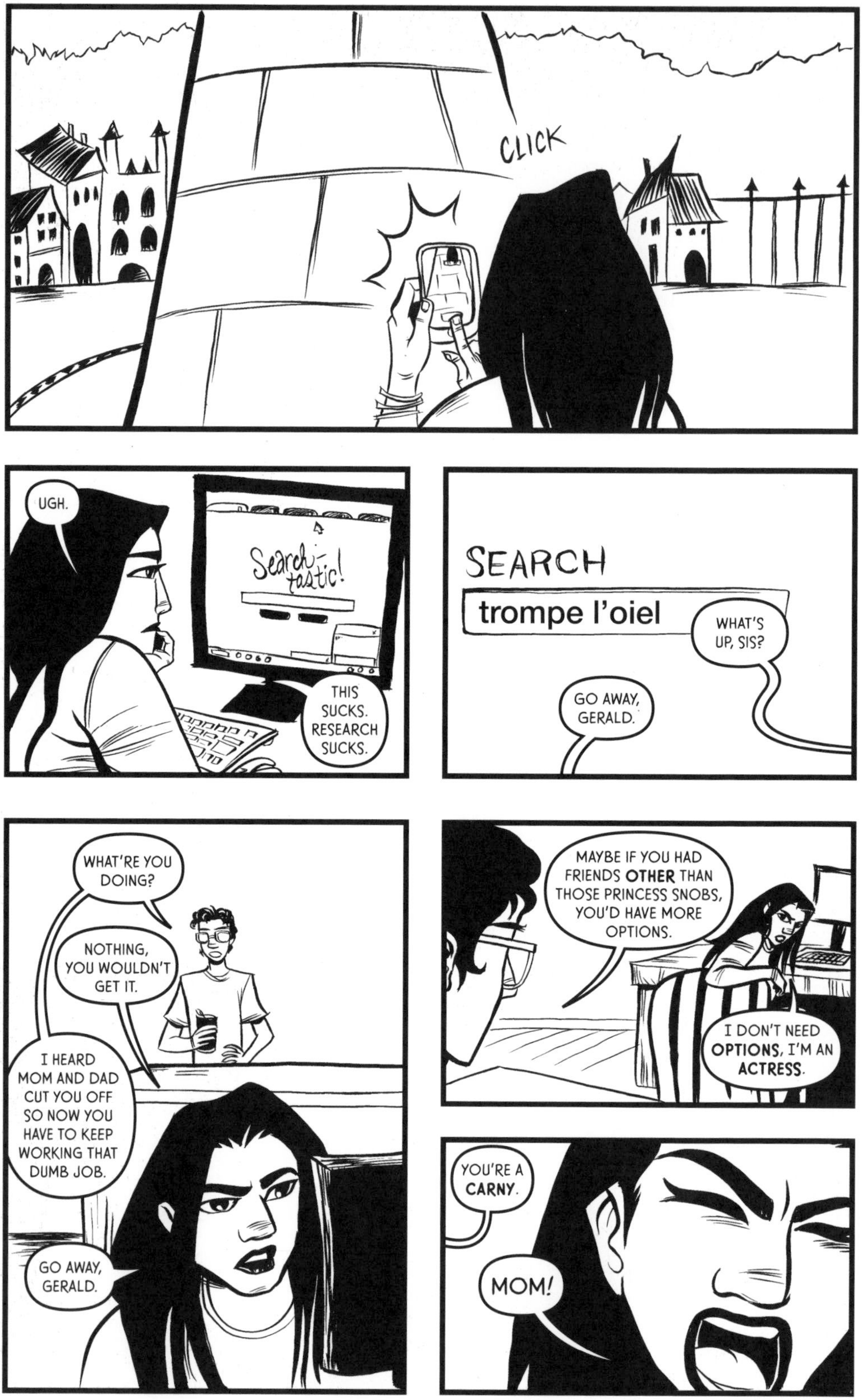

CLICK
UGH.
Search-tastic!
THIS SUCKS. RESEARCH SUCKS.
SEARCH
trompe l'oiel
WHAT'S UP, SIS?
GO AWAY, GERALD.
WHAT'RE YOU DOING?
NOTHING, YOU WOULDN'T GET IT.
I HEARD MOM AND DAD CUT YOU OFF SO NOW YOU HAVE TO KEEP WORKING THAT DUMB JOB.
GO AWAY, GERALD.
MAYBE IF YOU HAD FRIENDS **OTHER** THAN THOSE PRINCESS SNOBS, YOU'D HAVE MORE OPTIONS.
I DON'T NEED **OPTIONS**, I'M AN **ACTRESS**.
YOU'RE A **CARNY**.
MOM!

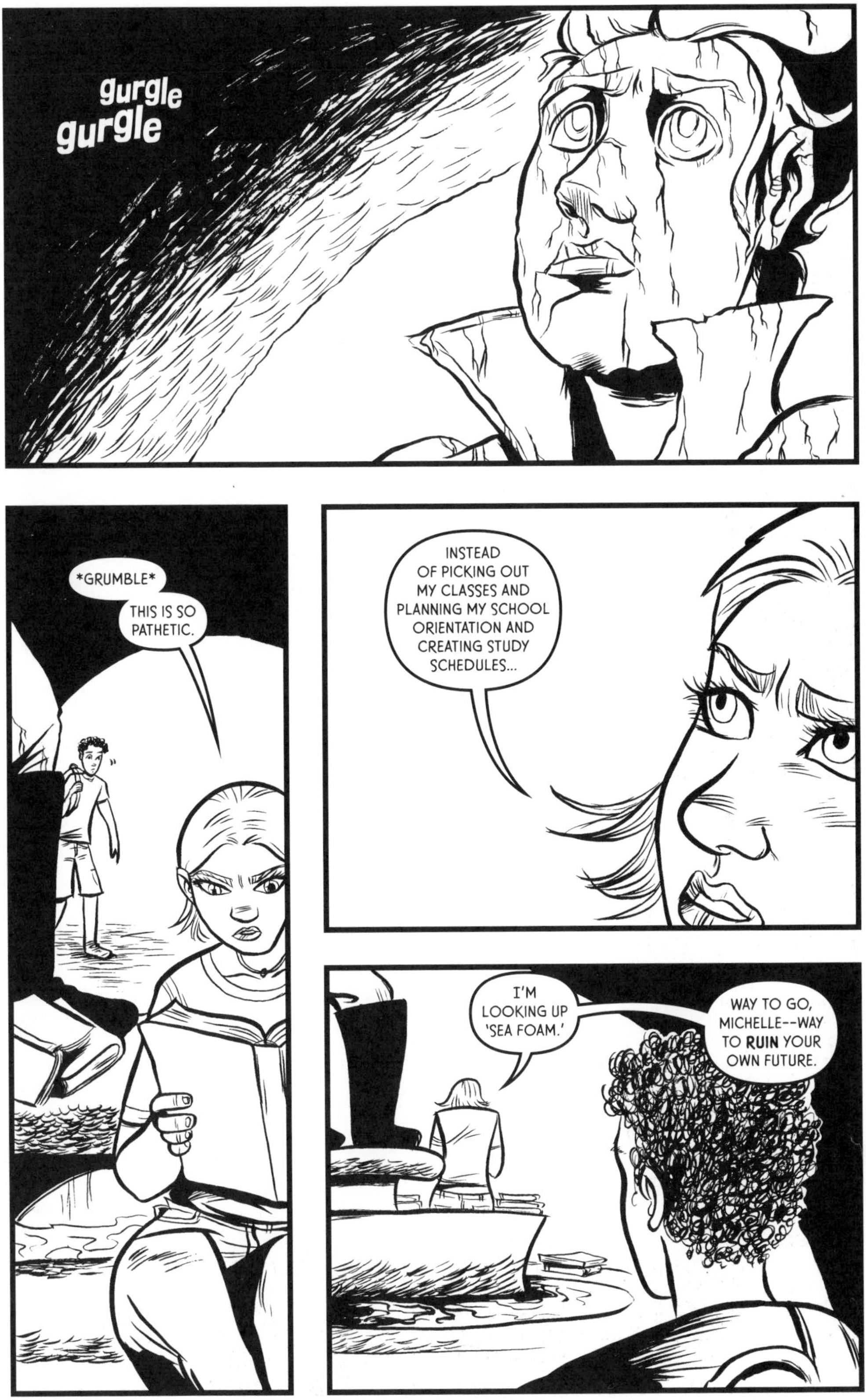
gurgle
gurgle
GRUMBLE
THIS IS SO PATHETIC.
INSTEAD OF PICKING OUT MY CLASSES AND PLANNING MY SCHOOL ORIENTATION AND CREATING STUDY SCHEDULES...
I'M LOOKING UP 'SEA FOAM.'
WAY TO GO, MICHELLE--WAY TO **RUIN** YOUR OWN FUTURE.

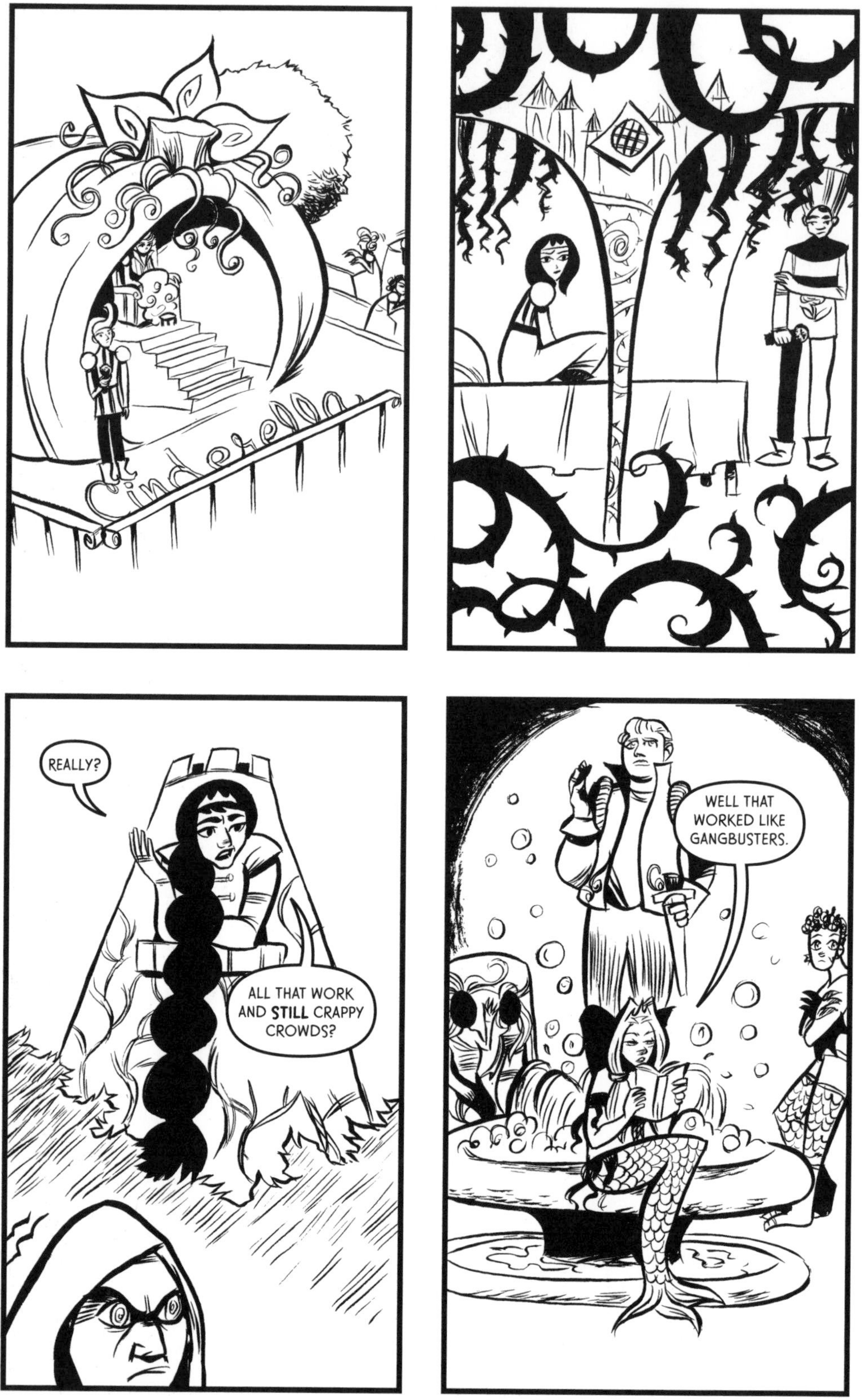
REALLY?
ALL THAT WORK AND STILL CRAPPY CROWDS?
WELL THAT WORKED LIKE GANGBUSTERS.

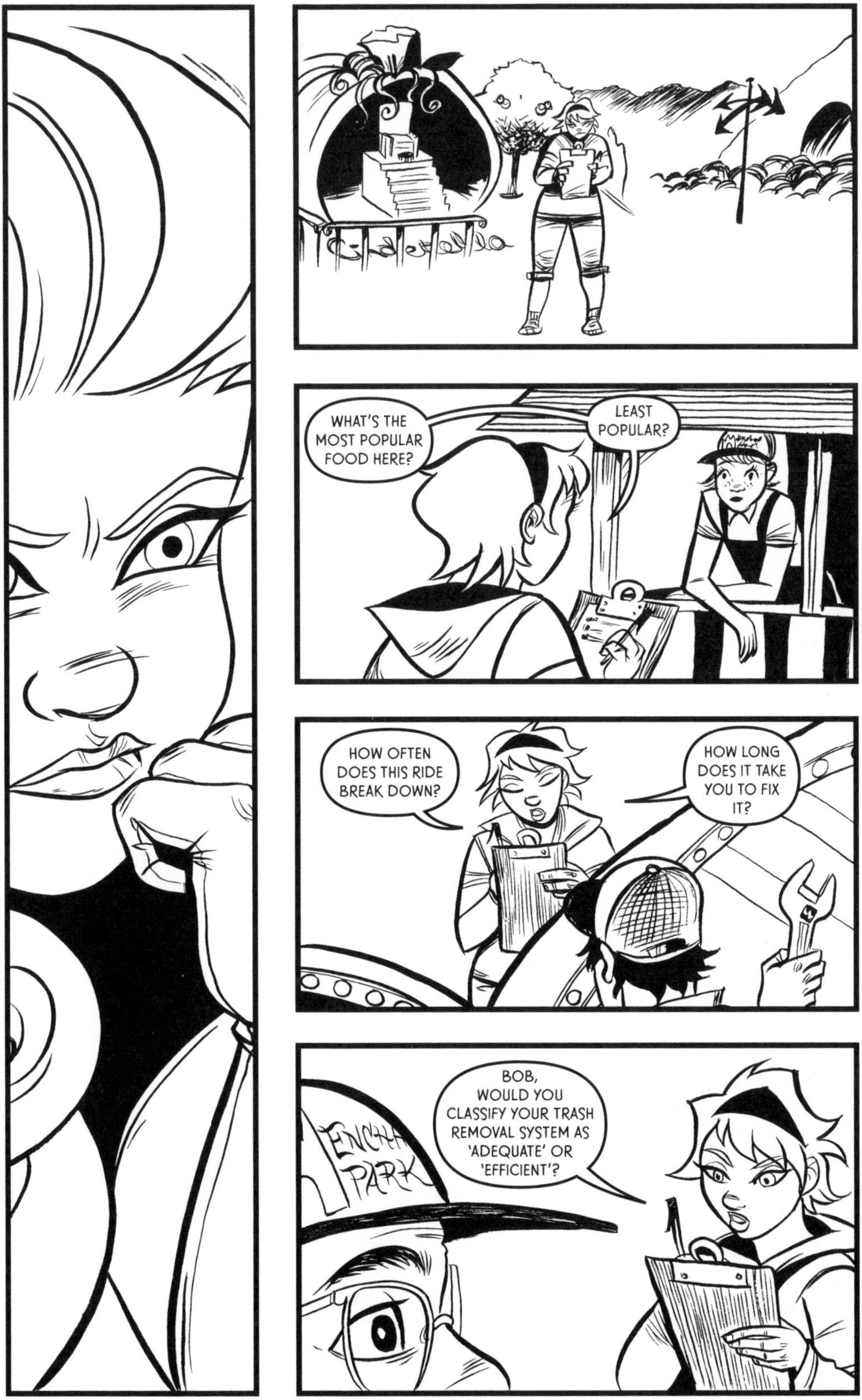
WHAT'S THE MOST POPULAR FOOD HERE?
LEAST POPULAR?
HOW OFTEN DOES THIS RIDE BREAK DOWN?
HOW LONG DOES IT TAKE YOU TO FIX IT?
BOB, WOULD YOU CLASSIFY YOUR TRASH REMOVAL SYSTEM AS 'ADEQUATE' OR 'EFFICIENT'?

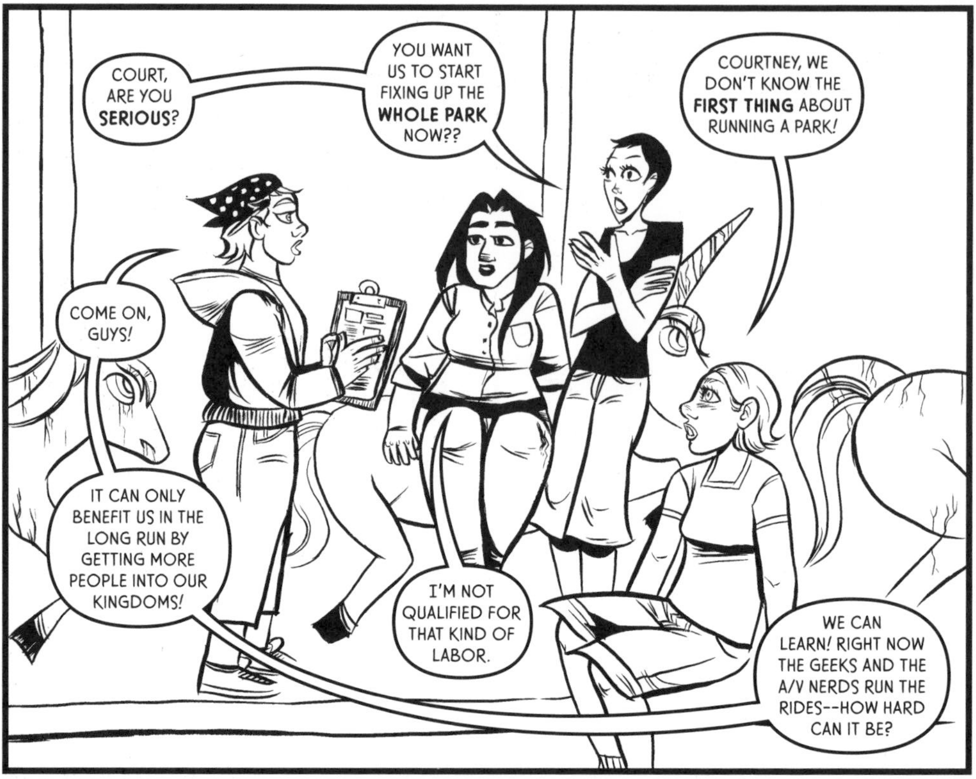
COURT, ARE YOU **SERIOUS**?
YOU WANT US TO START FIXING UP THE **WHOLE PARK** NOW??
COURTNEY, WE DON'T KNOW THE **FIRST THING** ABOUT RUNNING A PARK!
COME ON, GUYS!
IT CAN ONLY BENEFIT US IN THE LONG RUN BY GETTING MORE PEOPLE INTO OUR KINGDOMS!
I'M NOT QUALIFIED FOR THAT KIND OF LABOR.
WE CAN LEARN! RIGHT NOW THE GEEKS AND THE A/V NERDS RUN THE RIDES--HOW HARD CAN IT BE?

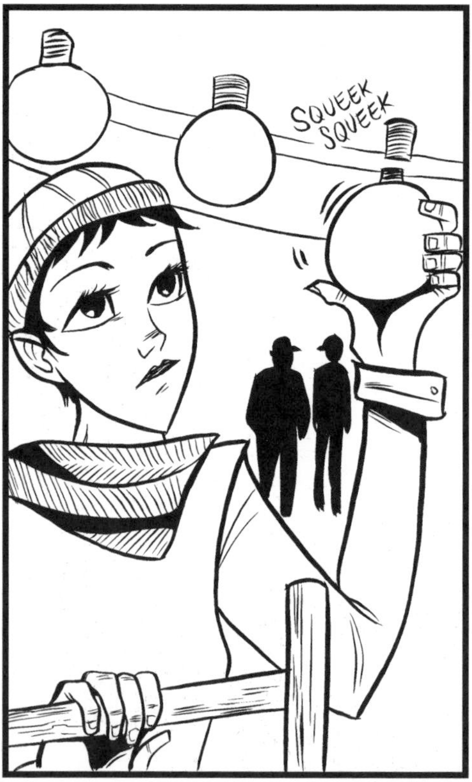
SQUEEK SQUEEK

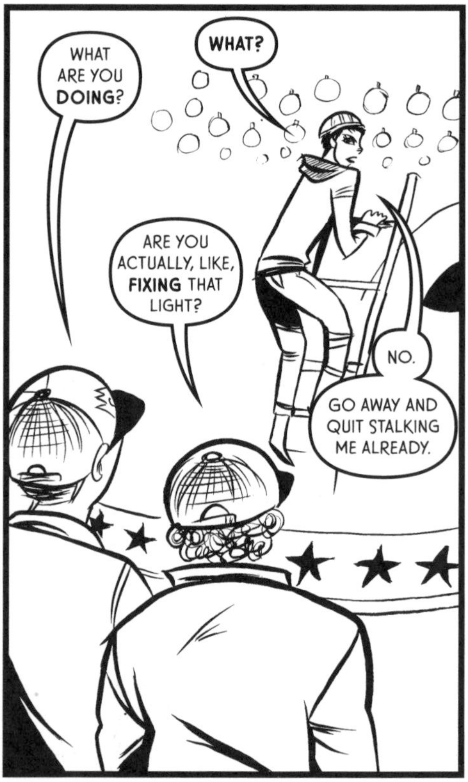
WHAT ARE YOU **DOING**?
WHAT?
ARE YOU ACTUALLY, LIKE, **FIXING** THAT LIGHT?
NO.
GO AWAY AND QUIT STALKING ME ALREADY.

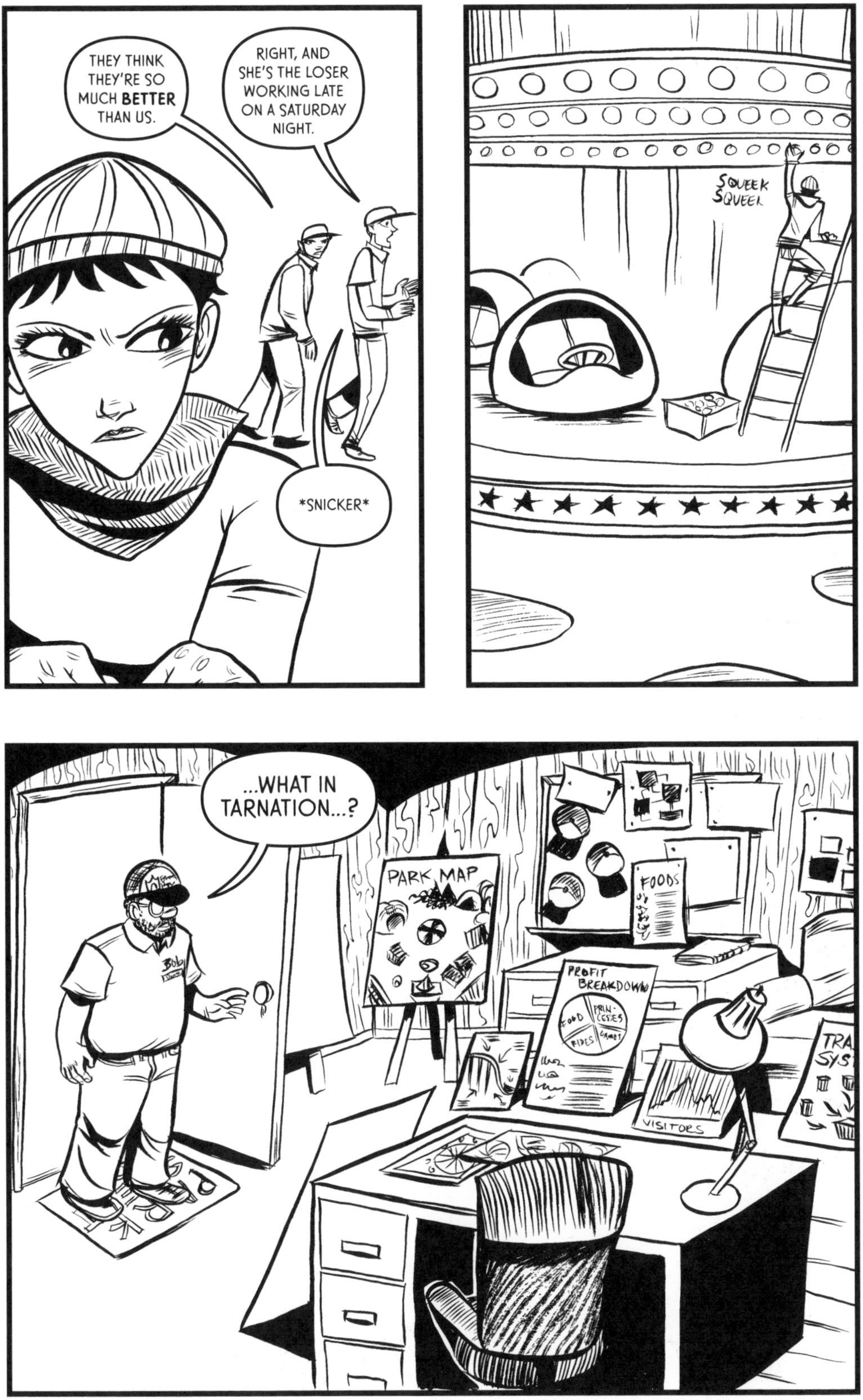
THEY THINK THEY'RE SO MUCH **BETTER** THAN US.
RIGHT, AND SHE'S THE LOSER WORKING LATE ON A SATURDAY NIGHT.
SNICKER
SQUEEK
SQUEEK
...WHAT IN TARNATION...?
Bob
PARK MAP
FOODS
PROFIT BREAKDOWN
FOOD
PRINCESSES
GAMES
RIDES
VISITORS

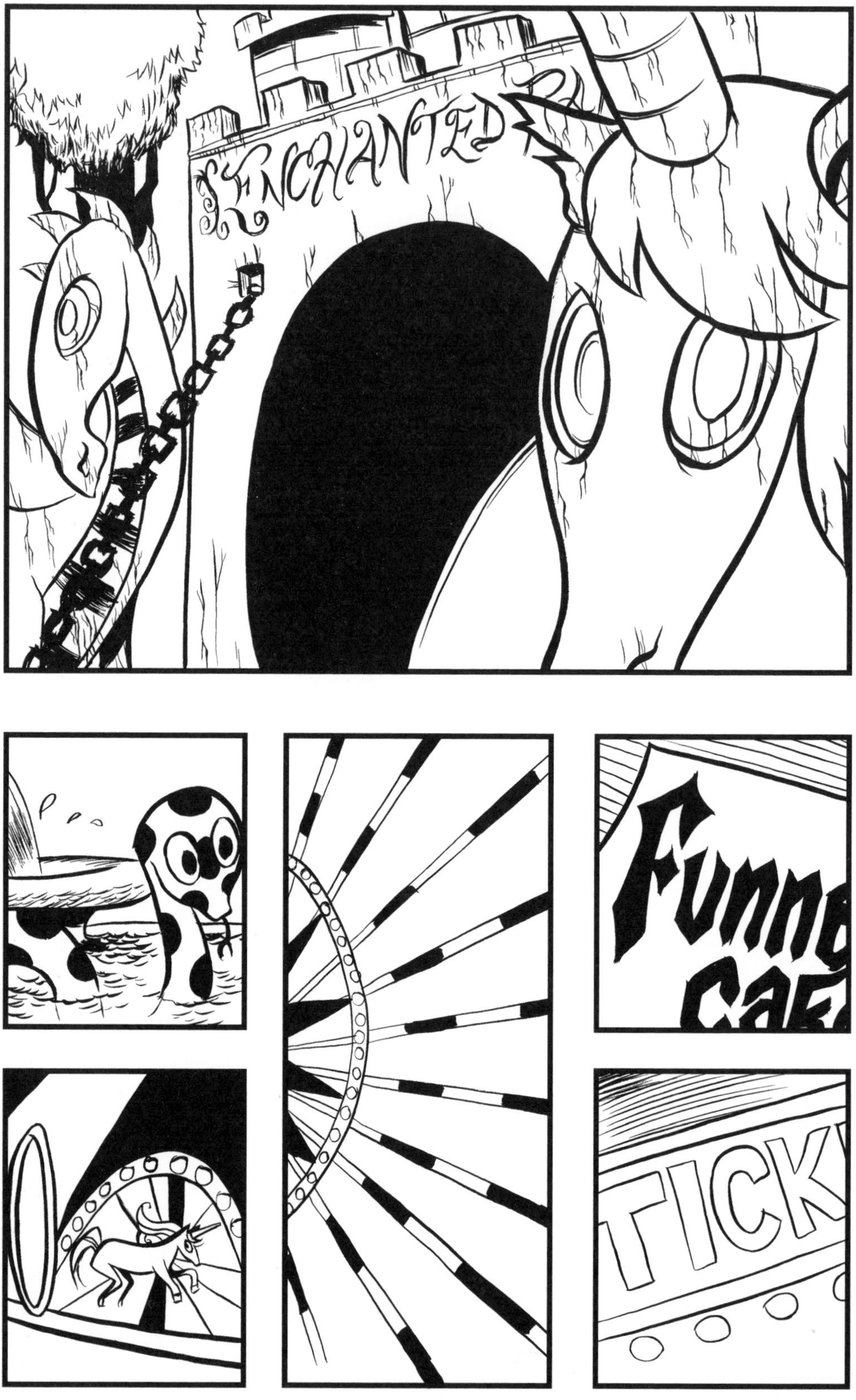
ENCHANTED
Funn
TICK

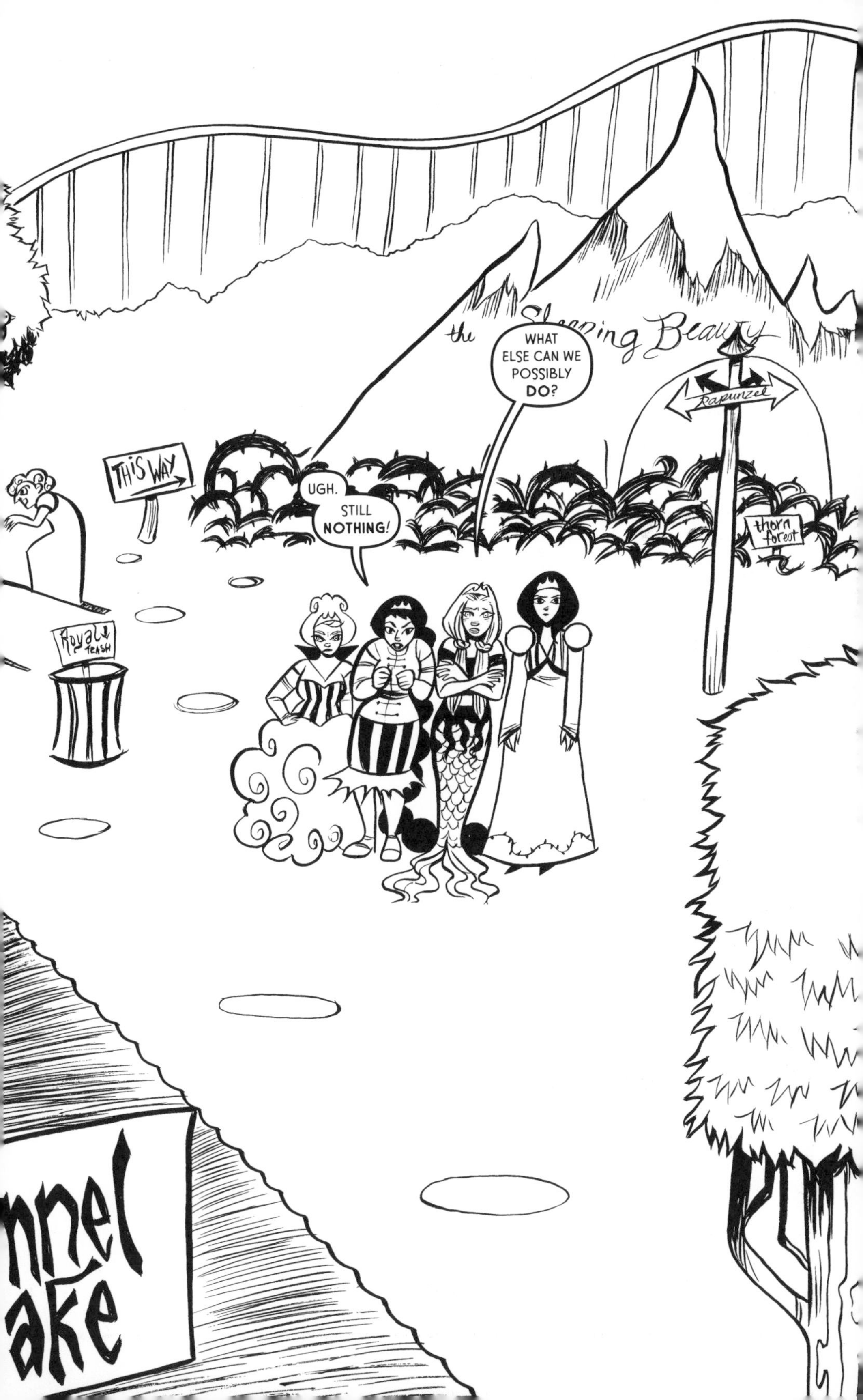

THIS WAY
Royal TRASH
UGH. STILL NOTHING!
WHAT ELSE CAN WE POSSIBLY DO?
Rapunzel
thorn forest

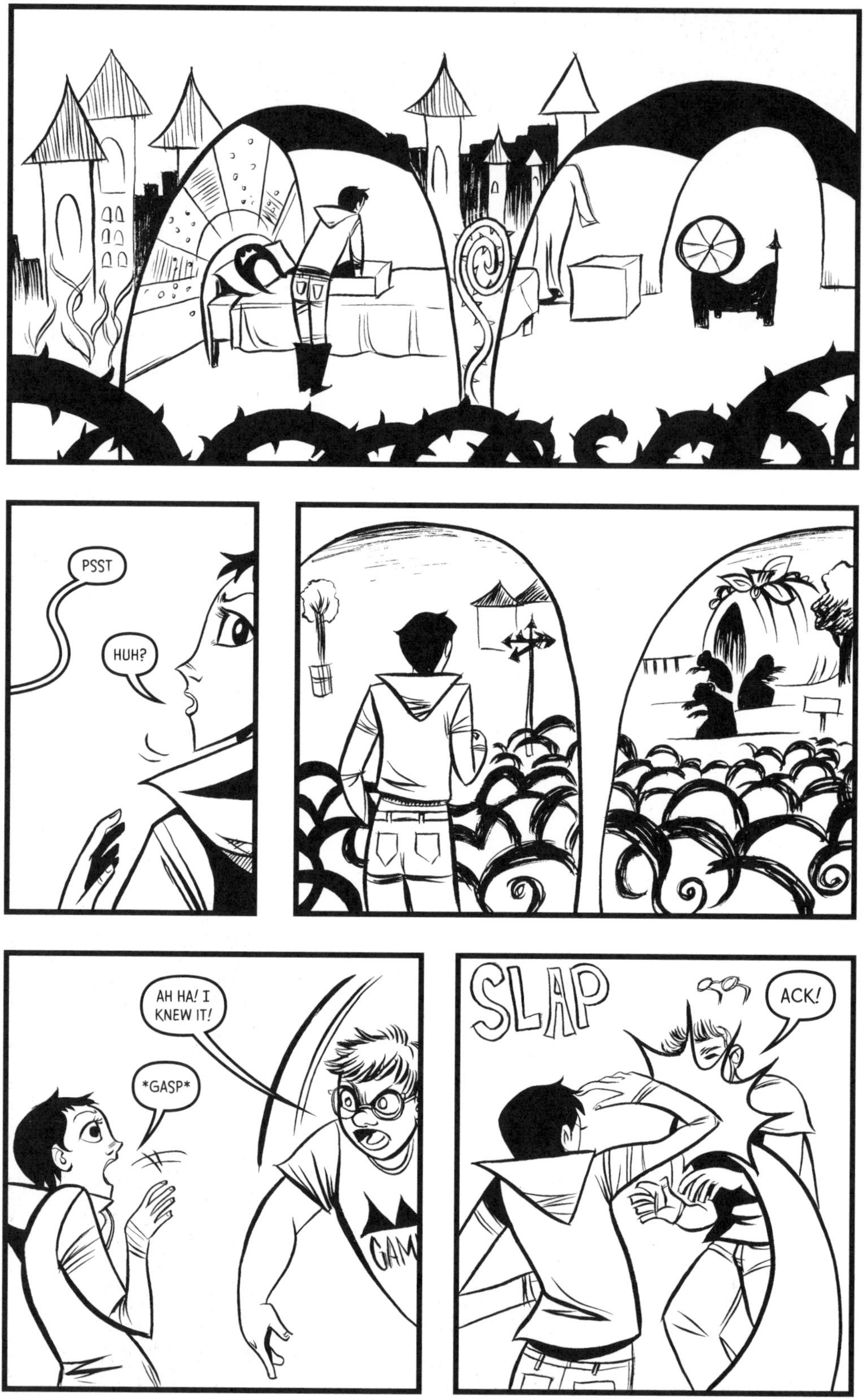
PSST
HUH?
AH HA! I KNEW IT!
GASP
GAM
SLAP
ACK!

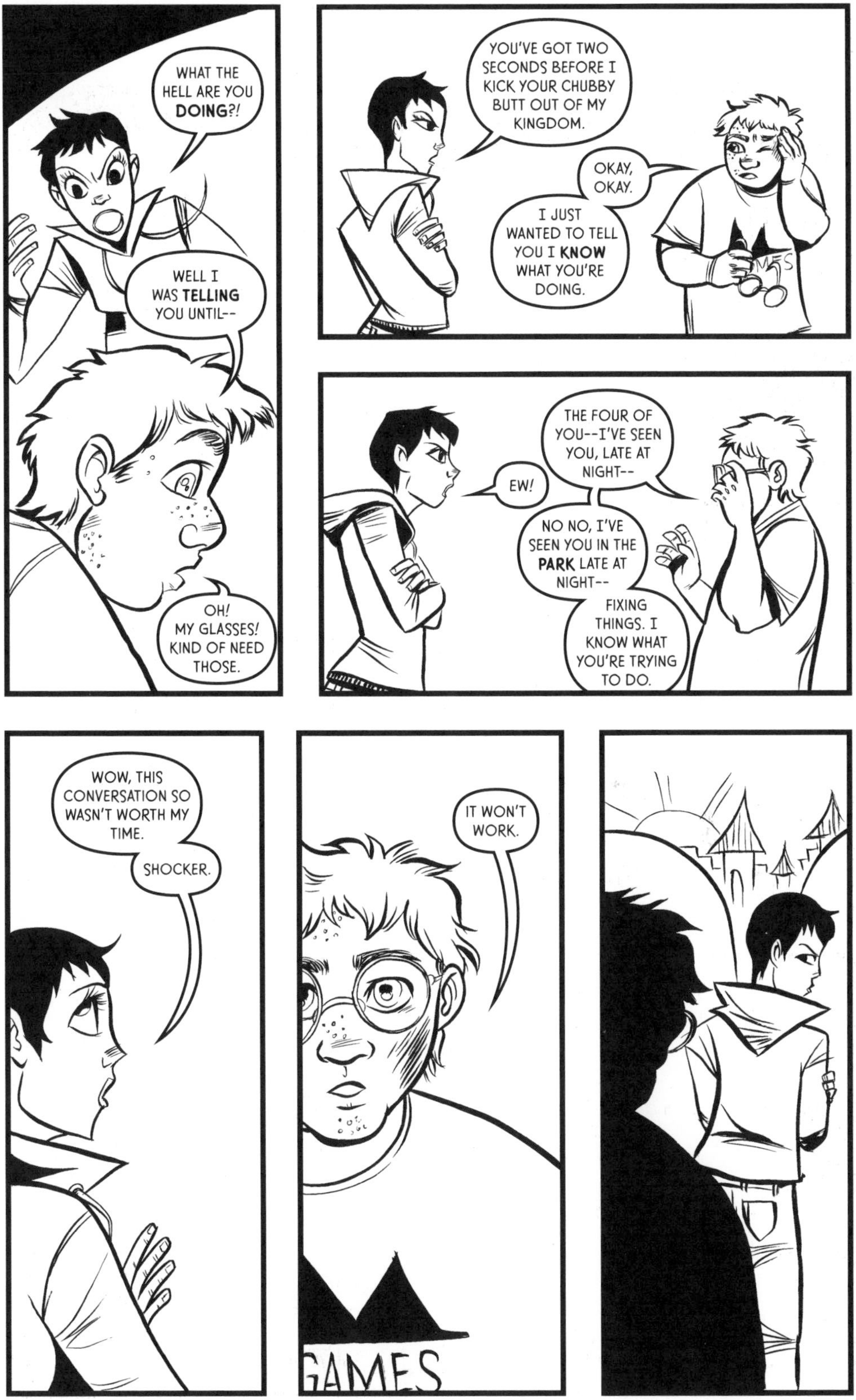
WHAT THE HELL ARE YOU **DOING**?!
WELL I WAS **TELLING** YOU UNTIL--
OH! MY GLASSES! KIND OF NEED THOSE.
YOU'VE GOT TWO SECONDS BEFORE I KICK YOUR CHUBBY BUTT OUT OF MY KINGDOM.
OKAY, OKAY.
I JUST WANTED TO TELL YOU I **KNOW** WHAT YOU'RE DOING.
THE FOUR OF YOU--I'VE SEEN YOU, LATE AT NIGHT--
EW!
NO NO, I'VE SEEN YOU IN THE **PARK** LATE AT NIGHT--
FIXING THINGS. I KNOW WHAT YOU'RE TRYING TO DO.
WOW, THIS CONVERSATION SO WASN'T WORTH MY TIME.
SHOCKER.
IT WON'T WORK.
GAMES

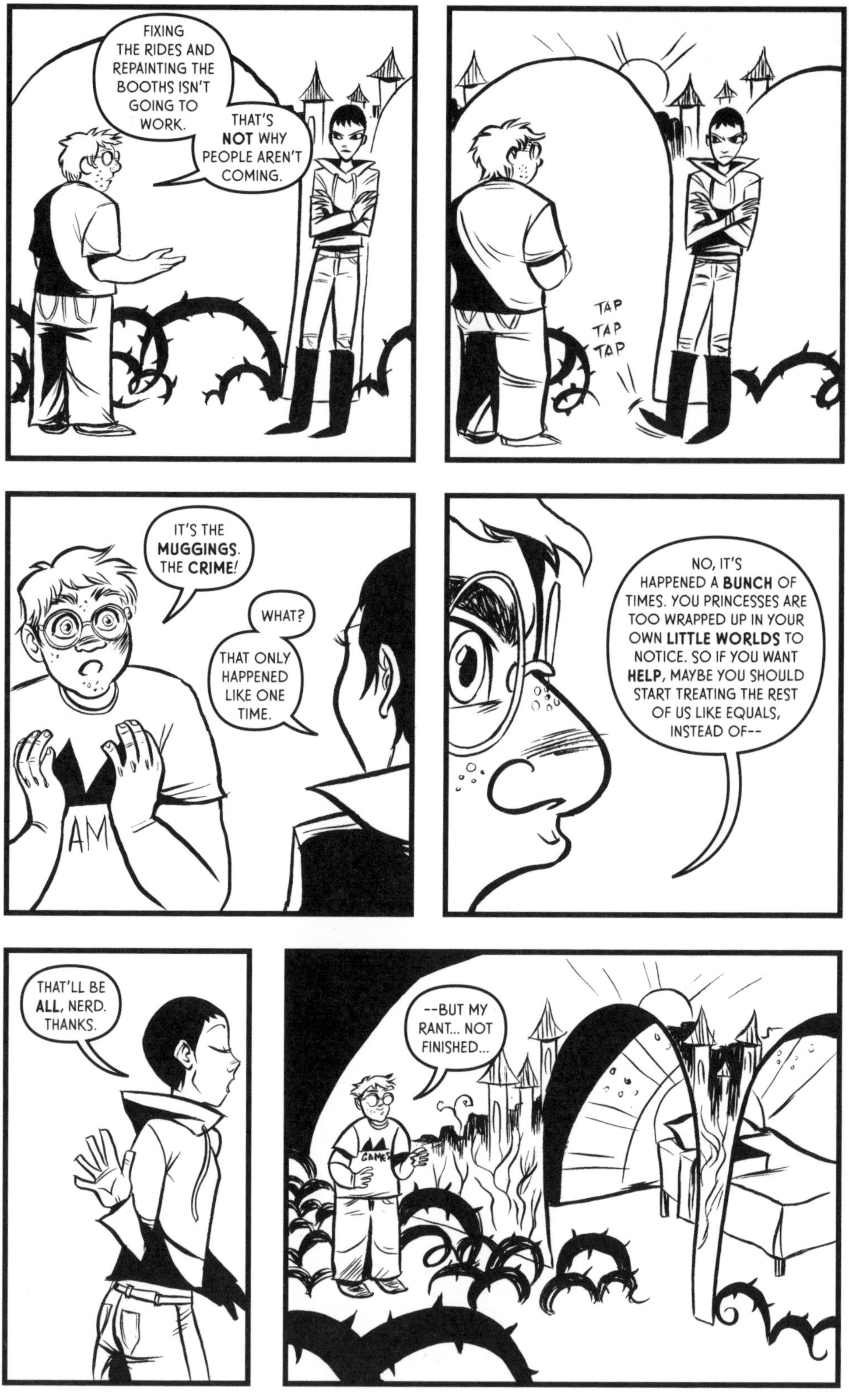
FIXING THE RIDES AND REPAINTING THE BOOTHS ISN'T GOING TO WORK.
THAT'S **NOT** WHY PEOPLE AREN'T COMING.
TAP TAP TAP
IT'S THE **MUGGINGS**. THE **CRIME**!
WHAT?
THAT ONLY HAPPENED LIKE ONE TIME.
NO, IT'S HAPPENED A **BUNCH** OF TIMES. YOU PRINCESSES ARE TOO WRAPPED UP IN YOUR OWN **LITTLE WORLDS** TO NOTICE. SO IF YOU WANT **HELP**, MAYBE YOU SHOULD START TREATING THE REST OF US LIKE EQUALS, INSTEAD OF--
THAT'LL BE **ALL**, NERD. THANKS.
--BUT MY RANT... NOT FINISHED...

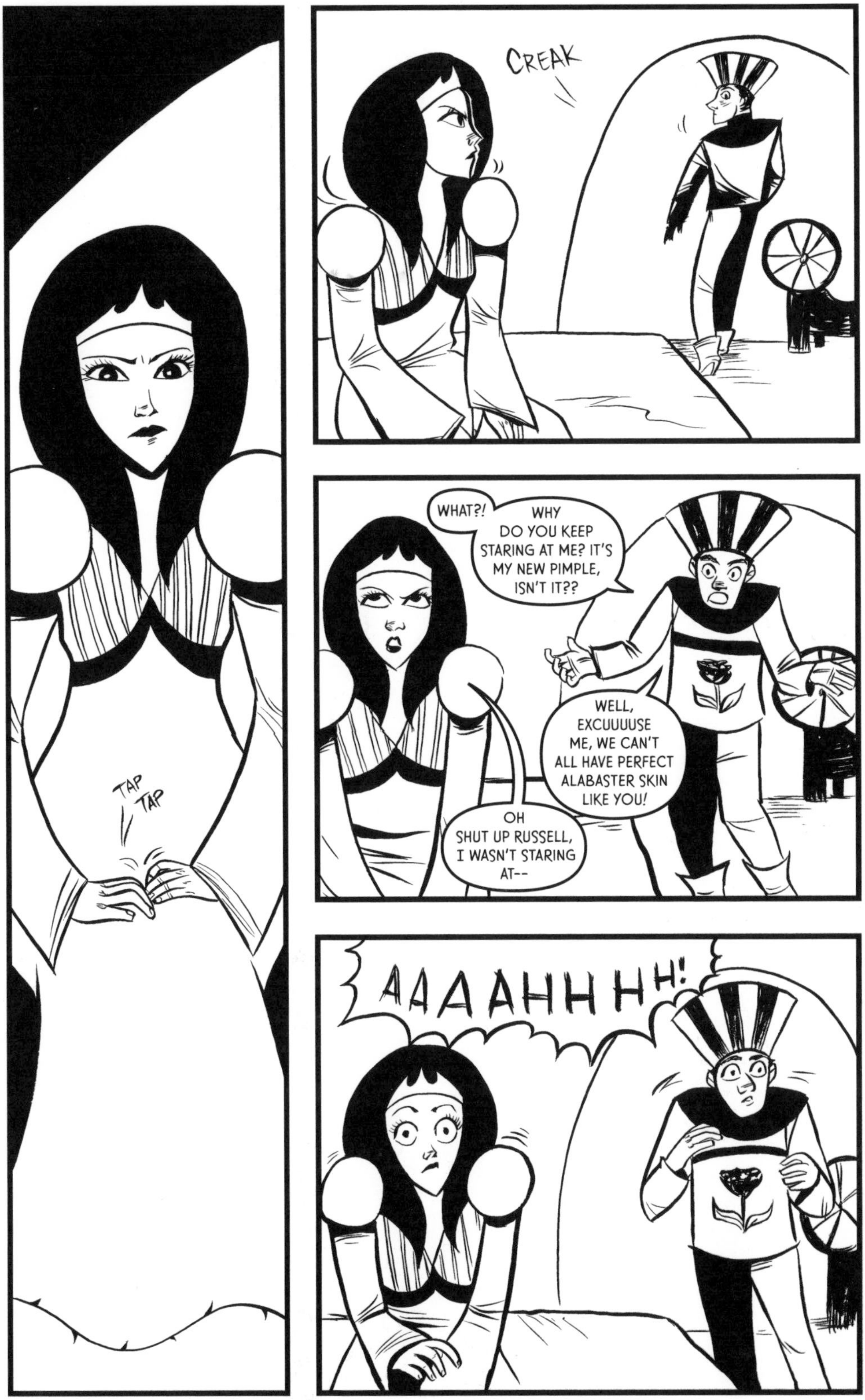
TAP TAP
CREAK
WHAT?!
WHY DO YOU KEEP STARING AT ME? IT'S MY NEW PIMPLE, ISN'T IT??
OH SHUT UP RUSSELL, I WASN'T STARING AT--
WELL, EXCUUUUSE ME, WE CAN'T ALL HAVE PERFECT ALABASTER SKIN LIKE YOU!
AAAAHHHH!

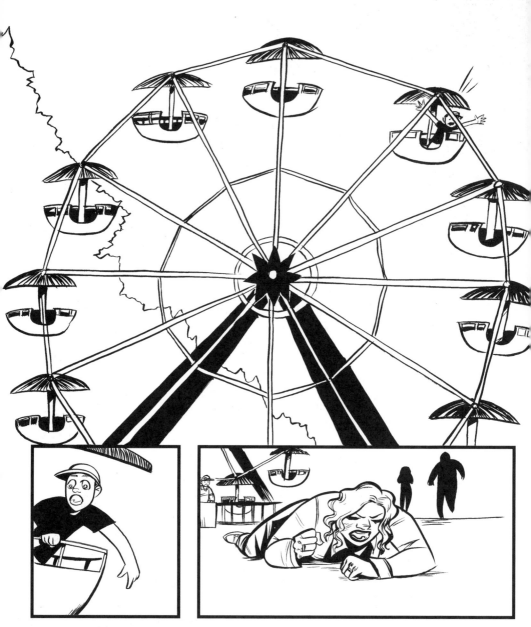

MR. MAYOR, HAS THE ENCHANTED PARK BECOME TOO DANGEROUS?

LIVE

IT'S DEFINITELY ON MY AGENDA TO DEAL WITH THIS GROWING... SITUATION IN THE PARK.

NEWS

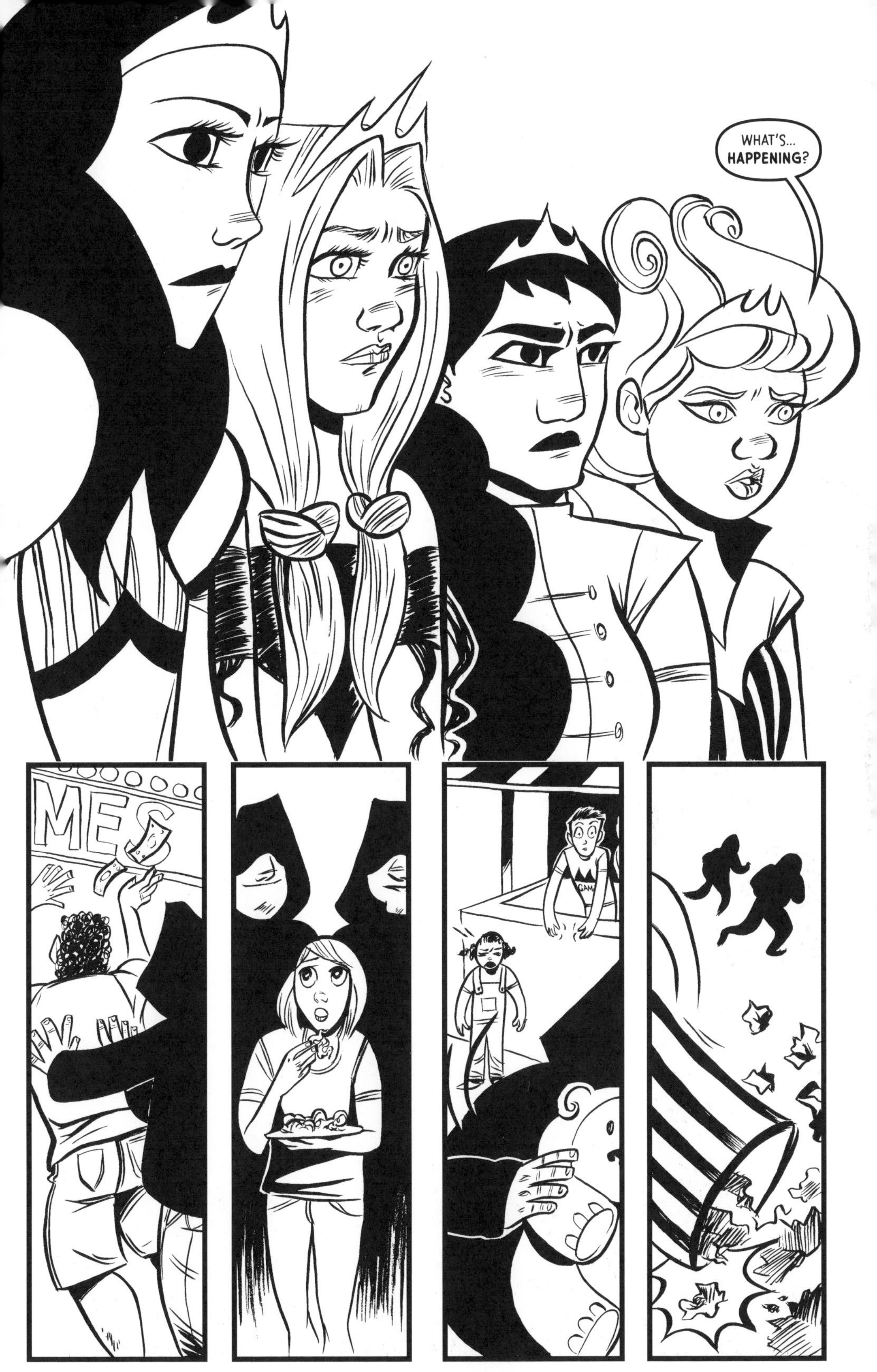
WHAT'S...
HAPPENING?
MES

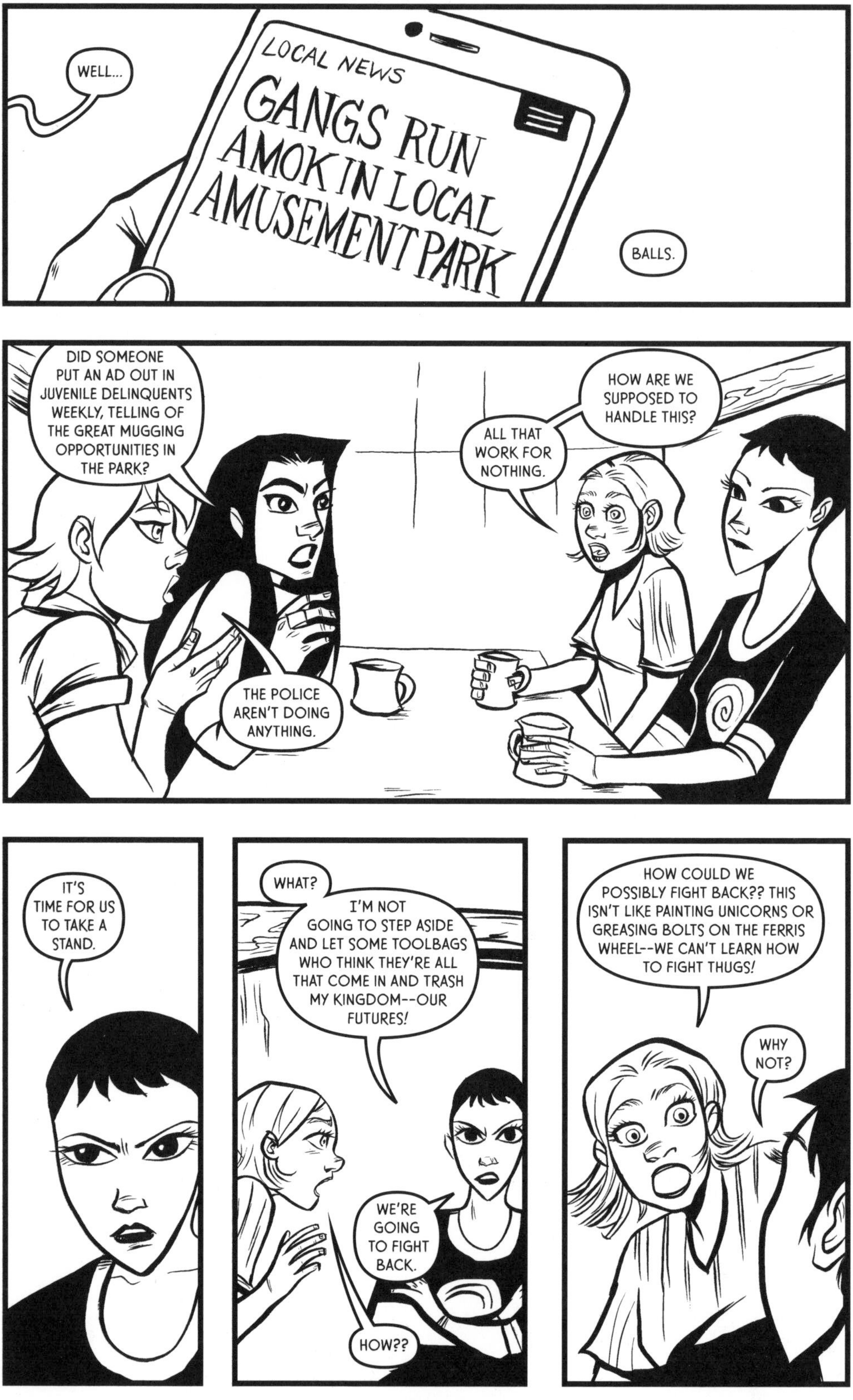
WELL...
LOCAL NEWS
GANGS RUN AMOK IN LOCAL AMUSEMENT PARK
BALLS.
DID SOMEONE PUT AN AD OUT IN JUVENILE DELINQUENTS WEEKLY, TELLING OF THE GREAT MUGGING OPPORTUNITIES IN THE PARK?
THE POLICE AREN'T DOING ANYTHING.
ALL THAT WORK FOR NOTHING.
HOW ARE WE SUPPOSED TO HANDLE THIS?
IT'S TIME FOR US TO TAKE A STAND.
WHAT?
I'M NOT GOING TO STEP ASIDE AND LET SOME TOOLBAGS WHO THINK THEY'RE ALL THAT COME IN AND TRASH MY KINGDOM--OUR FUTURES!
WE'RE GOING TO FIGHT BACK.
HOW??
HOW COULD WE POSSIBLY FIGHT BACK?? THIS ISN'T LIKE PAINTING UNICORNS OR GREASING BOLTS ON THE FERRIS WHEEL--WE CAN'T LEARN HOW TO FIGHT THUGS!
WHY NOT?

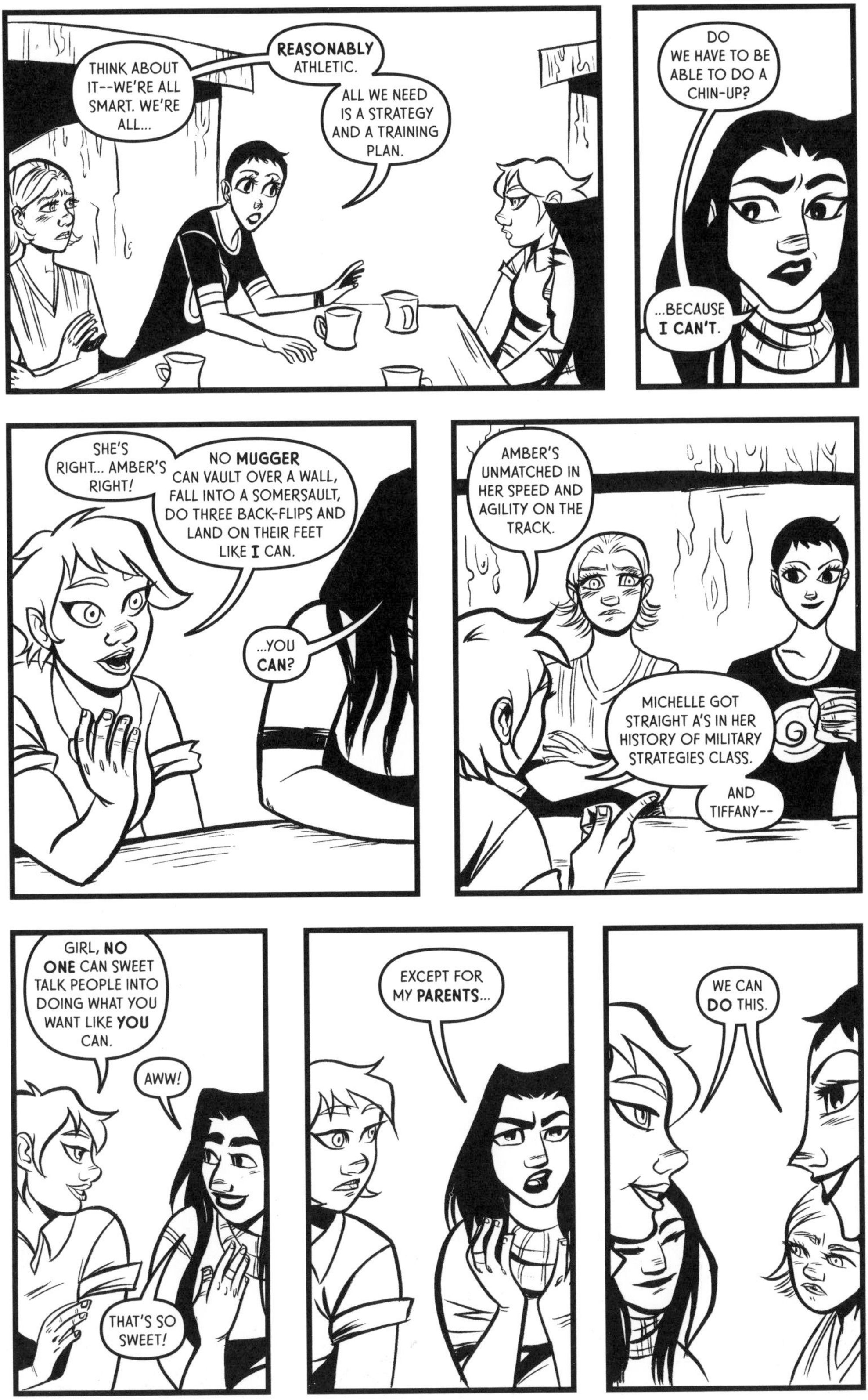
THINK ABOUT IT--WE'RE ALL SMART. WE'RE ALL...
REASONABLY ATHLETIC.
ALL WE NEED IS A STRATEGY AND A TRAINING PLAN.
DO WE HAVE TO BE ABLE TO DO A CHIN-UP?
...BECAUSE **I CAN'T**.
SHE'S RIGHT... AMBER'S RIGHT!
NO **MUGGER** CAN VAULT OVER A WALL, FALL INTO A SOMERSAULT, DO THREE BACK-FLIPS AND LAND ON THEIR FEET LIKE **I** CAN.
...YOU **CAN**?
AMBER'S UNMATCHED IN HER SPEED AND AGILITY ON THE TRACK.
MICHELLE GOT STRAIGHT A'S IN HER HISTORY OF MILITARY STRATEGIES CLASS.
AND TIFFANY--
GIRL, **NO ONE** CAN SWEET TALK PEOPLE INTO DOING WHAT YOU WANT LIKE **YOU** CAN.
AWW!
THAT'S SO SWEET!
EXCEPT FOR MY **PARENTS**...
WE CAN **DO** THIS.

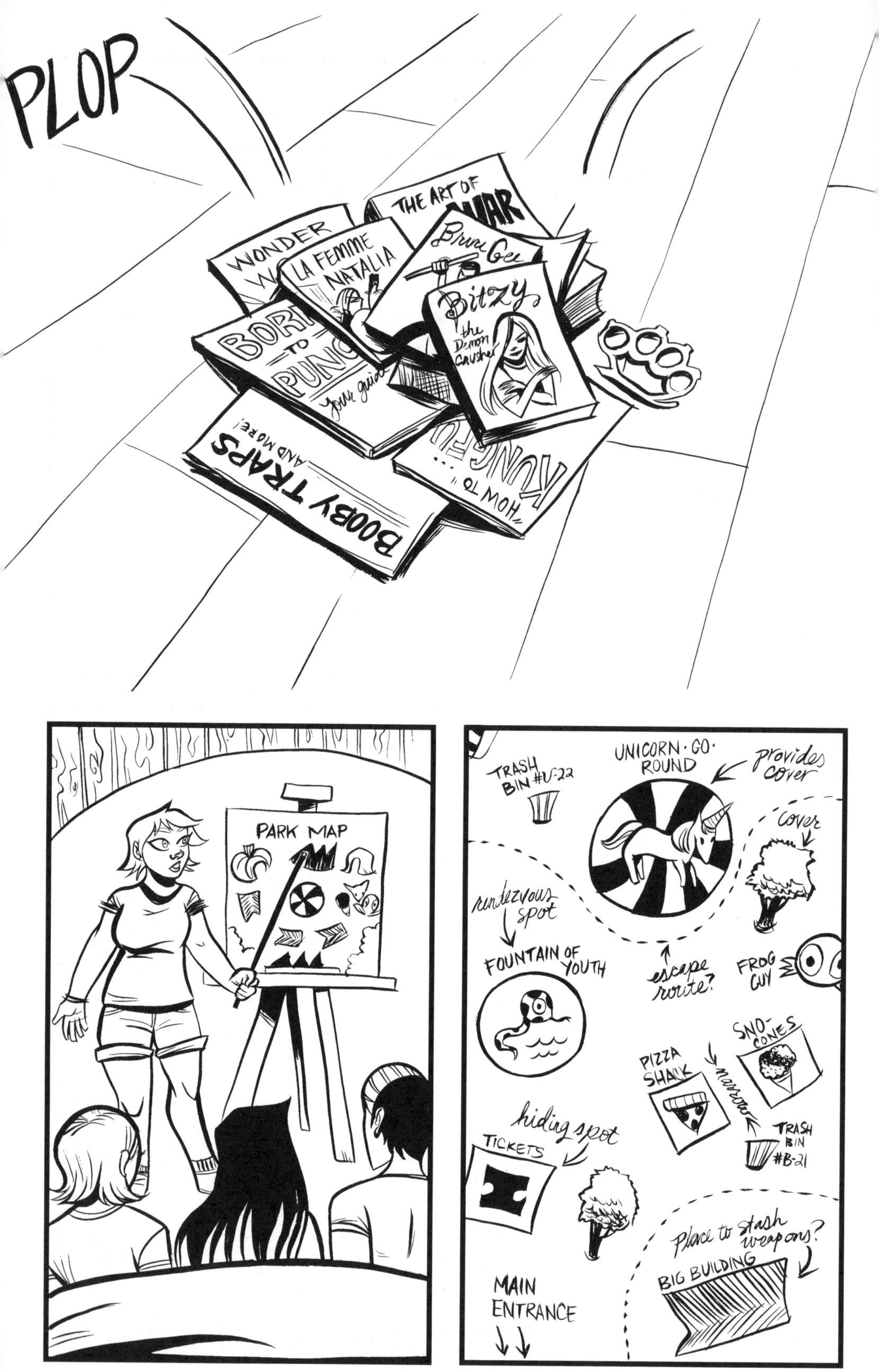
PLOP
WONDER
LA FEMME NATALIA
THE ART OF WAR
Bruce Lee
Bitzy the Demon Crusher
TO
your guide
BOOBY TRAPS AND MORE!
HOW TO
PARK MAP
UNICORN·GO·ROUND
provides cover
TRASH BIN #U-22
cover
rendezvous spot
FOUNTAIN OF YOUTH
escape route?
FROG GUY
SNO-CONES
PIZZA SHACK
TRASH BIN #B-21
hiding spot
TICKETS
Place to stash weapons?
BIG BUILDING
MAIN ENTRANCE

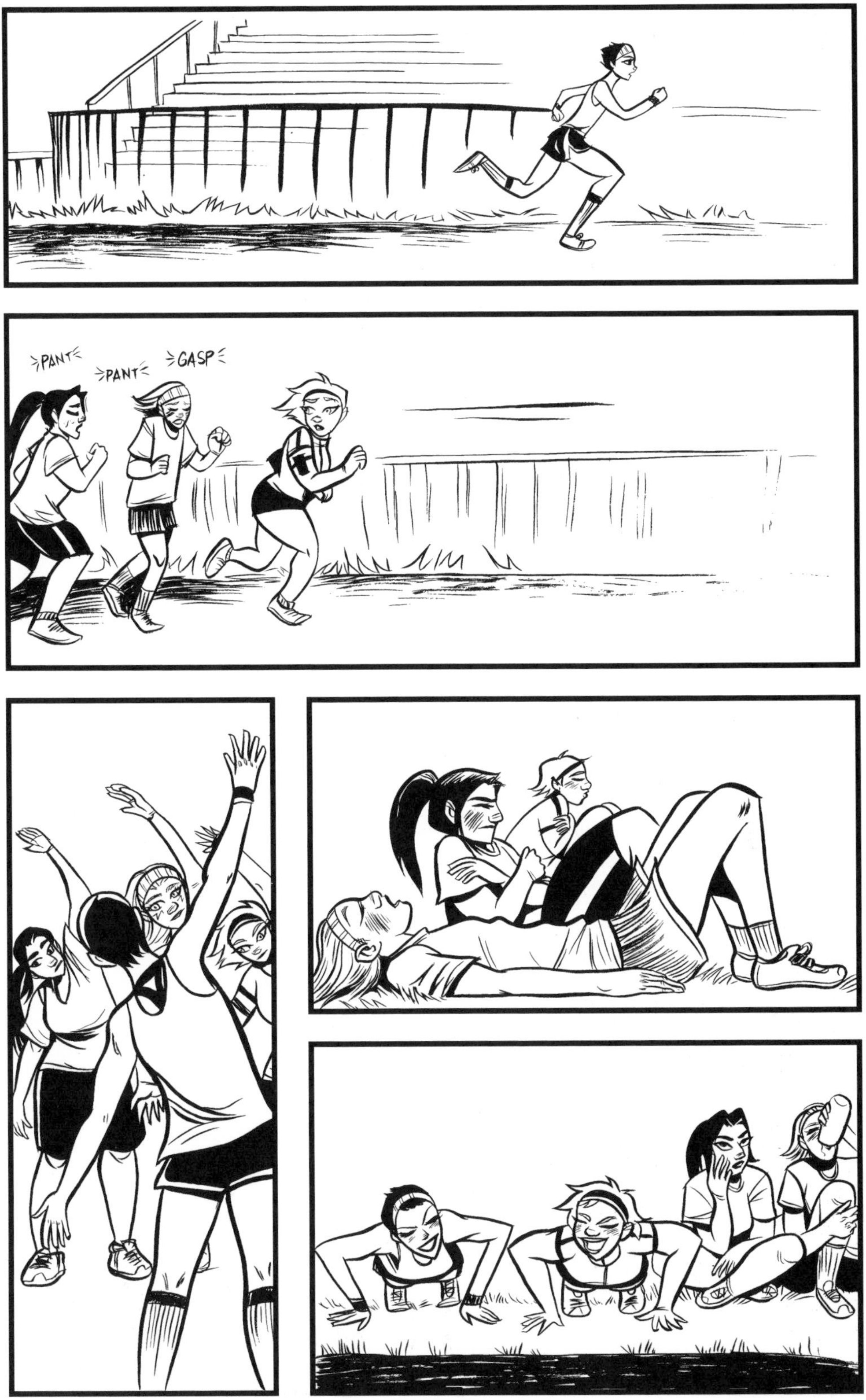
PANT
PANT
GASP

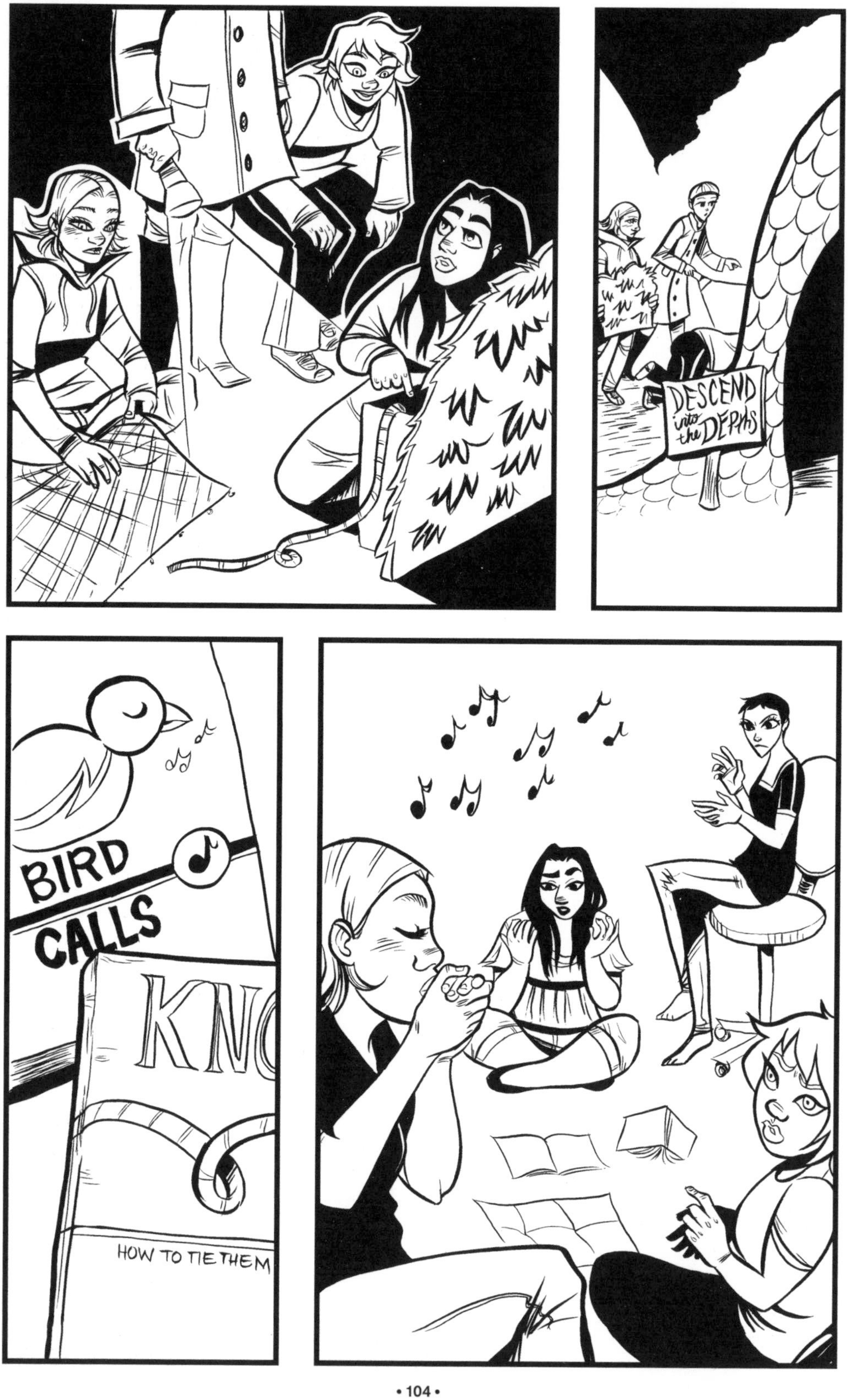
DESCEND into the DEPTHS
BIRD CALLS
KNO
HOW TO TIE THEM

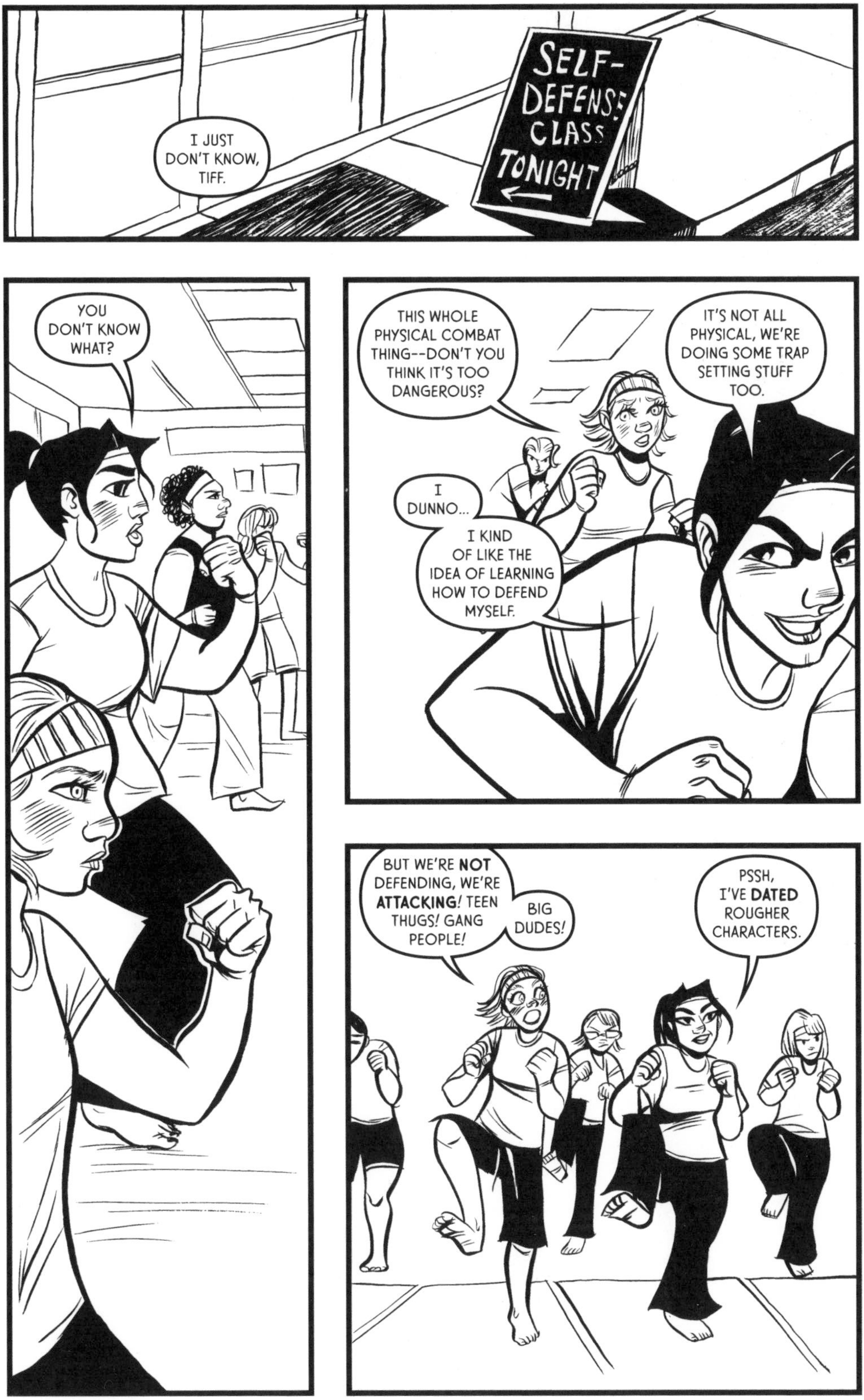
SELF-DEFENSE CLASS TONIGHT
I JUST DON'T KNOW, TIFF.
YOU DON'T KNOW WHAT?
THIS WHOLE PHYSICAL COMBAT THING--DON'T YOU THINK IT'S TOO DANGEROUS?
IT'S NOT ALL PHYSICAL, WE'RE DOING SOME TRAP SETTING STUFF TOO.
I DUNNO...
I KIND OF LIKE THE IDEA OF LEARNING HOW TO DEFEND MYSELF.
BUT WE'RE **NOT** DEFENDING, WE'RE **ATTACKING**! TEEN THUGS! GANG PEOPLE!
BIG DUDES!
PSSH, I'VE **DATED** ROUGHER CHARACTERS.

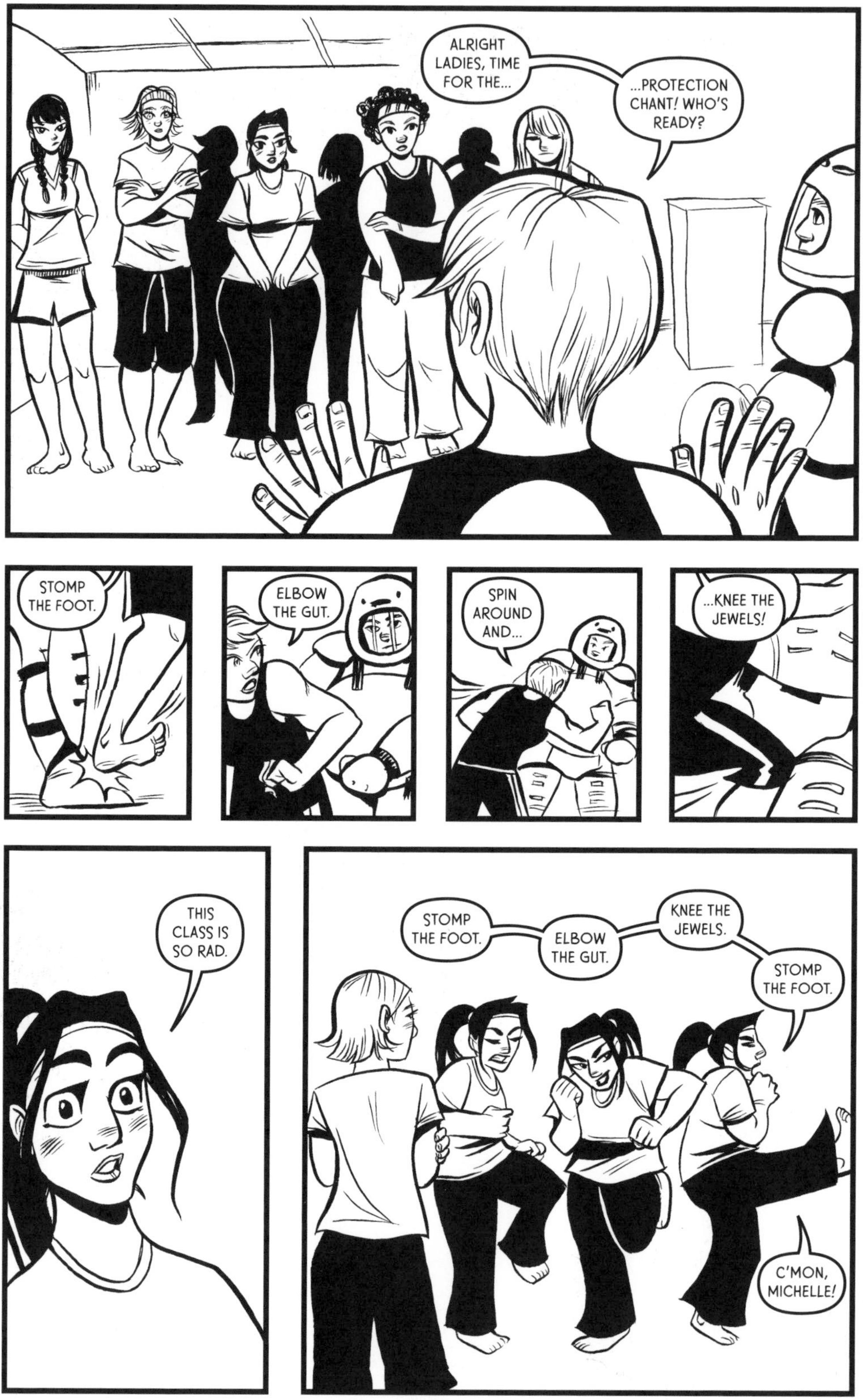
ALRIGHT LADIES, TIME FOR THE...
...PROTECTION CHANT! WHO'S READY?
STOMP THE FOOT.
ELBOW THE GUT.
SPIN AROUND AND...
...KNEE THE JEWELS!
THIS CLASS IS SO RAD.
STOMP THE FOOT.
ELBOW THE GUT.
KNEE THE JEWELS.
STOMP THE FOOT.
C'MON, MICHELLE!

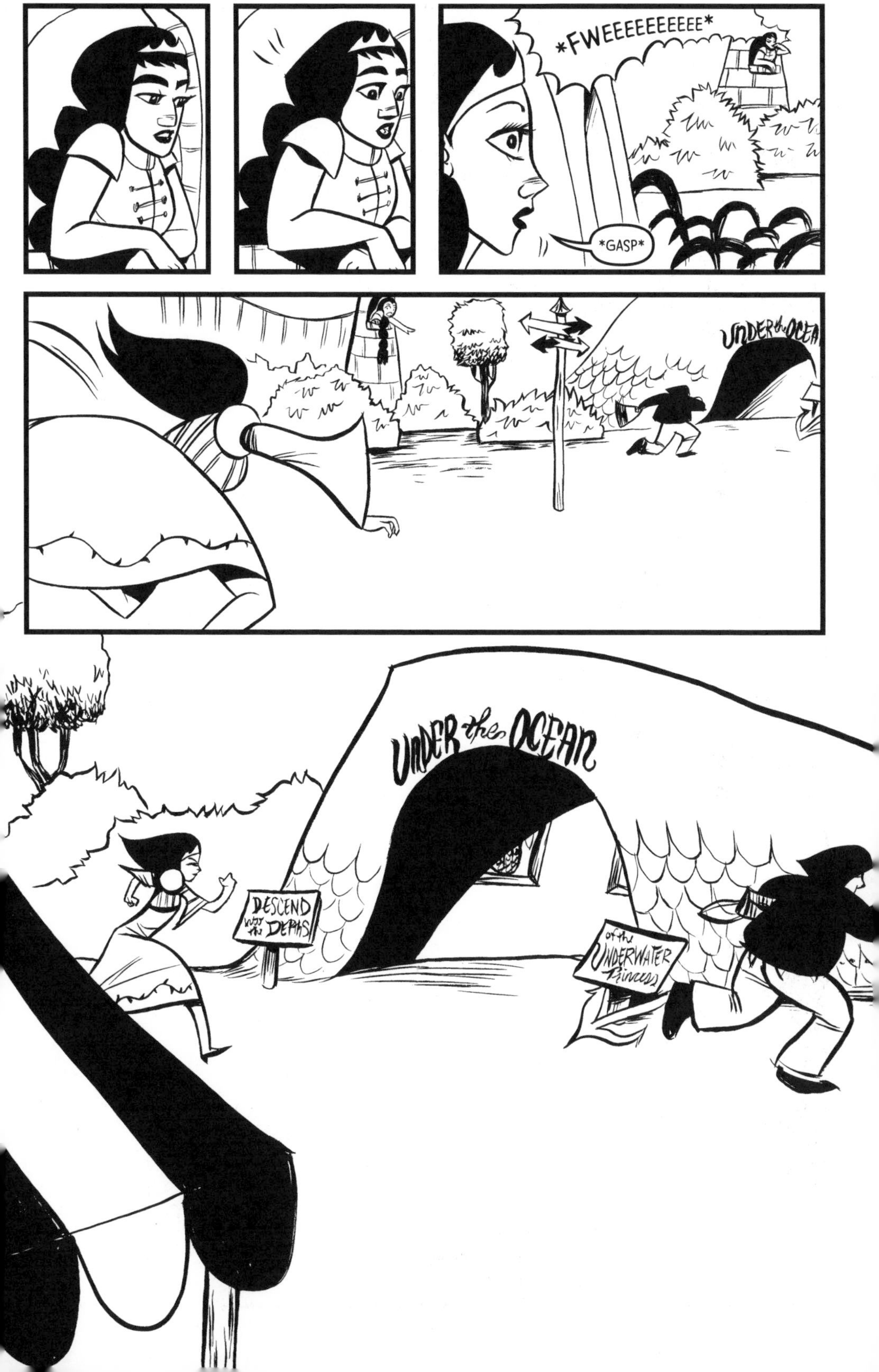
FWEEEEEEEEEE
GASP
UNDER the OCEA
UNDER the OCEAN
DESCEND
DEPTHS
of the
UNDERWATER
Princess

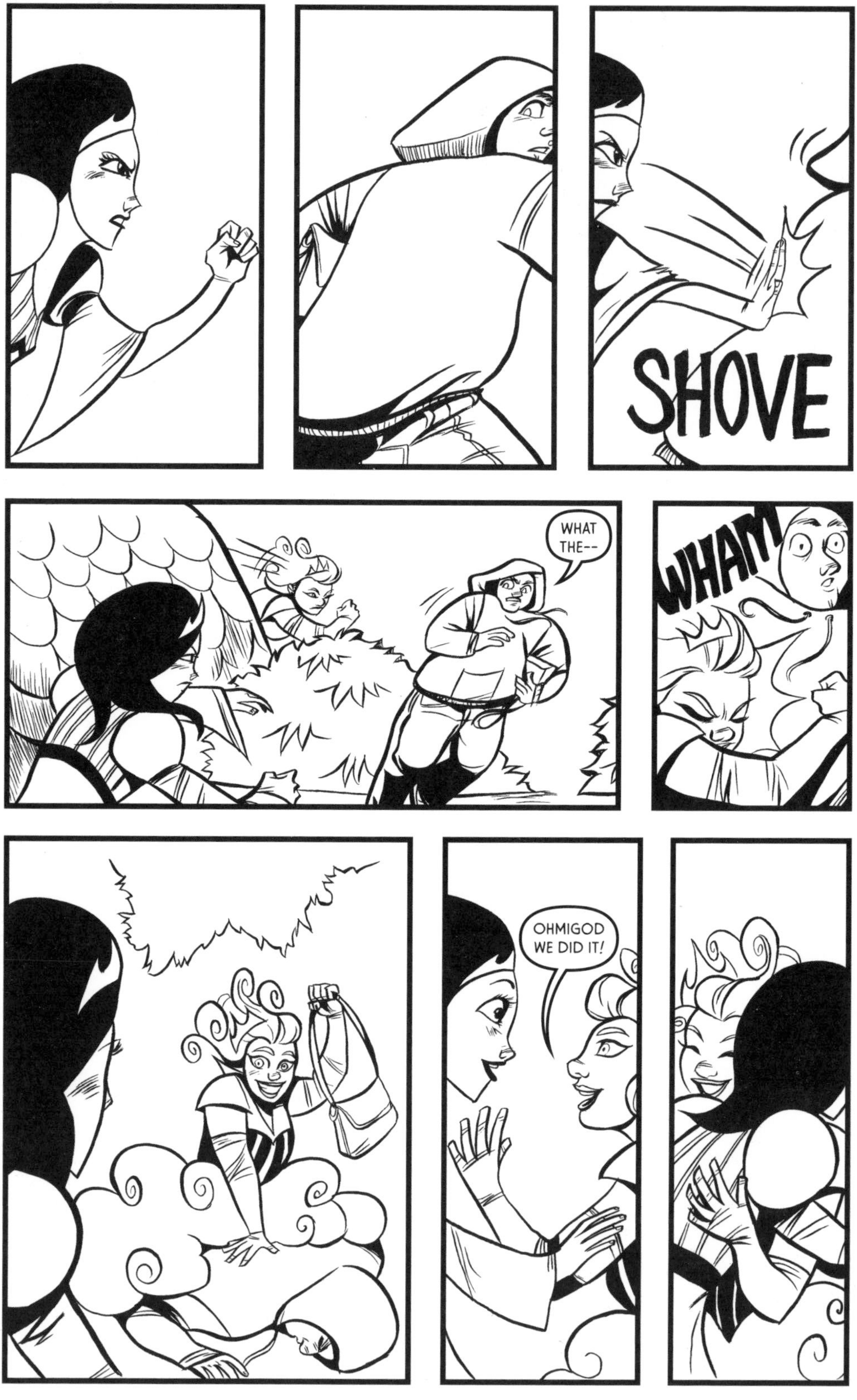
SHOVE
WHAT THE--
WHAM
OHMIGOD WE DID IT!

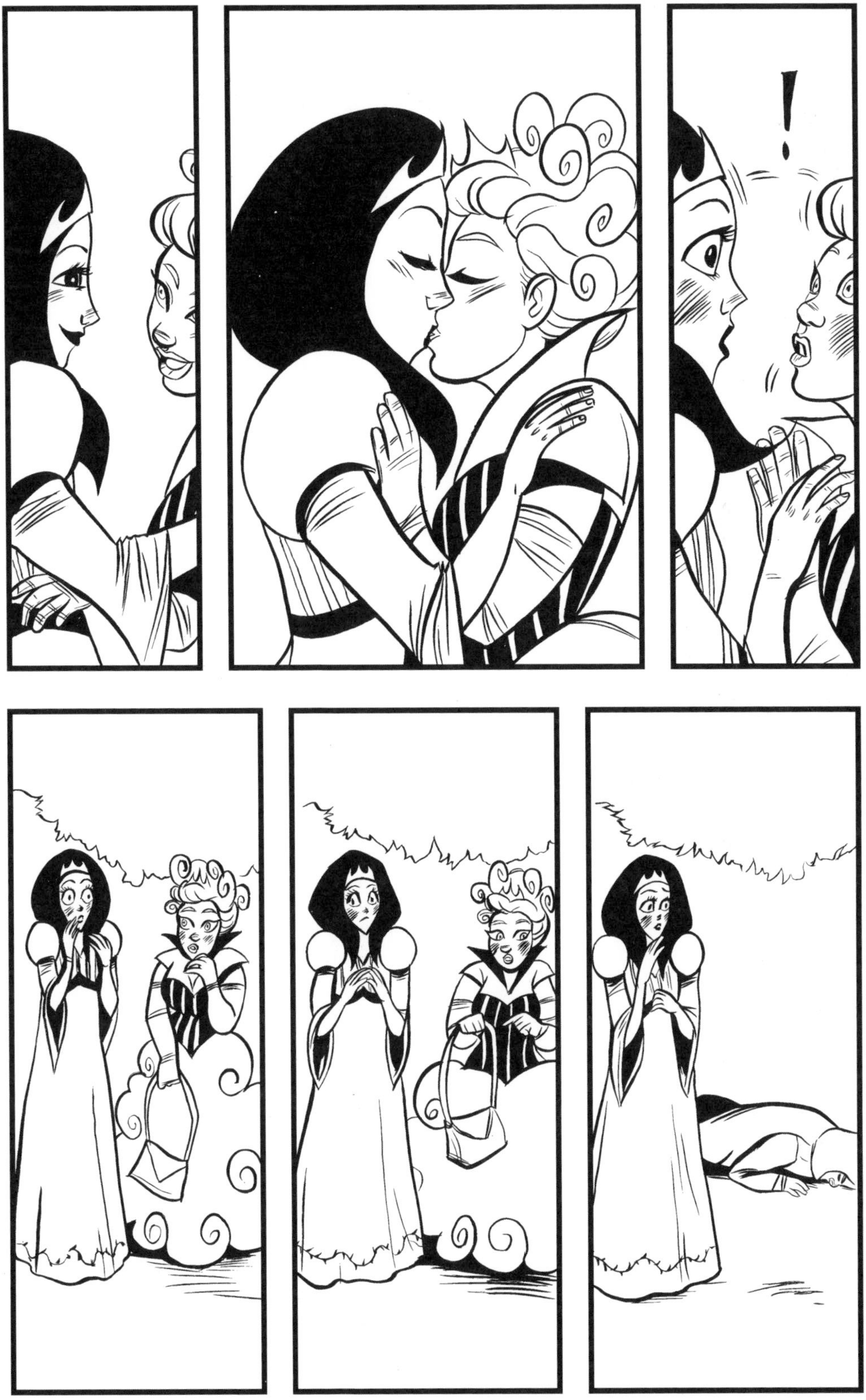
!

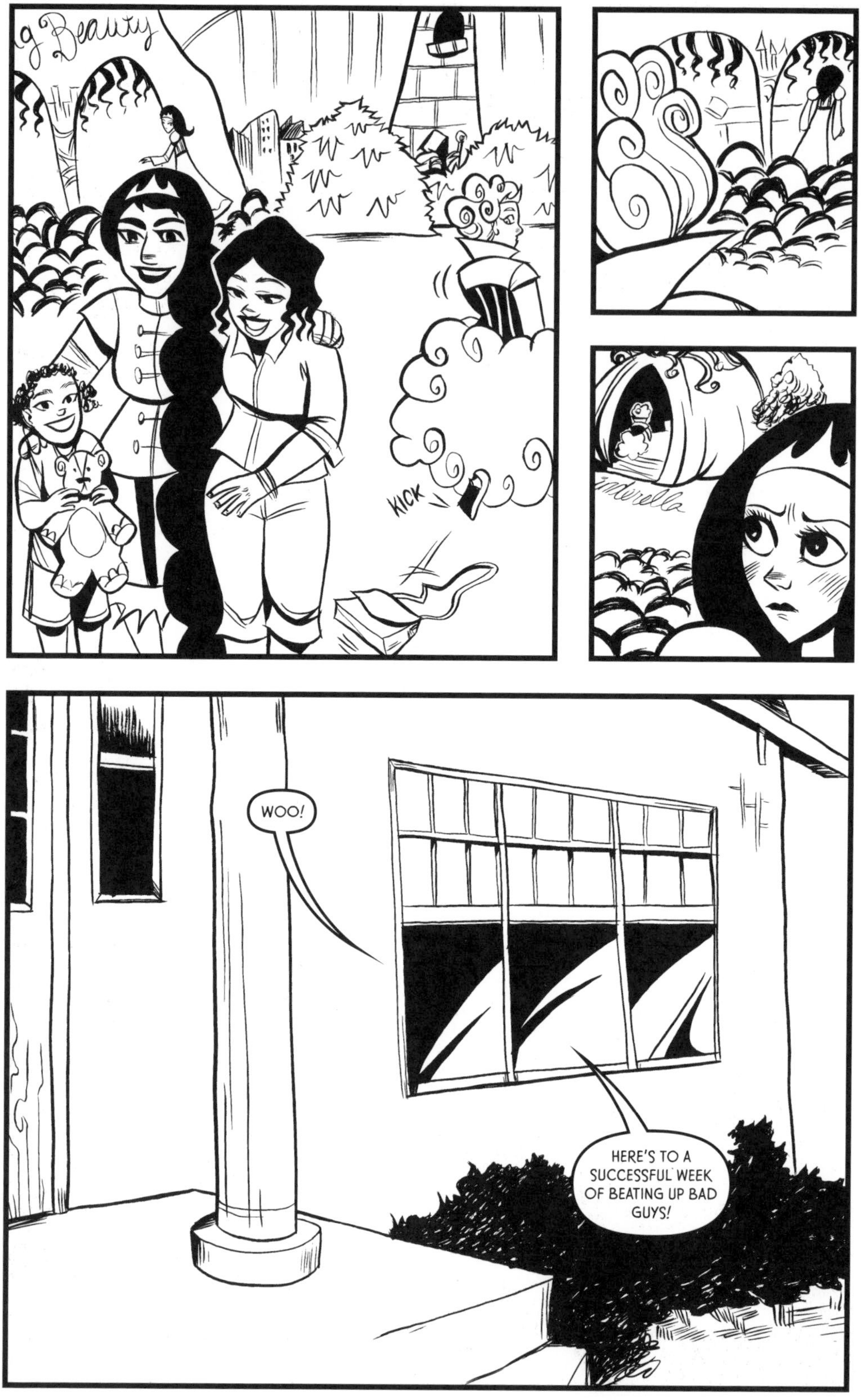
g Beauty
KICK
nderella
WOO!
HERE'S TO A SUCCESSFUL WEEK OF BEATING UP BAD GUYS!

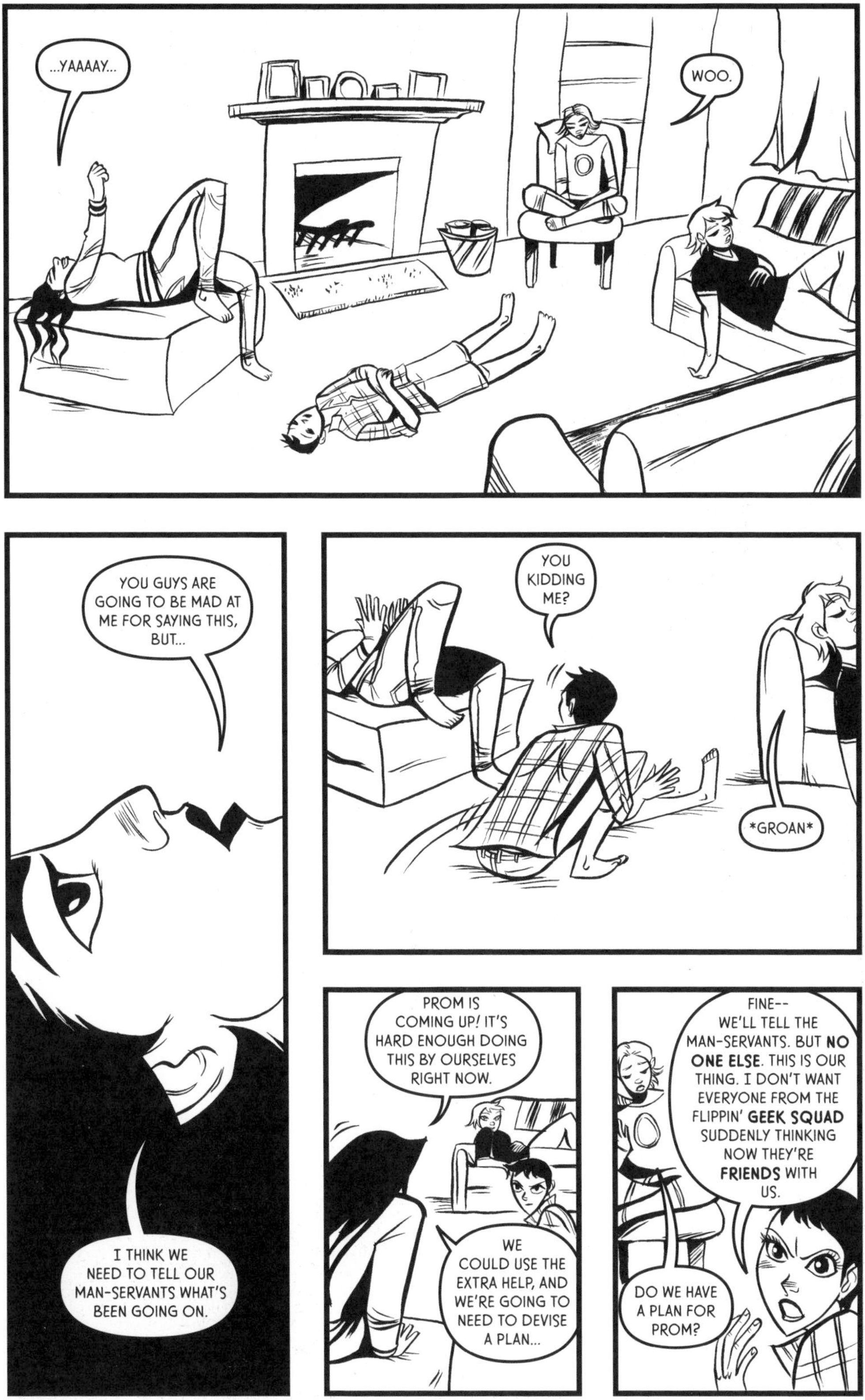
...YAAAAY...
WOO.
YOU GUYS ARE GOING TO BE MAD AT ME FOR SAYING THIS, BUT...
I THINK WE NEED TO TELL OUR MAN-SERVANTS WHAT'S BEEN GOING ON.
YOU KIDDING ME?
GROAN
PROM IS COMING UP! IT'S HARD ENOUGH DOING THIS BY OURSELVES RIGHT NOW.
WE COULD USE THE EXTRA HELP, AND WE'RE GOING TO NEED TO DEVISE A PLAN...
FINE-- WE'LL TELL THE MAN-SERVANTS. BUT **NO ONE ELSE**. THIS IS OUR THING. I DON'T WANT EVERYONE FROM THE FLIPPIN' **GEEK SQUAD** SUDDENLY THINKING NOW THEY'RE **FRIENDS** WITH US.
DO WE HAVE A PLAN FOR PROM?

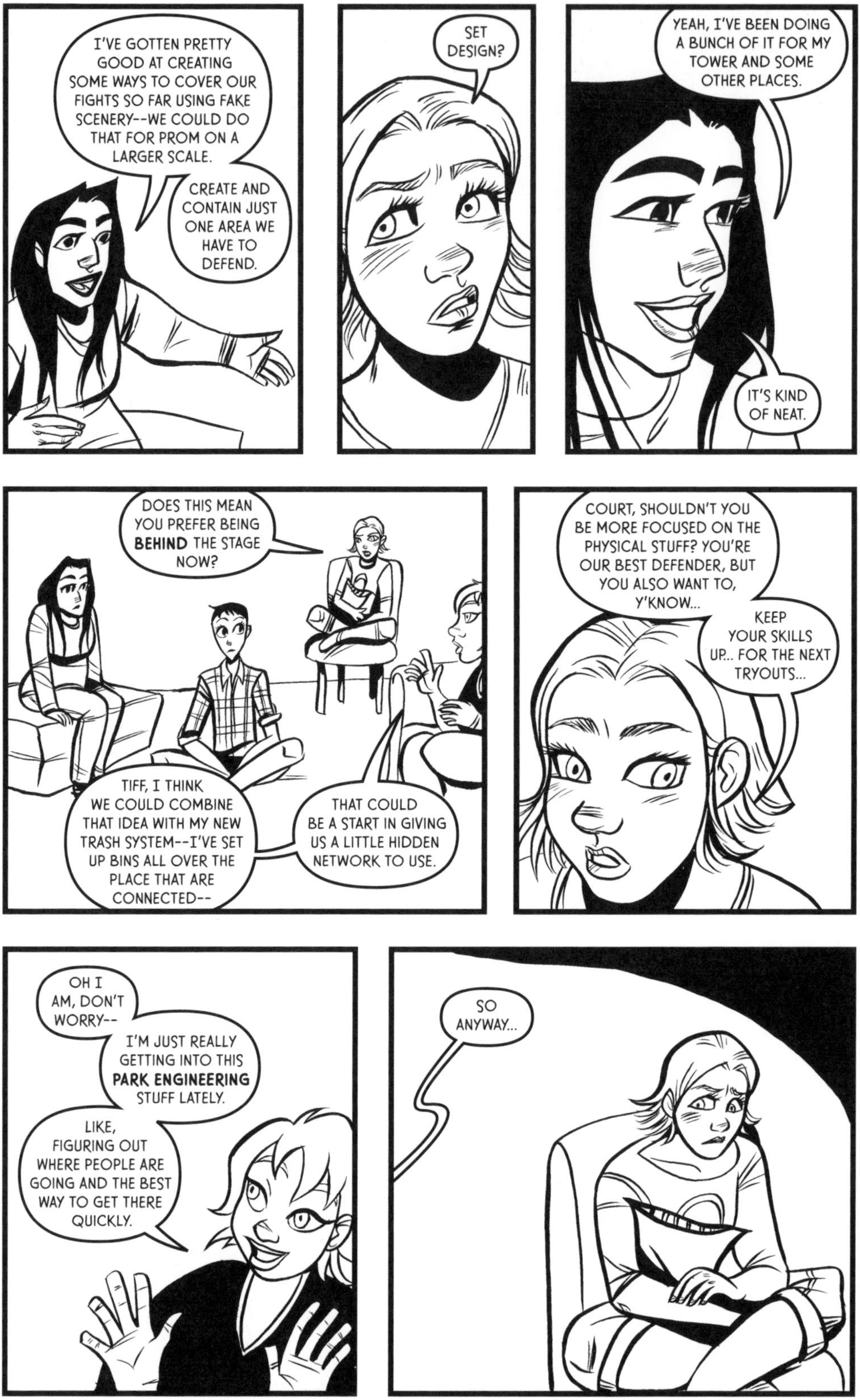
I'VE GOTTEN PRETTY GOOD AT CREATING SOME WAYS TO COVER OUR FIGHTS SO FAR USING FAKE SCENERY--WE COULD DO THAT FOR PROM ON A LARGER SCALE.
CREATE AND CONTAIN JUST ONE AREA WE HAVE TO DEFEND.
SET DESIGN?
YEAH, I'VE BEEN DOING A BUNCH OF IT FOR MY TOWER AND SOME OTHER PLACES.
IT'S KIND OF NEAT.
DOES THIS MEAN YOU PREFER BEING **BEHIND** THE STAGE NOW?
TIFF, I THINK WE COULD COMBINE THAT IDEA WITH MY NEW TRASH SYSTEM--I'VE SET UP BINS ALL OVER THE PLACE THAT ARE CONNECTED--
THAT COULD BE A START IN GIVING US A LITTLE HIDDEN NETWORK TO USE.
COURT, SHOULDN'T YOU BE MORE FOCUSED ON THE PHYSICAL STUFF? YOU'RE OUR BEST DEFENDER, BUT YOU ALSO WANT TO, Y'KNOW...
KEEP YOUR SKILLS UP... FOR THE NEXT TRYOUTS...
OH I AM, DON'T WORRY--
I'M JUST REALLY GETTING INTO THIS **PARK ENGINEERING** STUFF LATELY.
LIKE, FIGURING OUT WHERE PEOPLE ARE GOING AND THE BEST WAY TO GET THERE QUICKLY.
SO ANYWAY...

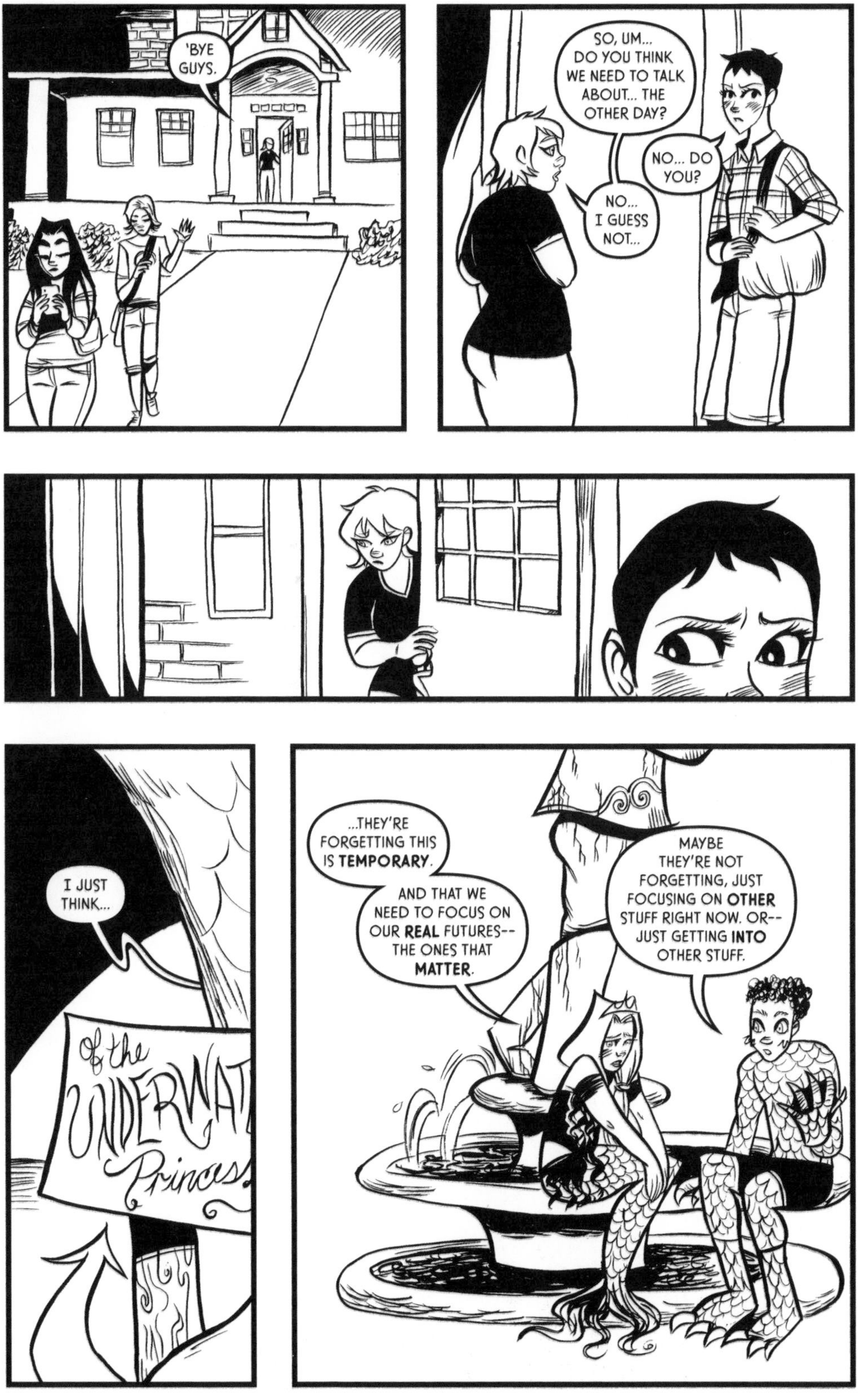
'BYE GUYS.
SO, UM... DO YOU THINK WE NEED TO TALK ABOUT... THE OTHER DAY?
NO... DO YOU?
NO... I GUESS NOT...
I JUST THINK...
Of the UNDERWAT Princes
...THEY'RE FORGETTING THIS IS **TEMPORARY**.
AND THAT WE NEED TO FOCUS ON OUR **REAL** FUTURES-- THE ONES THAT **MATTER**.
MAYBE THEY'RE NOT FORGETTING, JUST FOCUSING ON **OTHER** STUFF RIGHT NOW. OR-- JUST GETTING **INTO** OTHER STUFF.

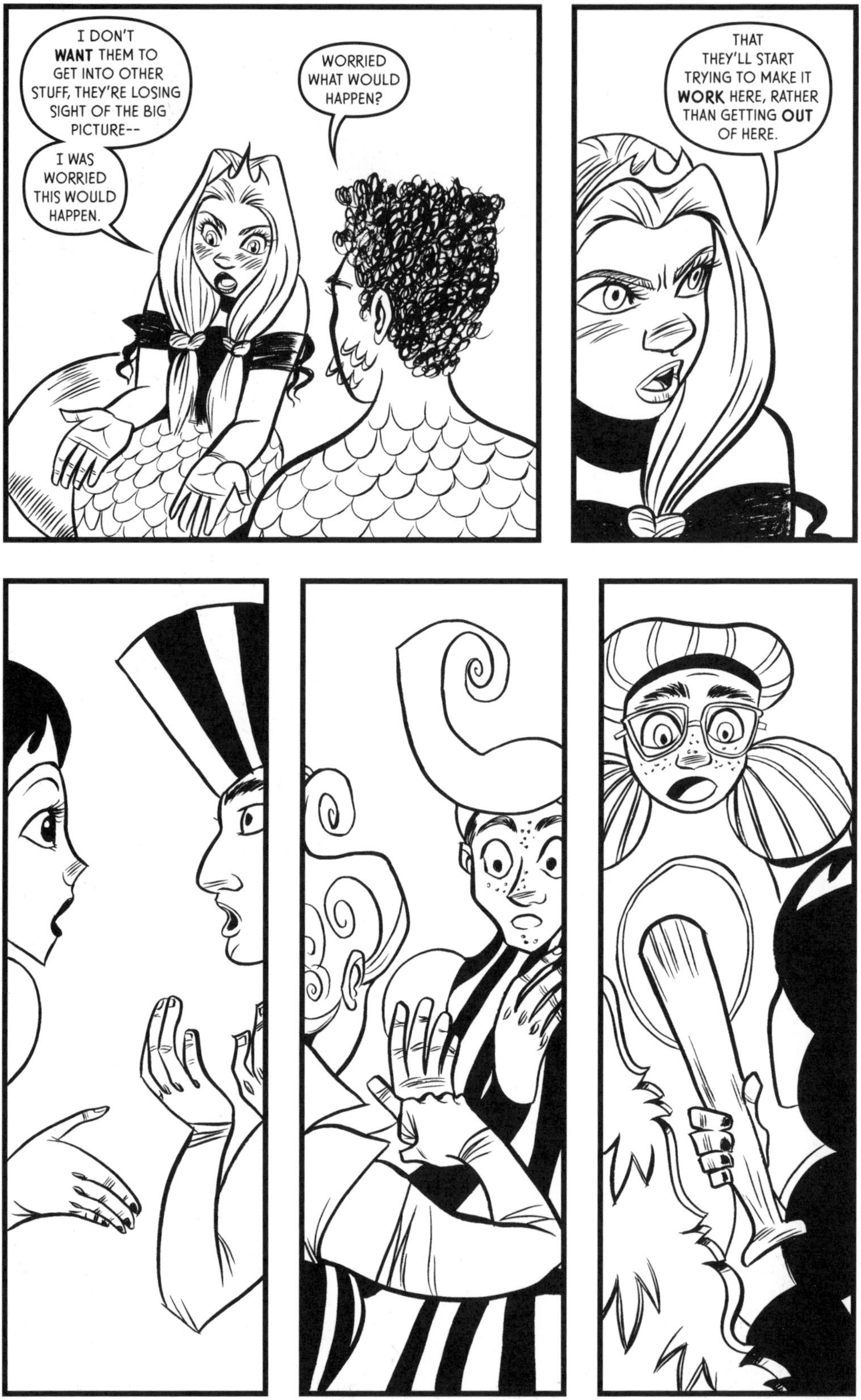
I DON'T **WANT** THEM TO GET INTO OTHER STUFF, THEY'RE LOSING SIGHT OF THE BIG PICTURE--
I WAS WORRIED THIS WOULD HAPPEN.
WORRIED WHAT WOULD HAPPEN?
THAT THEY'LL START TRYING TO MAKE IT **WORK** HERE, RATHER THAN GETTING **OUT** OF HERE.

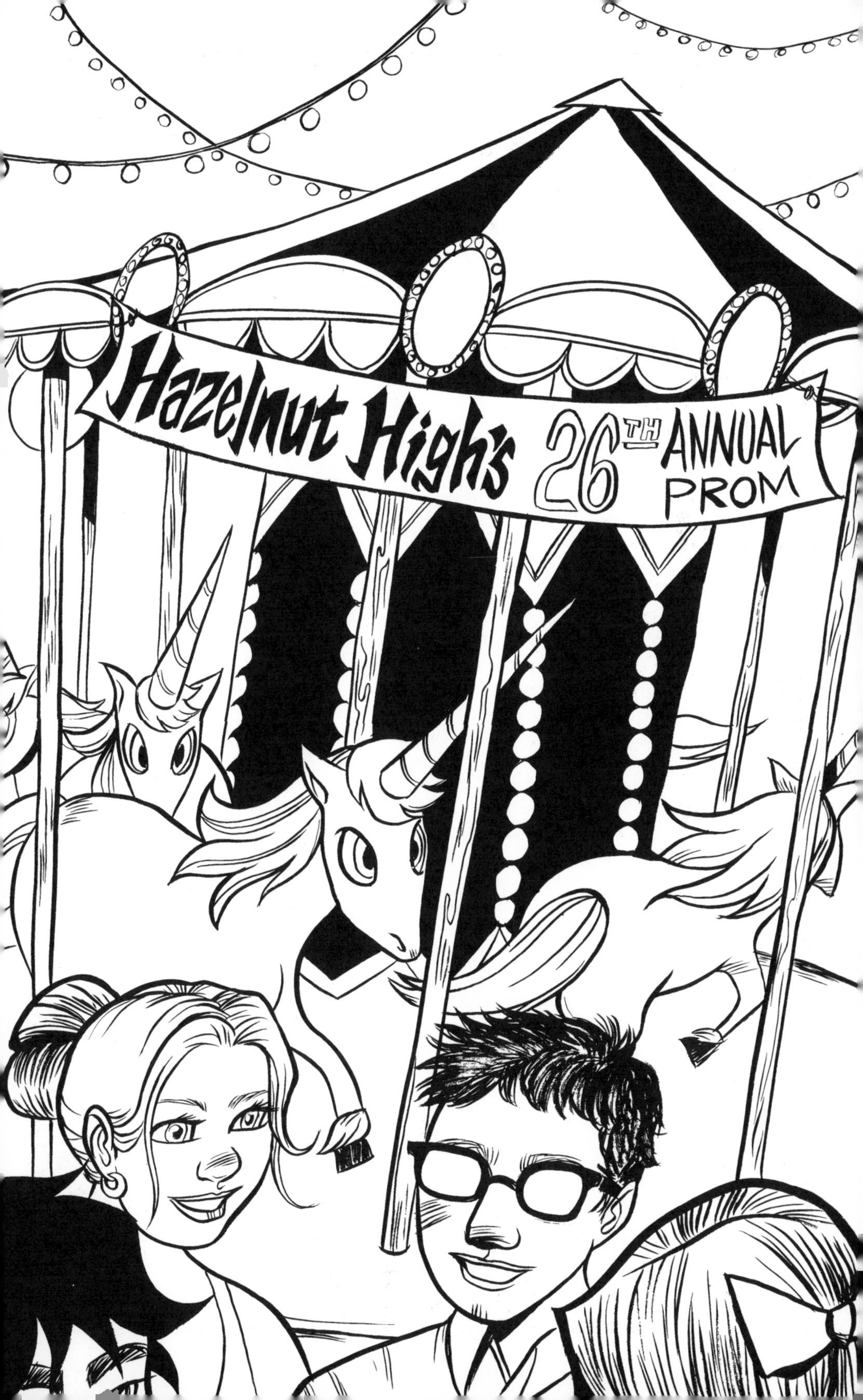
Hazelnut High's 26TH ANNUAL PROM

OKAY, GUYS, THIS IS IT.

PROM NIGHT. EVERYTHING NEEDS TO GO OFF WITHOUT A HITCH.

LET'S BRING IT IN.

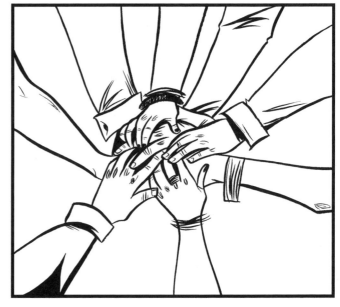

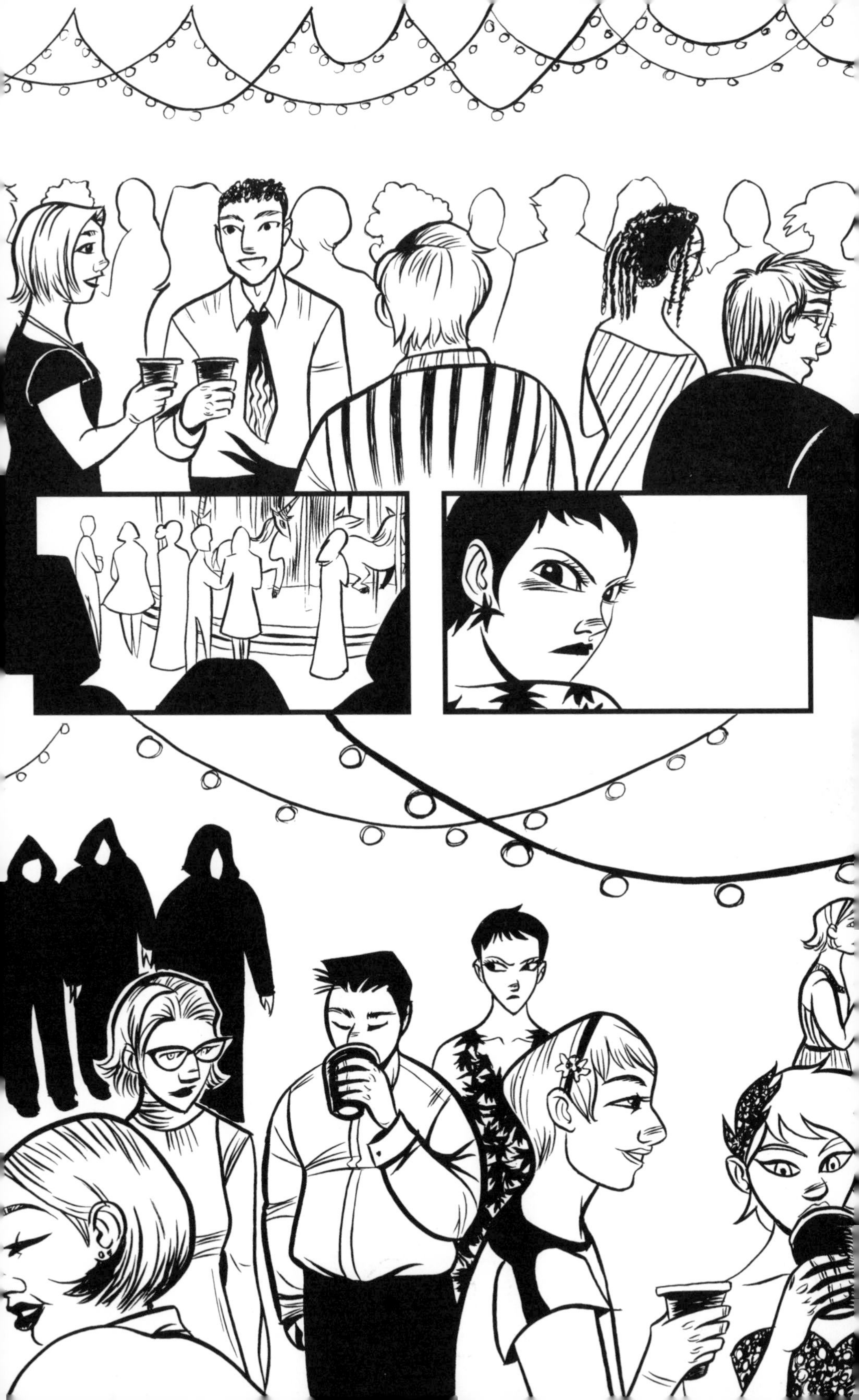

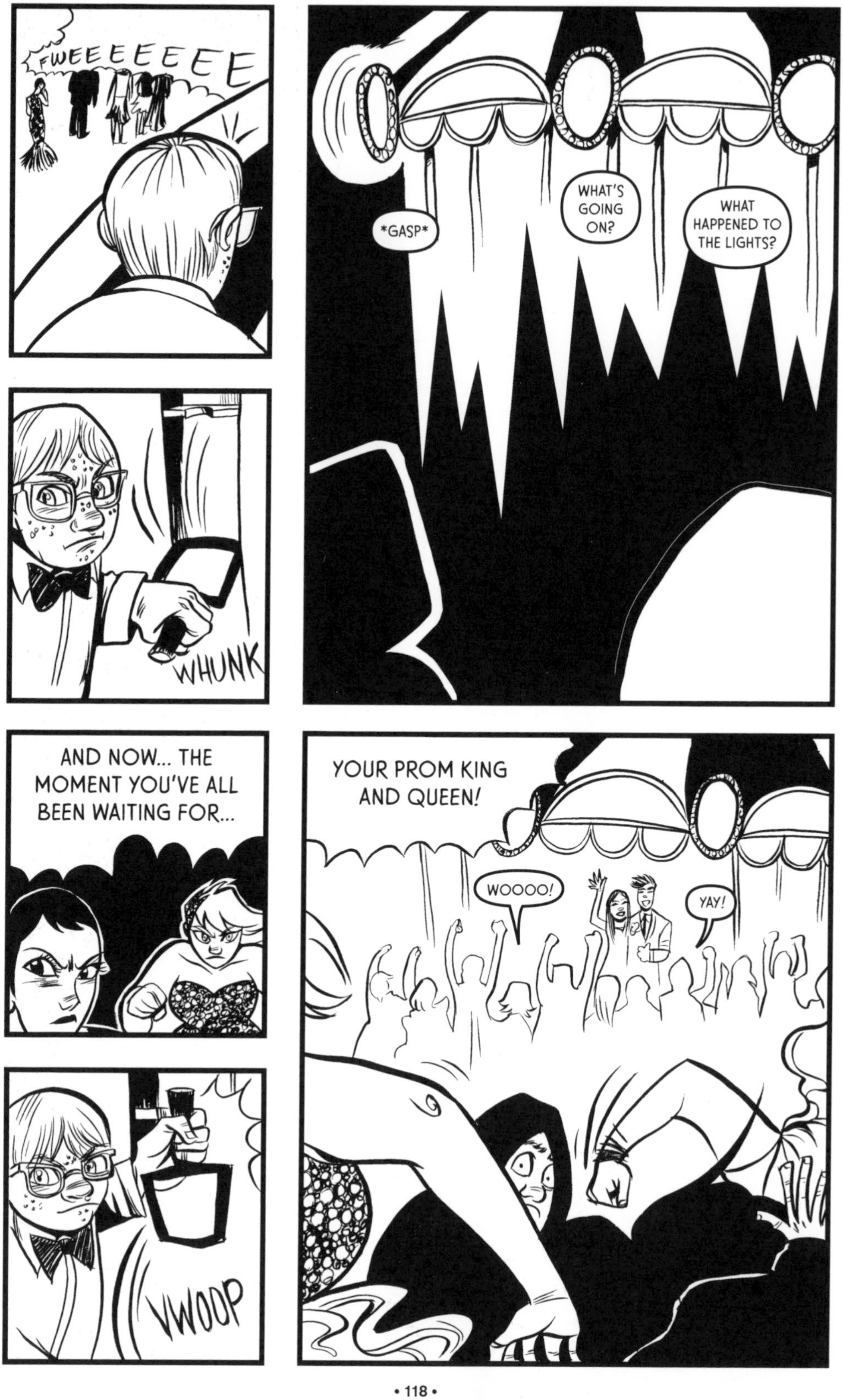
FWEEEEEEEE
WHUNK
AND NOW... THE MOMENT YOU'VE ALL BEEN WAITING FOR...
VWOOP
GASP
WHAT'S GOING ON?
WHAT HAPPENED TO THE LIGHTS?
YOUR PROM KING AND QUEEN!
WOOOO!
YAY!

ING

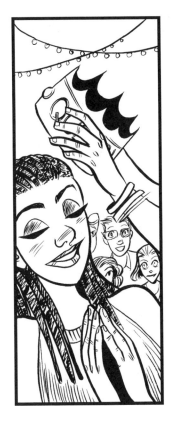

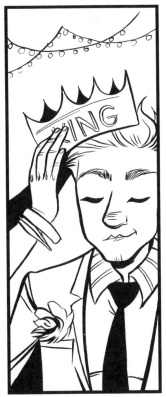

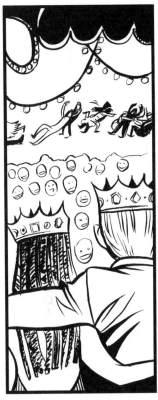

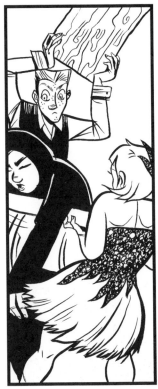

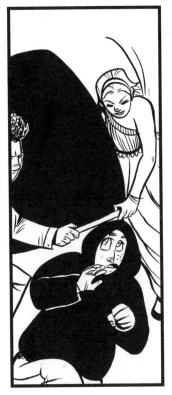

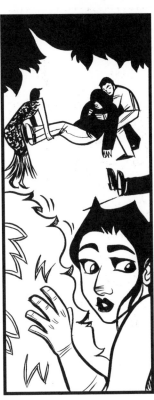

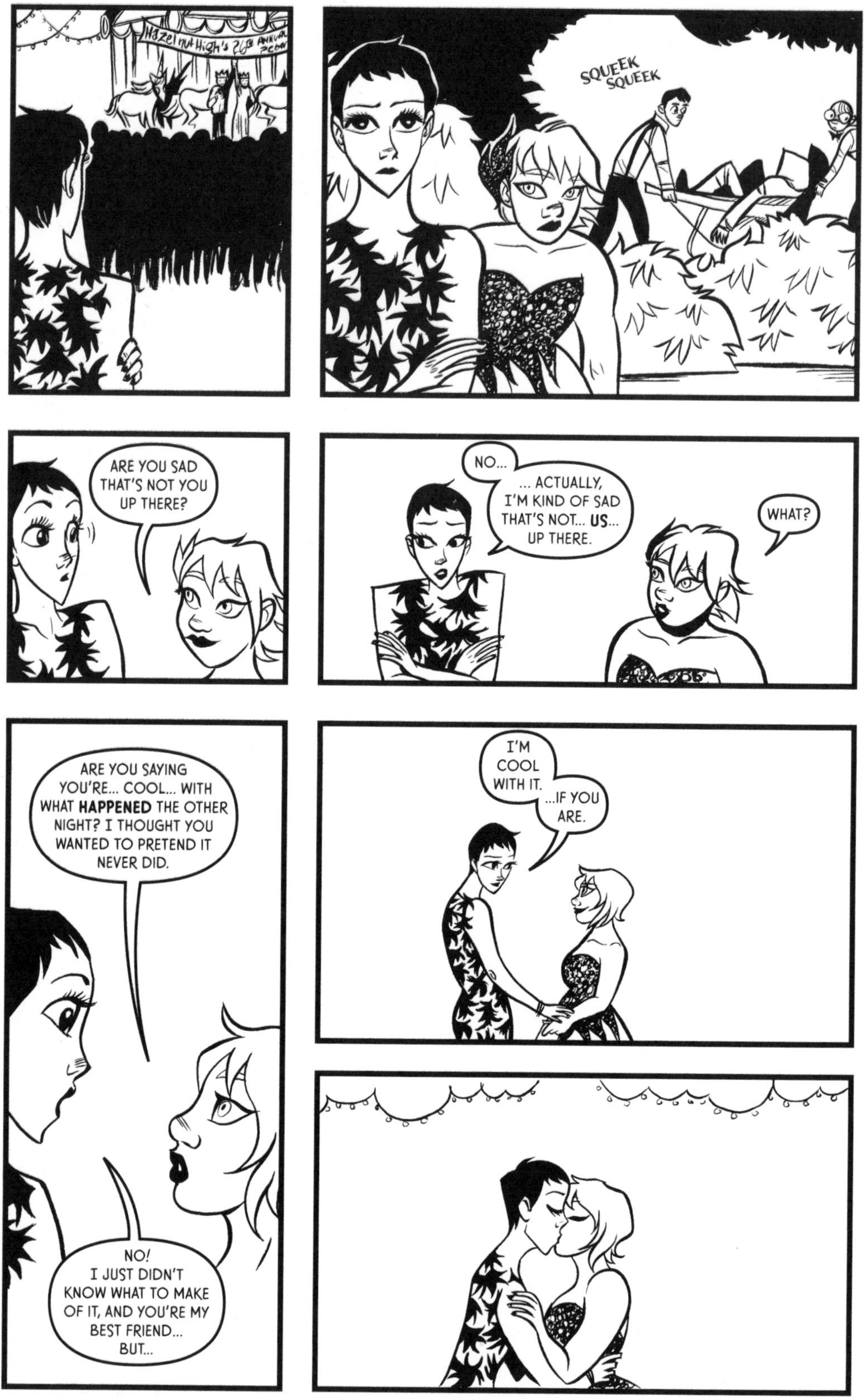
Hazelnut High's 26th Annual Peon
SQUEEK SQUEEK
ARE YOU SAD THAT'S NOT YOU UP THERE?
NO...
... ACTUALLY, I'M KIND OF SAD THAT'S NOT... **US**... UP THERE.
WHAT?
ARE YOU SAYING YOU'RE... COOL... WITH WHAT **HAPPENED** THE OTHER NIGHT? I THOUGHT YOU WANTED TO PRETEND IT NEVER DID.
NO! I JUST DIDN'T KNOW WHAT TO MAKE OF IT, AND YOU'RE MY BEST FRIEND... BUT...
I'M COOL WITH IT.
...IF YOU ARE.

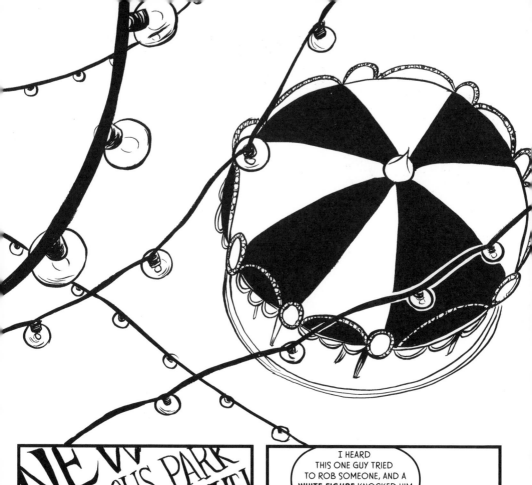

NEW DANGEROUS PARK GETS A LITTLE HE... FROM BEYOND?

...pectators at local Enchante... Amusement Park are witne... ghostly figures and apparit... what appears to be...fairy t... characters. Is the park fi... recent charges of local ... by resurrecting beings ... ...sion? Is the pa... ...nt India...

I HEARD THIS ONE GUY TRIED TO ROB SOMEONE, AND A **WHITE FIGURE** KNOCKED HIM OFF HIS FEET AND INTO A TRASHCAN.

IT'S SUPPOSED TO BE THE **NUMBER ONE** PLACE TO RECORD PARANORMAL ACTIVITY.

ALAN TOLD ME HE'S ALREADY HEARD CREEPY ELECTRONIC VOICE PHENOMENA (EVPS) TAKEN IN THE PARK OF **CONVERSATIONS** BETWEEN THE FAIRY TALE GHOSTS.

GASP

KNOCK IT OFF, TOM! WE'VE GOT TO GET IN THERE.

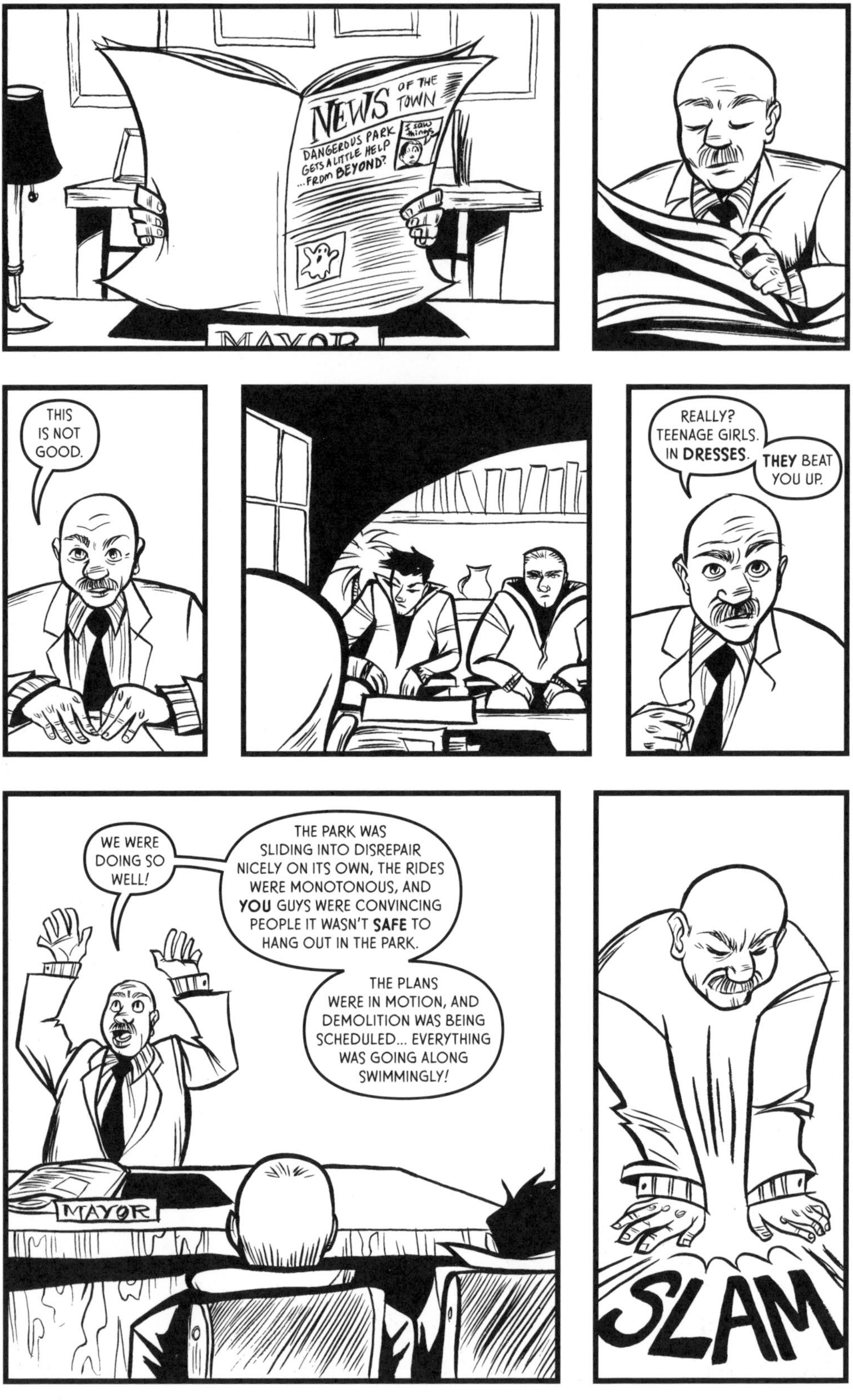

NEWS OF THE TOWN
DANGEROUS PARK GETS A LITTLE HELP ...FROM BEYOND?
I saw things
MAYOR
THIS IS NOT GOOD.
REALLY? TEENAGE GIRLS. IN DRESSES.
THEY BEAT YOU UP.
WE WERE DOING SO WELL!
THE PARK WAS SLIDING INTO DISREPAIR NICELY ON ITS OWN, THE RIDES WERE MONOTONOUS, AND YOU GUYS WERE CONVINCING PEOPLE IT WASN'T SAFE TO HANG OUT IN THE PARK.
THE PLANS WERE IN MOTION, AND DEMOLITION WAS BEING SCHEDULED... EVERYTHING WAS GOING ALONG SWIMMINGLY!
MAYOR
SLAM

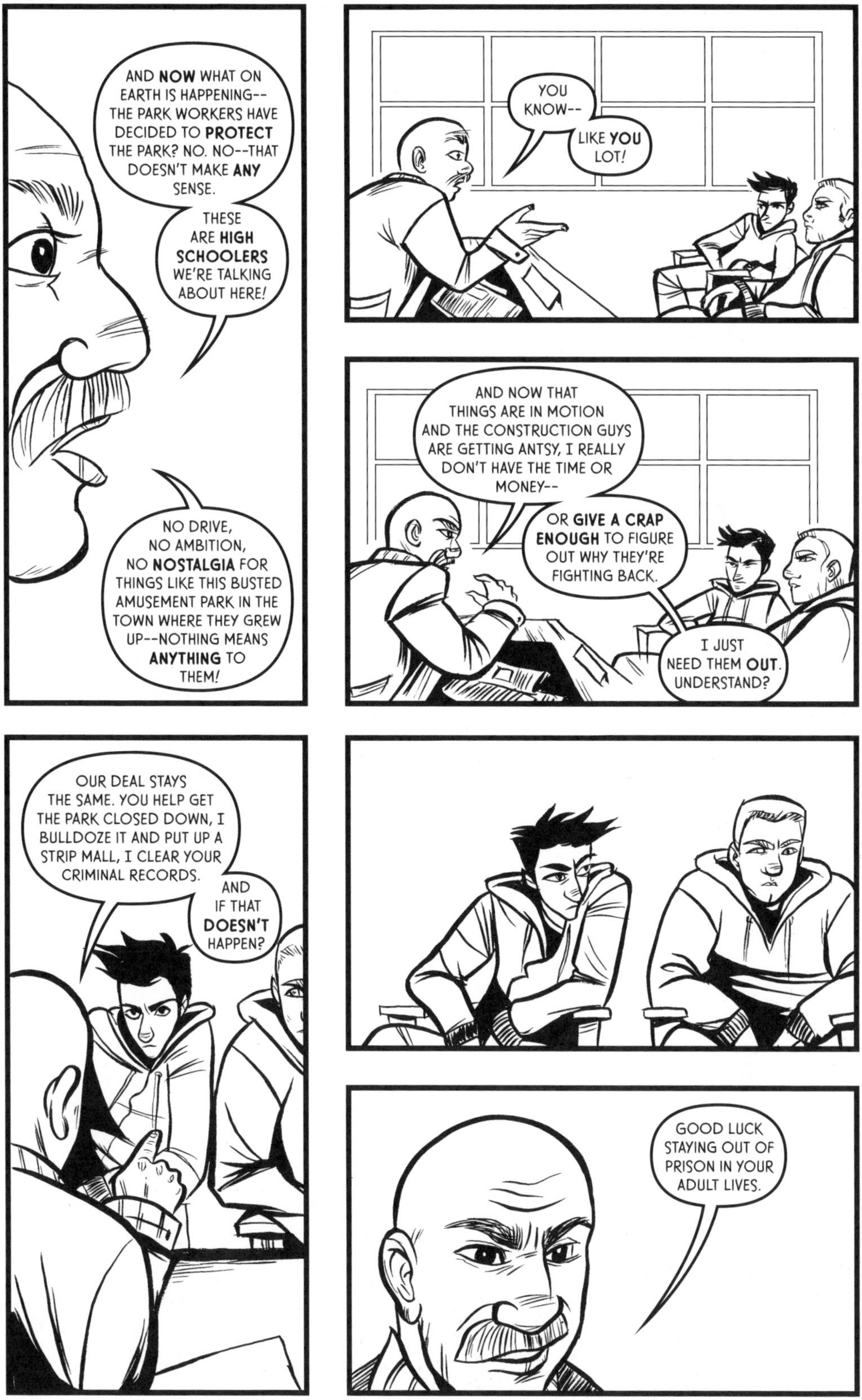
AND NOW WHAT ON EARTH IS HAPPENING-- THE PARK WORKERS HAVE DECIDED TO PROTECT THE PARK? NO. NO--THAT DOESN'T MAKE ANY SENSE.
THESE ARE HIGH SCHOOLERS WE'RE TALKING ABOUT HERE!
NO DRIVE, NO AMBITION, NO NOSTALGIA FOR THINGS LIKE THIS BUSTED AMUSEMENT PARK IN THE TOWN WHERE THEY GREW UP--NOTHING MEANS ANYTHING TO THEM!
YOU KNOW--
LIKE YOU LOT!
AND NOW THAT THINGS ARE IN MOTION AND THE CONSTRUCTION GUYS ARE GETTING ANTSY, I REALLY DON'T HAVE THE TIME OR MONEY--
OR GIVE A CRAP ENOUGH TO FIGURE OUT WHY THEY'RE FIGHTING BACK.
I JUST NEED THEM OUT. UNDERSTAND?
OUR DEAL STAYS THE SAME. YOU HELP GET THE PARK CLOSED DOWN, I BULLDOZE IT AND PUT UP A STRIP MALL, I CLEAR YOUR CRIMINAL RECORDS.
AND IF THAT DOESN'T HAPPEN?
GOOD LUCK STAYING OUT OF PRISON IN YOUR ADULT LIVES.

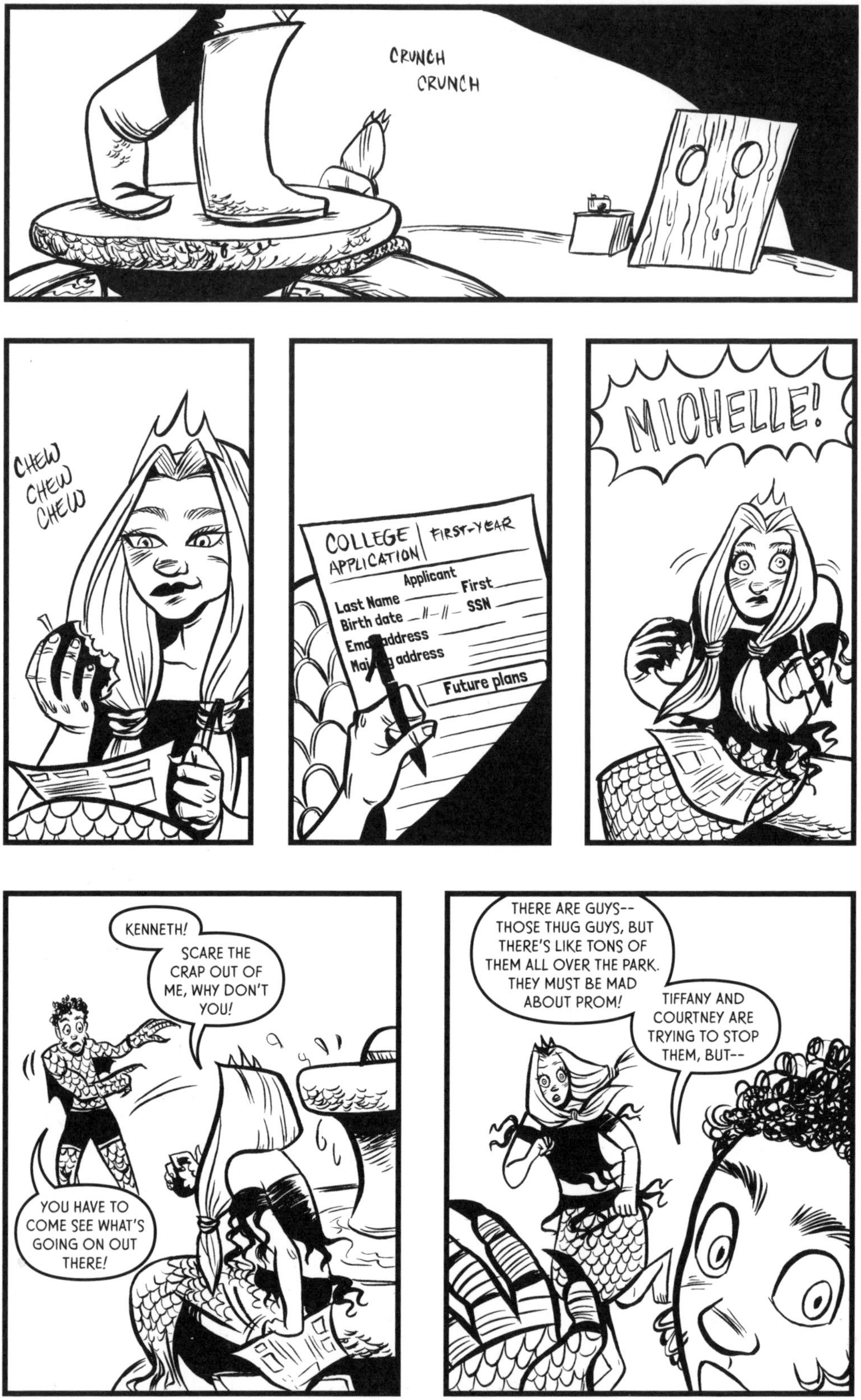
CRUNCH
CRUNCH
CHEW
CHEW
CHEW
COLLEGE APPLICATION
FIRST-YEAR
Applicant
Last Name
First
Birth date
SSN
Email address
Mailing address
Future plans
MICHELLE!
KENNETH!
SCARE THE CRAP OUT OF ME, WHY DON'T YOU!
YOU HAVE TO COME SEE WHAT'S GOING ON OUT THERE!
THERE ARE GUYS-- THOSE THUG GUYS, BUT THERE'S LIKE TONS OF THEM ALL OVER THE PARK. THEY MUST BE MAD ABOUT PROM!
TIFFANY AND COURTNEY ARE TRYING TO STOP THEM, BUT--

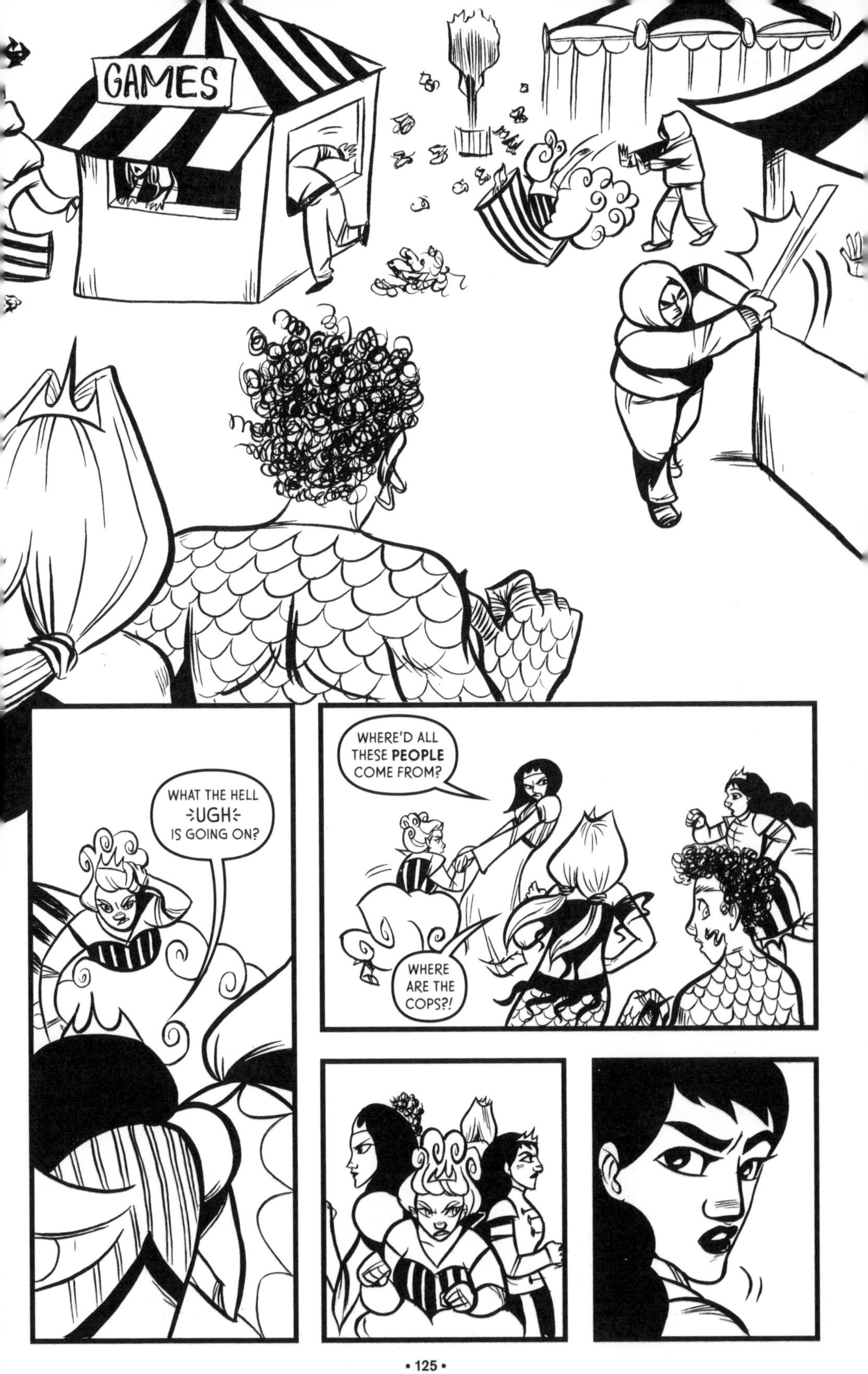
GAMES
WHAT THE HELL
=UGH=
IS GOING ON?
WHERE'D ALL THESE **PEOPLE** COME FROM?
WHERE ARE THE COPS?!

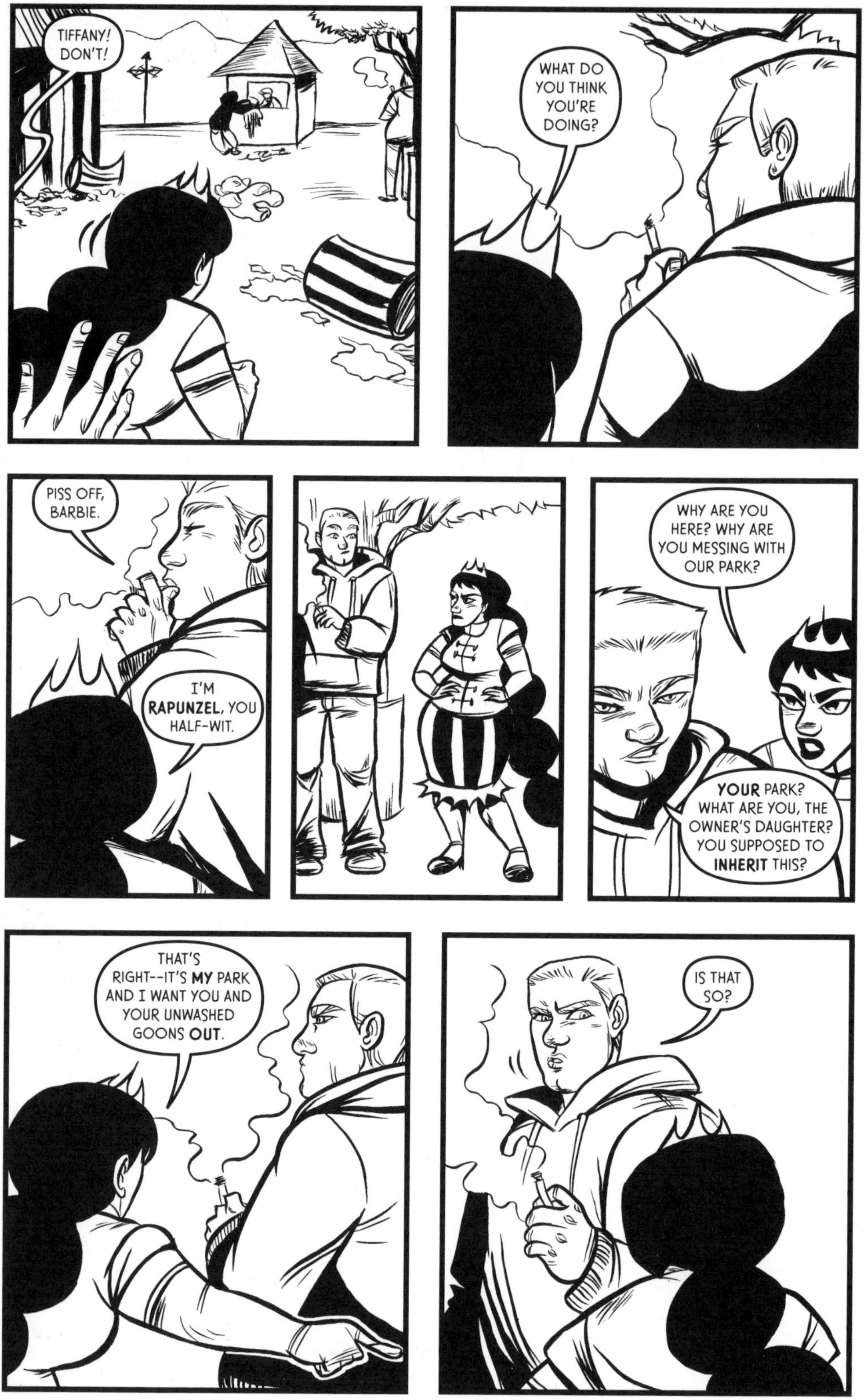
TIFFANY! DON'T!
WHAT DO YOU THINK YOU'RE DOING?
PISS OFF, BARBIE.
I'M **RAPUNZEL**, YOU HALF-WIT.
WHY ARE YOU HERE? WHY ARE YOU MESSING WITH OUR PARK?
YOUR PARK? WHAT ARE YOU, THE OWNER'S DAUGHTER? YOU SUPPOSED TO **INHERIT** THIS?
THAT'S RIGHT--IT'S **MY** PARK AND I WANT YOU AND YOUR UNWASHED GOONS **OUT**.
IS THAT SO?

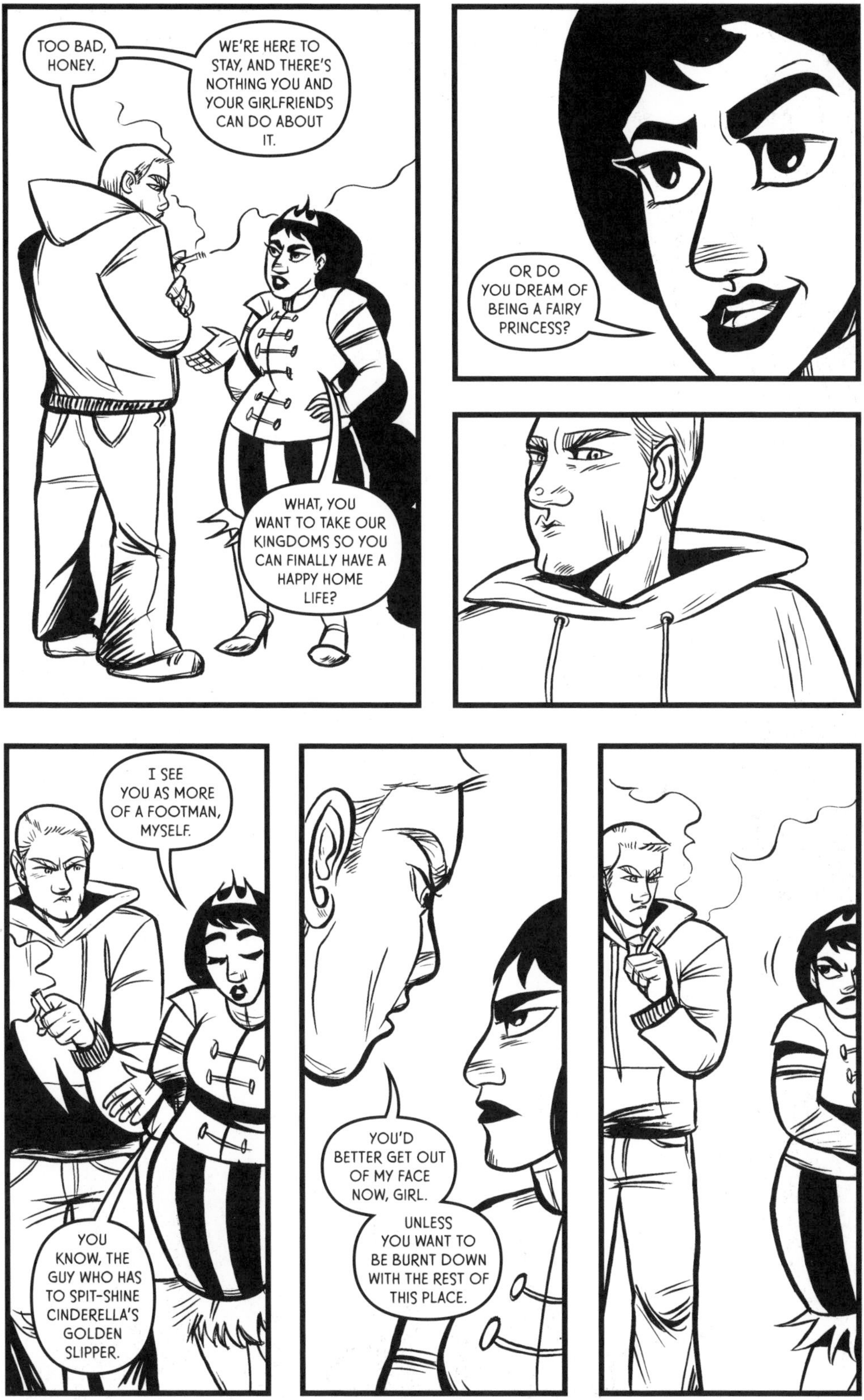
TOO BAD, HONEY.
WE'RE HERE TO STAY, AND THERE'S NOTHING YOU AND YOUR GIRLFRIENDS CAN DO ABOUT IT.
WHAT, YOU WANT TO TAKE OUR KINGDOMS SO YOU CAN FINALLY HAVE A HAPPY HOME LIFE?
OR DO YOU DREAM OF BEING A FAIRY PRINCESS?
I SEE YOU AS MORE OF A FOOTMAN, MYSELF.
YOU KNOW, THE GUY WHO HAS TO SPIT-SHINE CINDERELLA'S GOLDEN SLIPPER.
YOU'D BETTER GET OUT OF MY FACE NOW, GIRL.
UNLESS YOU WANT TO BE BURNT DOWN WITH THE REST OF THIS PLACE.

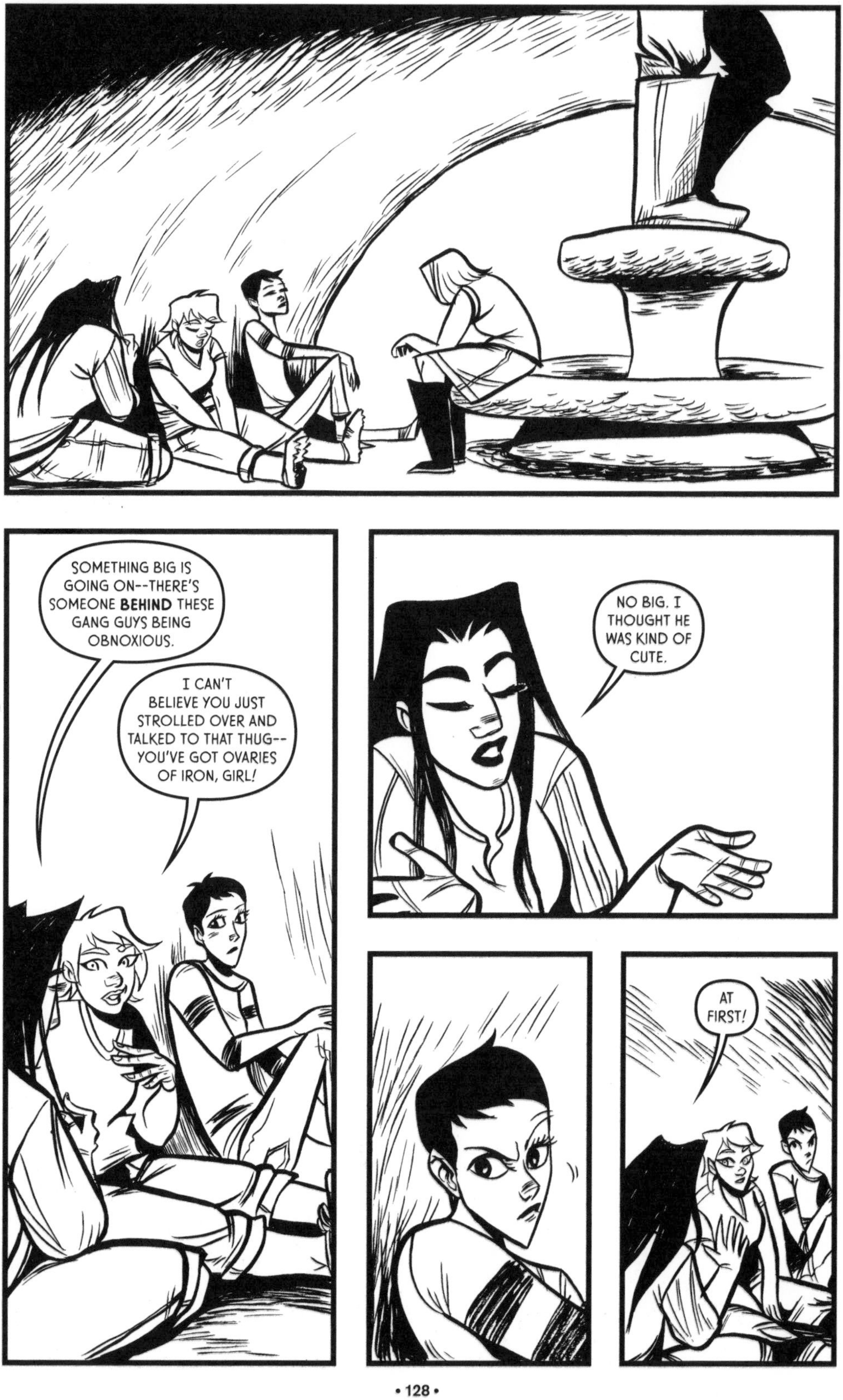
SOMETHING BIG IS GOING ON--THERE'S SOMEONE **BEHIND** THESE GANG GUYS BEING OBNOXIOUS.
I CAN'T BELIEVE YOU JUST STROLLED OVER AND TALKED TO THAT THUG--YOU'VE GOT OVARIES OF IRON, GIRL!
NO BIG. I THOUGHT HE WAS KIND OF CUTE.
AT FIRST!

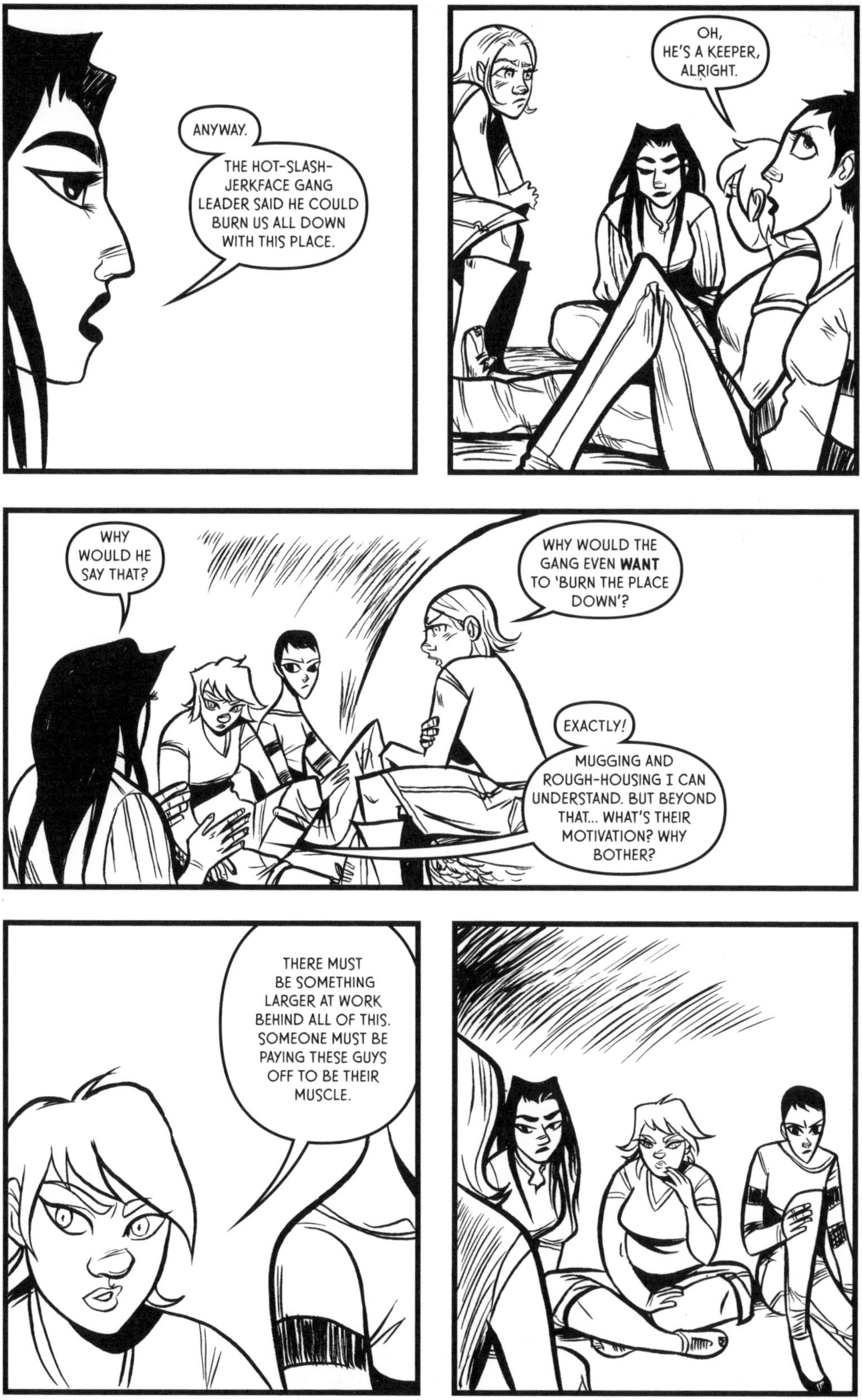
ANYWAY.
THE HOT-SLASH-JERKFACE GANG LEADER SAID HE COULD BURN US ALL DOWN WITH THIS PLACE.
OH, HE'S A KEEPER, ALRIGHT.
WHY WOULD HE SAY THAT?
WHY WOULD THE GANG EVEN **WANT** TO 'BURN THE PLACE DOWN'?
EXACTLY!
MUGGING AND ROUGH-HOUSING I CAN UNDERSTAND. BUT BEYOND THAT... WHAT'S THEIR MOTIVATION? WHY BOTHER?
THERE MUST BE SOMETHING LARGER AT WORK BEHIND ALL OF THIS. SOMEONE MUST BE PAYING THESE GUYS OFF TO BE THEIR MUSCLE.

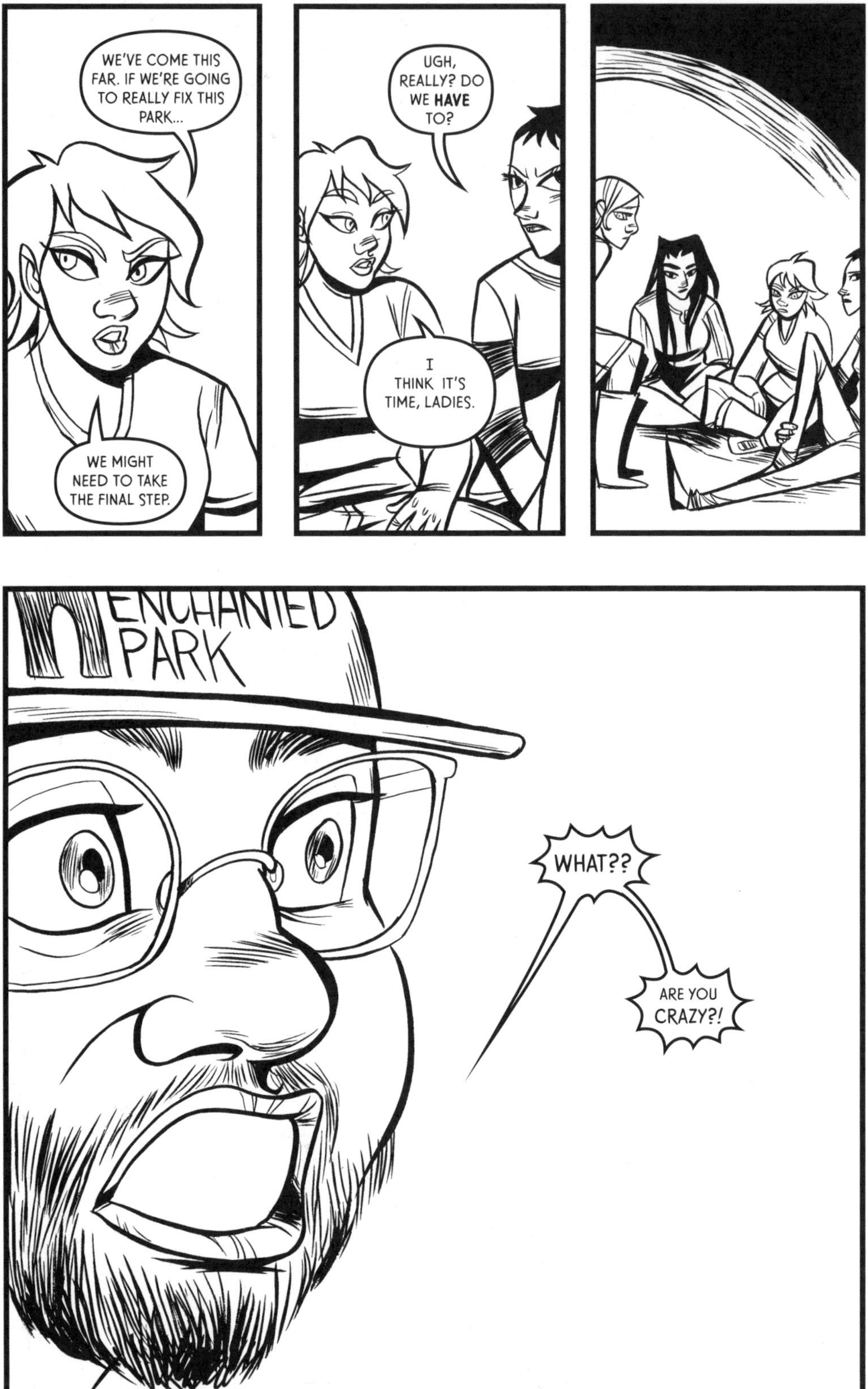
WE'VE COME THIS FAR. IF WE'RE GOING TO REALLY FIX THIS PARK...
WE MIGHT NEED TO TAKE THE FINAL STEP.
UGH, REALLY? DO WE **HAVE** TO?
I THINK IT'S TIME, LADIES.
ENCHANTED PARK
WHAT??
ARE YOU CRAZY?!

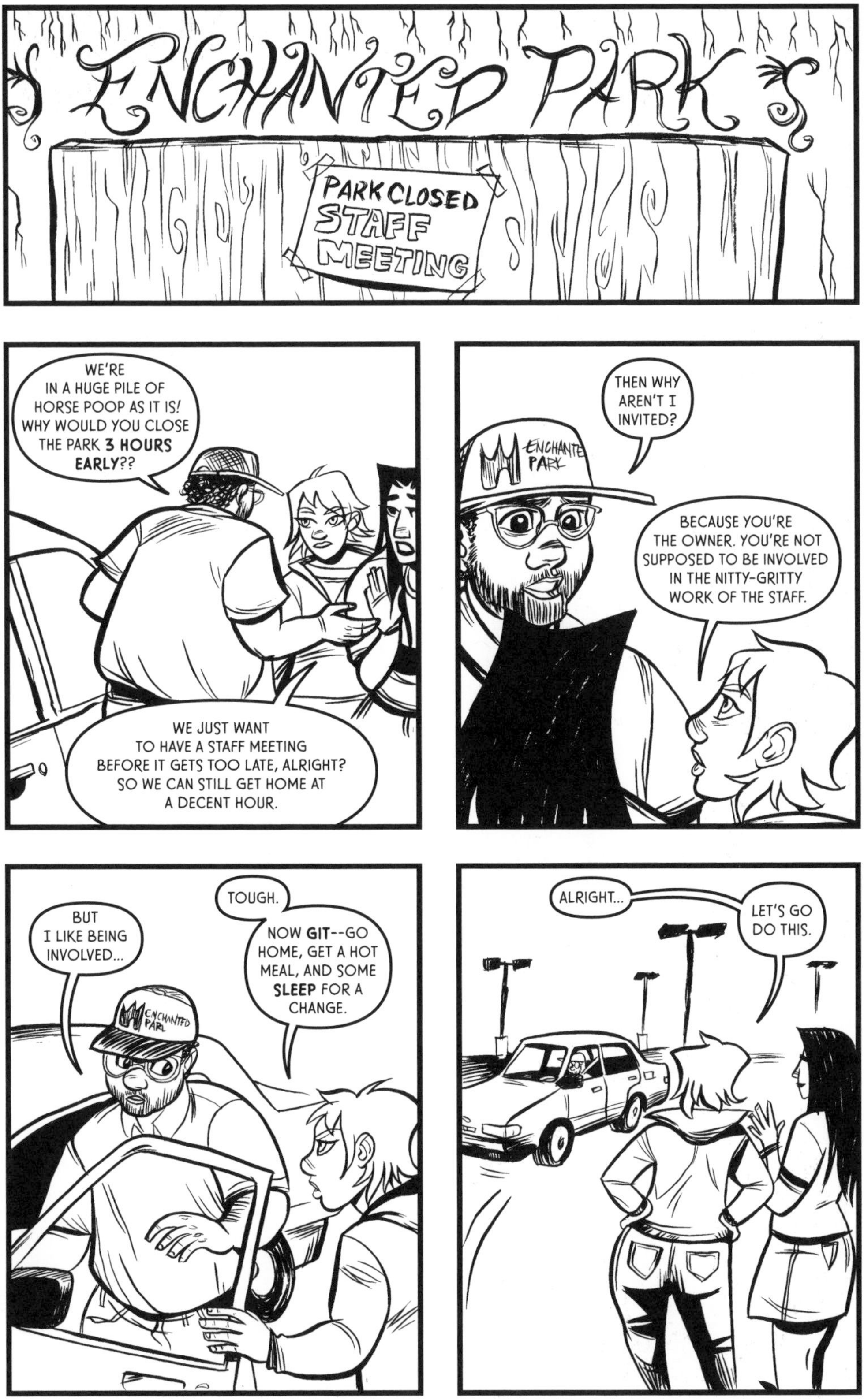
ENCHANTED PARK
PARK CLOSED STAFF MEETING
WE'RE IN A HUGE PILE OF HORSE POOP AS IT IS! WHY WOULD YOU CLOSE THE PARK **3 HOURS EARLY**??
WE JUST WANT TO HAVE A STAFF MEETING BEFORE IT GETS TOO LATE, ALRIGHT? SO WE CAN STILL GET HOME AT A DECENT HOUR.
THEN WHY AREN'T I INVITED?
BECAUSE YOU'RE THE OWNER. YOU'RE NOT SUPPOSED TO BE INVOLVED IN THE NITTY-GRITTY WORK OF THE STAFF.
BUT I LIKE BEING INVOLVED...
TOUGH.
NOW **GIT**--GO HOME, GET A HOT MEAL, AND SOME **SLEEP** FOR A CHANGE.
ALRIGHT...
LET'S GO DO THIS.

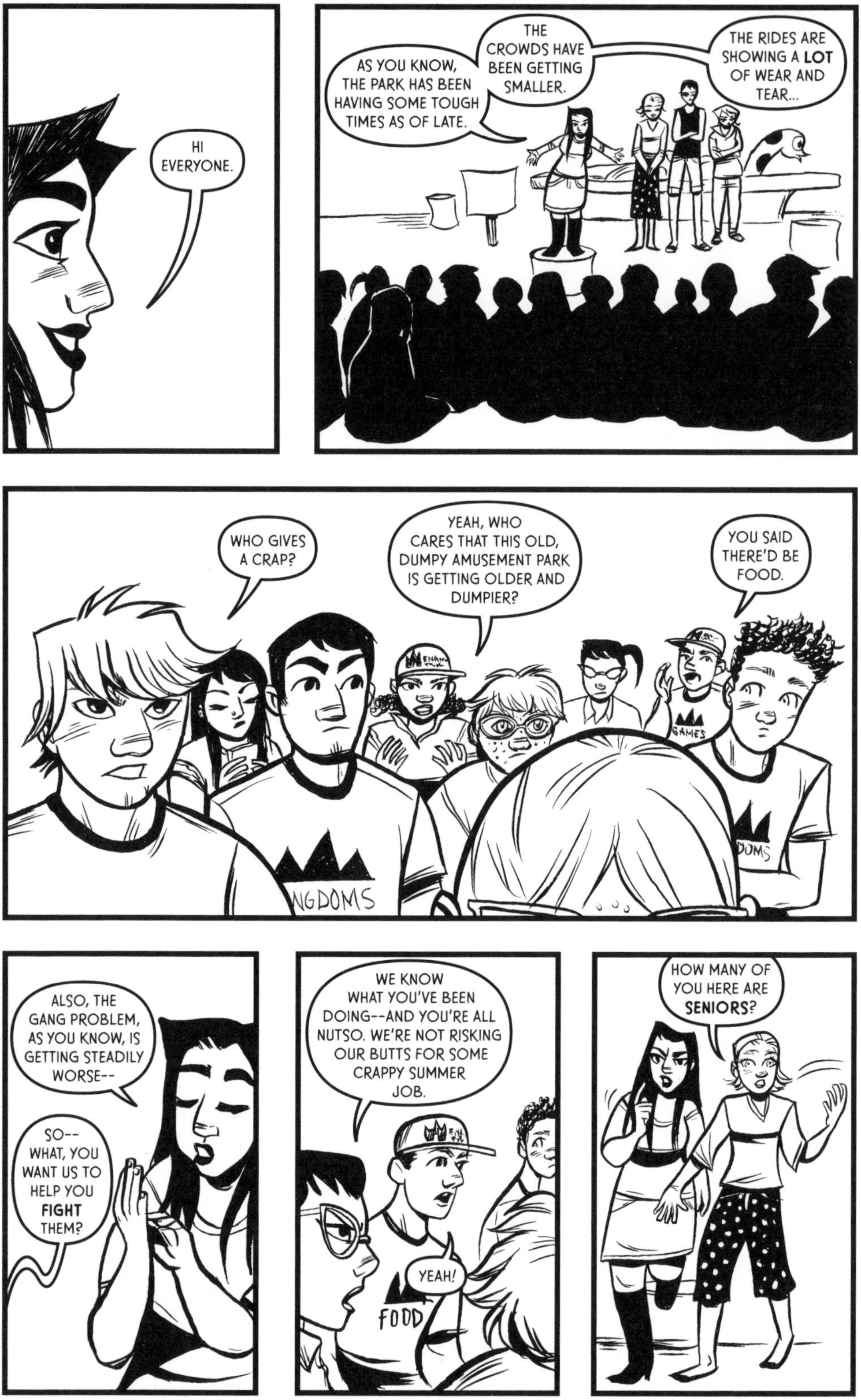
HI EVERYONE.
AS YOU KNOW, THE PARK HAS BEEN HAVING SOME TOUGH TIMES AS OF LATE.
THE CROWDS HAVE BEEN GETTING SMALLER.
THE RIDES ARE SHOWING A **LOT** OF WEAR AND TEAR...
WHO GIVES A CRAP?
YEAH, WHO CARES THAT THIS OLD, DUMPY AMUSEMENT PARK IS GETTING OLDER AND DUMPIER?
YOU SAID THERE'D BE FOOD.
NGDOMS
GAMES
DOMS
ALSO, THE GANG PROBLEM, AS YOU KNOW, IS GETTING STEADILY WORSE--
SO-- WHAT, YOU WANT US TO HELP YOU **FIGHT** THEM?
WE KNOW WHAT YOU'VE BEEN DOING--AND YOU'RE ALL NUTSO. WE'RE NOT RISKING OUR BUTTS FOR SOME CRAPPY SUMMER JOB.
YEAH!
FOOD
HOW MANY OF YOU HERE ARE **SENIORS**?

OK, NOW HOW MANY OF YOU AREN'T SENIORS, BUT KNOW WHAT YOU WANT TO DO WHEN YOU GRADUATE?

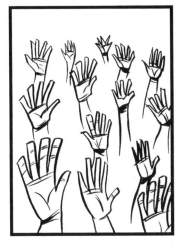

GLARE

WELL THE FOUR OF US THOUGHT WE KNEW WHAT WE WANTED TO DO, TOO.

MICHELLE...

YOU GUYS KNOW US, RIGHT? WE MAY BE POPULAR, AND NOT YOUR FRIENDS, BUT NO ONE HERE CAN SAY THAT THE FOUR OF US DON'T PUSH EVERYTHING TO THE **LIMIT**.

SO BORED.

SO WHEN THE FOUR OF US HOT, POPULAR GIRLS FOUND OUT THAT ALL OF OUR FUTURE PLANS WERE DESTROYED, ALL OF OUR DREAMS CRUSHED--

WE KNEW AT LEAST WE HAD THIS ONE THING TO FALL BACK ON.

THIS **ONE** THING IN OUR LIVES WE COULD **CONTROL**.

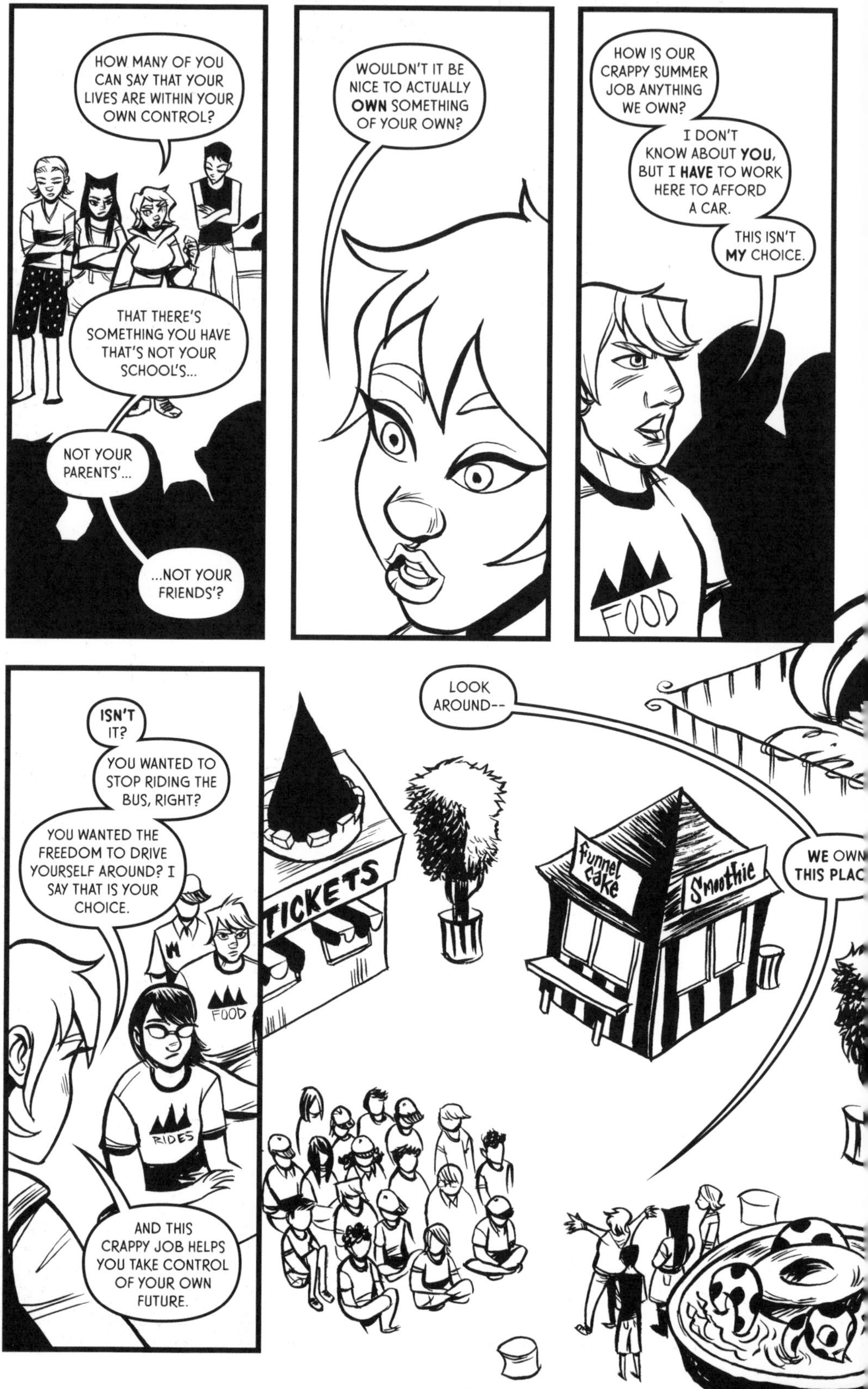

HOW MANY OF YOU CAN SAY THAT YOUR LIVES ARE WITHIN YOUR OWN CONTROL?
THAT THERE'S SOMETHING YOU HAVE THAT'S NOT YOUR SCHOOL'S...
NOT YOUR PARENTS'...
...NOT YOUR FRIENDS'?
WOULDN'T IT BE NICE TO ACTUALLY OWN SOMETHING OF YOUR OWN?
HOW IS OUR CRAPPY SUMMER JOB ANYTHING WE OWN?
I DON'T KNOW ABOUT YOU, BUT I HAVE TO WORK HERE TO AFFORD A CAR.
THIS ISN'T MY CHOICE.
FOOD
ISN'T IT?
YOU WANTED TO STOP RIDING THE BUS, RIGHT?
YOU WANTED THE FREEDOM TO DRIVE YOURSELF AROUND? I SAY THAT IS YOUR CHOICE.
FOOD
RIDES
AND THIS CRAPPY JOB HELPS YOU TAKE CONTROL OF YOUR OWN FUTURE.
LOOK AROUND--
TICKETS
funnel cake
Smoothie

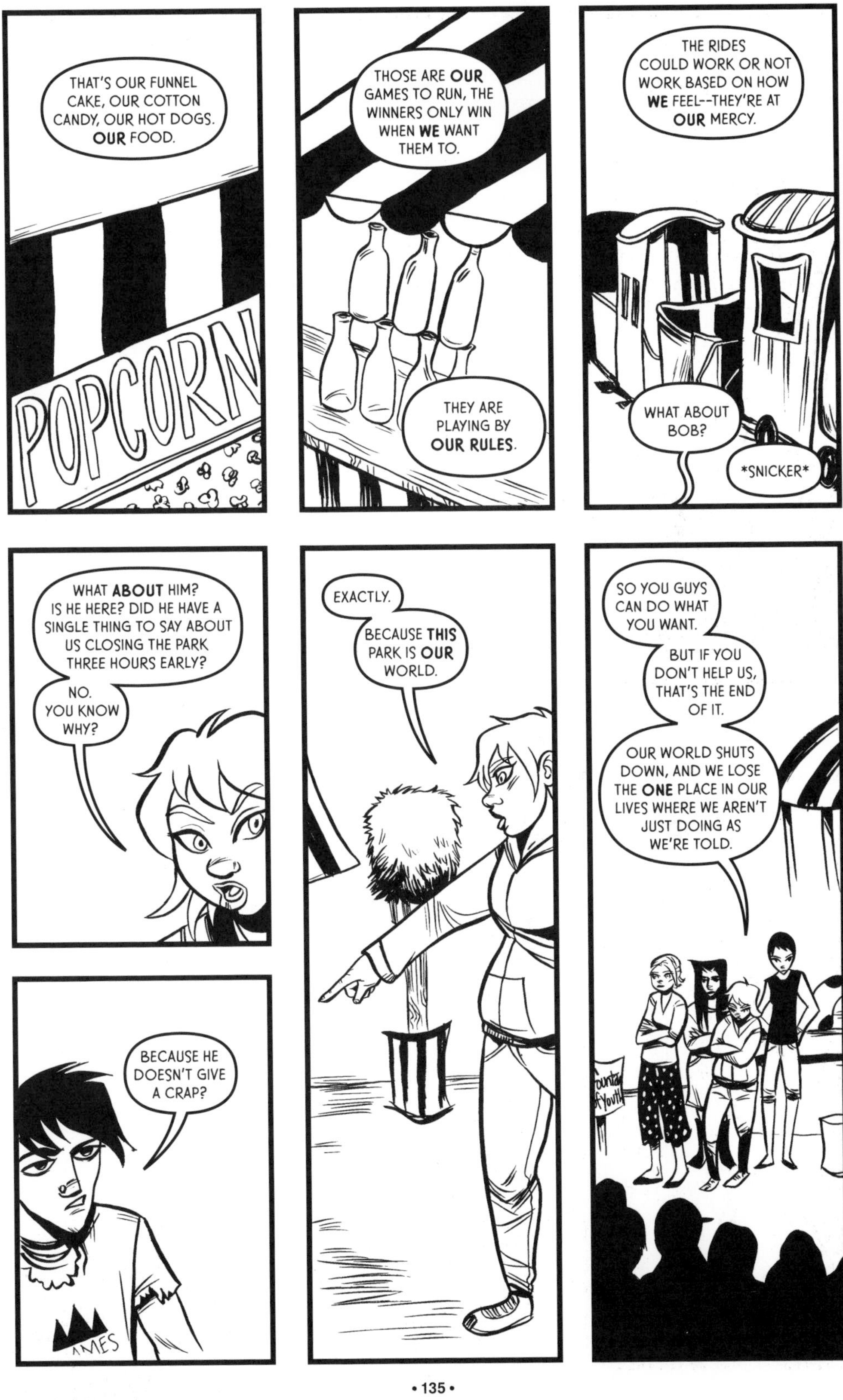

THAT'S OUR FUNNEL CAKE, OUR COTTON CANDY, OUR HOT DOGS. **OUR** FOOD.
POPCORN
THOSE ARE **OUR** GAMES TO RUN, THE WINNERS ONLY WIN WHEN **WE** WANT THEM TO.
THEY ARE PLAYING BY **OUR RULES**.
THE RIDES COULD WORK OR NOT WORK BASED ON HOW **WE** FEEL--THEY'RE AT **OUR** MERCY.
WHAT ABOUT BOB?
SNICKER
WHAT **ABOUT** HIM? IS HE HERE? DID HE HAVE A SINGLE THING TO SAY ABOUT US CLOSING THE PARK THREE HOURS EARLY?
NO. YOU KNOW WHY?
BECAUSE HE DOESN'T GIVE A CRAP?
AMES
EXACTLY.
BECAUSE **THIS** PARK IS **OUR** WORLD.
SO YOU GUYS CAN DO WHAT YOU WANT.
BUT IF YOU DON'T HELP US, THAT'S THE END OF IT.
OUR WORLD SHUTS DOWN, AND WE LOSE THE **ONE** PLACE IN OUR LIVES WHERE WE AREN'T JUST DOING AS WE'RE TOLD.

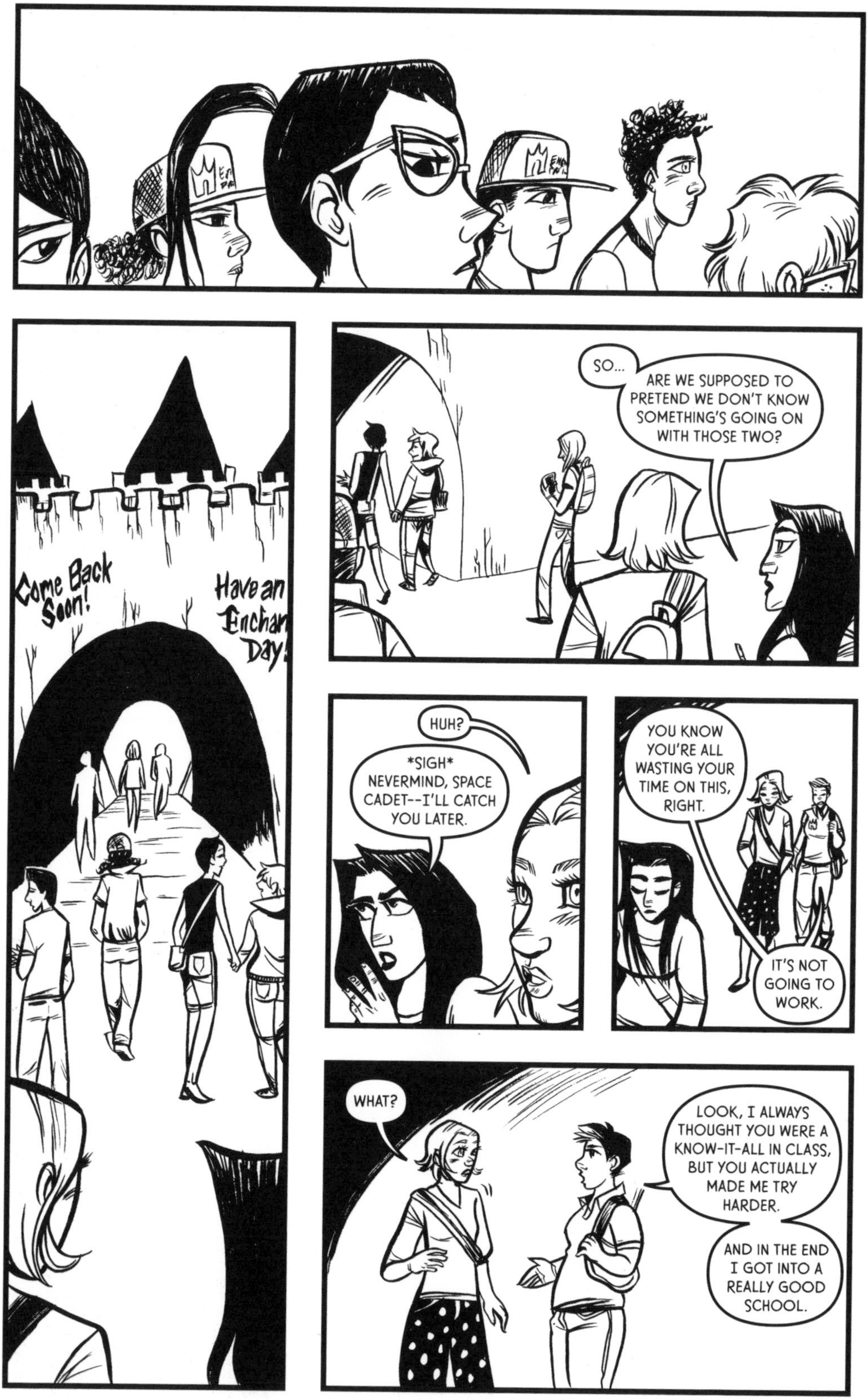
Come Back Soon!
Have an Enchan Day!
SO...
ARE WE SUPPOSED TO PRETEND WE DON'T KNOW SOMETHING'S GOING ON WITH THOSE TWO?
HUH?
SIGH NEVERMIND, SPACE CADET--I'LL CATCH YOU LATER.
YOU KNOW YOU'RE ALL WASTING YOUR TIME ON THIS, RIGHT.
IT'S NOT GOING TO WORK.
WHAT?
LOOK, I ALWAYS THOUGHT YOU WERE A KNOW-IT-ALL IN CLASS, BUT YOU ACTUALLY MADE ME TRY HARDER.
AND IN THE END I GOT INTO A REALLY GOOD SCHOOL.

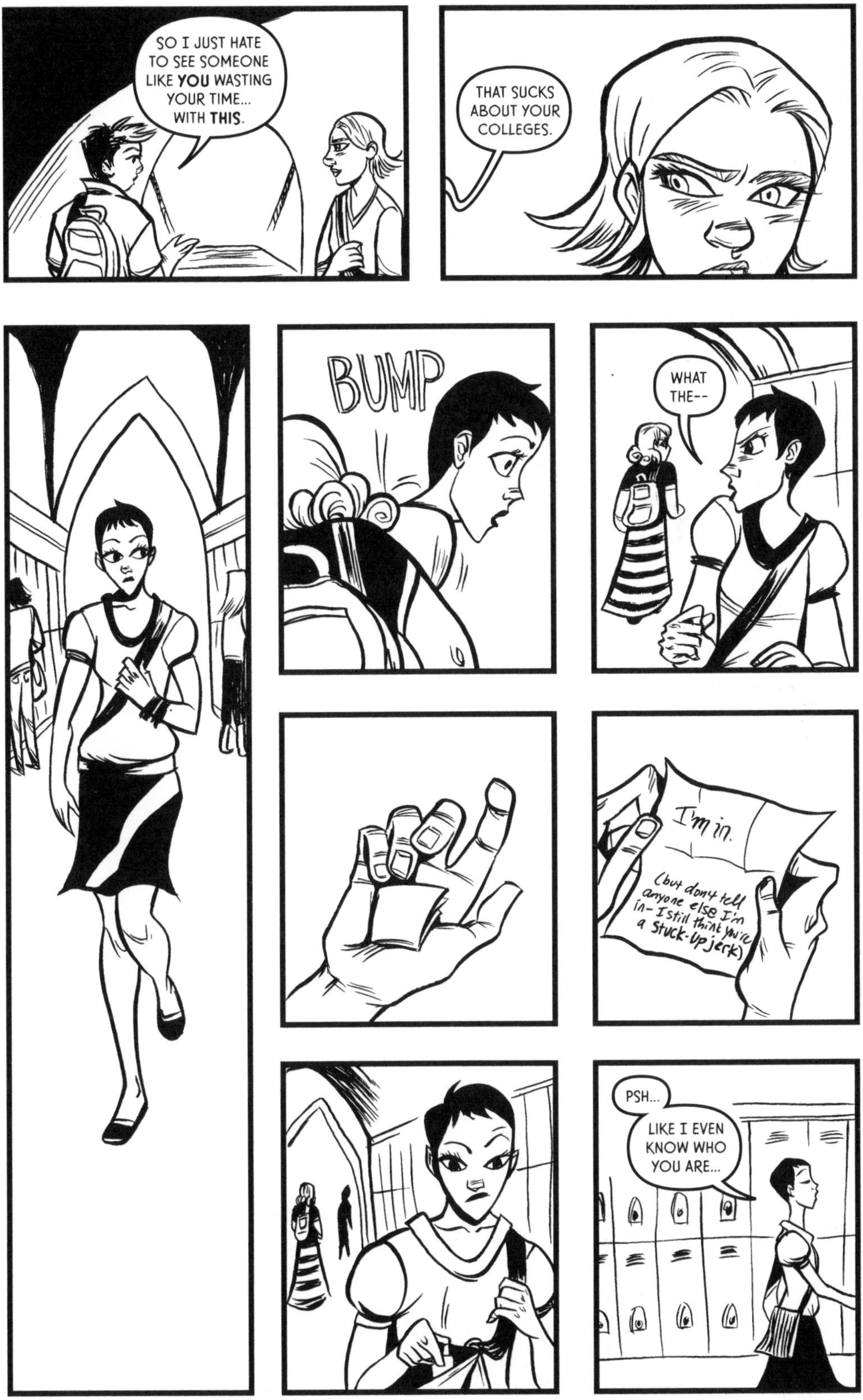
SO I JUST HATE TO SEE SOMEONE LIKE **YOU** WASTING YOUR TIME... WITH **THIS**.
THAT SUCKS ABOUT YOUR COLLEGES.
BUMP
WHAT THE--
I'm in.
(but don't tell anyone else I'm in- I still think you're a stuck-up jerk)
PSH...
LIKE I EVEN KNOW WHO YOU ARE...

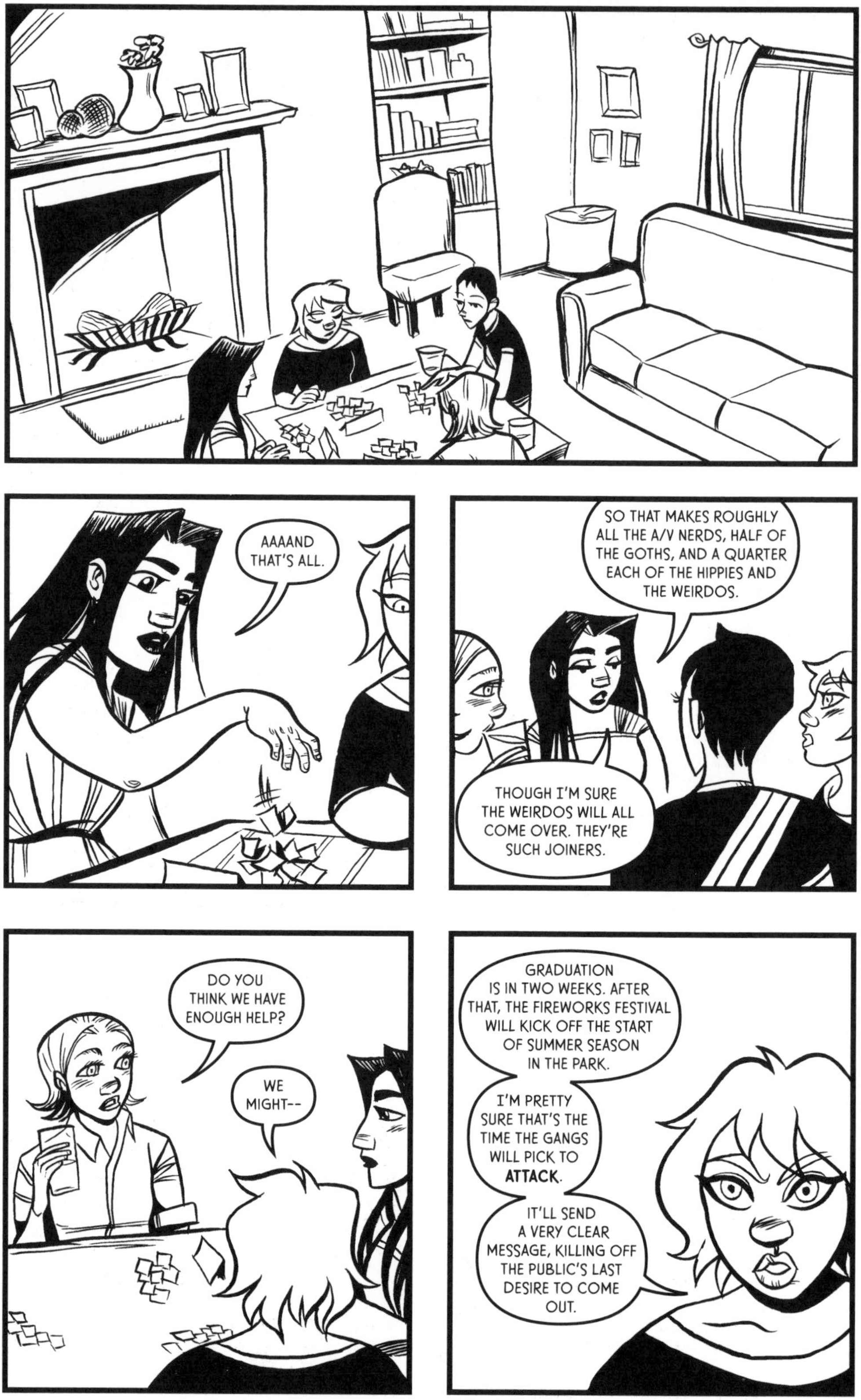
AAAAND THAT'S ALL.
SO THAT MAKES ROUGHLY ALL THE A/V NERDS, HALF OF THE GOTHS, AND A QUARTER EACH OF THE HIPPIES AND THE WEIRDOS.
THOUGH I'M SURE THE WEIRDOS WILL ALL COME OVER. THEY'RE SUCH JOINERS.
DO YOU THINK WE HAVE ENOUGH HELP?
WE MIGHT--
GRADUATION IS IN TWO WEEKS. AFTER THAT, THE FIREWORKS FESTIVAL WILL KICK OFF THE START OF SUMMER SEASON IN THE PARK.
I'M PRETTY SURE THAT'S THE TIME THE GANGS WILL PICK TO **ATTACK**.
IT'LL SEND A VERY CLEAR MESSAGE, KILLING OFF THE PUBLIC'S LAST DESIRE TO COME OUT.

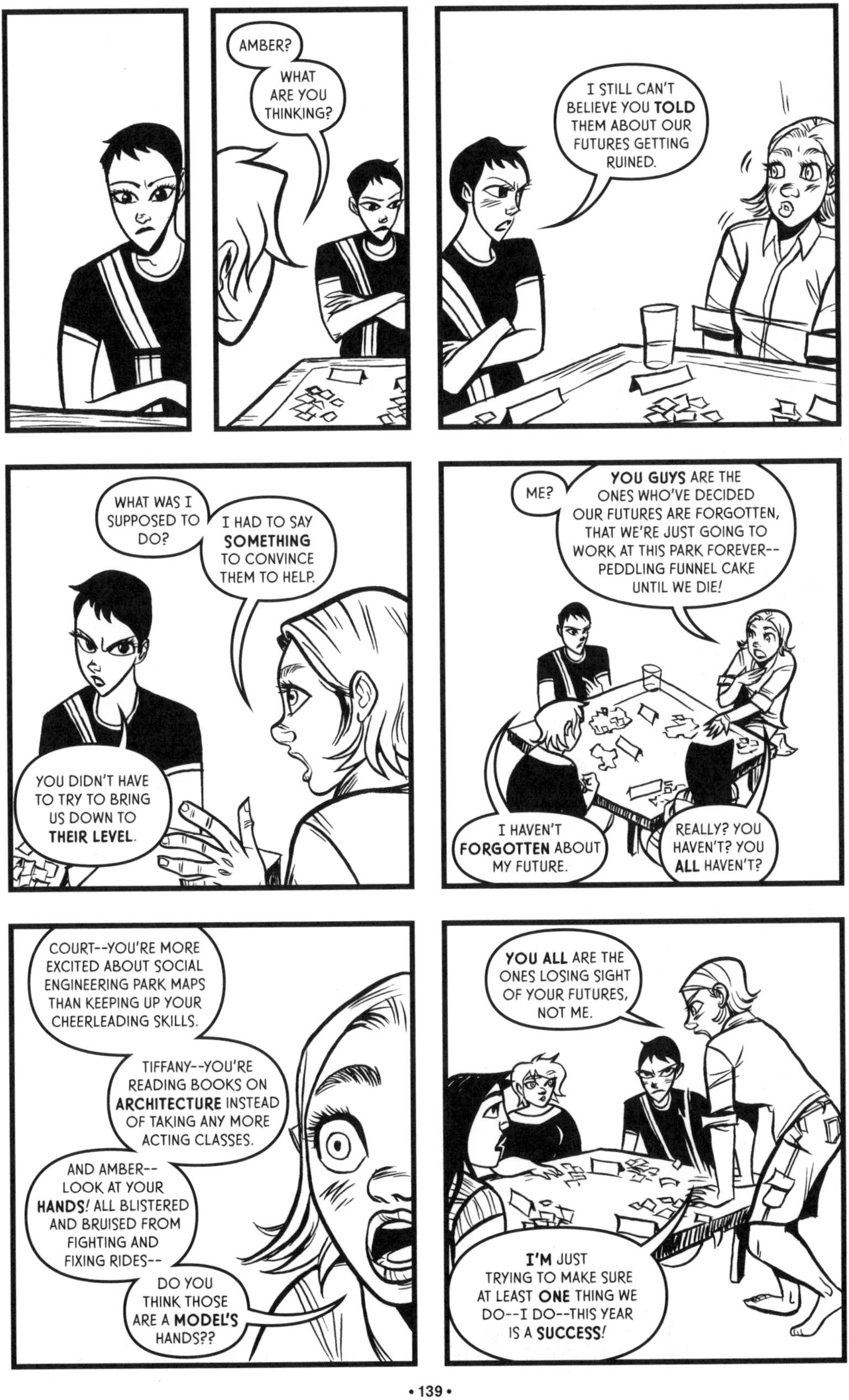
AMBER?
WHAT ARE YOU THINKING?
I STILL CAN'T BELIEVE YOU **TOLD** THEM ABOUT OUR FUTURES GETTING RUINED.
WHAT WAS I SUPPOSED TO DO?
I HAD TO SAY **SOMETHING** TO CONVINCE THEM TO HELP.
YOU DIDN'T HAVE TO TRY TO BRING US DOWN TO **THEIR LEVEL**.
ME?
YOU GUYS ARE THE ONES WHO'VE DECIDED OUR FUTURES ARE FORGOTTEN, THAT WE'RE JUST GOING TO WORK AT THIS PARK FOREVER-- PEDDLING FUNNEL CAKE UNTIL WE DIE!
I HAVEN'T **FORGOTTEN** ABOUT MY FUTURE.
REALLY? YOU HAVEN'T? YOU **ALL** HAVEN'T?
COURT--YOU'RE MORE EXCITED ABOUT SOCIAL ENGINEERING PARK MAPS THAN KEEPING UP YOUR CHEERLEADING SKILLS.
TIFFANY--YOU'RE READING BOOKS ON **ARCHITECTURE** INSTEAD OF TAKING ANY MORE ACTING CLASSES.
AND AMBER-- LOOK AT YOUR **HANDS**! ALL BLISTERED AND BRUISED FROM FIGHTING AND FIXING RIDES--
DO YOU THINK THOSE ARE A **MODEL'S** HANDS??
YOU ALL ARE THE ONES LOSING SIGHT OF YOUR FUTURES, NOT ME.
I'M JUST TRYING TO MAKE SURE AT LEAST **ONE** THING WE DO--I DO--THIS YEAR IS A **SUCCESS**!

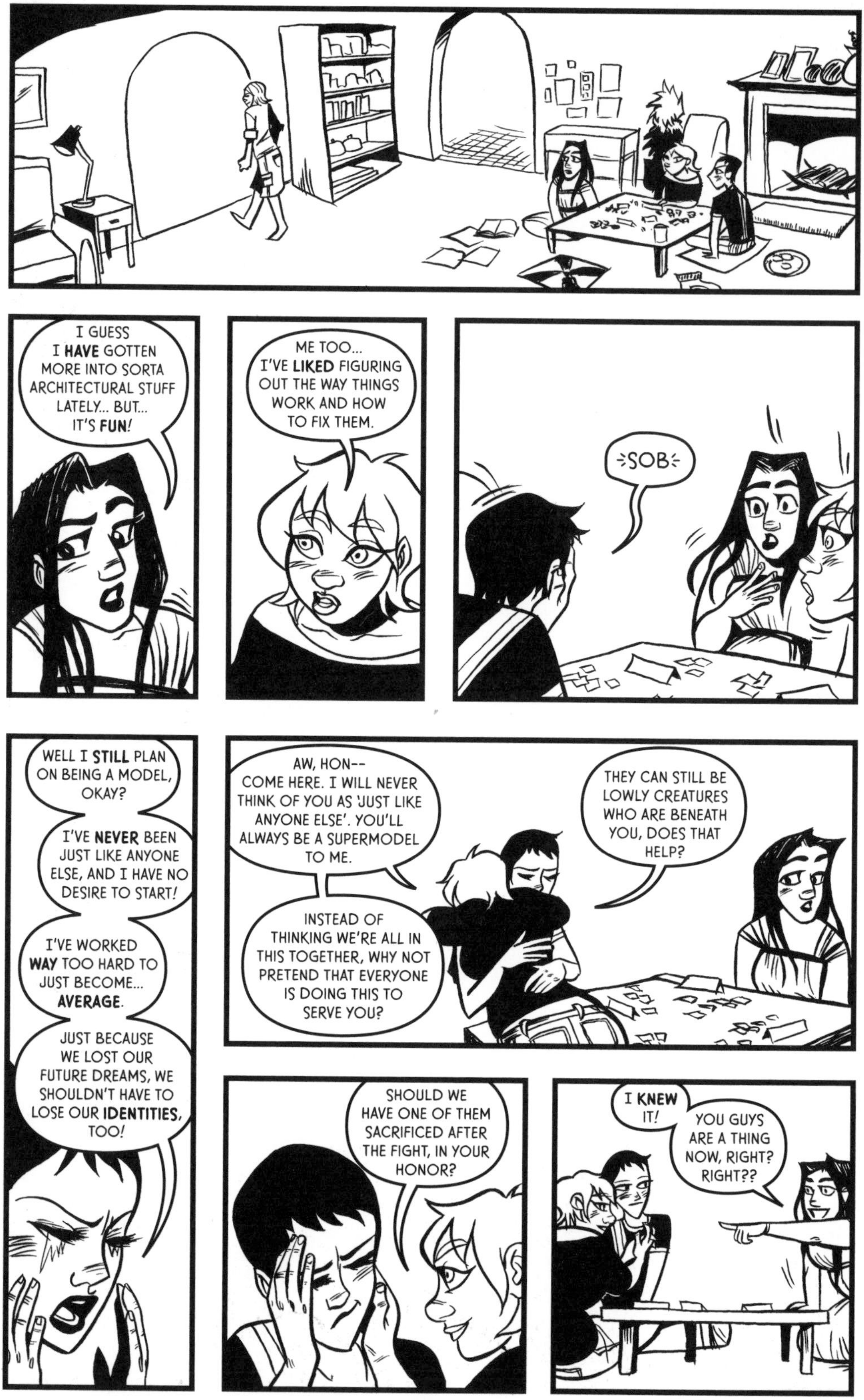
I GUESS I **HAVE** GOTTEN MORE INTO SORTA ARCHITECTURAL STUFF LATELY... BUT... IT'S **FUN**!
ME TOO... I'VE **LIKED** FIGURING OUT THE WAY THINGS WORK AND HOW TO FIX THEM.
SOB
WELL I **STILL** PLAN ON BEING A MODEL, OKAY?
I'VE **NEVER** BEEN JUST LIKE ANYONE ELSE, AND I HAVE NO DESIRE TO START!
I'VE WORKED **WAY** TOO HARD TO JUST BECOME... **AVERAGE**.
JUST BECAUSE WE LOST OUR FUTURE DREAMS, WE SHOULDN'T HAVE TO LOSE OUR **IDENTITIES**, TOO!
AW, HON-- COME HERE. I WILL NEVER THINK OF YOU AS 'JUST LIKE ANYONE ELSE'. YOU'LL ALWAYS BE A SUPERMODEL TO ME.
INSTEAD OF THINKING WE'RE ALL IN THIS TOGETHER, WHY NOT PRETEND THAT EVERYONE IS DOING THIS TO SERVE YOU?
THEY CAN STILL BE LOWLY CREATURES WHO ARE BENEATH YOU, DOES THAT HELP?
SHOULD WE HAVE ONE OF THEM SACRIFICED AFTER THE FIGHT, IN YOUR HONOR?
I **KNEW** IT!
YOU GUYS ARE A THING NOW, RIGHT? RIGHT??

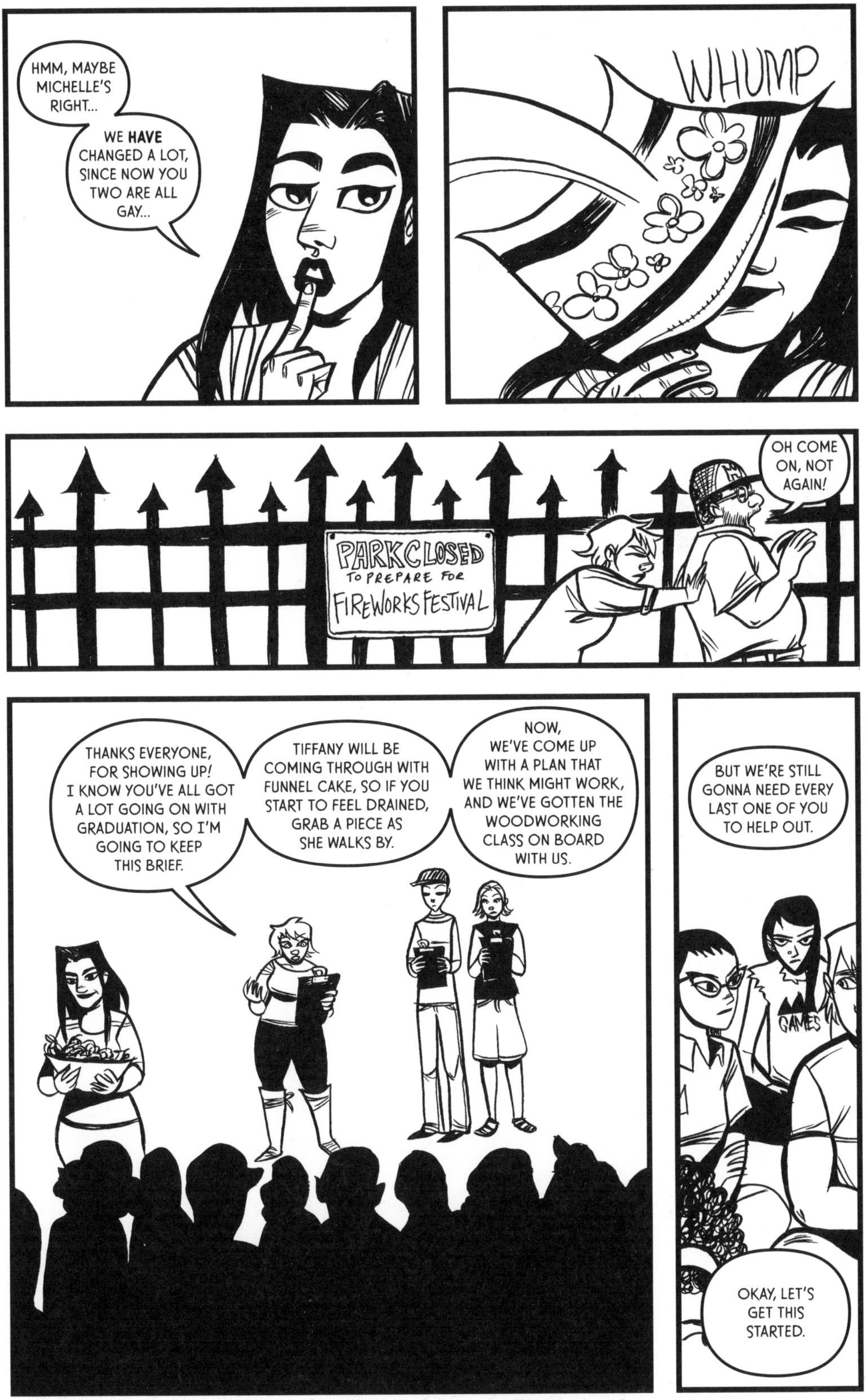
HMM, MAYBE MICHELLE'S RIGHT...
WE **HAVE** CHANGED A LOT, SINCE NOW YOU TWO ARE ALL GAY...
WHUMP
OH COME ON, NOT AGAIN!
PARK CLOSED TO PREPARE FOR FIREWORKS FESTIVAL
THANKS EVERYONE, FOR SHOWING UP! I KNOW YOU'VE ALL GOT A LOT GOING ON WITH GRADUATION, SO I'M GOING TO KEEP THIS BRIEF.
TIFFANY WILL BE COMING THROUGH WITH FUNNEL CAKE, SO IF YOU START TO FEEL DRAINED, GRAB A PIECE AS SHE WALKS BY.
NOW, WE'VE COME UP WITH A PLAN THAT WE THINK MIGHT WORK, AND WE'VE GOTTEN THE WOODWORKING CLASS ON BOARD WITH US.
BUT WE'RE STILL GONNA NEED EVERY LAST ONE OF YOU TO HELP OUT.
GAMES
OKAY, LET'S GET THIS STARTED.

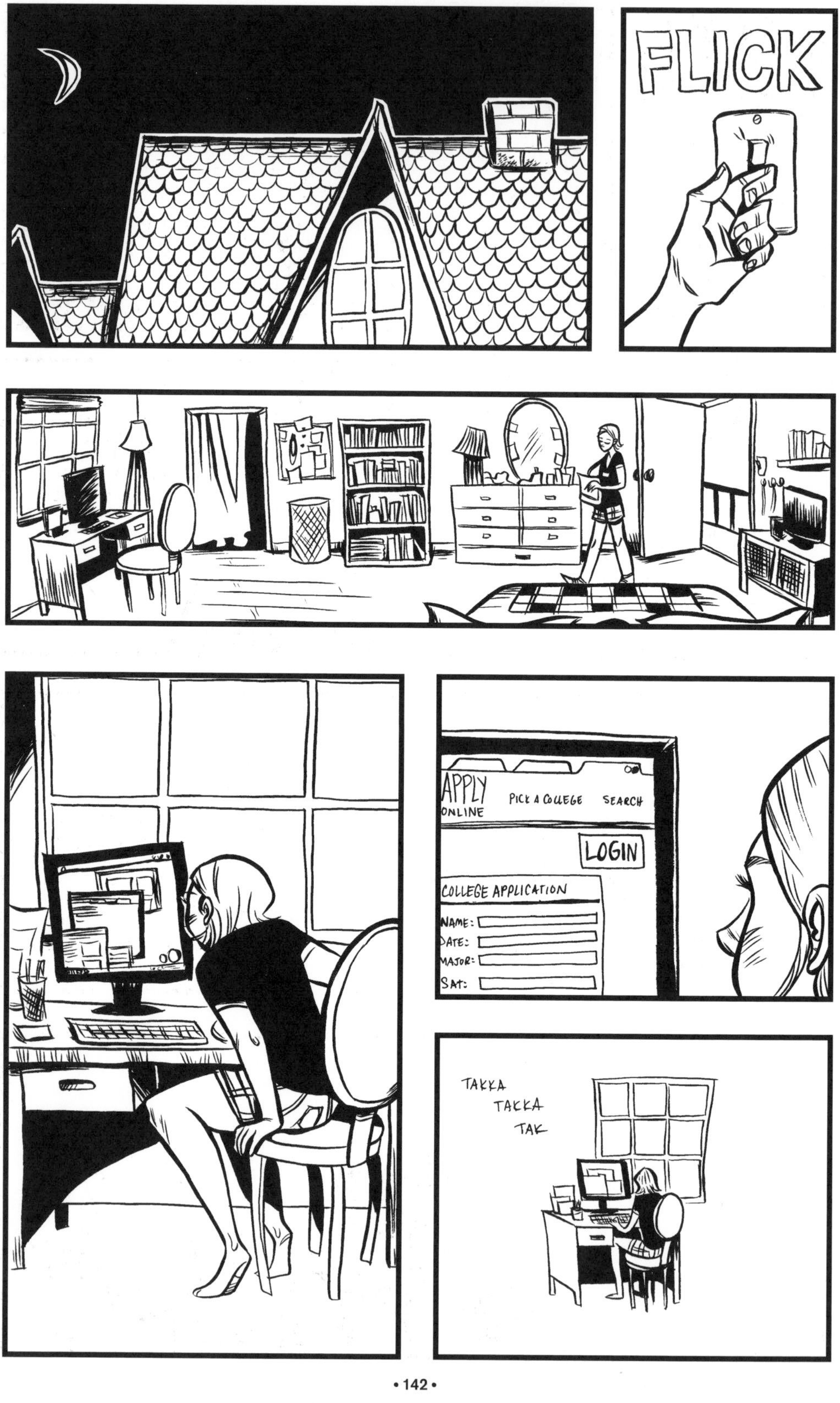
FLICK
APPLY
ONLINE
PICK A COLLEGE
SEARCH
LOGIN
COLLEGE APPLICATION
NAME:
DATE:
MAJOR:
SAT:
TAKKA
TAKKA
TAK

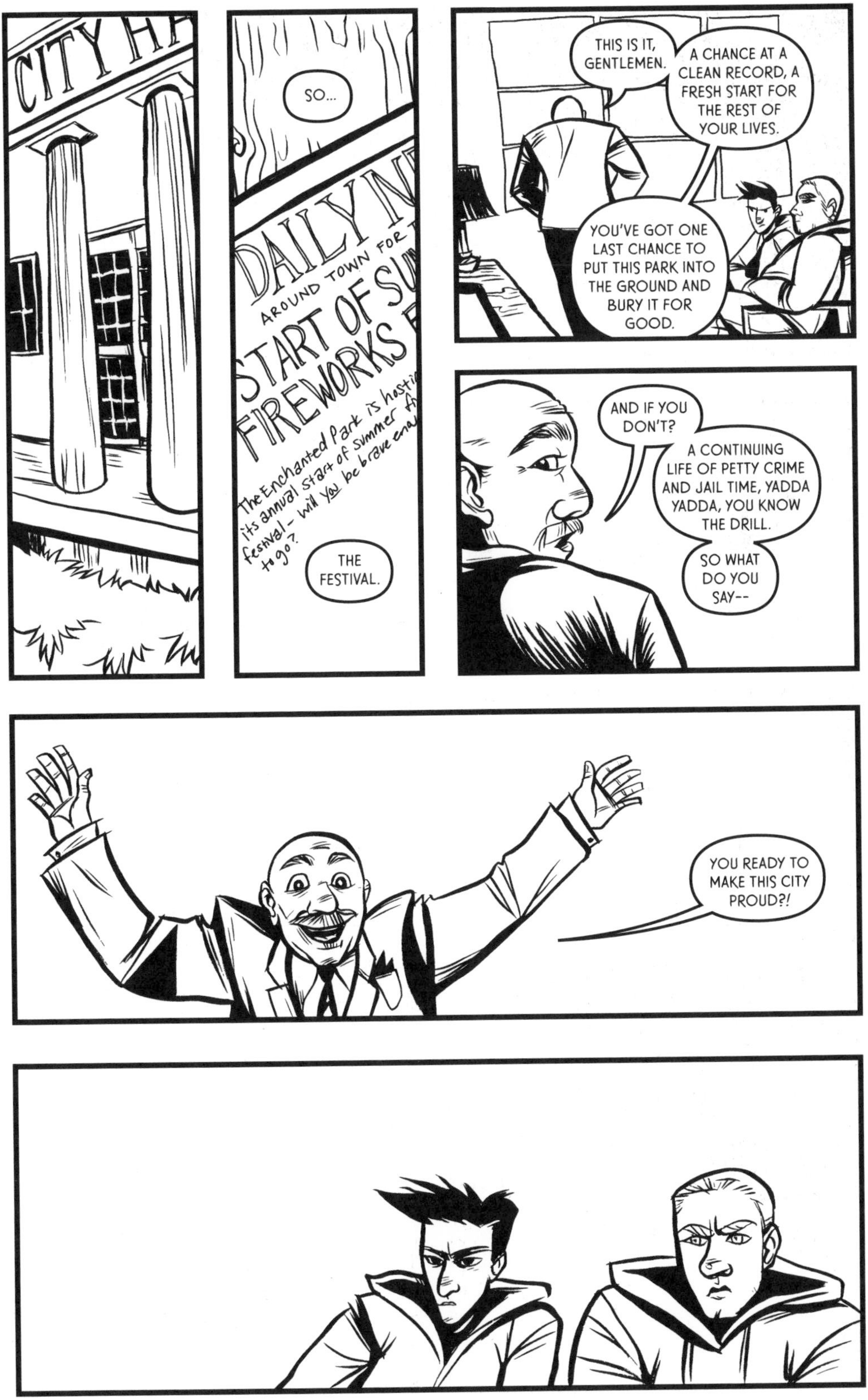
CITY H
SO...
DAILY N
AROUND TOWN FOR
START OF SU
FIREWORKS F
The Enchanted Park is hostin
its annual start of summer fe
festival - will you be brave enou
to go?
THE FESTIVAL.
THIS IS IT, GENTLEMEN.
A CHANCE AT A CLEAN RECORD, A FRESH START FOR THE REST OF YOUR LIVES.
YOU'VE GOT ONE LAST CHANCE TO PUT THIS PARK INTO THE GROUND AND BURY IT FOR GOOD.
AND IF YOU DON'T?
A CONTINUING LIFE OF PETTY CRIME AND JAIL TIME, YADDA YADDA, YOU KNOW THE DRILL.
SO WHAT DO YOU SAY--
YOU READY TO MAKE THIS CITY PROUD?!

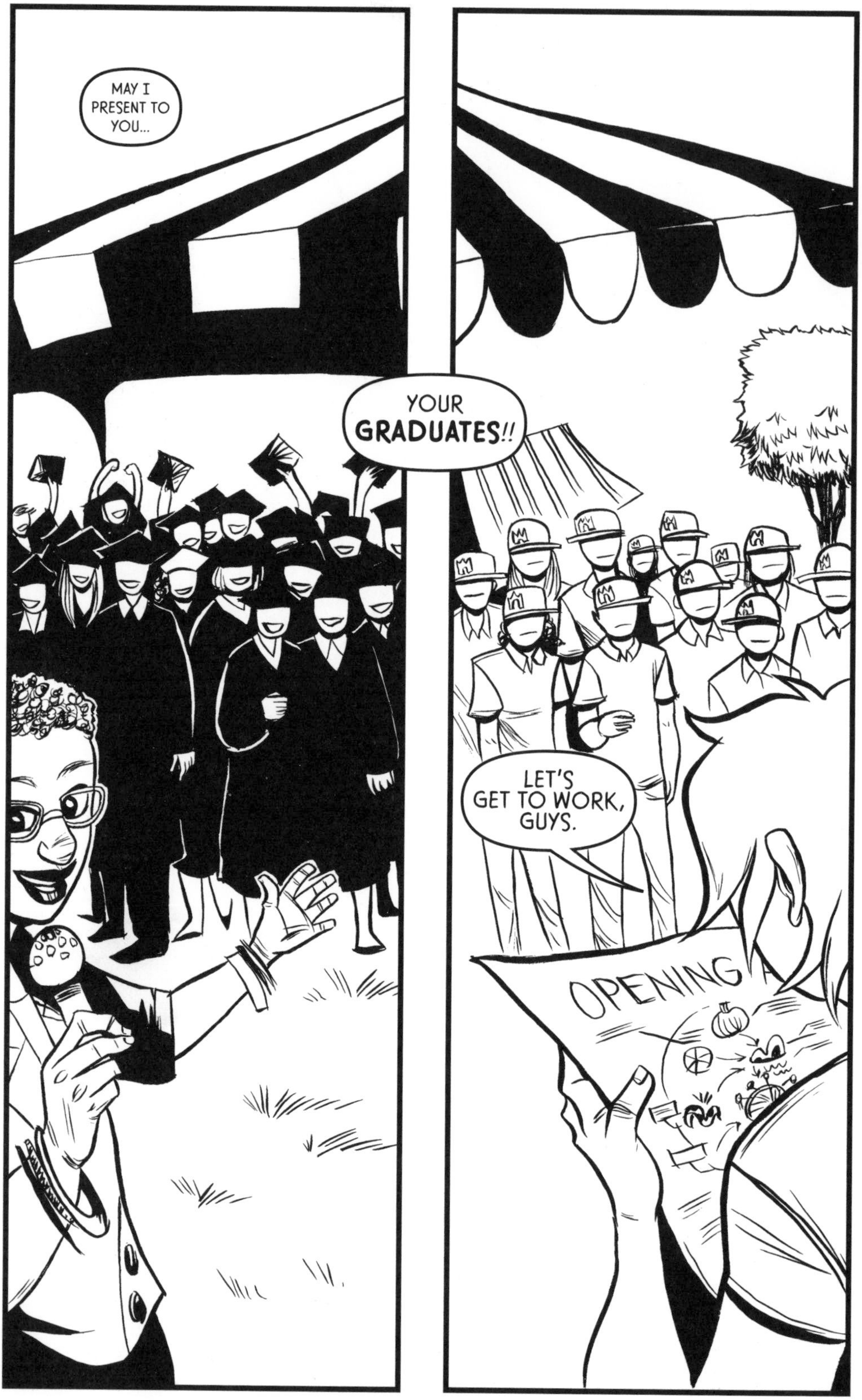
MAY I PRESENT TO YOU...
YOUR GRADUATES!!
LET'S GET TO WORK, GUYS.
OPENING

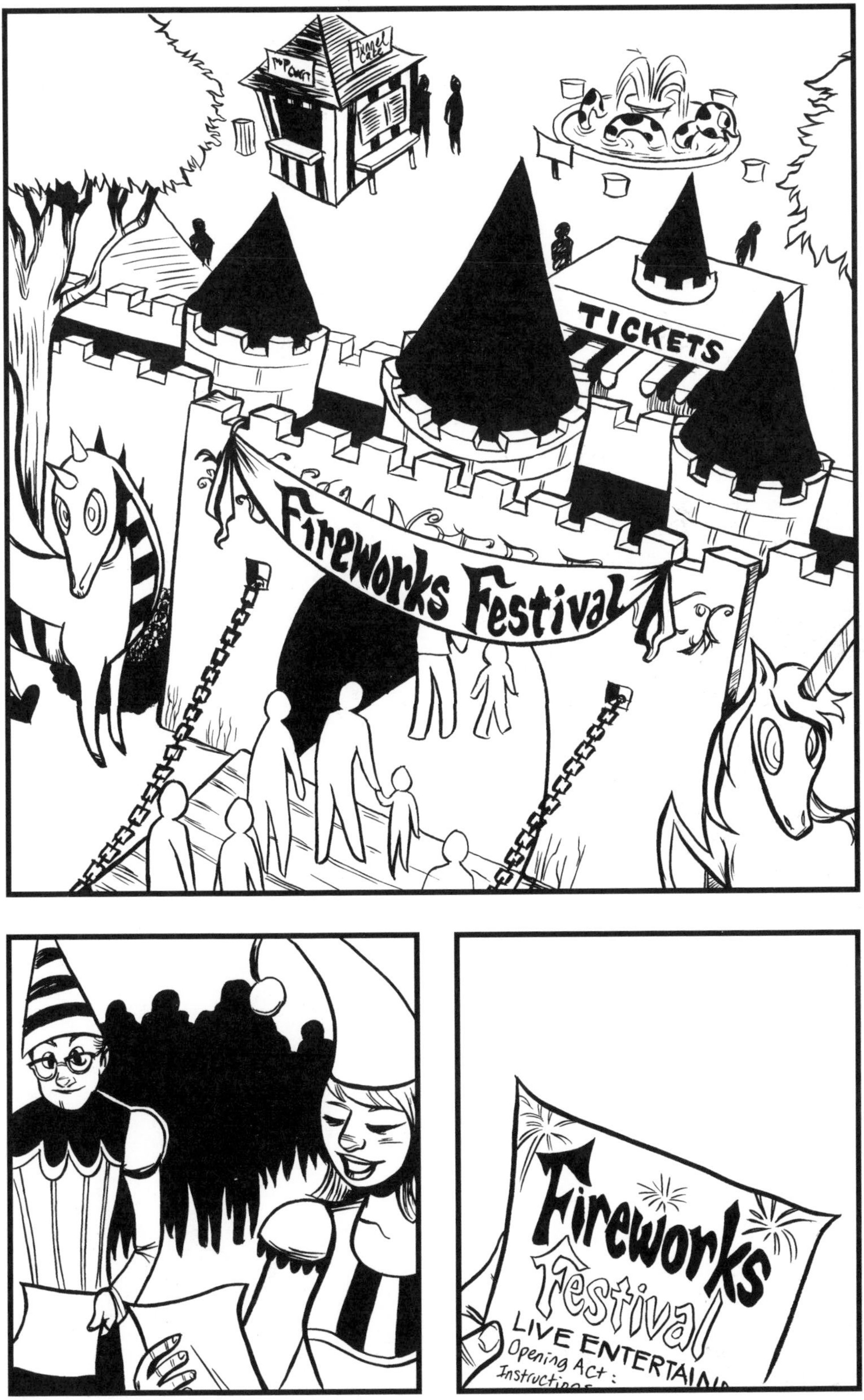
TICKETS
Fireworks Festival
Fireworks Festival
LIVE ENTERTAIN
Opening Act :

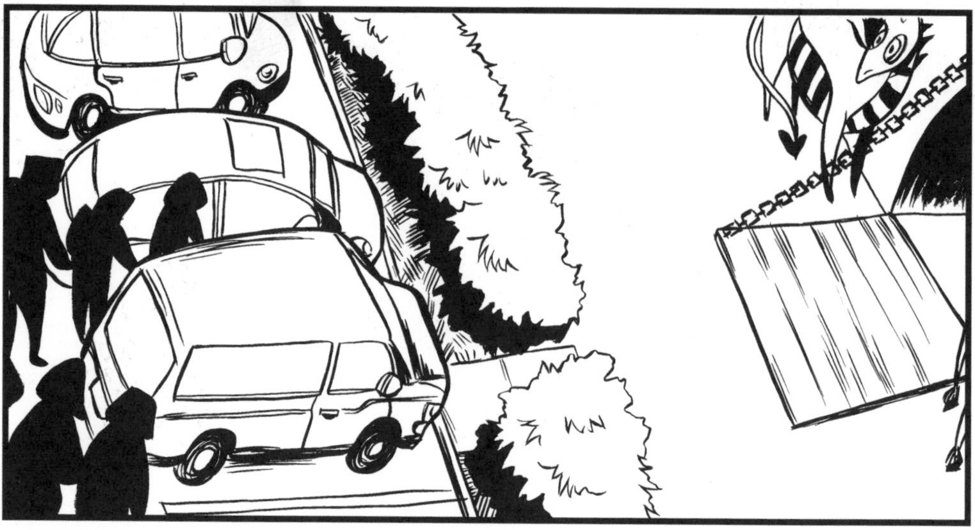

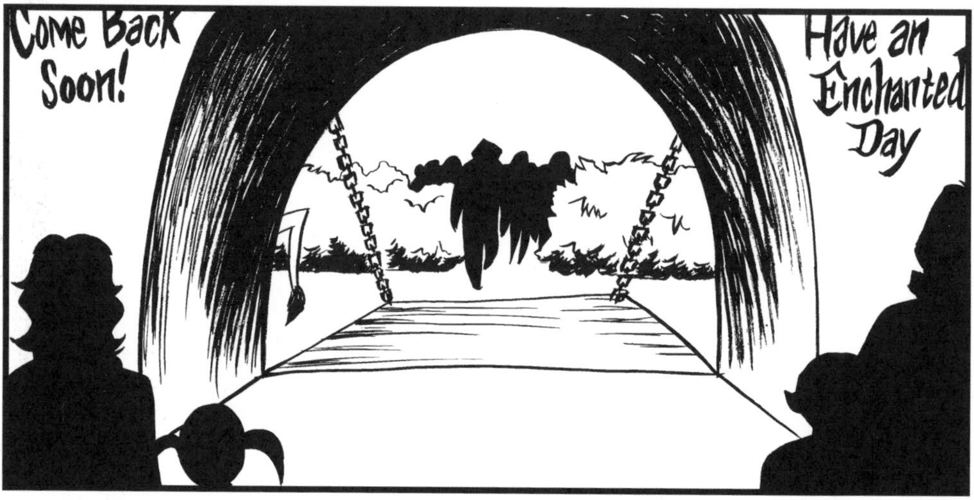
Come Back Soon!
Have an Enchanted Day

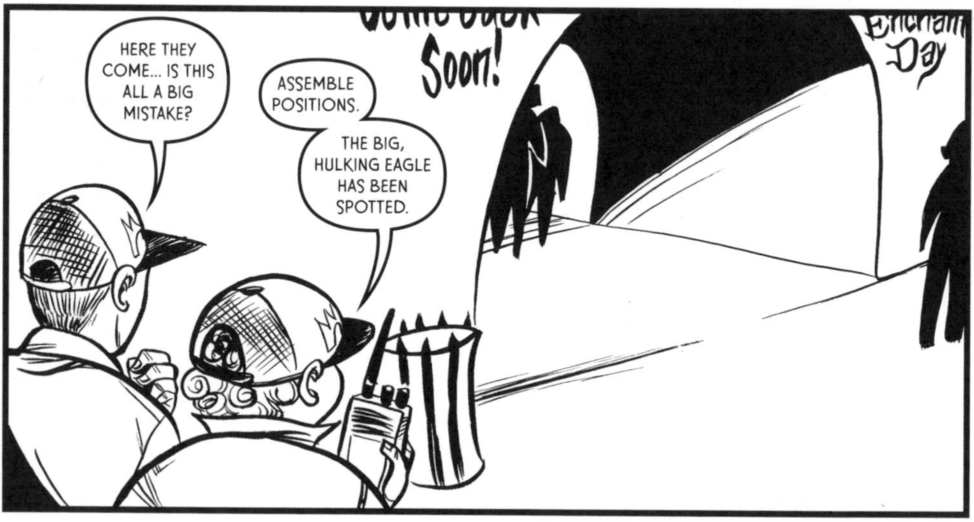
Soon!
Day
HERE THEY COME... IS THIS ALL A BIG MISTAKE?
ASSEMBLE POSITIONS.
THE BIG, HULKING EAGLE HAS BEEN SPOTTED.

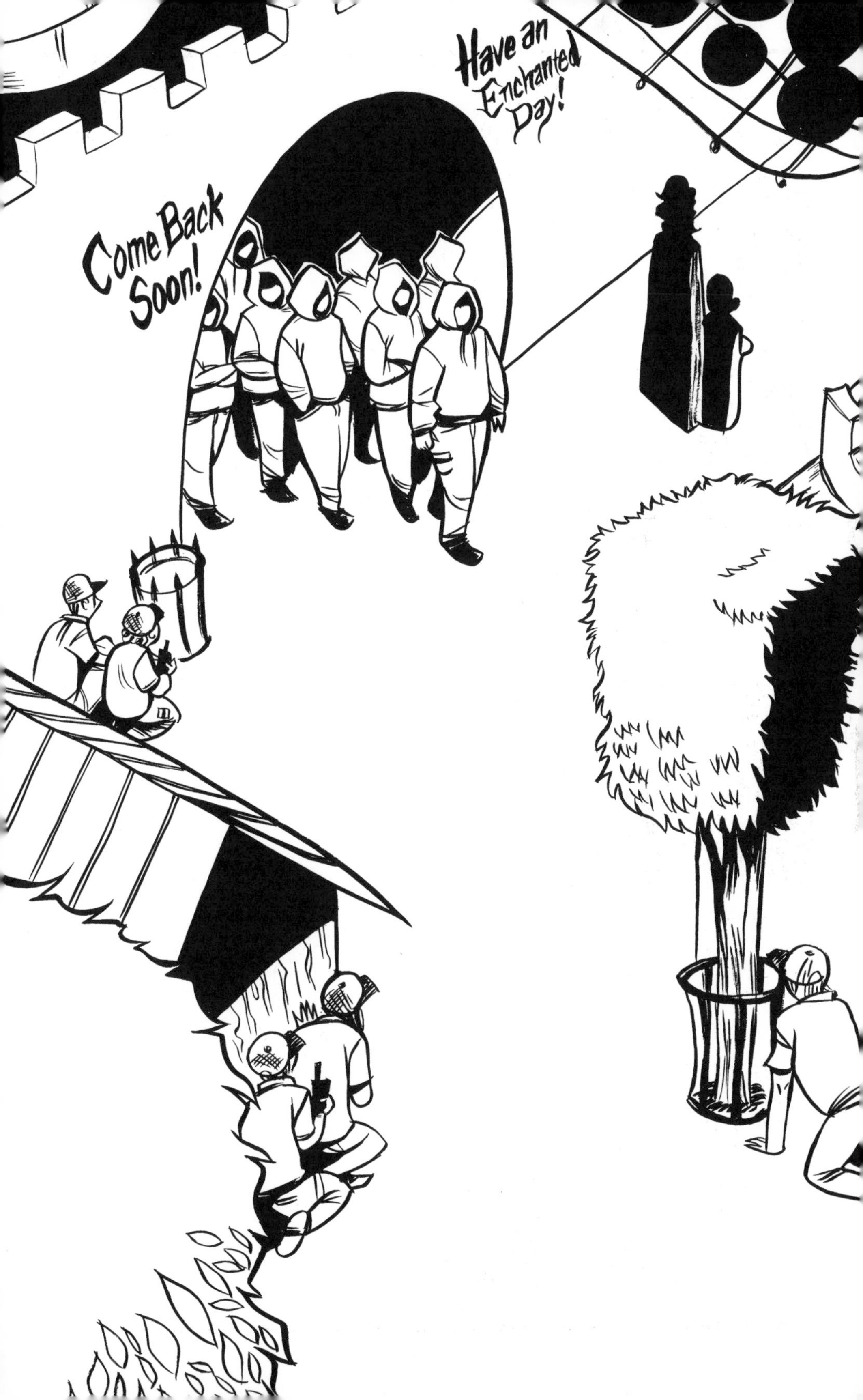
Have an Enchanted Day!
Come Back Soon!

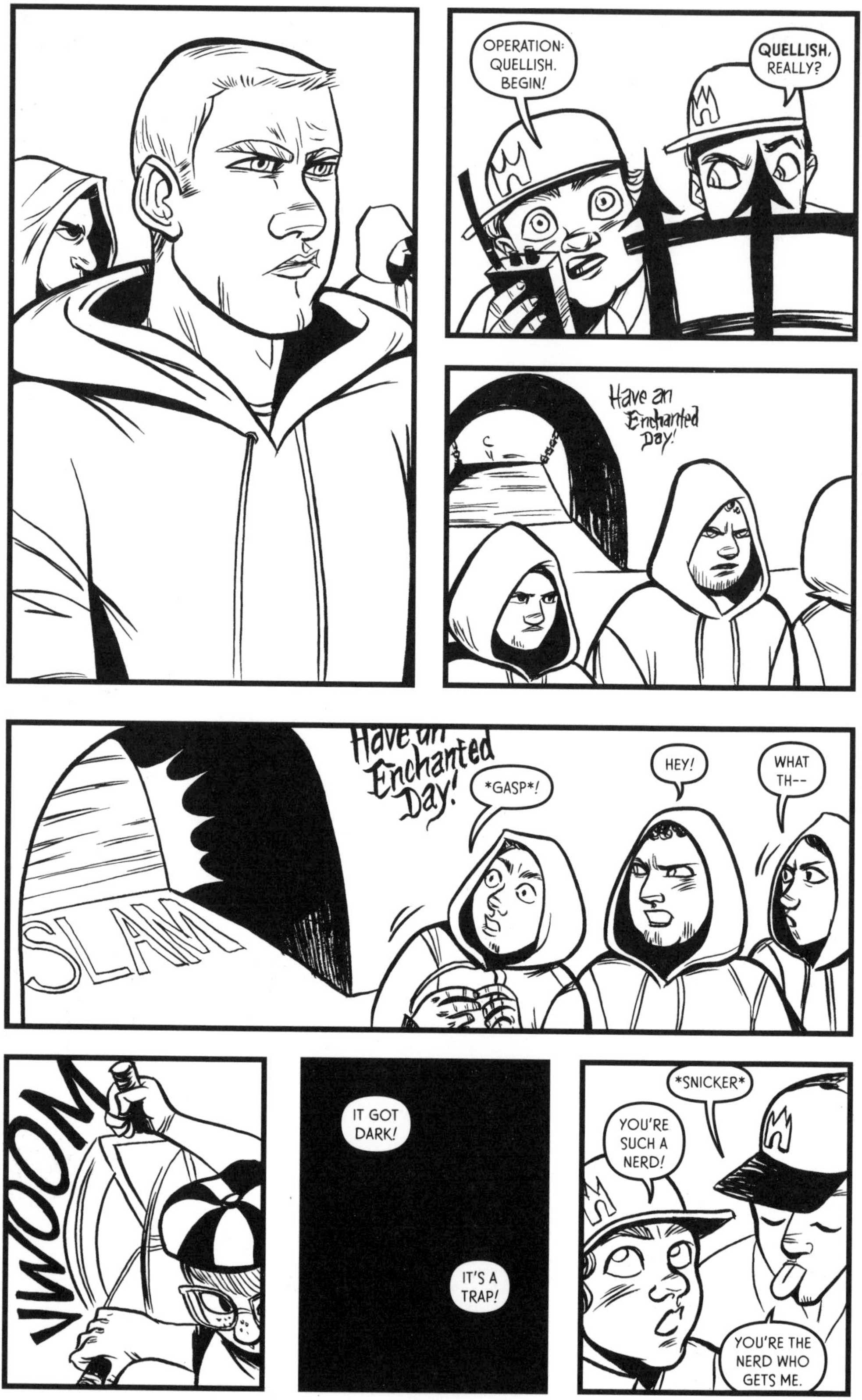
OPERATION: QUELLISH. BEGIN!
QUELLISH, REALLY?
Have an Enchanted Day!
Have an Enchanted Day!
SLAM
GASP!
HEY!
WHAT TH--
VWOOM
IT GOT DARK!
IT'S A TRAP!
YOU'RE SUCH A NERD!
SNICKER
YOU'RE THE NERD WHO GETS ME.

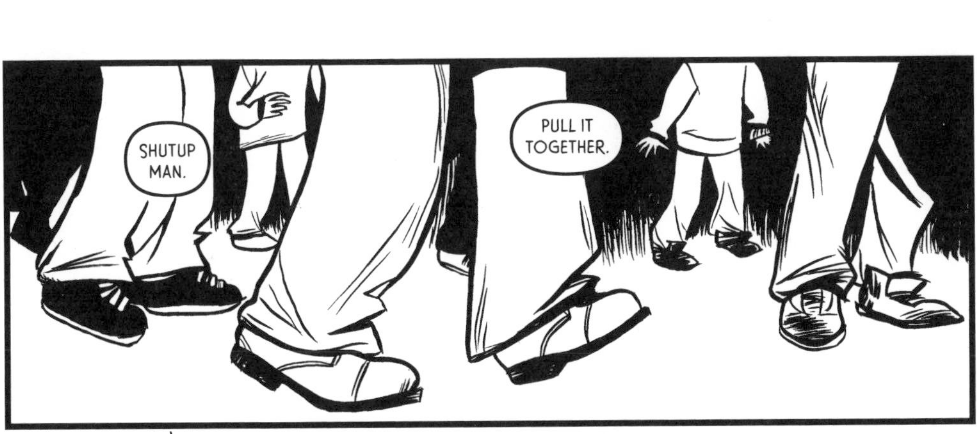
SHUTUP MAN.
PULL IT TOGETHER.

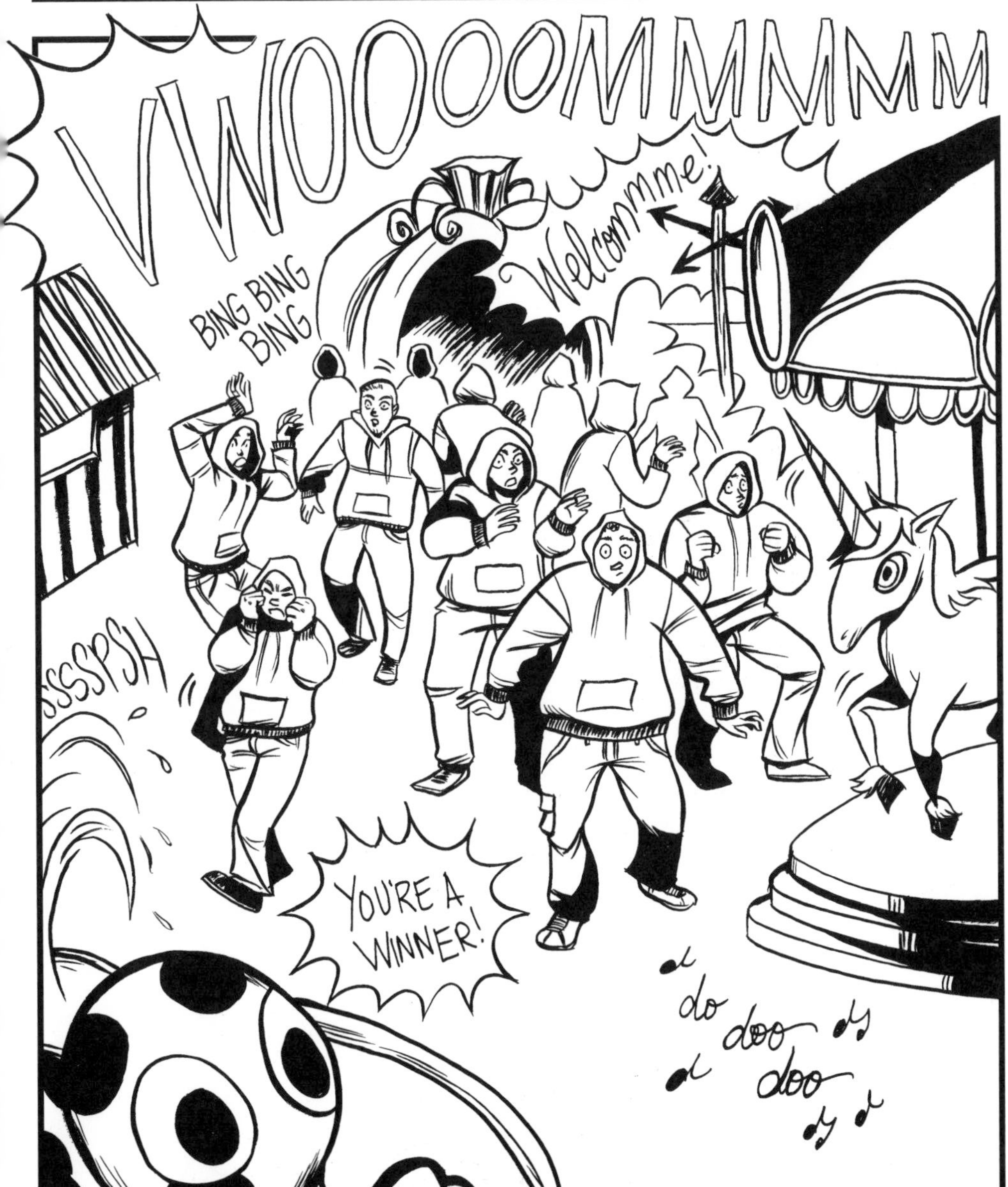
VWOOOOOMMMMMM
Welcommme!
BING BING BING
SSSSPSH
YOU'RE A WINNER!
do doo doo

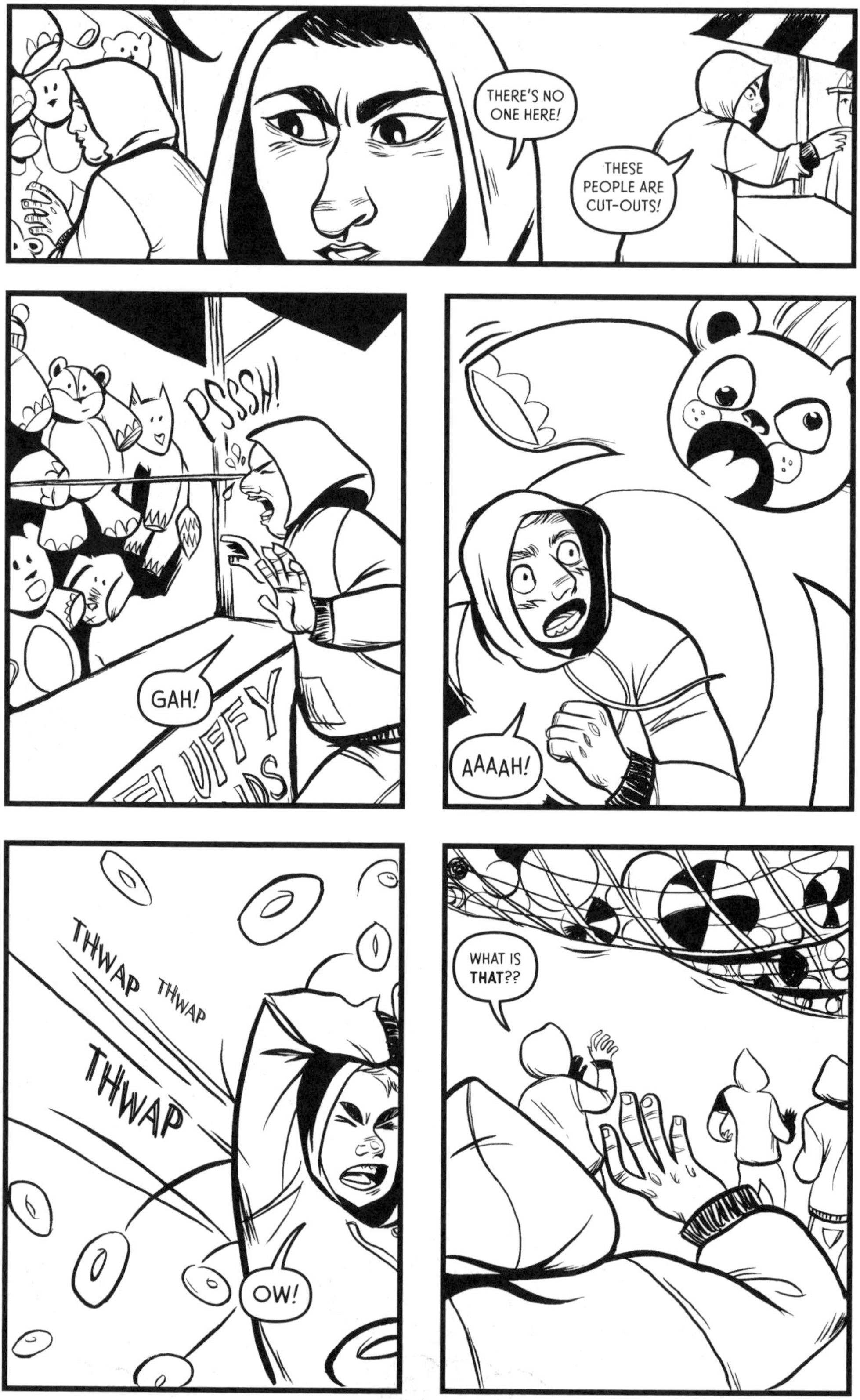
THERE'S NO ONE HERE!
THESE PEOPLE ARE CUT-OUTS!
PSSSH!
GAH!
AAAAH!
THWAP THWAP
THWAP
OW!
WHAT IS THAT??

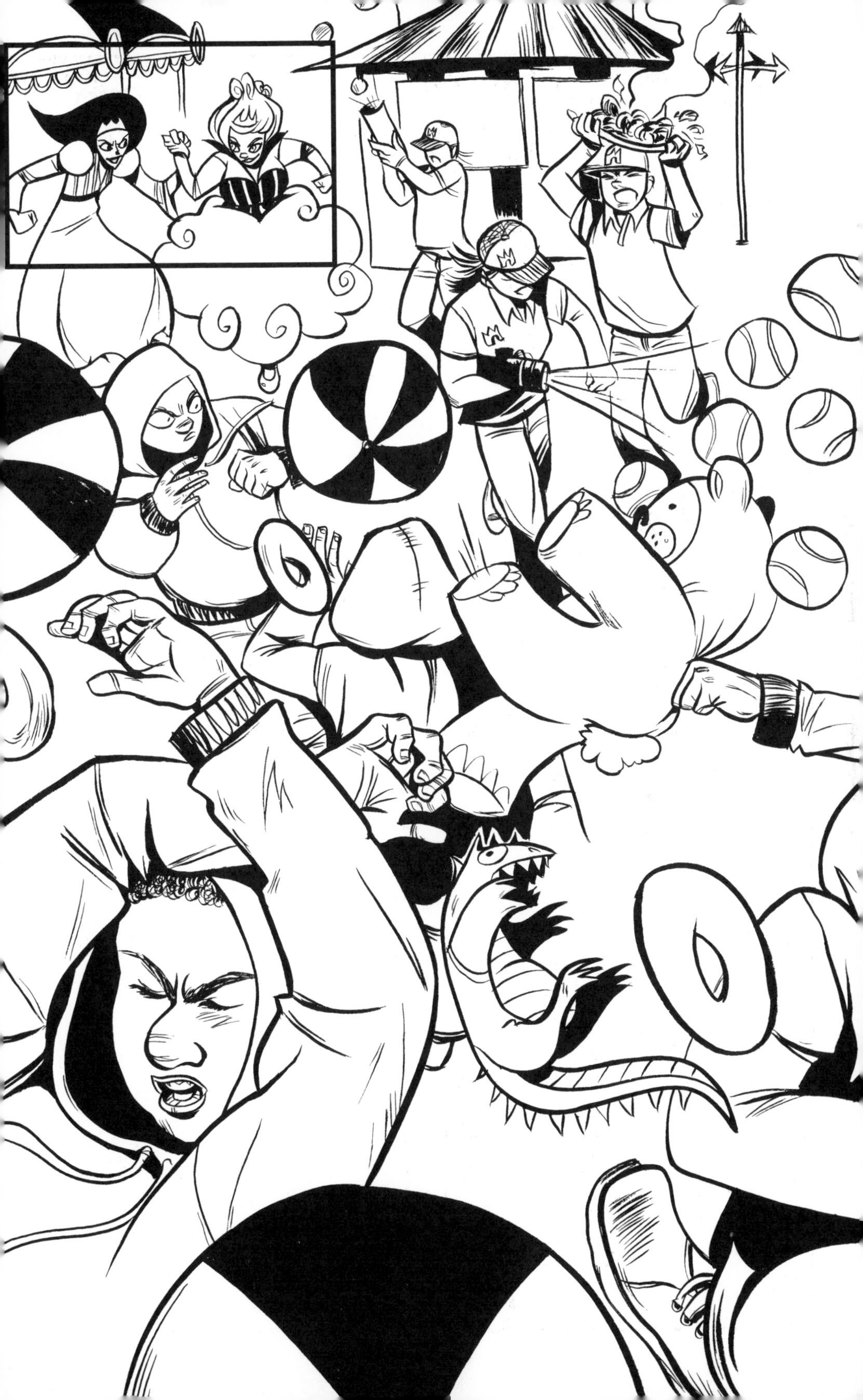

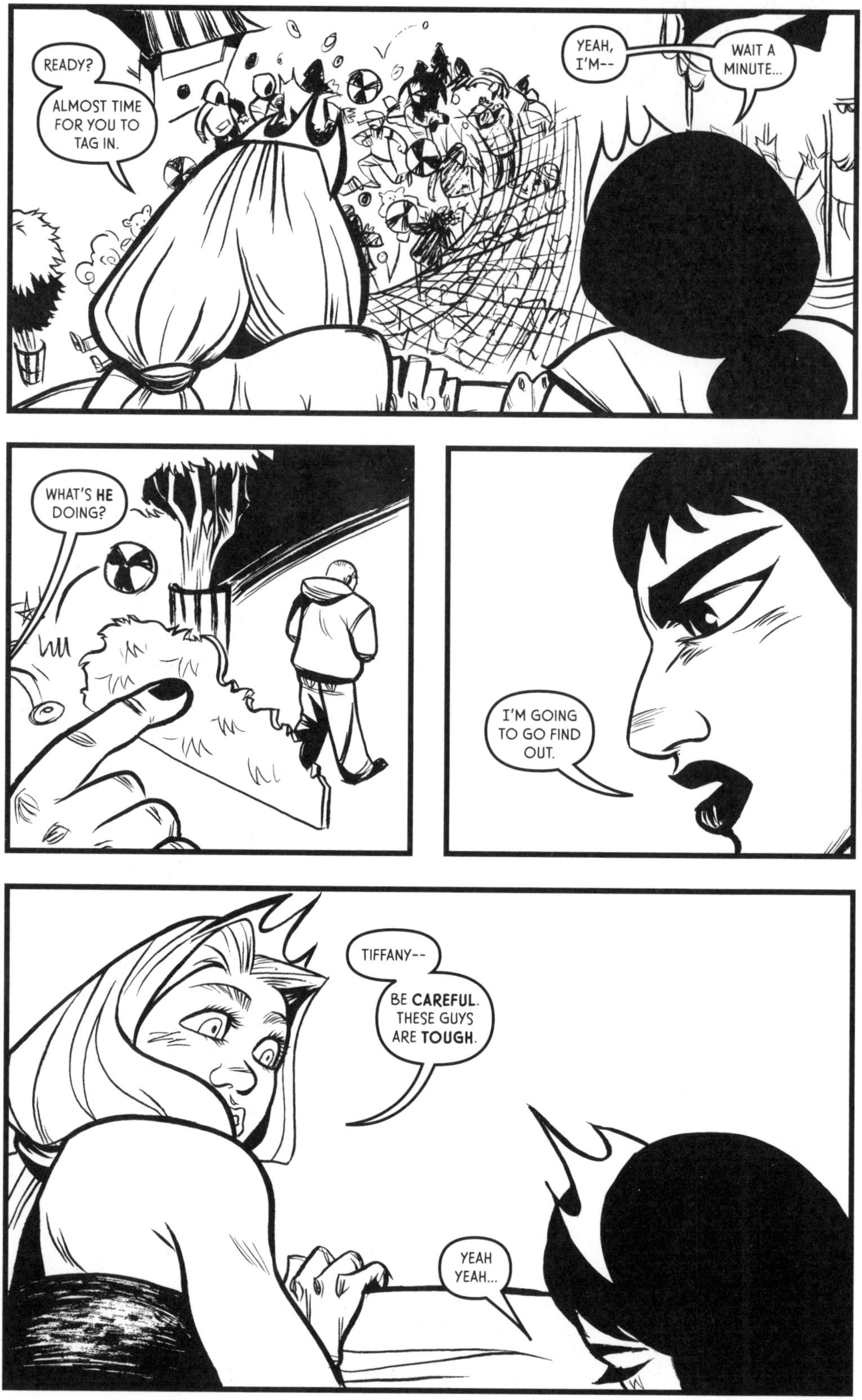
READY?
ALMOST TIME FOR YOU TO TAG IN.
YEAH, I'M--
WAIT A MINUTE...
WHAT'S **HE** DOING?
I'M GOING TO GO FIND OUT.
TIFFANY--
BE **CAREFUL**. THESE GUYS ARE **TOUGH**.
YEAH YEAH...

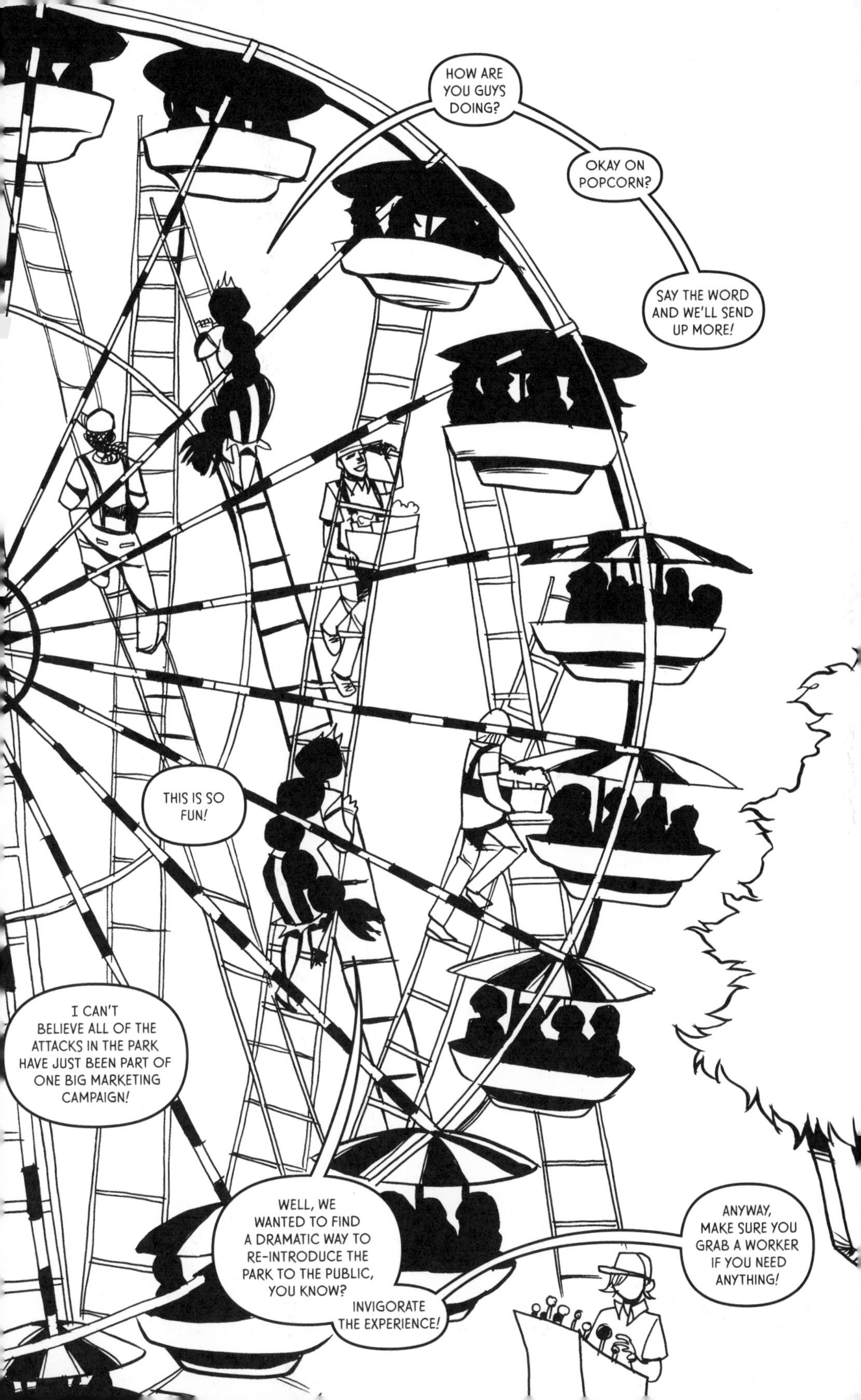
HOW ARE YOU GUYS DOING?
OKAY ON POPCORN?
SAY THE WORD AND WE'LL SEND UP MORE!
THIS IS SO FUN!
I CAN'T BELIEVE ALL OF THE ATTACKS IN THE PARK HAVE JUST BEEN PART OF ONE BIG MARKETING CAMPAIGN!
WELL, WE WANTED TO FIND A DRAMATIC WAY TO RE-INTRODUCE THE PARK TO THE PUBLIC, YOU KNOW?
INVIGORATE THE EXPERIENCE!
ANYWAY, MAKE SURE YOU GRAB A WORKER IF YOU NEED ANYTHING!

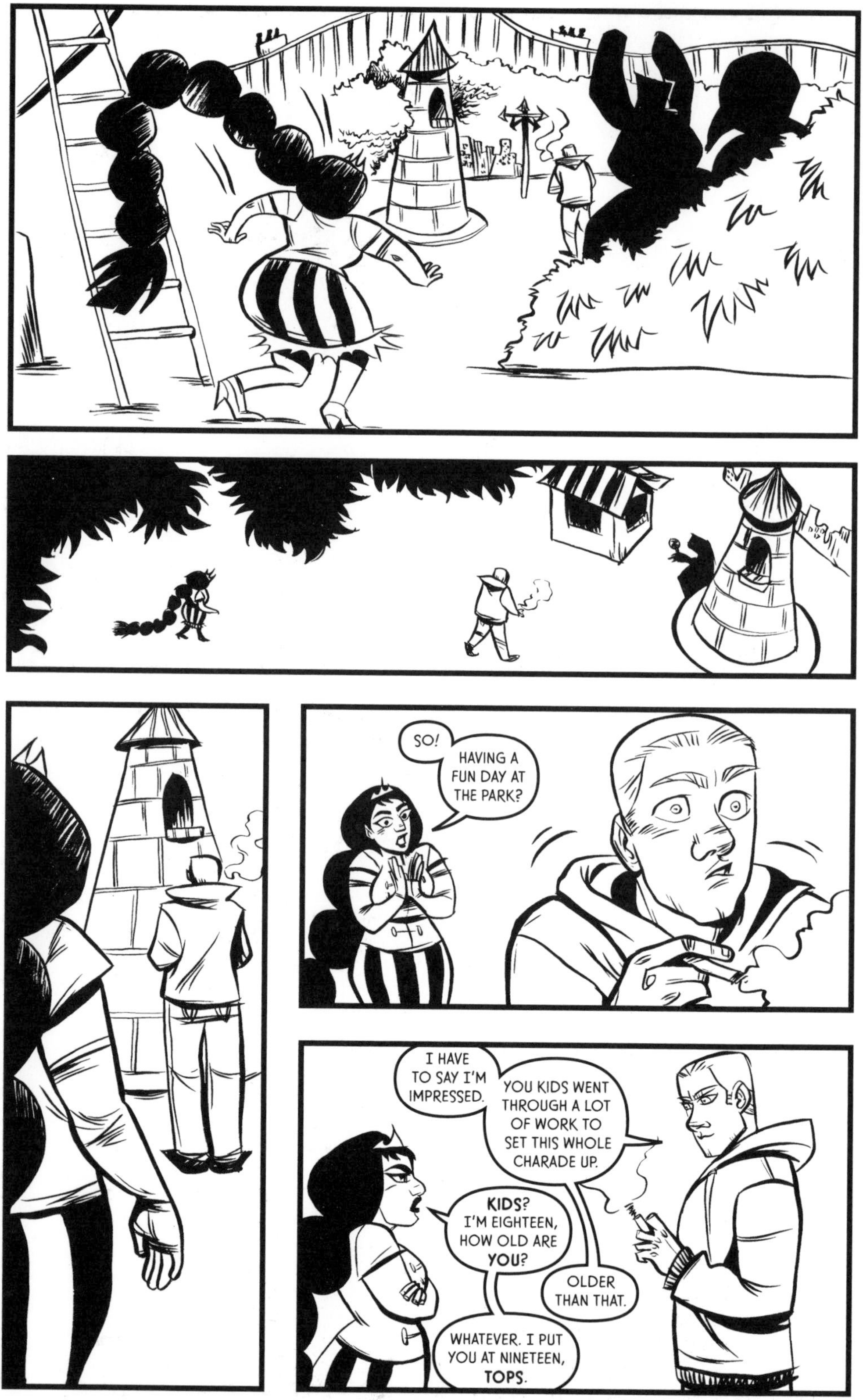
SO!
HAVING A FUN DAY AT THE PARK?
I HAVE TO SAY I'M IMPRESSED.
YOU KIDS WENT THROUGH A LOT OF WORK TO SET THIS WHOLE CHARADE UP.
KIDS? I'M EIGHTEEN, HOW OLD ARE YOU?
OLDER THAN THAT.
WHATEVER. I PUT YOU AT NINETEEN, TOPS.

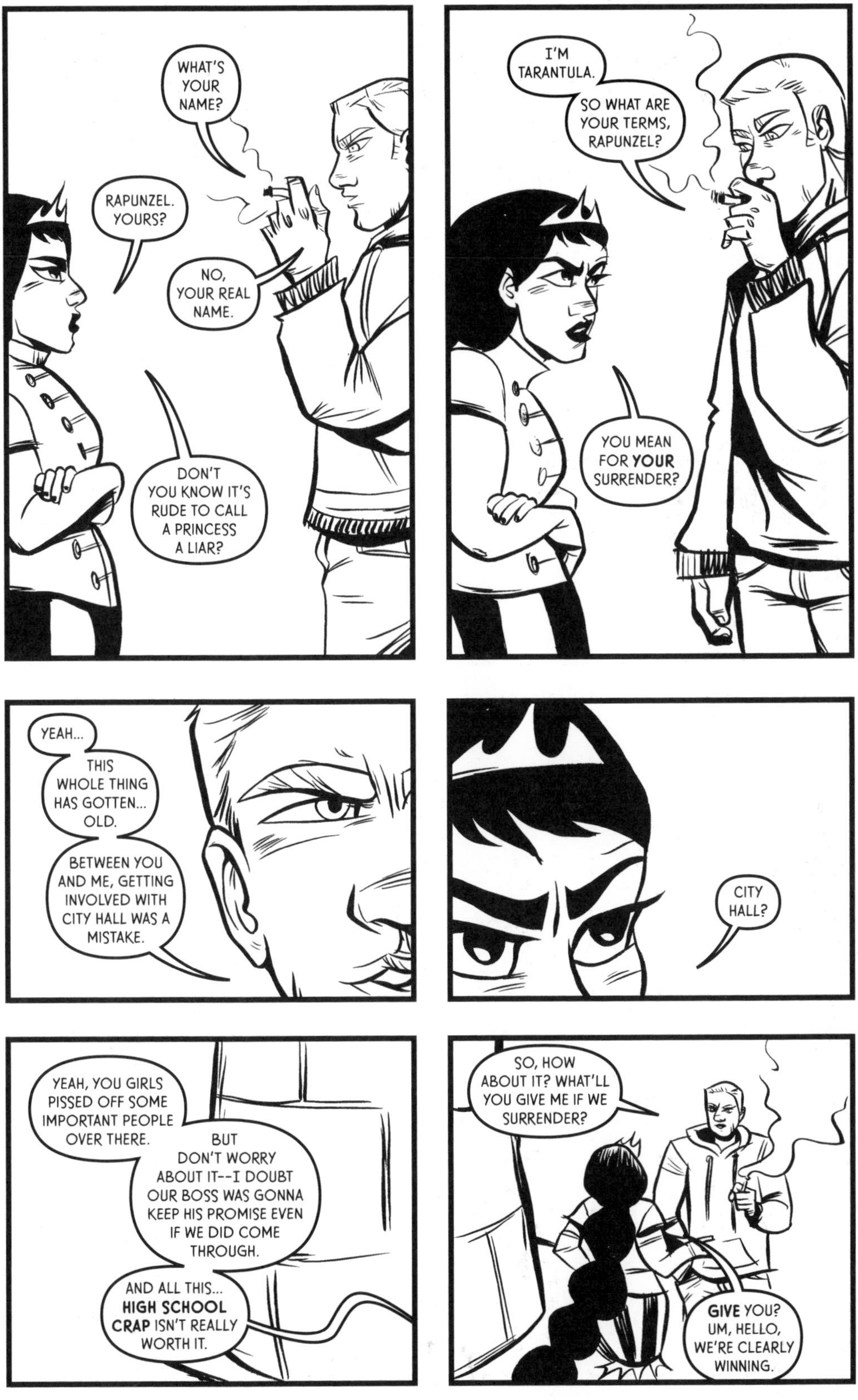
WHAT'S YOUR NAME?
RAPUNZEL. YOURS?
NO, YOUR REAL NAME.
DON'T YOU KNOW IT'S RUDE TO CALL A PRINCESS A LIAR?
I'M TARANTULA.
SO WHAT ARE YOUR TERMS, RAPUNZEL?
YOU MEAN FOR **YOUR** SURRENDER?
YEAH...
THIS WHOLE THING HAS GOTTEN... OLD.
BETWEEN YOU AND ME, GETTING INVOLVED WITH CITY HALL WAS A MISTAKE.
CITY HALL?
YEAH, YOU GIRLS PISSED OFF SOME IMPORTANT PEOPLE OVER THERE.
BUT DON'T WORRY ABOUT IT--I DOUBT OUR BOSS WAS GONNA KEEP HIS PROMISE EVEN IF WE DID COME THROUGH.
AND ALL THIS... **HIGH SCHOOL CRAP** ISN'T REALLY WORTH IT.
SO, HOW ABOUT IT? WHAT'LL YOU GIVE ME IF WE SURRENDER?
GIVE YOU? UM, HELLO, WE'RE CLEARLY WINNING.

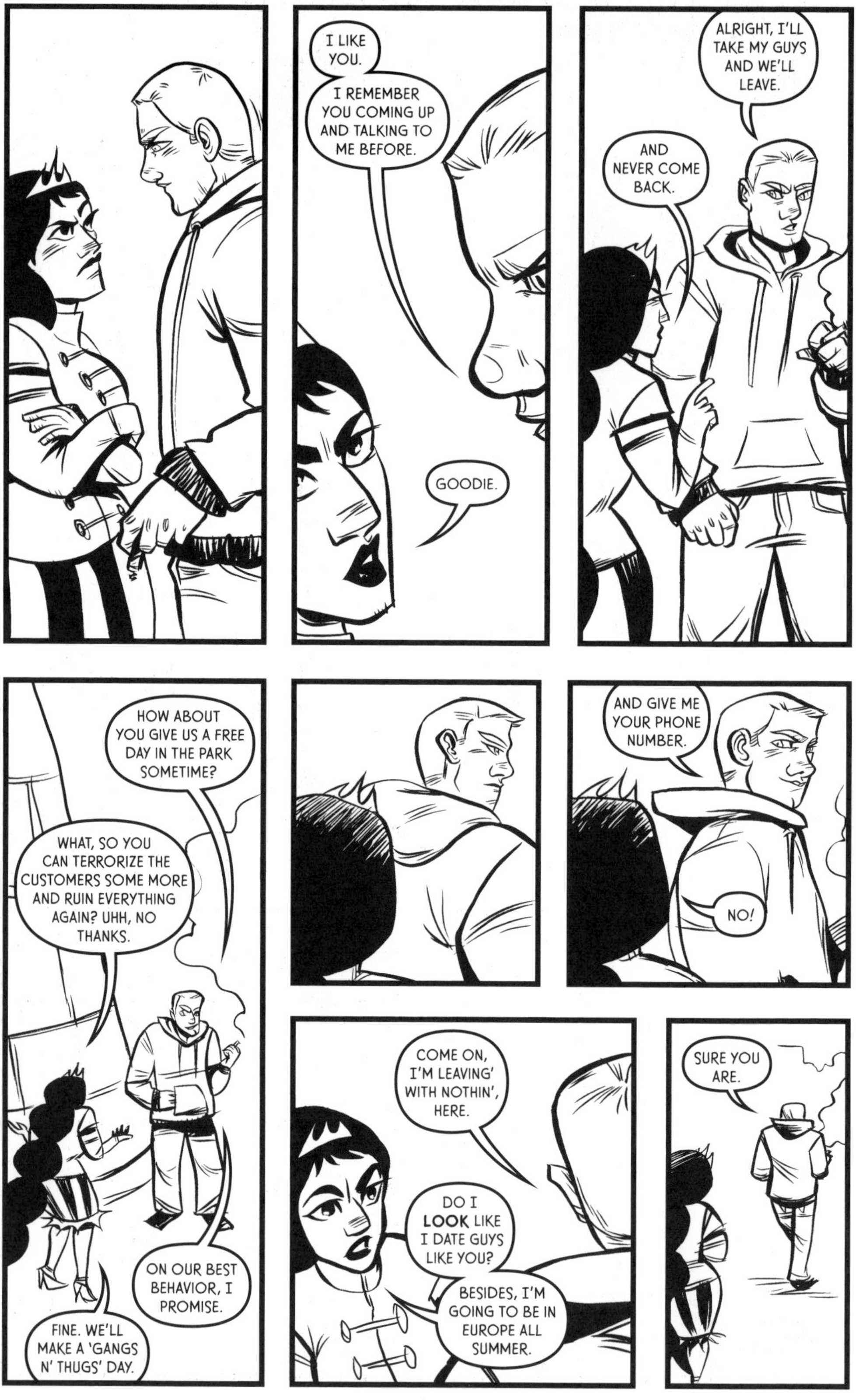
I LIKE YOU.
I REMEMBER YOU COMING UP AND TALKING TO ME BEFORE.
GOODIE.
ALRIGHT, I'LL TAKE MY GUYS AND WE'LL LEAVE.
AND NEVER COME BACK.
HOW ABOUT YOU GIVE US A FREE DAY IN THE PARK SOMETIME?
WHAT, SO YOU CAN TERRORIZE THE CUSTOMERS SOME MORE AND RUIN EVERYTHING AGAIN? UHH, NO THANKS.
ON OUR BEST BEHAVIOR, I PROMISE.
FINE. WE'LL MAKE A 'GANGS N' THUGS' DAY.
AND GIVE ME YOUR PHONE NUMBER.
NO!
COME ON, I'M LEAVING' WITH NOTHIN', HERE.
DO I **LOOK** LIKE I DATE GUYS LIKE YOU?
BESIDES, I'M GOING TO BE IN EUROPE ALL SUMMER.
SURE YOU ARE.

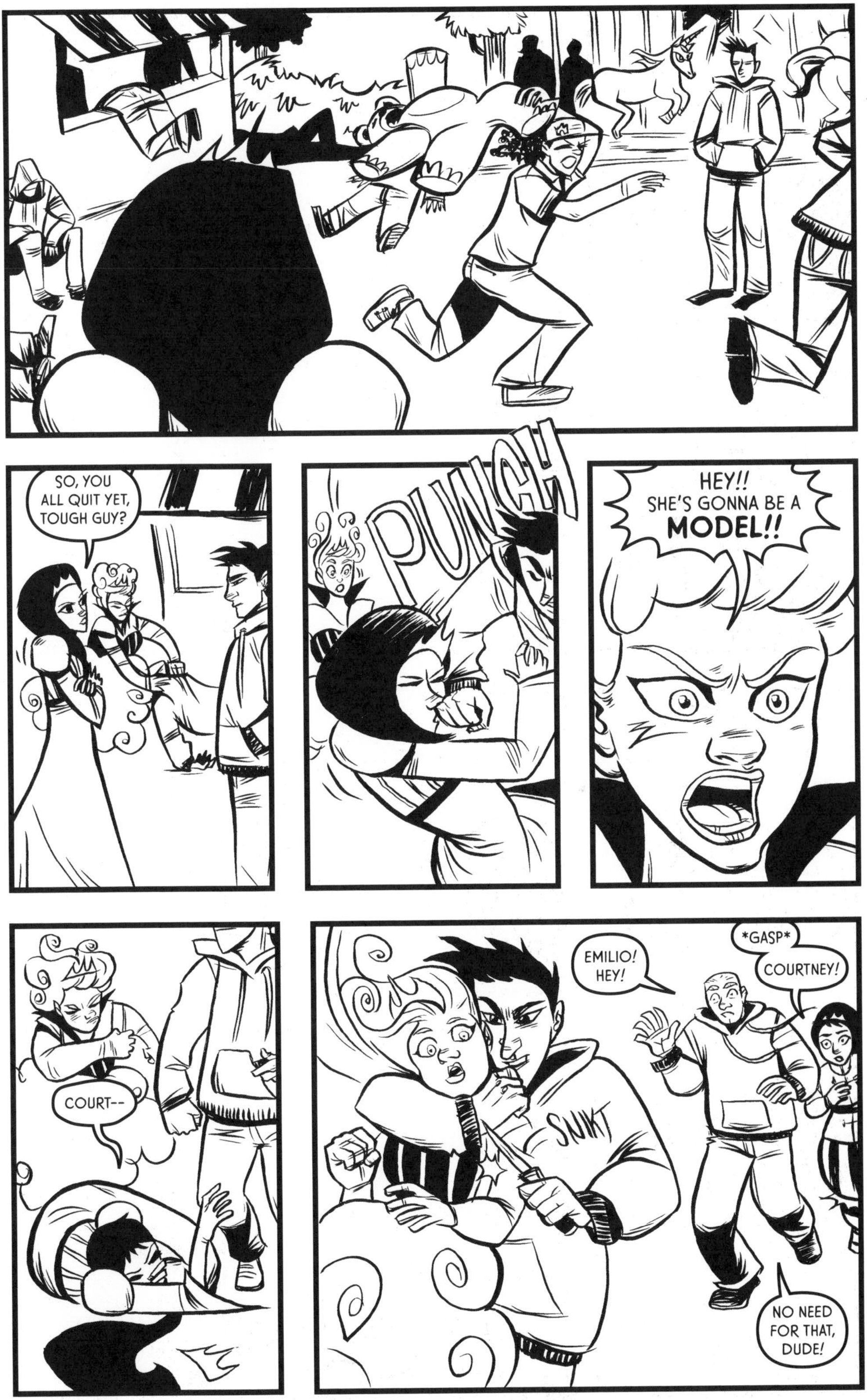
SO, YOU ALL QUIT YET, TOUGH GUY?
PUNCH
HEY!! SHE'S GONNA BE A MODEL!!
COURT--
SNIKT
EMILIO! HEY!
GASP
COURTNEY!
NO NEED FOR THAT, DUDE!

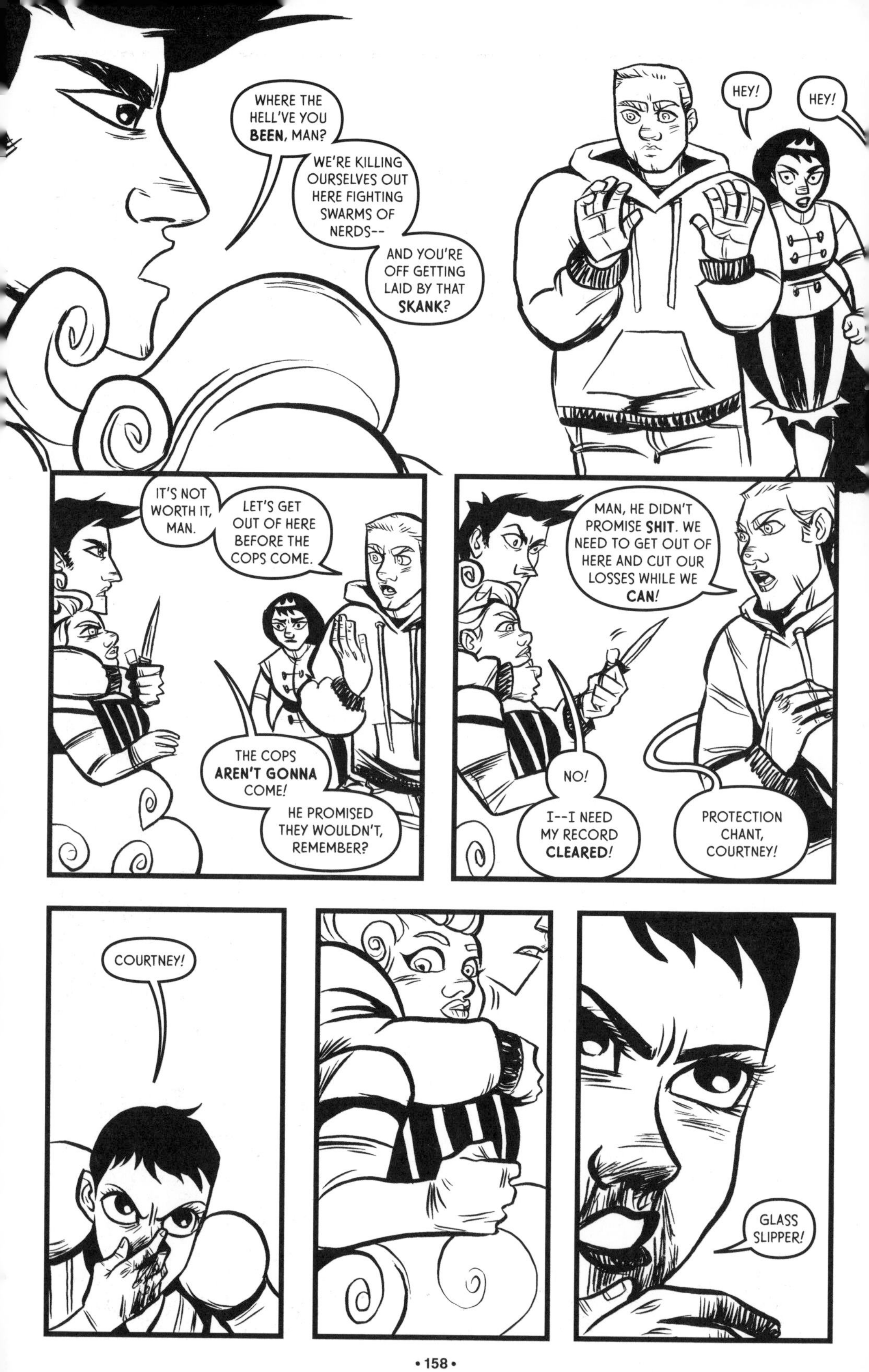
WHERE THE HELL'VE YOU BEEN, MAN?
WE'RE KILLING OURSELVES OUT HERE FIGHTING SWARMS OF NERDS--
AND YOU'RE OFF GETTING LAID BY THAT SKANK?
HEY!
HEY!
IT'S NOT WORTH IT, MAN.
LET'S GET OUT OF HERE BEFORE THE COPS COME.
THE COPS AREN'T GONNA COME!
HE PROMISED THEY WOULDN'T, REMEMBER?
MAN, HE DIDN'T PROMISE SHIT. WE NEED TO GET OUT OF HERE AND CUT OUR LOSSES WHILE WE CAN!
NO!
I--I NEED MY RECORD CLEARED!
PROTECTION CHANT, COURTNEY!
COURTNEY!
GLASS SLIPPER!

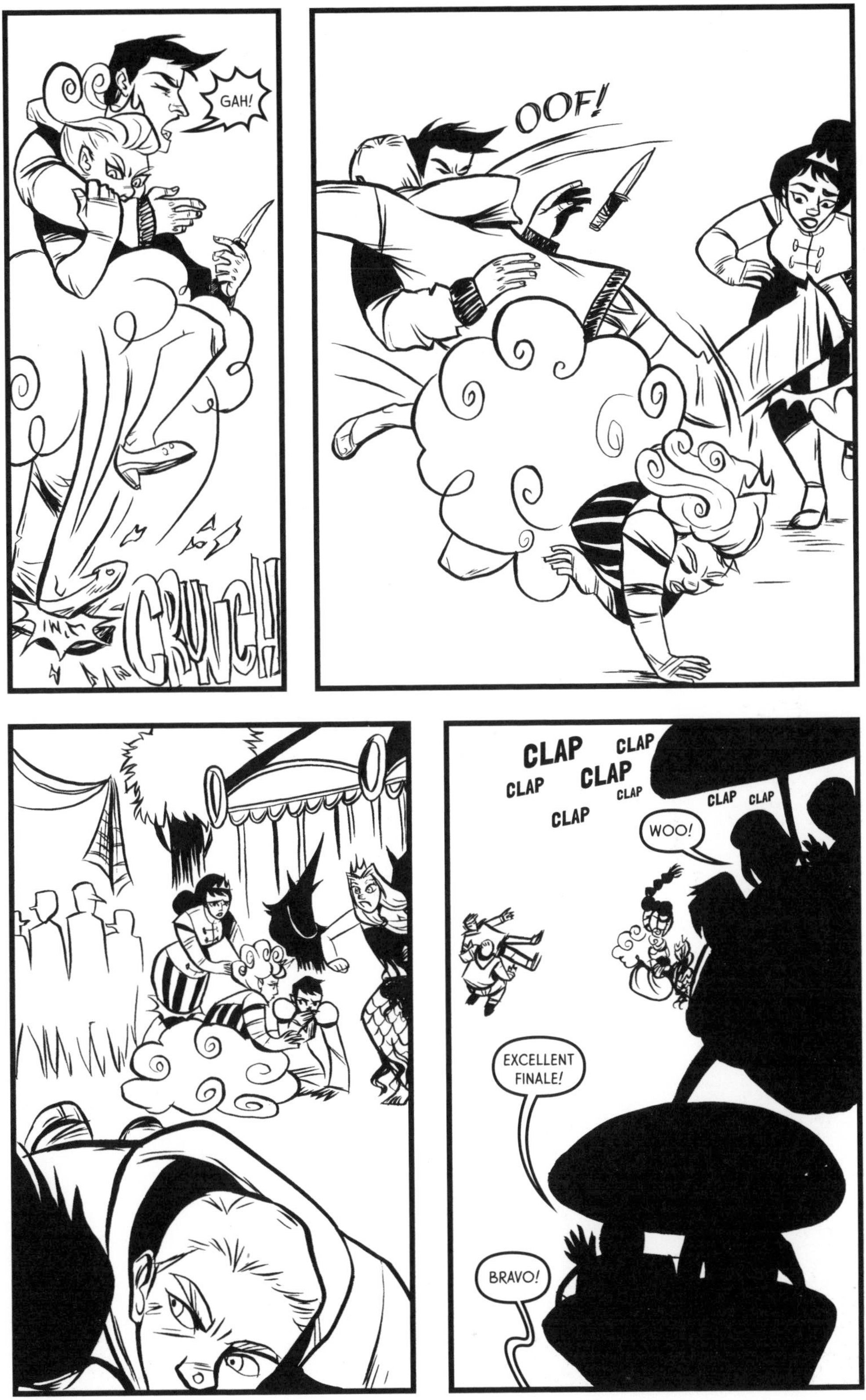
GAH!
CRUNCH
OOF!
CLAP CLAP
CLAP CLAP
CLAP CLAP
CLAP
CLAP CLAP
WOO!
EXCELLENT FINALE!
BRAVO!

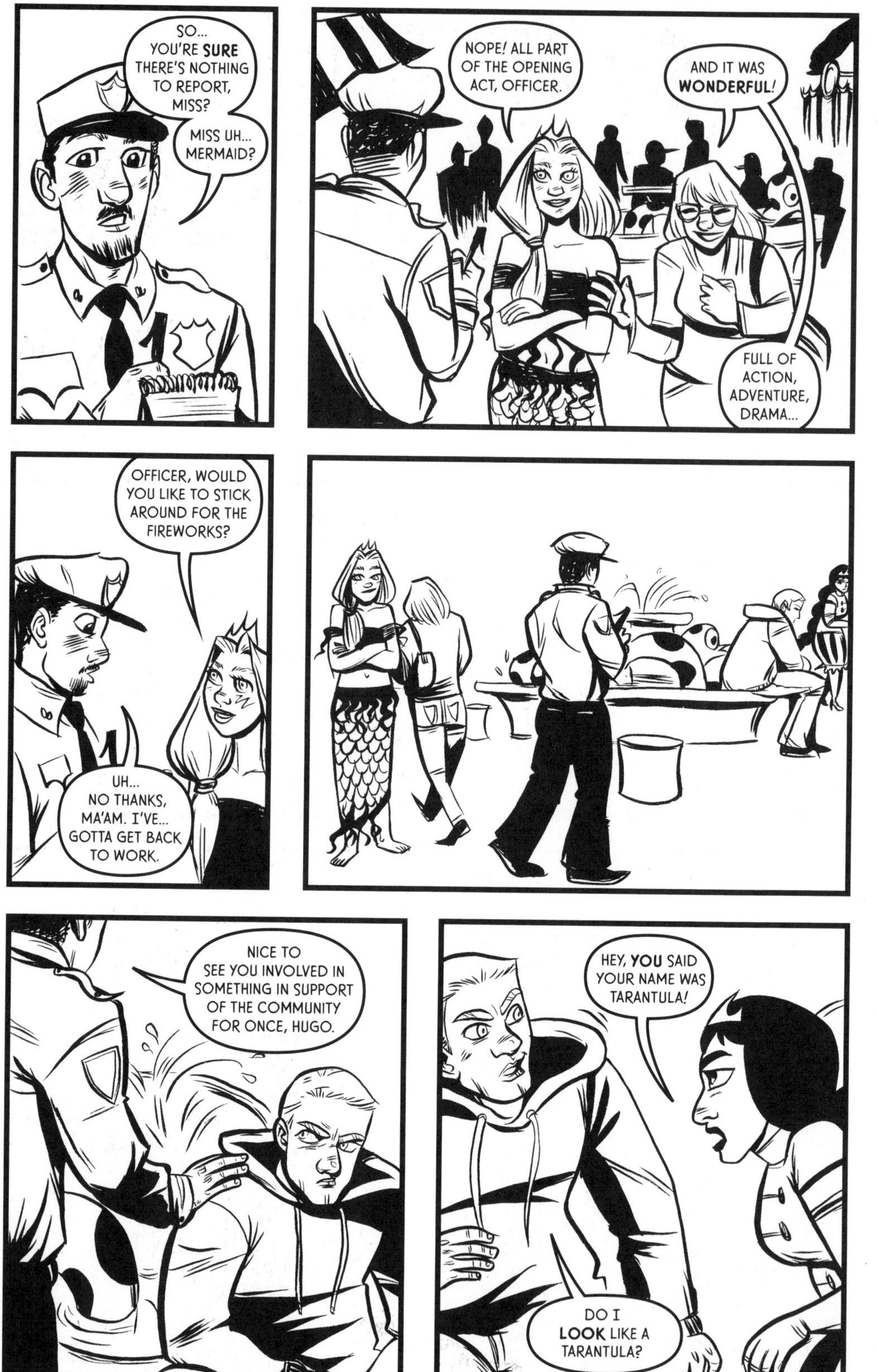

SO... YOU'RE **SURE** THERE'S NOTHING TO REPORT, MISS?
MISS UH... MERMAID?
NOPE! ALL PART OF THE OPENING ACT, OFFICER.
AND IT WAS **WONDERFUL**!
FULL OF ACTION, ADVENTURE, DRAMA...
OFFICER, WOULD YOU LIKE TO STICK AROUND FOR THE FIREWORKS?
UH... NO THANKS, MA'AM. I'VE... GOTTA GET BACK TO WORK.
NICE TO SEE YOU INVOLVED IN SOMETHING IN SUPPORT OF THE COMMUNITY FOR ONCE, HUGO.
HEY, **YOU** SAID YOUR NAME WAS TARANTULA!
DO I **LOOK** LIKE A TARANTULA?

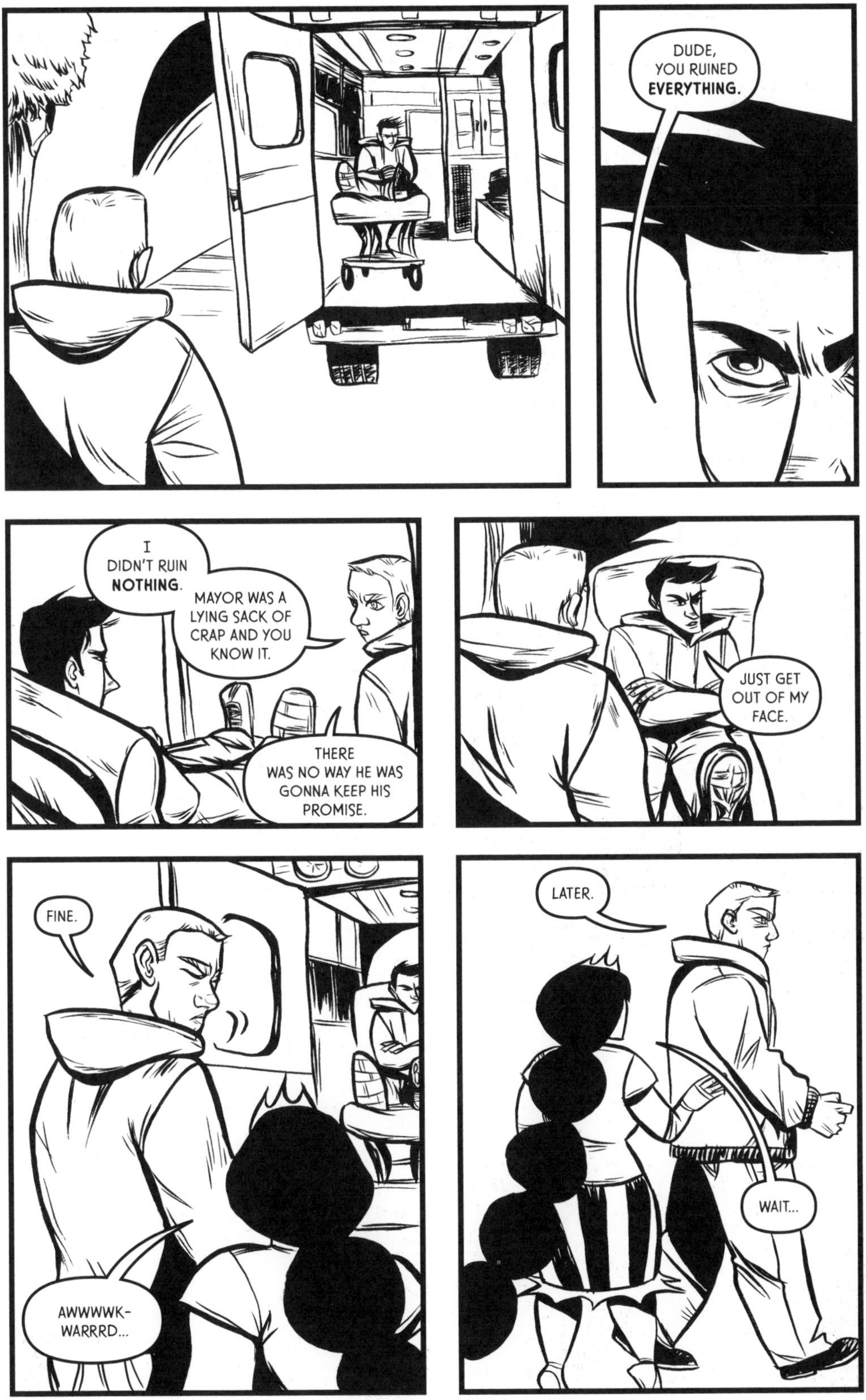
DUDE, YOU RUINED EVERYTHING.
I DIDN'T RUIN NOTHING.
MAYOR WAS A LYING SACK OF CRAP AND YOU KNOW IT.
THERE WAS NO WAY HE WAS GONNA KEEP HIS PROMISE.
JUST GET OUT OF MY FACE.
FINE.
AWWWWK-WARRRD...
LATER.
WAIT...

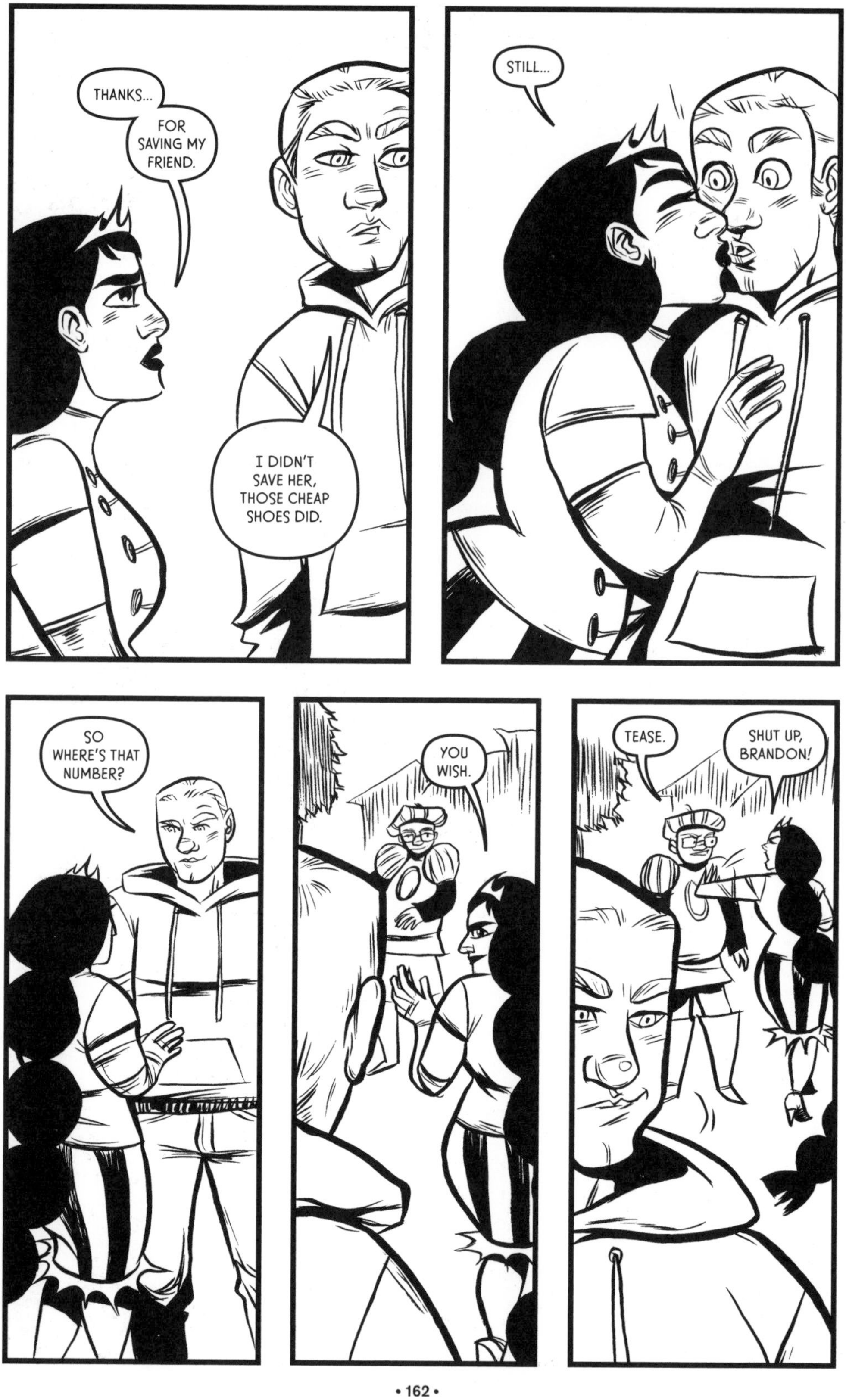
THANKS...
FOR SAVING MY FRIEND.
I DIDN'T SAVE HER, THOSE CHEAP SHOES DID.
STILL...
SO WHERE'S THAT NUMBER?
YOU WISH.
TEASE.
SHUT UP, BRANDON!

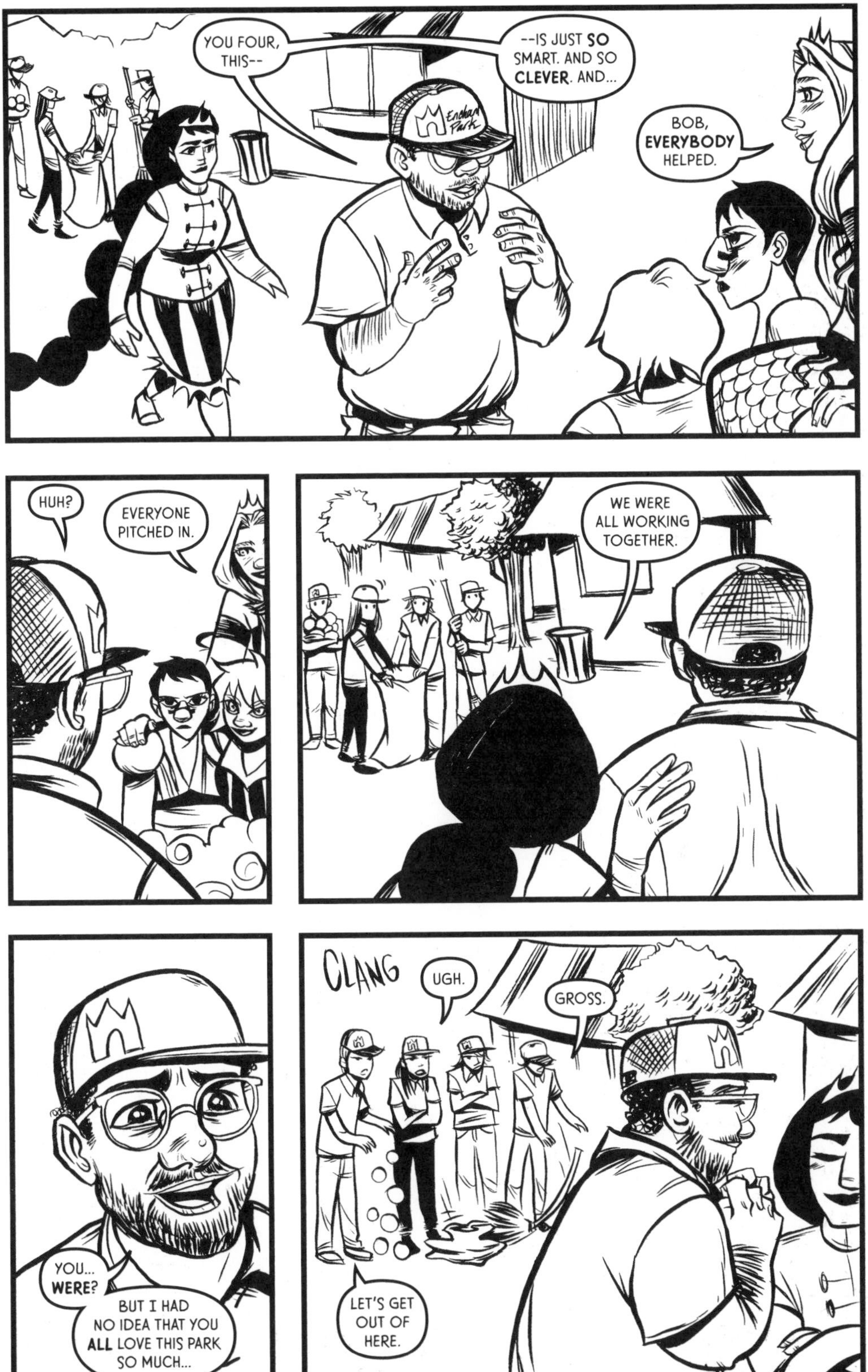

YOU FOUR, THIS--
--IS JUST **SO** SMART. AND SO **CLEVER**. AND...
BOB, **EVERYBODY** HELPED.
HUH?
EVERYONE PITCHED IN.
WE WERE ALL WORKING TOGETHER.
YOU... **WERE**?
BUT I HAD NO IDEA THAT YOU **ALL** LOVE THIS PARK SO MUCH...
CLANG
UGH.
GROSS.
LET'S GET OUT OF HERE.

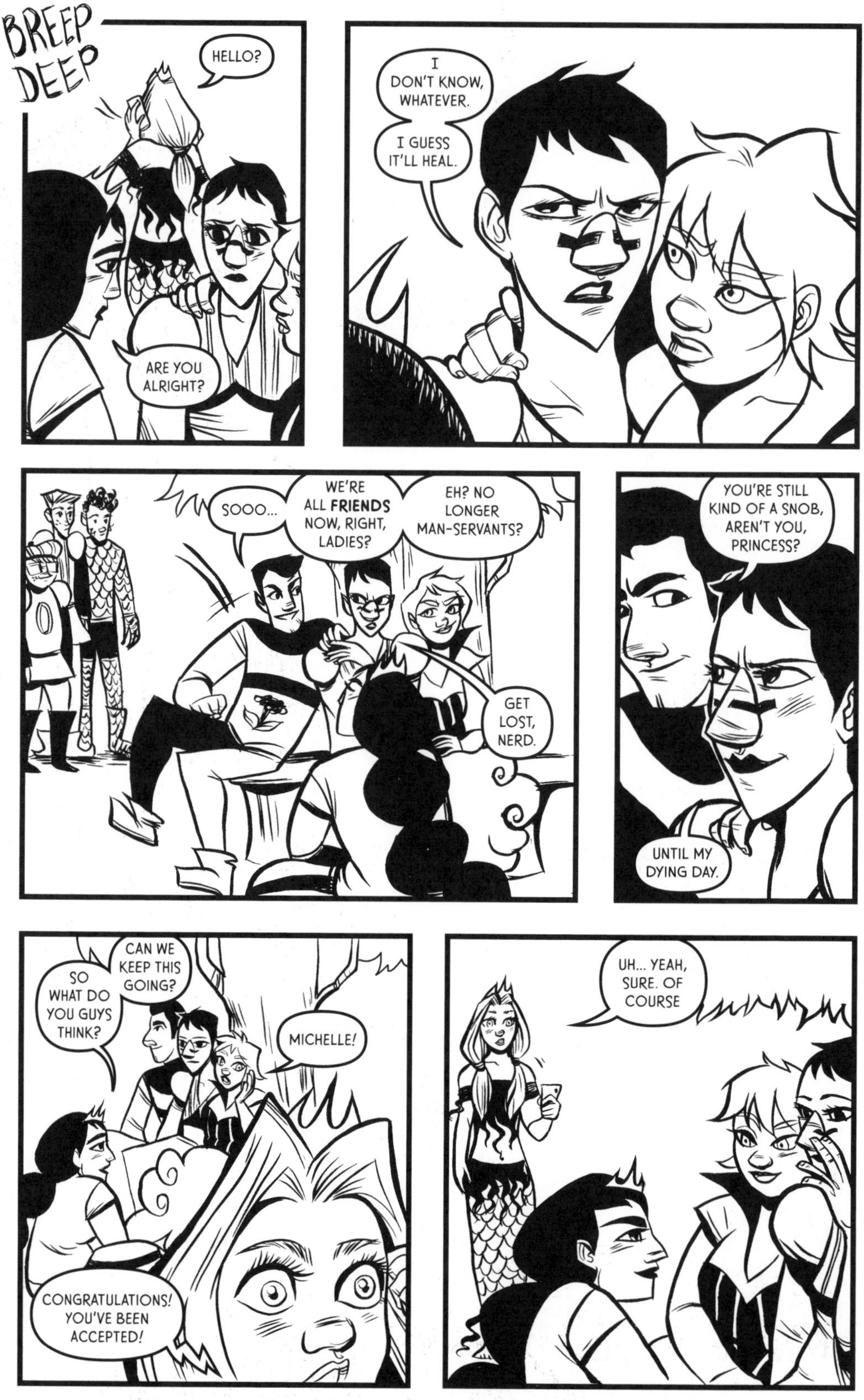
BREEP DEEP
HELLO?
ARE YOU ALRIGHT?
I DON'T KNOW, WHATEVER.
I GUESS IT'LL HEAL.
SOOO...
WE'RE ALL **FRIENDS** NOW, RIGHT, LADIES?
EH? NO LONGER MAN-SERVANTS?
GET LOST, NERD.
YOU'RE STILL KIND OF A SNOB, AREN'T YOU, PRINCESS?
UNTIL MY DYING DAY.
SO WHAT DO YOU GUYS THINK?
CAN WE KEEP THIS GOING?
MICHELLE!
CONGRATULATIONS! YOU'VE BEEN ACCEPTED!
UH... YEAH, SURE. OF COURSE

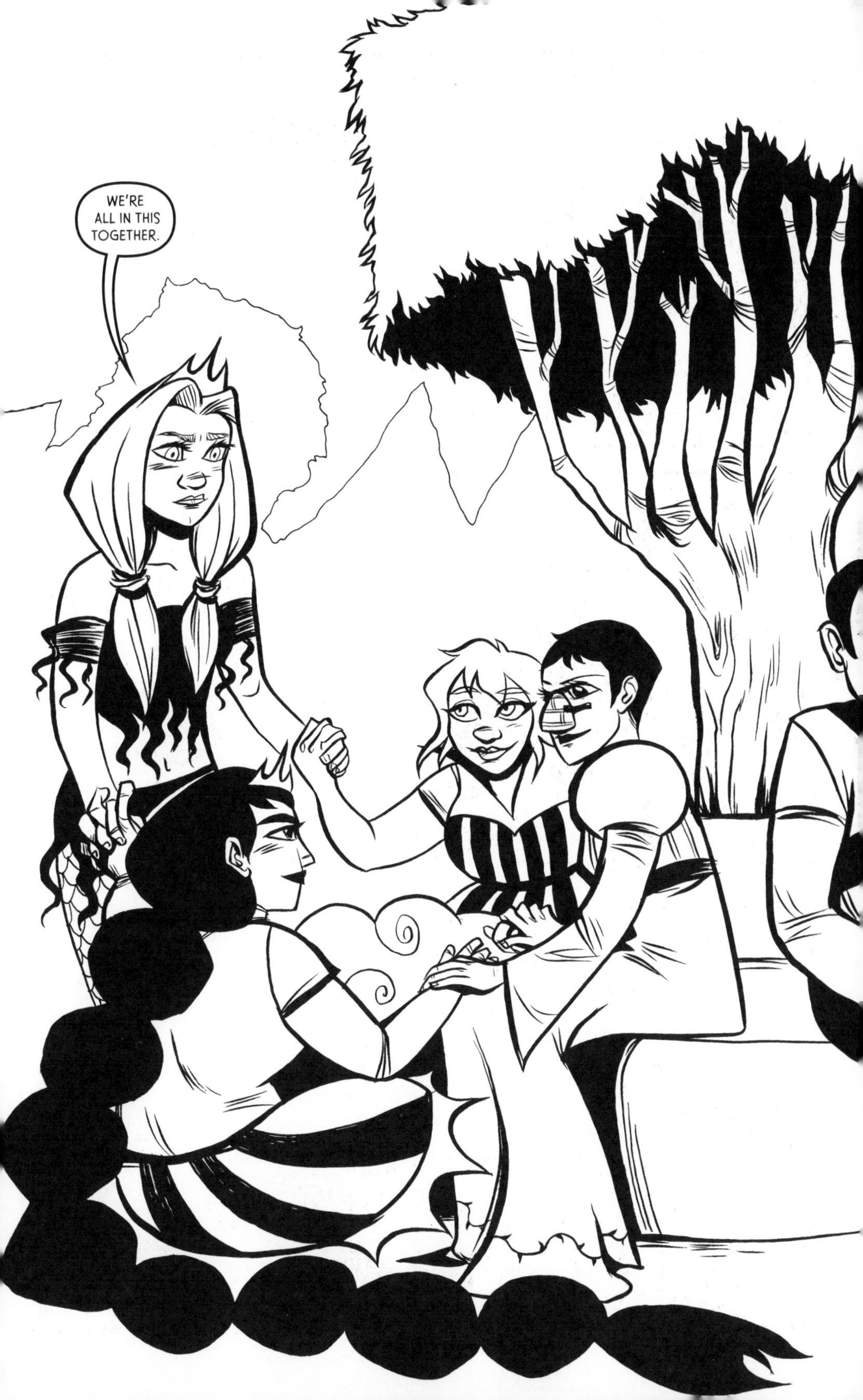
WE'RE ALL IN THIS TOGETHER.

Monica Gallagher

is an avid lipstick wearer and former rollergirl who currently lives in Baltimore with her husband and their two dueling cats. She finds all amusement parks to be delightfully creepy and is completely convinced that the creature statues come to life in the middle of the night. Stumbling through mirrored funhouses is one of her all-time favorite activities, however if her stomach even catches a glimpse of a roller coaster, it's allllll over. Monica's work has been previously published in Oni Press's *JAM! Tales from the World of Roller Derby* and *Glitter Kiss*. To check out Monica's weekly webcomic *Bonnie N. Collide, Nine to Five* as well as her other work, visit www.eatyourlipstick.com.

. . . .

Acknowledgements

Special thanks to my super special comics pals for their encouragement, critiquing, and loving pushes: Tim Fish, Mike DiMotta, Mr. Phil Jackson, Danielle Corsetto, and Greg Lockard.

Happy thanks to all my dear friends who put up with progress spreadsheet reports and complaints on drawing ferris wheels: Heather Johnson, Jessie Williams, Erin Whitehead, Lauren Summers, Dan Williford, Matt Hollis, Lisa Lunt, Lani Paulik, Heather Scher, Sean Gallagher, Jim & Sandie Gallagher, Mary Beth & Molly Manarchy, and Becky & Kyle McArthur.

And most of all big thanks to my hubs Dennis for his patience and insight throughout revisions, and for giving the book a title.

more from monica and oni press

Glitter Kiss
By Adrianne Ambrose
& Monica Gallagher
176 pages, Softcover
ISBN 978-1-62010-082-0

Jam! Tales from the World of Roller Derby
192 pages, Softcover
ISBN 978-1-934964-14-9

Princess Ugg: Volume One
By Ted Naifeh
120 pages, Softcover
ISBN 978-1-62010-178-0

A Boy & A Girl
By Jamie S. Rich
& Natalie Nourigat
176 pages
Softcover & Hardcover
ISBN 978-1-62010-089-9

Buzz
By Ananth Panagariya
& Tessa Stone
176 pages
Softcover & Hardcover
ISBN 978-1-62010-088-2

Spell Checkers: Volume One
By Jamie S. Rich,
Nicolas Hitori De & Joëlle Jones
152 pages, Softcover
ISBN 978-1-934964-32-3

**Bad Machinery, Volume One:
The Case of the Team Spirit**
By John Allison
144 pages
Softcover & Hardcover
ISBN 978-1-62010-084-4